# MAKE YOUR OWN
# CLASSIC BEARS

# MAKE YOUR OWN
# CLASSIC BEARS

## 14 HEIRLOOM DESIGNS

## ·JULIA JONES·

CRESCENT BOOKS
NEW YORK · AVENEL, NEW JERSEY

*For Charlotte Brandrick and her brother George*

First published in Great Britain in 1994 by Anaya Publishers Ltd.,
Strode House, 44-50 Osnaburgh Street, London NW1 3ND

This 1994 edition published by Crescent Books, distributed by
Outlet Book Company, Inc., a Random House Company,
40 Engelhard Avenue, Avenel, New Jersey 07001.

Random House
New York • Toronto • London • Sydney • Auckland

Designer: Clare Clements
Photographer: Jon Stewart
Front cover picture: Tim Hill
Stylist: Barbara Stewart
Artwork: Anthony Duke

ISBN 0-517-10205-6

Typeset in Great Britain by Litho Link Ltd, Welshpool, Powys
Colour reproduction by J. Film Process, Singapore
Printed and bound by Dai Nippon Printing Co. Ltd, Hong Kong

*Page 1: A rare Steiff teddy bear circa 1906.*
*Page 2 (opposite title page): Julia Jones' 1920s German Bear.*
*See pages 48 to 53 for instructions.*
*Page 3 (title page): Julia Jones' American Bear.*
*See pages 82 to 87 for instructions.*

# CONTENTS

# INTRODUCTION

*The earliest advertisement for teddy bears appeared in 1909. The Christmas novelty gift offered by Morrells of Oxford Street, London, that year was "Old Mistress Teddy that lived in a shoe", together with twelve baby bears, a sledge, ladder and even some bottles and bowls, all packaged together in a large crimson shoe.*

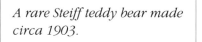

*A rare Steiff teddy bear made circa 1903.*

The wonderful, lovable, loyal and friendly teddy bear is probably one of the most enduring treasures of childhood. Even most adults would not be embarrassed to admit their secret fondness for an old, worn bear. Ever since teddy bears gained popularity in the early part of the century, they have appeared as mascots and talismans, going into battle with their owners, facing the stresses of examinations and featured in countless songs, books and verses.

The teddy bear came into the world in 1903. Since its conception it has been made in all shapes, sizes and colors with numerous expressions and capable of a wide range of actions.

This book looks at the classic bear and how it has evolved over the years. On the following pages, bears reminiscent of early examples can be made using modern materials and traditional methods. No complex needlework skills are necessary to produce wonderful collectors' bears, just straightforward sewing techniques.

### DEFINING A CLASSIC BEAR
A classic bear has well-defined characteristics. It has slightly curved paws, which taper at the ends. Its feet are long in relation to its overall height; to the purist this ratio is set at 5:1. High quality felt or velvet oval or triangular pads complete the feet. It either has no claws or ones stitched in black wool or cotton thread. Its head is rather small and triangular – it may or may not have a central gusset – with a long, pointed muzzle. Its head and limbs are invariably attached to its body with hardboard or cardboard discs and split pins. Black boot button eyes are the hallmark of a traditional bear, with a nose and mouth either embroidered with black thread or conveyed by an oval of black leather.

### TEDDY BEAR HISTORY
Although there are numerous stories surrounding the birth of the bear, it is probably accurate to attribute the lovable teddy to two simultaneous sources: America and Germany.

The American tale is perhaps the most entertaining, although not strictly documented. Certainly, a Russian immigrant shopkeeper, Morris Michtom, conceived the idea for a cuddly bear after seeing the now famous cartoon of President Roosevelt refusing to shoot a tethered bear cub. As Michtom's wife was a skilled toymaker, she set about creating what we now refer to as a Michtom teddy (see page 36).

The legend runs that the enterprising Michtom sent one of her bears to the president with the request to name the bear "teddy" after Roosevelt's first name, Theodore. The President allegedly consented and "Teddy's bear" was born.

Meanwhile, in Germany a young seamstress had begun to make soft toys. The girl was Margarete Steiff and so popular were her designs that by the close of the 19th century, she had become firmly established as a leading toymaker. It was her nephew Richard who brought the idea of a soft toy bear to Margarete's attention. Looking for a boy's alternative to the doll, Richard thought a bear might be the answer. After various modifications and some setbacks, the Steiff factory produced "Friend Petz" in time for the Leipzig Toy Fair of 1903.

Evidently no one seemed interested in little Friend Petz until the last day of the Fair. Hermann Berg, an American buyer for a New York company, approached the Steiffs, complaining that there was little new or interesting that year. Richard showed him the small bear and it is said that he was so delighted he placed an order for 3,000.

And so the teddy bear had arrived. The new toy had such an impact that suppliers just could not keep up with demand. By the 1920s, and despite the interruption of World War I, firms in Britain had sprung up to manufacture these creatures. While U.S. bears stayed more or less at home, German bears were exported around the world.

The shape of bears has evolved gradually over the years and makers have experimented with different colors, shapes and fabrics. The modern bear has mostly lost its jointed limbs and hump, and its body and face is rounder, but the basic appeal remains the same.

## COLLECTING BEARS

Today, old bears have become most collectable and many are quite valuable. The main factors governing the price of a bear are its condition, quality, rarity value and desirability. In older bears look for the soft colors of old mohair (black being the exception), straw or wood wool stuffing and wooden boot button eyes which should be deeply set. The body should display a well-defined hump. As early bears were designed to stand on all fours, they should have long arms, extending half way down their legs.

Personal preferences for bears vary considerably from collector to collector. Only you can decide the style and decade which appeals most, but always beware of impulse buys. Check the facts before making a decision and determining a fair price. But when the choice has been made, make the most of the bear you have the privilege of owning!

## MAKING BEARS

There is now a growing interest worldwide not only for collecting bears but also making them in the traditional manner. On the following pages, you will find 14 bears – all with full patterns and clear instructions.

Even complete beginners will achieve remarkable success with their first bear by following the step-by-step instructions closely, while experienced bear-makers will find the useful tips contained throughout this book a stimulus to their creativity.

There is also scope to vary each bear, so that a tremendous range and variety of styles can be achieved, needing only a little imagination and confidence. Once the basic steps have been mastered, the desire to experiment will naturally develop. Making any bear and watching its personality develop as you work is rewarding and great fun.

However, when first making a particular bear, it is best to use the recommended fabric. Bears made up in different fabrics or colors will look quite unlike the ones illustrated. For the more experienced this can be one of the delights of making your own Classic Bears!

*The classic bears in this book are not designed as toys for small children. If, however, one of them is to be made for a small child, it must conform to all toy safety standards.*

*Manufacturers were quick to realize the marketing potential of the endearing "teddy" bear and over the years its form has appeared in the trademarks of many companies. Teddies have been used to promote all manner of products, as widely diverse as ladies' hosiery, balloons and coal!*

# MATERIALS
# AND EQUIPMENT

*Occasionally a nose molded from leather or gutta-percha (a natural resin exuded from various Malaysian trees) can be found on a classic collectors' bear.*

Classic bears have always been made from natural materials such as wool, mohair, angora and cashmere, with fillings of wood wool or straw. The eyes were almost always fashioned from black wooden boot buttons, though occasionally beads or metal discs were used. Most paw and foot pads were made from good quality felt. Other features, such as mouths and claws where included, were embroidered with simple stitches such as straight stitch, using cotton or wool embroidery threads.

During the world wars some resourceful people, faced with limited supplies of material, resorted to using sheepskin and surviving examples have a very unusual and distinctive look. A small number of early bears, with a somewhat unappealing appearance, were manufactured from burlap, a fabric coarsely woven from jute. This gave a hairless and slightly abrasive feel to a creature primarily designed to be cuddled.

In this section, the more recognizable and available materials are described, together with the essential tools, equipment, materials and fittings required to make authentic collectors' bears today.

### TOOLS AND EQUIPMENT

The following are all the simple tools and equipment you will need when making a classic bear using the techniques described in the section called Classic Bear-making. They are listed in the order in which they will be required.

**Graph paper** The pattern pieces on grids in this book are designed to be transferred to graph paper (or pattern paper) with 1in (2.5cm) squares. Should you wish to reduce or enlarge the size of a bear, you can use smaller or larger sized squared paper.

*Never use ballpoint pens when marking templates of pattern pieces, as they will leave a mark which may be transferred accidentally to the right side of the fabric and will be impossible to remove.*

**Tracing paper** Ideally use a heavy-weight tracing paper for transferring the pattern outlines when making templates. Do not be tempted to economize by buying a lighter weight tracing paper as this may distort slightly or tear during use.

**Pencils** A selection of hard and soft lead pencils are needed for making the pattern-piece templates and also for marking fabric. In many cases, a soft lead pencil will seem the most suitable choice for marking fabrics.

**A French curve** This is a flexible plastic rod which may be helpful in joining the marks smoothly when drawing pattern-piece shapes on graph paper.

*When marking dark fabrics for bear-making, colored pencils or chalk can be used.*

**Masking tape** Masking tape is used to hold the tracing paper in position while the outlines are transferred to the templates.

**Non-smudge ink pen** When marking templates with a pen, it is essential to use one that will not smudge.

**Cardboard** Thin white cardboard is needed for making semi-permanent templates which can be used many times. Any type of lightweight cardboard can be used, provided it is clean and fairly stiff.

8

**Craft scissors** Short round-ended scissors are needed for cutting paper or cardboard.

**Tailor's chalk and dressmaker's marker pens** Both tailor's chalk and dressmaker's marker pens are useful when marking fabric around the templates. Tailor's chalk is most suitable for dark fabrics and it will brush out easily after use. Dressmaker's marker pens are also used to label and mark fabric pieces. Usually pale blue in color, they work well on most fabrics, but the manufacturer's instructions must be carefully followed to avoid leaving stains on some fabrics.

**Dressmaking scissors** Dressmaking scissors are used for cutting fur fabric, suedette, leather and all other bear-making fabrics. Ideally, these should be 7–8in (18–21cm) long and have offset handles.

**Embroidery scissors** Fine-bladed, sharp embroidery scissors are useful for cutting around small pattern pieces, negotiating sharp angles and for all embroidery work.

**Pins** Long, slim dressmaker's pins are required to hold seams together before tacking (basting). As an extra safety precaution, colored glass-headed pins can be used. Either way, count the number of pins used as you work and be sure to remove them all as soon as possible.

**Sewing machine and needles** Although it is perfectly possible to make any of the bears in this book without the aid of a sewing machine, it is assumed that most readers will have access to one and instructions are written accordingly. A ball-point or sharp sewing-machine needle can be used for fur fabrics, velvet and velveteens; and a wedge point for leather or suede. The machine needle size depends on the fabric thickness and a size 14 to 16 will suit most fabrics. A heavy-weight leather or suede will require a size 16 to 18.

**Needles** A variety of needles will be necessary for the various hand-sewing and embroidery techniques used to make a classic bear. Besides the obvious choice of sharps and embroidery needles for general work, it is necessary to use a 3in (7.5cm) darning needle which is slim enough not to snag or distort the fabric when inserting eyes. A toymaker's or packing needle is useful for ladder stitching openings after stuffing. Alternatively, a fine curved upholstery needle will serve equally well.

**Seam ripper** A seam ripper is useful for unpicking seams quickly to undo errors, but great care must be used not to tear or cut the fabric.

**Fine crochet hook or bodkin** Either a fine crochet hook or a bodkin can be used for teasing out pile trapped in machine-stitched seams. A knitting needle could also be used, but it is likely to bend during use.

**Stiletto or awl** A stiletto (or awl) is used for making holes in fur fabric or cardboard templates. However, if this is not available, a fine knitting needle can be used instead.

**A stuffing stick** A strong stick is necessary to ensure that any filling medium can be tightly packed into even the smallest corners. A cheap alternative to a custom-made stuffing stick can be made from an 8in (20cm) length of ⅜in (1cm) dowelling, smoothly sanded before use. Stuffing sticks can also be used to assist in the turning of small limbs and the pushing out of noses and feet. Orange (manicure) sticks are useful when working on tiny bears.

**Tape measure** A tape measure is needed for measuring the positions for eyes, ears and nose.

*Do not be tempted to cut paper with dressmaking or embroidery scissors, as this will quickly blunt their blades.*

*"T" pins are useful for holding bear ears in position before stitching.*

*Any hand-stitched seams in bear-making must be very accurately and firmly worked to withstand the pressure exerted during the stuffing process.*

*The handle of a wooden spoon or a chopstick could be used as stuffing stick in bear-making.*

*Pliers are useful for flattening the wire on the back of some glass eyes, to aid their insertion through the fabric.*

*If any of the bears in this book is to be made for a child, it is essential that a suitable, non-flammable fabric is used.*

*As synthetic fur fabrics are much cheaper than natural fur fabrics, it may be wise for a beginner to practice with these first.*

*The mohair plush originally used by all German makers in the manufacture of their bears is believed to have been woven exclusively in Yorkshire, England.*

**Pliers** Long-nosed pliers are essential for bending split pins when assembling crown joints and for pulling a needle through the fabric when required.

**Wire cutters** These are used for cutting the joining wire found on some glass eyes and for cutting through wrongly assembled joints in order to release them.

**Teasel brush** A teasel or soft bristle nail brush is useful to help ease trapped strands from machine-stitched seams or to fluff up the pile on a finished bear. On crushed mohair it is better to use a soft nail brush, rather than the wire teasel type, as this will not disturb the distinctive antique appearance of the fabric.

## FABRICS AND THREADS

There are many types of fabric to choose from, both traditional and modern, and these can vary enormously in price and quality. The work entailed when making a classic bear demands that you use the best possible material to produce an heirloom. Fur fabrics are either woven or knitted and the materials used for the pile may be synthetic or natural. Obviously, the choice for a classic bear would be for a natural and traditional material such as mohair, wool or cashmere.

**Plush** The word "plush" is a term often applied to fur fabrics. This simply means that the fabric has a nap which is softer and longer than velvet. Plush is usually manufactured from silk, cotton or wool and will produce an authentic and lovable bear.

**Synthetic furs** Synthetic furs are usually produced with a knitted backing, which is not ideally suited to the production of a collectors' bear. Knitted fabrics do not withstand stress and are inclined to give and pull out of shape during stuffing, whereas natural fibers such as mohair, alpaca, silk and wool have a woven backing that will withstand pressure, resulting in a better quality and firmer bear.

The pile length of each type of fabric can vary considerably, as does its quality and softness, and these factors will also determine the look of your finished bear.

Two of the bears in this book – the 1950s British Bear and the 1940s American Bear have been made with manmade fabrics. Although both bears can, of course, also be made up using an alternative, natural fabric for a more traditional appeal. If you have never made a soft toy before, use a good quality synthetic fabric and follow the step-by-step classic bear instructions carefully to produce results that should be very satisfying. Keep in mind the possibility of stretching, however, when the stuffing stage is reached.

**Non-pile fabrics** The patterns in this book can be also used for a modern approach to bear-making, using techniques such as quilting or patchwork and fabrics such as silk, cotton or linen. A good-quality German felt can also be used to produce a hairless bear, but in this case avoid any pattern with a very thin body, arms or legs, as the bear's thinness will be accentuated by its lack of fur!

**Mohair pile fabrics** Classic teddies were and still are, in general, made from mohair fabric. This is obtained from the coat of the Angora goat, which is woven into soft luxurious fabric. The process of making mohair fabrics for bears can take as long as six weeks and this explains their relatively high cost. A mohair substitute, made from a mixture of wool and cotton, is obtainable.

**Fur fabric widths** Fur fabric is generally woven in widths of 54in (137cm) and a 16in (41cm) bear would require ½yd (45cm) of this. If you intend to make several bears, it is possible, by careful placing of the pattern pieces, to economize on fabric, cutting several from 1yd (91cm). Different widths of fabric will, of course, need differing lengths. If in doubt, cut a sheet of paper to the required width and arrange the templates on this, measuring the depth of fabric required to cut them all satisfactorily.

**Felt** Traditional bears always had felt paw and foot pads, usually of beige, black or cream. Felt is easily and quickly cut and has no pile or right and wrong side. Consequently, pattern pieces can be fitted jigsaw-like onto the fabric resulting in very little waste.

*To the right are some fur fabrics currently available for classic bear-making. Also shown are fabrics used for pads, such as felt and suedette.*

*The felt used for classic bear paws should always be the best quality. Today the best felt is manufactured in Germany.*

*Embroidery threads such as stranded cotton (floss) or pearl cotton are often used for embroidering the features on contemporary collectors' teddy bears.*

*Turn to page 112 for a list of specialist suppliers who sell classic bear fabrics, fittings, and filling or stuffing.*

*When buying any filling or stuffing sold for soft toys, always read the label on the packaging so that you are aware of the safety standard information.*

**Velveteens and Velvets** Velveteen was used for paws and pads for many bears in the period from 1910 to 1940. It is a cotton pile fabric, similar in appearance to velvet, but with a much shorter nap or pile. Because velveteen is harder to find today, velvet is often used in its place on classic bears.

**Suede and leather** Ovals for noses, paw and foot pads can be cut from suede or leather. The most usual colors are light beige, brown or black. Old, worn gloves can be successfully recycled for this purpose. Suede could be used for any of the bear pads in this book.

**Suedette** This fabric is manufactured to resemble suede. It can be purchased in a variety of colors and is extremely easy to cut and sew.

**Threads** All-purpose sewing thread (no. 30) of the same color as the fabric is required for machine stitching classic bears. In addition, a heavy-duty or buttonhole thread is required for some sewing jobs such as attaching the eyes and ears securely, or for machine stitching large bears or heavy-weight leather or suede. Cotton or wool embroidery threads are the most suitable choices for embroidering features.

## BEAR FILLING OR STUFFING

Wood wool was traditionally used for the heirloom bears and most modern collectors' bears are still stuffed with it. Occasionally referred to as "Excelsior", wood wool is made of long, thin fine-quality wood shavings. Kapok, sometimes called "silk cotton", took over from wood wool as the most popular medium for stuffing toys from the 1940s until the advent of man-made fibers.

**Kapok** This is a natural material similar to cotton, and is formed from the short fibers which surround the seeds of a tropical tree. If you are stuffing a large bear with kapok remember that it is relatively heavy, and it may be advisable to combine kapok with some other medium. Asthma sufferers are advised to wear a mask when using kapok, as the fine strands and dust can prove irritating.

**Sheep's wool** This can be collected from hedges and barbed wire fences or bought in a fleece. With careful washing it will make a wonderful filling material and can be teased out gently to fill tiny corners. As it is possible to get a rash from unwashed sheep's wool, it is advisable to wear rubber gloves while collecting and washing. Make sure that wool prepared at home is thoroughly dry before use.

**Wood wool** This can be ordered from specialist suppliers (see page 112) and will usually be packaged in a plastic bag or sack. As soon as it is delivered, it should be emptied into a large cardboard box or wooden tea chest, as storage in plastic may cause dampness and rotting.

Wood wool is sold in a semi-compressed state and the blocks should be lightly teased out to their full volume just before use. Check carefully and remove any large wood shavings before beginning to stuff a bear.

For smooth finish paws, feet and muzzles should be stuffed with a small amount of synthetic filling to give a softer feel, before completing the stuffing using wood wool.

**Manmade fibers** A variety of manmade fibers are available for soft toy making – the most commonly used is polyester or terylene (Dacron). When purchasing it is essential to specify whether a soft or firm fill is required for the bear in question. Terylene produces a loose, open and fairly resilient stuffing medium, while polyester has less crimp and will need slightly more to produce the same results.

**Foam rubber** Never be tempted to use the brightly colored pieces of foam rubber sold in some stores as a suitable medium for stuffing good quality toys. Although it has the advantage of being cheap, readily available and hygienic, it also has a nasty habit of sticking to the inside of the fabric and will make the finished bear very heavy and shapeless.

### BEAR FITTINGS

The fittings used for classic bears – such as eyes, joints and growlers – can be purchased from specialist suppliers (see page 112). Remember that the bear instructions in this book are for traditional collectors' bears which are not suitable for small children. If you intend to make toys for children, strict safety regulations must be adhered to and only fittings which comply with these regulations can be used.

**Eyes** Following tradition, all classic bears made for the collector's market are fitted with boot button or glass eyes. A careful search through boxes of odds and ends at antique and estate sales will sometimes be rewarded by discovering wooden boot button eyes. Failing that, specialist suppliers sell reproduction boot button eyes in sizes ranging from ¼in (7mm) to ⅝in (16mm).

Safety eyes, made of plastic, can be found in craft shops or mail order catalogues. They range in size from ⅜in (9 mm) to 1¼in (45mm) and are made in various colors, including amber, brown and black. It is possible to purchase a special tool to help to exert pressure when assembling safety eyes. It is not essential, however, as an empty sewing cotton spool can be employed in much the same manner.

**Joints** Most classic bears are assembled using crown joints. These come in different sizes. Bears made for children must be fitted with the correct safety-locking plastic joints.

**Growler boxes** This can be fitted to most bears to provide a voice. A growler is made from a cylindrical cardboard container with holes at one end like a pepper pot. It has a weight inside which, when the bear is tipped backwards, presses on a small bellows, forcing air through its reed to produce a sound similar to a short growl. These teddy bear "voices" were introduced in 1908, but were later replaced with cheaper, mass produced "squeakers".

It is wise to purchase a growler from a specialist bear supplier. Otherwise, listen to its sound carefully – you may find that your bear sounds more like a cow or a duck!

**Squeakers** A squeaker is comprised of a small bellows, which, when pressed, forces air through a reed, emitting a high-pitched note.

**Tinklers** A tinkler is a simple device made from a cardboard cylinder containing steel pins of various lengths. A weight is suspended from one end and when the cylinder is rolled, this hits the pins, making a soft tinkling sound.

**Musical boxes** Musical boxes were first included in bears during the 1920s. Today, musical boxes suitable for insertion in soft toys are enclosed in a small tin and have a key for winding which is fitted to a screw. (See page 27 for inserting a musical box in a teddy bear.)

*Never use any fittings either outside or inside a teddy bear that is to be given to a child unless these fittings comply with toy safety regulations.*

*Growlers, tinklers and musical boxes can only be inserted into bears big enough to accommodate them. Bears containing any of these items should be well stuffed with wood wool.*

# CLASSIC
# BEAR-MAKING

The traditional techniques for making classic bears are outlined here in these detailed step-by-step instructions. Before making any of the bears featured in this book, you will need to read this chapter. When a bear has a special feature not included in these general directions, the necessary techniques are outlined in the individual instructions.

### PREPARING THE TEMPLATES

The first stage in the process of bear-making is preparing the pattern-piece templates. The pattern pieces for most of the bears in this book have been drawn on a grid with squares representing 1in (2.5cm). These pieces must be transferred onto graph paper with 1in (2.5cm) squares, then onto tracing paper and finally onto thin, stiff cardboard. To make a bigger or smaller bear than the recommended one, a graph paper with different sized squares can be used. The pattern pieces can also be reduced or enlarged on a photocopier.

*The pattern pieces for the Miniature Bear and the 1980s Bear are given actual size (see pages 54 and 100)*

1 To transfer the pattern shapes to graph paper, first note where each curved line crosses the sides of a square. Make a light mark at these points on the graph paper before drawing in the finished curves. An artist's flexible plastic rod may be helpful in joining the marks smoothly. When all the shapes have been transferred to graph paper, transfer all pattern markings, labels and, most importantly, the name of the bear.

2 Trace each pattern shape onto tracing paper, using a soft lead pencil and a firm hand. Transfer all pattern markings in the same way. Turn over the tracing paper and lay it over a piece of cardboard, securing it with masking tape. Using a hard lead pencil, go over the traced outlines and markings, thus transferring them to the cardboard. Repeat this process for each pattern shape, fitting the pieces closely together.

3 Set aside the tracing paper and, using a fine non-smudge pen, reinforce the traced lines and markings on all of the templates. Still using the pen, insert all remaining labels. Then cut out each template, using craft scissors. Cut smoothly and accurately, as the quality of the templates will affect the quality of your bear. Using a stiletto, push holes through templates at all dart points and at the positions for arm and leg joints.

## TRANSFERRING PATTERN SHAPES TO FUR FABRIC

Before beginning to outline the pattern shapes onto your fur fabric, first check that you have the required number of templates. (You will notice that your templates are mirror images of the shapes in the book because the tracing paper was turned over to transfer the pieces to the template cardboard.)

The type of fabric from which each pattern piece is to be cut is clearly marked on each piece. How many pieces to cut from a template and whether to reverse a piece (for a right and left side) is also indicated. All this should be checked carefully after the pieces have been drawn, but before cutting, paying attention to the direction of the pile.

The minimum amount of fabric required for each bear is given in the Materials list accompanying each set of instructions. If more material has to be purchased than is necessary to cut a particular bear, it may be possible, by careful arrangement of the pattern pieces, to cut a second smaller bear from the surplus. In any event, do not throw the remnants and scraps away. These can be stored, for future use.

It may be necessary to try various layouts to achieve the most economical use of fabric, but experience will quickly make this apparent. It is not possible, as with dress patterns, to work on folded fabric, cutting two pieces at a time. You must therefore remember to reverse the template in order to form "pairs" of pattern pieces where necessary.

Most of the patterns in this book require two body sections, two side head sections, one head gusset, as well as two inner arms, two outer arms, two inner legs, two outer legs, two paw pads and two foot pads. The paw and foot pad pieces will be cut from suedette, leather, velvet or felt as instructed.

Do not use a ballpoint pen to mark any fabric. It may smudge and would undoubtedly stain the material, which could spoil the finished bear. Note that all seam allowances are included in the templates.

*Using templates (instead of paper patterns) allows for more accurate bear-making. Templates can also be re-used many times.*

*When fur fabric or velvet is stroked, the pile or "nap" lies smoothly or it ruffles, depending on the direction in which it lies. The pile on a bear should always run downwards from head to toe, except on the top of the muzzle and the ears. If in any doubt check the direction in which the fur runs on a dog or cat!*

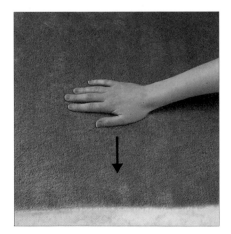

1 First spread the fur fabric out on a large flat surface (such as a table or a clean floor), face up. Check the direction of the nap or pile by stroking the fur flat, noting the direction it runs.

2 Turn the fur fabric face down, so that the pile of the fur runs towards you. Then carefully draw a few large arrows showing the direction of the fur pile, using tailor's chalk.

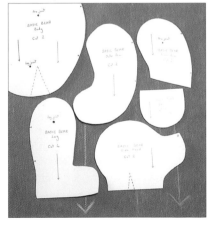

3 Arrange the templates on the fabric, being sure to match the directional arrows to the direction of the pile. Pattern pieces should always be cut on a single layer of fur fabric.

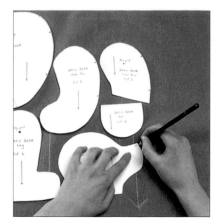

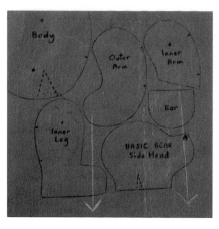

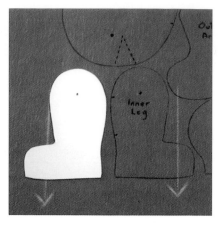

4 When you have decided on the layout, you can begin tracing the shapes. Carefully holding each template firmly in place with one hand, draw around the edge of each template, using tailor's chalk, a marker pen or a soft lead pencil.

5 Transfer onto the fabric all markings for openings, arm and leg joint positions, dart points, seam labels and any notches. Then label each piece with the part name, e.g. "inner arm", "leg", "head gusset", "paw pad", "body", etc.

6 Prepare remaining pieces in the same way, reversing templates where necessary so that there is a "right" and "left" side of head or an "inner" and "outer" arm, etc. After completion, check that you have the correct number of cut pieces.

### CUTTING FABRICS

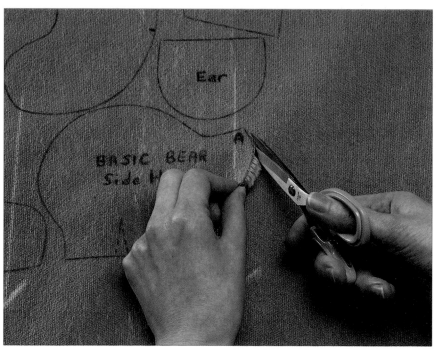

*Remember that the seam allowances are already included inside the pattern-piece outlines.*

When absolutely sure that the pattern pieces are drawn correctly, lay the fabric right side down on a firm surface. Then using sharp, pointed dressmaking scissors, push the point through the fabric and carefully cut out each drawn shape. Rather than cutting through both the fabric and the fur pile, try to cut only the ground fabric, leaving the fur to be teased apart. On small or complex shapes, it may be easier to use sharp embroidery scissors.

As each piece is cut, check that it is correctly labelled and that all necessary instructions have been transferred. As you work, place all the cut pieces in a clean self-seal plastic bag or a paper bag, keeping identical pieces together.

Your bear's velvet, suedette or leather foot and paw pads should be traced onto the wrong side of the fabric in the same way as the pattern pieces were transferred to the fur, taking the direction of the nap into account in the case of the velvet. Felt has no right and wrong side and the shapes can be transferred to either side of felt.

Using small, sharp scissors, cut very carefully around each paw and foot pad shape, being sure to keep closely to the outlines.

It may be advisable, when using especially soft fabrics, to cut paw and foot pads out again in a medium weight interfacing, which can then be tacked (basted) to the outer fabric to give additional body.

### SEWING THE PATTERN PIECES

As fur fabric has a habit of "slipping", all pattern pieces should be pinned together first before tacking (basting), using long, slim pins placed at right angles to the seams. After careful pinning, the pieces should be tacked (basted), using long running stitches. It is helpful to tuck the pile inwards between the two edges of fabric while tacking (basting).

If the pattern pieces do not fit exactly, use pins and tacking (basting) stitches to ease the longer edge gently before machine stitching. The dense pile of fur fabric can, fortunately, be used to cover a number of minor mishaps! This does not mean, however, that anything but the greatest care should be taken when stitching, as the ultimate character of your bear will be affected by your attention to detail.

When machine stitching, added strength can be given to a seam by turning the fabric and running a second row of stitches back along the original seamline. To secure the thread ends, always backstitch at the beginning and end of a machine-stitched seam.

All seam allowances are ¼in (7mm) on bears unless otherwise stated. References to the seamline apply to an imaginary line at this distance from the cutting edge.

*In the instructions given for each bear, the word "stitch" means pin, then tack (baste) and then machine stitch, unless the instructions state otherwise.*

*After each seam has been machine stitched, any pile trapped in the seams should be gently teased out using a bodkin or stiletto. (See also "teasel brush" on page 10.)*

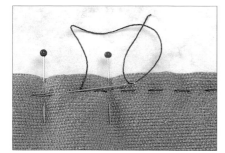

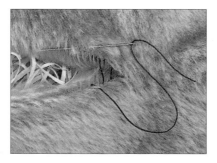

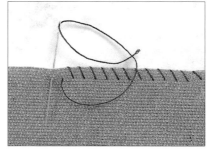

**Running stitch** is the simplest of the hand-stitching techniques used in bear-making. It is used for tacking (basting) and for stay stitching along some fur-fabric edges before the seams are machine stitched.

**Ladder stitch** is used for closing openings after stuffing. It is worked by taking a tiny stitch alternately on each side of the seam. After every few stitches the thread should be pulled firmly to close the seam.

**Oversewing** (overcast stitches) can be used along the raw edges of fabrics that are likely to fray. Never use oversewing stitches to close openings as they will form an ugly ridge, in which the stitches will show.

## STITCHING THE BEAR'S HEAD

**1** Some bear heads do not have shaping darts, but if there are any they may be stitched first before joining head pieces. Fold together the dart gusset of each side head section and pin. Tack (baste) outside the dart line from the tip of the dart to the fabric edge. Machine stitch the dart. Remove tacking (basting).

**2** Do not slash darts, but press them down firmly (away from the muzzle) using a thumb and forefinger (index finger). Using heavy-duty thread, knotted and doubled, stay stitch along the lower neck edge with short, even running stitches. This will prevent the raw edge from stretching out of shape.

**3** Place the side head sections right sides together and pin and tack (baste) the lower muzzle seam which goes from the tip of the nose to the neck. Machine stitch this seam, remembering to always start and finish each seam with a few backstitches. Remove tacking (basting) stitches.

**4** If any darts appear on the head gusset pattern piece, stitch these in the manner described in Step 1. Using heavy-duty thread, stay stitch along the seamline on both long edges of the gusset. The fitting of the head gusset is critical for the finished head shape. Great care should be taken to make sure that the gusset does not stretch out of shape. (As you join the gusset, it may be helpful to turn the head right side out occasionally to check the balance and shape of the muzzle and head.)

**5** Pin the head gusset to one side of the head, easing to fit where necessary. Make sure that the center notch on the nose tip of the gusset is lined up accurately with the center of the lower muzzle seam. When you are entirely satisfied with the fit and shape of the seam, tack (baste) the gusset and the side of the head together just inside the seamline, using small running stitches. The seam may need to taper towards the nose tip. Join on the second side of the head in the same way.

**6** When completely satisfied with the easing and shaping of these seams, machine stitch from the point of the nose to the back neck edge on each side of the gusset, starting the machine stitching as close as possible to the muzzle seam on each side of the nose notch. Remove the tacking (basting) stitches and trim the seams around the nose to ⅛in (3mm) to ensure a smooth muzzle. (Be careful when trimming not to cut the seam.) Set the head section aside for stuffing later.

STITCHING THE BEAR'S BODY

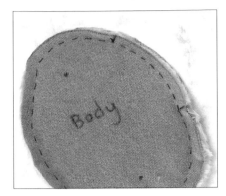

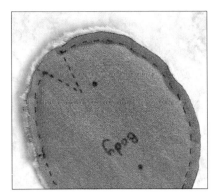

1 The bear body-shapes vary, and some have an upper and lower dart on each of the two body sections. Before joining the body pieces, stay stitch along the seamline of the back opening on each of the two pieces, using heavy-duty thread and small running stitches. Place the body sections right sides together, matching any notches. If there are no darts, simply pin, tack

(baste) and machine stitch body pieces together, leaving an opening for stuffing (above left). If there are body darts (above right), pin from the edges of the upper dart around to the edges of the lower dart. Tack (baste), then machine stitch center front seam and center back seam, each from dart to dart, leaving opening for stuffing. Remove tacking (basting).

*Some bears have four body sections. In these cases, the side seams should be joined first to create a left and right body section. The general instructions can then be followed to complete the body.*

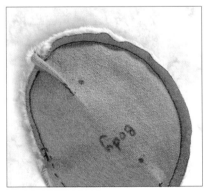

2 To complete a body with darts, flatten the top body section across the seamline, placing the top dart edges together. Pin and tack (baste) this dart from the farthest point to the seam edge. Remove the pins and machine stitch, again starting from its farther point to the seam edge. Then remove tacking (basting) stitches. The tiny space left where the four seams meet will provide the hole for the bear's head joint.

3 Flatten the dart seam towards the back of the body, using the pressure from the thumb and forefinger (index finger). Do not be tempted to slash or cut these darts as this may seriously weaken the fabric. Pin, tack (baste) and machine stitch the dart at the lower body edge in the same way. As there are no joints to be attached here, try to make all machine stitching lines coincide as closely as possible. Set body aside for stuffing later.

*Most of the bears have seam allowances of ¼ in (7mm). Check individual instructions for seam allowances for the two smallest bears (pages 54 and 100).*

### ATTACHING PAW PAD TO INNER ARM

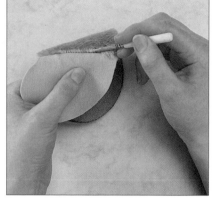

*Unless great care is exercised, a smooth fabric such as suedette tends to slide across the surface of a fur fabric during the pinning and tacking (basting) process.*

**1** Take an inner arm and a paw pad section and, with the right sides together, pin and tack (baste) along this seamline. Machine stitch and remove tacking (basting) stitches. Trim the seam close to the machine stitching and press the seam upwards towards the top of the arm, using the thumb and forefinger (index finger).

**2** Tease the pile from the seamline using a bodkin or stiletto and brush the fur lightly. If using a teasel brush, avoid scratching or pulling the fabric of the paw. This is particularly important when using suede, leather or felt. (Only use a teasel brush if instructed.) Join the second inner arm and paw pad sections in the same way.

### STITCHING THE BEAR'S ARMS

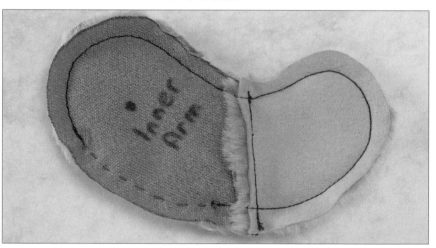

*The finished seam between the paw pad and the arm should face upwards towards the top of the arm to prevent it showing through on the smooth surface of the paw.*

Stay stitch the stuffing opening along the seamline on both the inner and outer arms. Place a front and back arm section right sides together, ensuring that the seamline of the paw is pressed upwards. Pin and tack (baste) all around the arm, leaving the stay stitched edge open. Starting from the edge of the stuffing opening, machine stitch around the arm, paying particular attention to the paw seams. Trim the seams where necessary and turn the arm right side out. Tease any trapped pile from the seamline. Make the second arm in the same way and set both arms aside for stuffing later.

### STITCHING THE BEAR'S LEGS

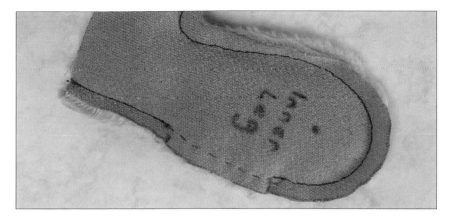

Stay stitch along the seamline of the stuffing opening on the inner and outer leg sections. Place these right sides together, and pin carefully, taking care to align each lower straight edge of the foot correctly. Tack (baste), then machine along the seamline around the leg section, leaving the lower edge and stuffing opening unstitched. Remove the tacking (basting) stitches. Turn the leg right side out and pull any trapped pile from the seamlines. Turn the leg inside out once more.

*Before machine stitching, all stuffing openings on the bear pattern pieces are stay stitched using a heavy-duty sewing thread.*

### ATTACHING THE BEAR'S FOOT PADS

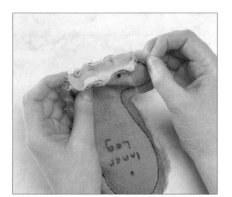

1 Place a foot pad within the oval formed by the lower straight edge of the foot, lining up the front and back notches with the front and back seamlines. Pin the pad in position. It may be necessary to stretch the fur fabric slightly to take in the curve of the oval smoothly. Using very small running stitches, tack (baste) around the pad, trying to maintain its oval shape as much as possible. Tack (baste) each side of the foot separately, starting and ending at a seamline and leaving seam free.

2 Remove the pins and turn the leg right side out to check that the pad is correctly placed. When you are completely satisfied, turn the leg inside out and machine stitch the pad, again working each side of the foot separately and ending and starting stitching as close as possible to the seamlines. Remove the tacking (basting) stitches, turn the leg right side out and brush out the pile on all the seams. Make the second leg in the same way and set both legs aside for stuffing later.

*The foot-pad seam is worked in two sections on either side of the leg seams to avoid having to stitch through two thicknesses of fur fabric. The foot-pad seam allowance is tapered as it approaches the leg seams.*

*When positioning the bear's eyes, the aim is to achieve a pleasing symmetry and an endearing expression.*

*If the special "eye tool" for inserting safety eyes is not available, a sturdy wooden sewing thread reel (spool) can be placed over the shank behind the washer to give extra support.*

### BEAR EYES

Both plastic teddy-bear safety eyes and traditional glass or boot button eyes come in various sizes. Altering the size and position of the eyes will greatly alter the expression of the finished bear. For instance, large eyes will give a bright, wide-awake look to your bear. By careful positioning these can be made to give the impression of slight surprise. Whatever the size of the eyes, try out various positions before deciding, then mark the center position of each eye using a glass-headed pin.

Glass and boot button eyes are inserted after the head has been stuffed (see opposite page), but safety eyes are inserted before the head is stuffed. For inserting safety eyes, turn the head right side out and make a tiny hole by easing the fabric threads aside with a stiletto or bodkin. Push the shank of the eye through to the wrong side. Then press down the securing washer over the shank as firmly as possible. It is possible to purchase a small strip of metal with two small holes, known as an "eye tool" or "flat safety tool" which will help to give additional pressure on the washer.

### STUFFING THE BEAR'S HEAD

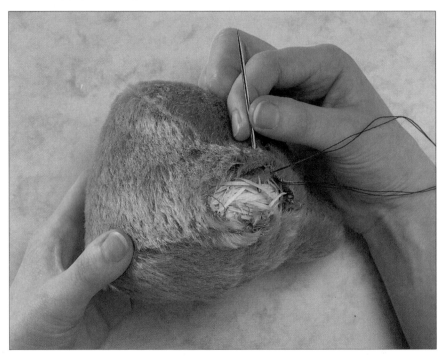

*Polyester filling, or stuffing, is used in conjunction with traditional wood wool to achieve a smoother finish on your collectors' bear.*

Begin by rolling a small amount of polyester filling between the palms of your hands to form a small ball. Then, using a stuffing stick, push the ball into the muzzle of the bear to begin to shape the nose section. Continue to fill the muzzle in this way, using your hands to mold and shape the bear from the outside. When the nose and muzzle are well shaped and firm, continue to stuff the head, using wood wool and working from the muzzle upwards, outwards and downwards. When sufficient filling has been added to the head, thread a darning needle with a doubled and knotted length of heavy-duty thread. Run this around the neck opening, using medium-length straight stitches. Do not fasten off the thread.

## INSERTING THE NECK CROWN JOINT

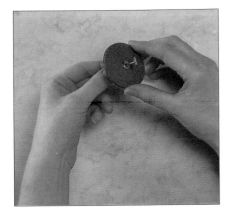 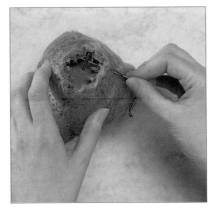 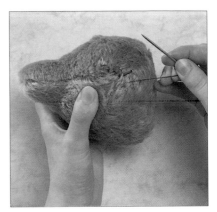

**1** Assemble the first part of the larger crown joint by threading a washer and one hardboard disc onto the split pin. (While inserting the crown joint in Step 2, check that there is sufficient stuffing behind it to hold it securely in position when the neck opening is closed.)

**2** Push the head of the split pin, the washer and the hardboard disc into the neck opening of the bear's head. The joint should sit above the line of running stitches. Take up the needle and heavy-duty thread and draw up the running stitches quite tightly, to hold the joint firmly in place.

**3** Take long stitches backwards and forwards through the fur fabric and across the joint around the split pin. Pull these stitches tightly and secure with a few stitches, before cutting the thread. Pull the split pin firmly to ensure that its head is sitting against the enclosed hardboard disc.

## FIXING GLASS OR BOOT BUTTON EYES

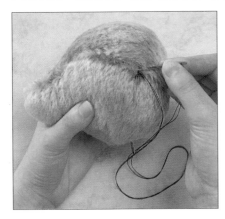  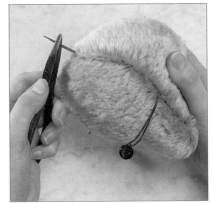

**1** Before fixing the bear's eyes, determine the exact positions of eyes and ears. Thread a long darning needle or bodkin with a long, doubled length of heavy-duty thread, knotting this several times at the end. Take the needle through the head from the position of the left ear seamline to the position of the left eye, bringing the needle through the fabric and pulling the thread slightly to tighten the tension.

**2** Using a stiletto, push aside the ground fabric warp and weft threads from around the needle thread, thus making a small hole through which the "bail" or loop of the eye can be passed. Thread the first eye onto the needle and take it down the thread to push the "bail" firmly through the fabric. Take the needle back through this hole and across the muzzle to surface at the position of the second eye.

**3** Repeat the last step for the second eye, but finish by taking the needle through the head to the position of the seamline of the right ear. Tighten the thread to pull in both eyes, forming a slight depression in each to provide the eye socket. Anchor the thread firmly by making several small straight stitches in one place on the ear line and cut off the working thread close to the fabric.

## STITCHING AND ATTACHING THE BEAR'S EARS

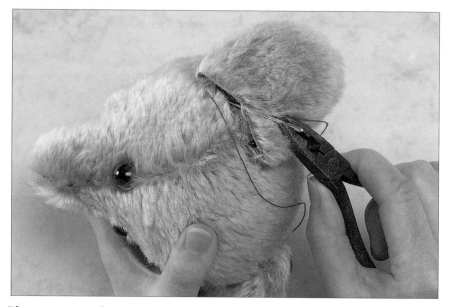

*The ears are attached using oversewing (also called overcasting) stitches. Before stitching them in place, check that they are symmetrical and give the bear the right appearance.*

Place two ear shapes right sides together. Pin, tack (baste) and machine stitch around the upper curve. Make the other ear in the same way and turn both right side out.

Then pin the back edge of each ear to the head. Using heavy-duty thread, stitch from the center point of one ear to the outer edge, using small oversewing (overcast) stitches pulled tightly. At the outer edge, tuck in the seam edges and stitch them inside the ear line. Secure with a few stitches and cut the thread. Re-join the thread to the center of the ear and work to the opposite edge in the same way. Turn under a tiny seam on the front edge of the ear and oversew this in position, working from the center outwards each time. Repeat for the second ear.

### PLACING THE NECK JOINT IN THE BODY

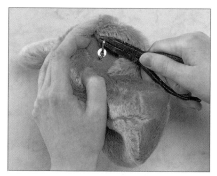

*Each classic bear requires five crown joints. The four smallest are for the legs and arms and the largest for the neck. The head is attached before the arms and legs.*

1 Before the body is stuffed, the crown joints are fitted. Use a stiletto to ease aside the seam stitching gently at the center top point of the body section. Insert the legs of the split pin through this hole and turn the top section of the body inside out.

2 Finish assembling the crown joint by threading on the second hardboard disc followed by a washer. Using sharp-nosed pliers, curl one pin over tightly, so that it sits against the washer and disc. Curl the second pin and check that the joint is firm.

## STUFFING ARMS AND LEGS AND INSERTING CROWN JOINTS

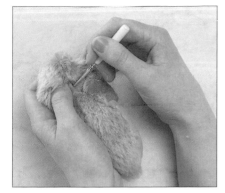

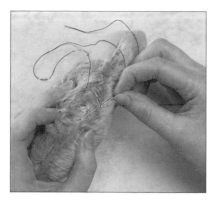

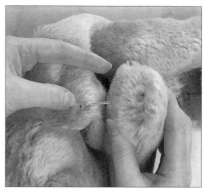

**1** Stuff both arms and legs to within 2in (5cm) of the joint mark. From inside, push a stiletto through this joint mark, carefully easing apart the threads of the fabric. Make a hole large enough for the split pin to fit. Assemble the remaining joints, threading on a washer and a disc. Push these through the holes in the arms and legs.

**2** Finish stuffing each limb, packing the filling behind and around each hardboard disc until the required shape and firmness is achieved. Using matching sewing thread, ladder stitch the stuffing openings firmly closed on both arms and both legs, pushing in extra filling with the stuffing stick or a knitting needle as required while stitching.

**3** Using a stiletto as before, make holes and insert the split pins at the points marked for placing both arms and legs on the bear's body. Thread on the second hardboard disc followed by a washer. Then complete the crown joints as described in Step 2 for the neck joints (see opposite page), making sure that each joint is firm.

## STUFFING AND CLOSING THE BEAR'S BODY

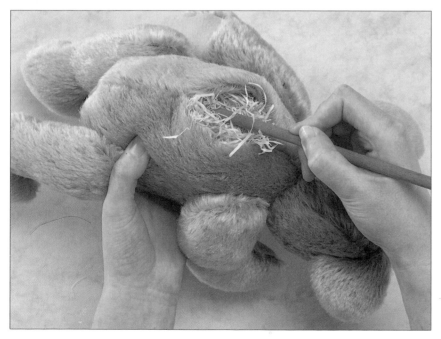

When all the joints are securely placed, stuff the body very firmly, pushing the stuffing down into position and shaping the bear as you work. (Before closing bear, see page 27 about growlers, squeakers, etc.) Ladder stitch the back opening of the bear closed, pulling the stitches firmly and fastening off securely.

*The ladder stitching should not be visible on the surface of the bear.*

25

## TRIMMING THE BEAR'S MUZZLE

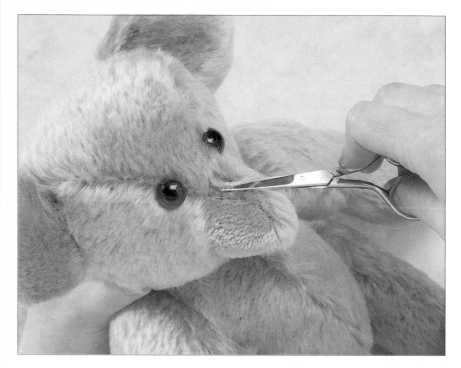

*Great care should be taken when trimming any of the fur pile on your classic bear. Before beginning, test your trimming skills on a fur-fabric scrap or remnant.*

If it is called for in the individual bear instructions, trim the pile around the muzzle. Use fine embroidery scissors and cut a little at a time until the required effect is achieved. For a traditional look, the muzzle should be trimmed all around to the point where the face begins to spread and flatten out. If in doubt, proceed very slowly and carefully, checking from time to time that the balance is correct.

## EMBROIDERING THE BEAR'S FEATURES

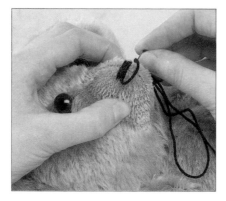

*Worked in satin stitch, the bear's nose is usually a rectangular shape, but other shapes include hearts, triangles and ovals.*

1 Embroidering features is the last stage in the bear-making process. With embroidery thread, embroider the nose in the desired shape, using closely worked satin stitches. It may be necessary to use pliers to pull the needle through when embroidering over seamlines.

2 Using straight stitches and embroidery thread, embroider the mouth. Experience will show the style of mouth you prefer to create the right expression for your classic bear. If in doubt, unpick the mouth stitches and try again until you are completely satisfied with the result.

## GROWLERS

For the ultimate touch of nostalgia a growler could be inserted in your bear before the stuffing opening on the body is closed. Growlers are best fitted in bears filled with wood wool, which, when tightly packed, will support their weight.

To insert a growler box, cut a circle of calico of sufficient size to enclose the growler completely. Place the growler, hole-end down in the center of the calico fabric, pulling up the edges and gathering these over the opposite end. Wrap heavy-duty thread around the ends of the fabric a few times and tie off securely.

Fill half the body of the bear with wood wool, packing it tightly into the lower section. Insert the growler so that the flat side is against the center back of the body. Using a darning needle and heavy-duty thread, stitch the calico neatly to the fur fabric with tiny stitches that should be invisible on the right side. Finish off firmly. Continue to stuff the bear with wood wool, making sure this is tightly packed around the growler. Close the opening in the usual way with ladder stitching (see page 25).

## SQUEAKERS

Bears fitted with squeakers should be soft enough to press and should not be laundered. A squeaker should be wrapped in calico and placed inside the bear in a similar manner to a growler (see instructions above), making sure that the reed is facing outwards.

## TINKLERS

A tinkler, like a growler or a squeaker, must be inserted in a teddy bear before the stuffing opening on the bear's body is closed. It should be placed right in the middle of the bear. The bear should be large and well stuffed with wood wool.

## MUSICAL BOXES

Before a musical box can be inserted in a bear, a calico cover should be made for it. The cover should have a hole through which the screw can be pushed. The calico is then stitched to the back of the bear in a similar manner to a growler, with the screw facing the fur fabric. A stiletto can then be used to make a hole through which to push the screw before the key is replaced. As with other "voices", the bear should be firmly stuffed with wood wool which will hold the movement rigidly in position.

*When making collectors' bears always use the best quality bear fittings.*

*Below are shown (from left to right and interspersed with sewing equipment) wood wool, eyes, hardboard crown joints, a teasel brush, plastic squeakers, a growler box and a musical box.*

# BEAR CARE AND REPAIR

Both new and old classic bears should be looked after carefully in order to preserve them in the best possible condition. The high acid content of straw and wood wool stuffing can cause bears to rot and the natural fibers used in their textiles can dry with age, making them prone to tear at the slightest pressure.

Strong sunlight or artificial light that contains ultraviolet rays can also prove damaging, so always keep bears away from prolonged exposure.

*Before attempting to use a vacuum cleaner to remove dust from a classic bear, cover the hose nozzle with a piece of net or gauze*

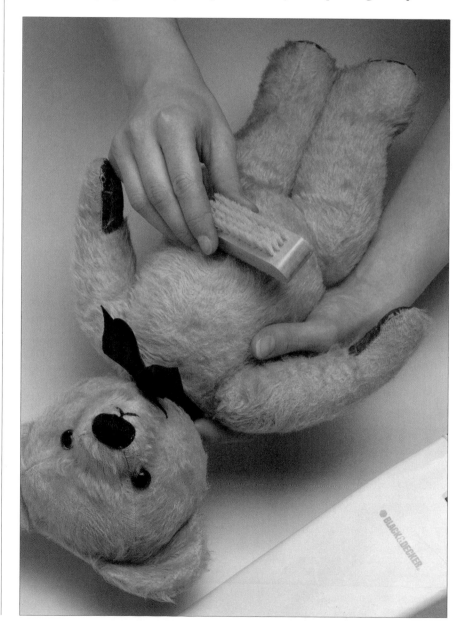

*Read the instructions for cleaning classic bears on the opposite page before brushing a valuable bear.*

For a permanent display of bears it is best to use a tungsten light bulb. Fluctuations in temperature should also be avoided, so remember to keep bears away from any source of heat, such as a radiator, convection heater or even hot water pipes.

Collectors' bears should always be handled with clean hands and in the case of valuable bears, it is wise to wear cotton gloves. The grime and acid on the hands can inflict untold damage on delicate fabrics.

### CLEANING CLASSIC BEARS

Dust can also prove a problem. It too has a high acid content and bears on display should be vacuumed regularly to remove any particles that may have settled. To minimize the risk of damaging the bear, cover the hose nozzle of the vacuum cleaner with a piece of fine net or gauze, which can be held in place with an elastic band. Then run the nozzle gently over the bear, taking extra care around the eyes, over the embroidered areas and along the seams – all places where dust is most likely to settle.

It is possible to freshen the fur pile of a bear by scrubbing it gently with a soft toothbrush or natural bristle nail brush which has been dipped in a very weak solution of detergent. The liquid type used for washing delicate clothes is best. Great care must be taken not to let the water soak into the backing fabric, as this might be absorbed into the wood wool filling. The fur can then be wiped gently with a clean, damp cloth until both the detergent and grime have been removed. It cannot, however, be stressed strongly enough that you should not attempt to wash a valuable bear without seeking advice from an expert such as the curator of a museum specializing in childhood toys and memorabilia. Specialist companies are now developing dry-cleaning fluids for bears and the manufacturers' instructions should always be followed carefully.

### REPAIRING BEARS

Restorers who specialize in repairing the wear and tear inflicted by the years can also be found. Unless you are very sure of what you are doing, or the bear is of little value, do not attempt do-it-yourself repairs.

Obviously, seams can be restitched using a good quality thread and a ladder-stitch technique and eyes can be replaced using reproduction glass boot buttons or modern amber ones. However, never make a repair or alteration that cannot be easily removed, thus restoring the bear to its original condition. This is particularly true of replacement paw and foot pads.

### STORING BEARS

A well-loved collectors' bear that is beginning to show its age should be wrapped in acid-free tissue paper and stored in a sturdy cardboard box. On no account should it be wrapped in polythene or plastic. It is possible that an old bear may have had its stuffing eaten by mites, in which case the seams should be opened gently, and the remaining stuffing removed. The bear should then be treated with a suitable proprietary insect repellant before being restuffed with wood wool and its seams restitched. Again, if in any doubt, it is always wise to consult an expert before attempting any repairs.

*Remember that collectors' bears and the bears in this book should not be given to small children to play with, as they do not comply with toy safety regulations.*

*Take good care of your traditionally made teddy bears and they will be a joy for collectors in the future.*

# EARLY BLACK BEAR

*The bear pictured here was inspired by early black bears. Made from black bouclé woven fabric, it is 16in (41cm) tall and has a black velvet muzzle and pads.*

Some years before the official birth of the teddy bear in 1903, both stuffed and wooden bears were being sold as toys. Unlike the teddies of later years, these bears were made to sound fierce and lifelike with a sinister growl; hardly the cuddly confidante of childhood!

These forerunners of the modern teddy were based on the bears of the wild. Known as "bruins", they stood on all fours and usually had a humped back. Often they were made from real fur; they had snarling expressions and some even had clockwork mechanisms to open their mouths in a realistic growl.

Some of these lifelike bears were muzzled and chained, resembling the dancing bears of middle European countries of the time. These poor bears stared through sad eyes over the straps and harnesses used to fetter them.

By today's more enlightened standards we look at these early examples of bears as being pathetic and miserable! They certainly were not made to be cuddled and loved.

Russian children of the time were no strangers to bears in captivity. One particular bear – Mishka – is traditional to Russian folklore and is looked upon as part of the national heritage. (More recently he appeared as the national emblem for the Moscow Olympic games held in 1980). Certainly, carved wooden bears that could perform simple tricks were produced in Russia, alongside somersaulting bears and bears that could walk across the floor. Once again, these were amusing pieces, but far removed from the teddy bear.

There was also a range of German-produced bears known as Peter bears. With their rolling eyes, moving tongues and bared teeth, they would probably have startled most adults, let alone a small child! Examples of these ferocious animals still exist, and although they post date early teddy bear manufacturing by a couple of decades (historians put their production around 1925,) they are more advanced and more frightening versions of the original bruins.

Although we tend to think of teddy bears in golden plush fur

fabric, many early bears were black or dark brown. In the dawn of teddy bear production, black and dark brown bears were still popular, particularly with German manufacturers. Unlike their predecessors, these are proper teddies with all the charm of their breed. The bear featured here is reminiscent of a Steiff bear produced in 1912 which, in fact, had beige felt pads and glowing, red tinted eyes (they were shiny black buttons on circles of orange felt). The ferocious Victorian bruins would, almost without exception, have had black glass eyes and dark paw and foot pads.

Early bears were intended to issue a fierce growl, although often it sounded more as though they were mooing! Although this bear has a friendly disposition, a growling voicebox would add to its authenticity and old-fashioned appeal.

A growler can be inserted quite easily – instructions on how to do this appear on page 27.

## Materials

*½yd (45cm) of 54in (137cm) wide black bouclé woven fabric with man–made pile*
*9in (23cm) square of black velvet*
*Tacking (basting) thread*
*Matching sewing thread*
*Matching heavy-duty thread*
*One 2½in (64mm) hardboard crown joint*
*Four 2in (50mm) hardboard crown joints*
*Small amount of "firm-fill" polyester filling (stuffing)*
*1½ lb (680g) wood wool*
*Two ⅝in (17mm) black boot button eyes*
*One skein black "pearl cotton" embroidery thread*

MAKING THE EARLY BLACK BEAR

Before starting to make the bear, carefully read the chapter on Classic Bear-making. Following the step-by-step instructions there, make the 10 templates, cut out the fabric pieces and assemble the bear, taking into consideration the special points below. Take care to keep your working surfaces as clean as possible at all times.

This bouclé fabric is not easy to sew and beginners are advised to practice on the more usual fur pile fabrics before attempting a bear of this type. The backing fabric is quite stiff and it may be necessary to use a pair of pliers and a stronger needle (such as a darner) when hand stitching or tacking (basting). The pile is not so easily trapped in the seams, but these should be checked and any caught threads teased out using a bodkin or stiletto. Do not use a teasel brush on bouclé fabrics.

The muzzle of this bear is cut out separately in velvet. Before sewing the head gusset to the side-of-head pieces following the step-by-step instructions, join the two velvet side-muzzle pieces to the two side-of-head pieces (seams B-C). Then join the velvet top muzzle to the head gusset (seam B-B).

As velvet tends to "slip" as it is machine sewn, it is advisable to hand stitch paw and foot pads, using a doubled thread and a firm backstitch. Tack (baste) both paw and foot pads in position as shown in the step-by-step instructions on page 21 for foot pads, using smaller and closer stitches than normal.

The eyes are placed on the head gusset seam, so that their lower edges are 1in (2.5cm) from the start of the velvet muzzle.

The ears should be set towards the back of the head across the gusset seams and at a slight angle with the lower edges tilting forwards a little.

The nose is worked in horizontal satin stitches across the seam at the end of the muzzle, forming a rectangle about ¾in (2cm) wide and ¼in (7mm) deep. Using two strands of pearl cotton, work a ½in (12mm) straight stitch downwards from the nose along the lower muzzle seam. Then work a ⅝in (18mm) straight stitch to either side to form the mouth.

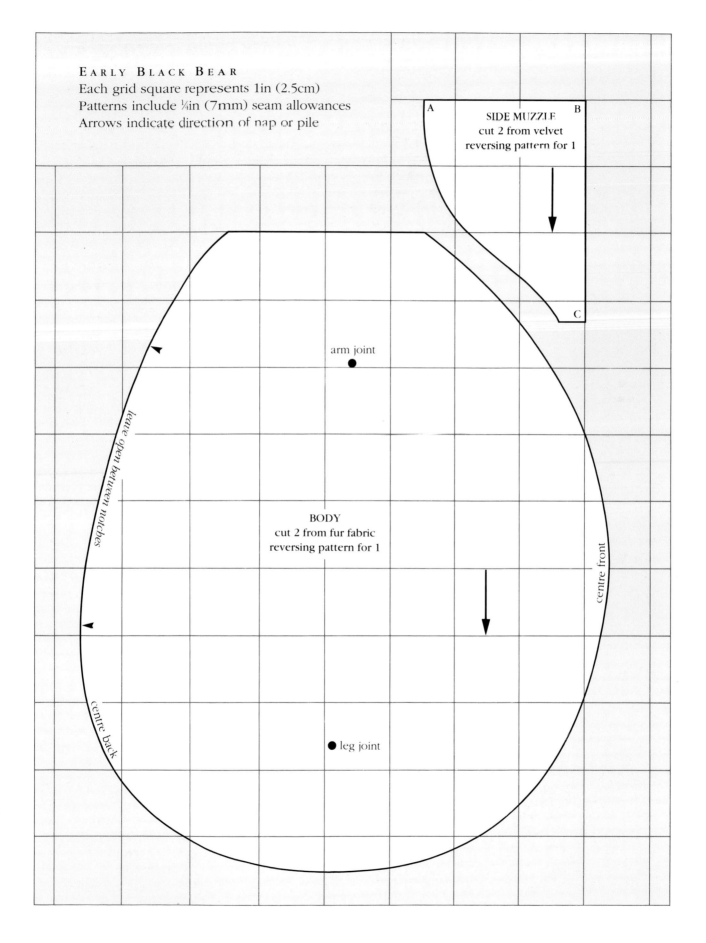

EARLY BLACK BEAR
Each grid square represents 1in (2.5cm)
Patterns include ¼in (7mm) seam allowances
Arrows indicate direction of nap or pile

A　B
SIDE MUZZLE
cut 2 from velvet
reversing pattern for 1

C

arm joint

leave open between notches

BODY
cut 2 from fur fabric
reversing pattern for 1

centre front

centre back

● leg joint

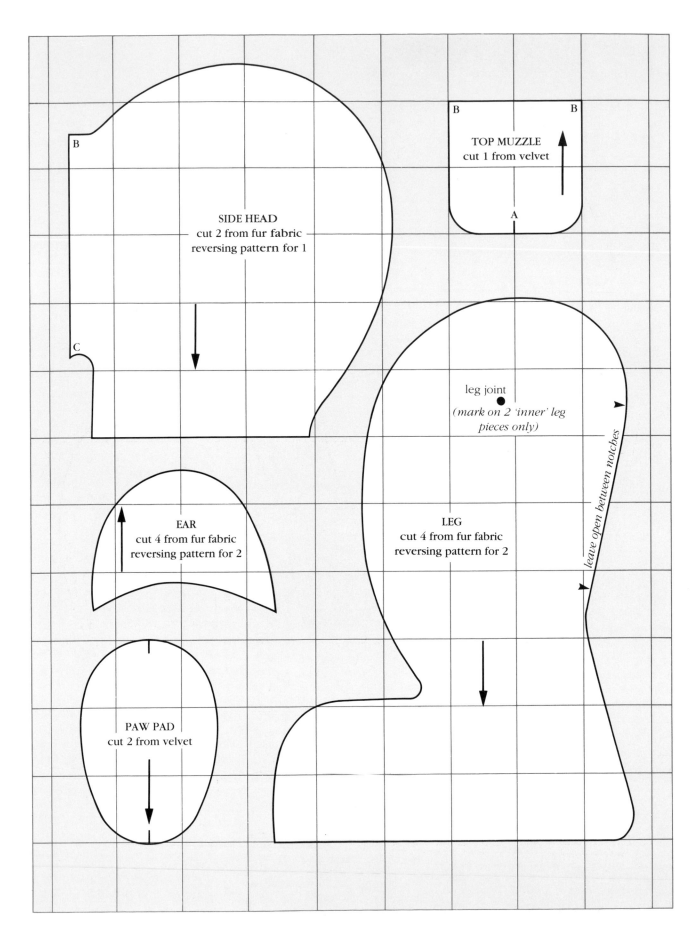

SIDE HEAD
cut 2 from fur fabric
reversing pattern for 1

B

C

TOP MUZZLE
cut 1 from velvet

B                    B

A

leg joint
(mark on 2 'inner' leg
pieces only)

leave open between notches

EAR
cut 4 from fur fabric
reversing pattern for 2

LEG
cut 4 from fur fabric
reversing pattern for 2

PAW PAD
cut 2 from velvet

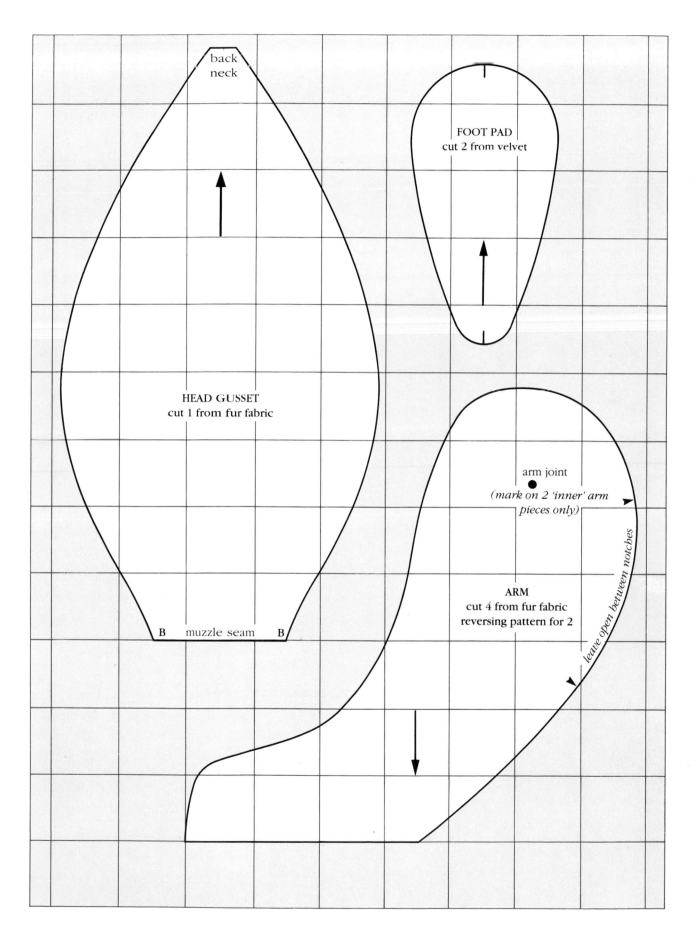

back neck

FOOT PAD
cut 2 from velvet

HEAD GUSSET
cut 1 from fur fabric

arm joint
*(mark on 2 'inner' arm pieces only)*

ARM
cut 4 from fur fabric
reversing pattern for 2

*leave open between notches*

B    muzzle seam    B

# MICHTOM BEAR

The creation of a jointed, mohair pile bear was the inspiration of a Russian immigrant to the United States named Morris Michtom.

Michtom ran a small candy store in Brooklyn with his wife, Rose, a skilled toymaker and seamstress. Many of her toys adorned the shop window to encourage customers inside.

The enterprising Mr. Michtom seized upon the idea of the toy bear while reading the *Washington Evening Post* one November day in 1902. A political cartoon, showing President Theodore Roosevelt refusing to shoot a tethered bear cub, gave Michtom the idea for an endearing toy bear. Michtom persuaded his wife to make a prototype cuddly bear. It was to be the first of many.

The original Michtom bear was made from golden plush mohair. It stood 21in (53cm) tall, with long, rather thin, arms and legs which had pale felt paws embroidered with black, straight-stitched claws. The bear's large, rounded ears were set on the sides of its head and it viewed the world from small, black, boot button eyes. The rather pensive and woebegone expression of Rose Michtom's toy bear proved an instant success.

The shrewd Mr. Michtom, so the story goes, sent a presentation bear to the White House asking for permission to name it in honor of the President. "I don't believe that my name will do much for the image of your stuffed bear," President Roosevelt allegedly replied, "but you have my permission to use it".

Whether Teddy Roosevelt's name did, in fact, do much, or whether the lovable little bear with its big round ears simply caught the imagination of the public does not really matter. "Teddy's bear" was taken into the hearts and homes of many American families.

The Michtom bear was soon being distributed through wholesalers Butler Brothers, and from these simple beginnings the hugely successful Ideal Novelty and Toy Company was formed in Brooklyn.

In fact, so successful was the Michtom's teddy that many imitators jumped on the bear bandwagon, producing teddy bear lookalikes.

Certainly, by 1907, teddy bears had taken America by storm. Although teddy bear history is poorly documented, evidence of

these creatures' popularity was immortalized in the much-loved music, *Teddy Bears' Picnic*, composed in this year by W. J. Bratton. The lyrics to the piece were added later.

One of the original Michtom bears now resides at the Smithsonian Institute in Washington, D.C., but you can make your own version displaying some of its charming characteristics by using the following pattern instructions.

The Michtom bear, like most bears in this book, can be stuffed with either a polyester or wood wool filling (stuffing). The latter creates a lot of dust, so asthma sufferers would be advised to wear a mask when using it.

## Materials

*½yd (.45m) of 54in (137cm) wide honey-gold mohair with ⅜in (9mm) pile*
*Small square of mushroom-colored suedette*
*Tacking (basting) thread*
*Matching sewing thread*
*Matching heavy-duty thread*
*One 2in (50mm) hardboard crown joint*
*Four 1⅜in (36mm) hardboard crown joints*
*Small amount of "firm-fill" polyester filling (stuffing)*
*1½lb (680g) wood wool*
*Two ½in (14mm) black buttons for eyes*
*One skein black "stranded cotton" embroidery thread*

### MAKING THE MICHTOM BEAR

Before starting to make the bear, carefully read the chapter on Classic Bear-making. Following the step-by-step instructions there, make the 10 templates, cut out the fabric pieces and assemble the bear, taking into consideration the special points below. Take care to keep your working surfaces as clean as possible at all times.

When using wood wool, always stuff the point of the muzzle, the feet and front paws with polyester filling (stuffing) first. This will ensure a smooth and even shape. Additional wood wool can be added to give extra firmness, but the smoother polyester should always remain as a protective layer beneath the fabric.

After stuffing and before finally closing the back opening, use polyester filler to pad out the hump and back curve fully.

If you wish to use black buttons for the eyes, it may be necessary to enlarge the stiletto hole by carefully cutting a few strands of ground fabric to enable the shank of the button to slip through. The eyes should be set just below the head gusset seam lines, level with the lower edge of the ears.

The claws are formed by embroidering three straight stitches on each foot pad and four straight stitches on each paw pad, using six strands of black stranded cotton embroidery thread.

The ears should be positioned from the head gusset seam downwards following the stitching line of the lower dart.

The nose is worked in horizontal satin stitches across the seam at the end of the muzzle, forming a rectangle about ⅝in (16mm) wide and ½in (12mm) deep. Using 6 strands of stranded cotton, work a ¼in (7cm) straight stitch downwards from the nose along the lower muzzle seam; then work a ½in (12mm) straight stitch to either side to form the mouth.

Finally, trim the fur pile back close around the whole of the muzzle. The pile around the teddy bear's eyes should also be trimmed lightly to expose them fully.

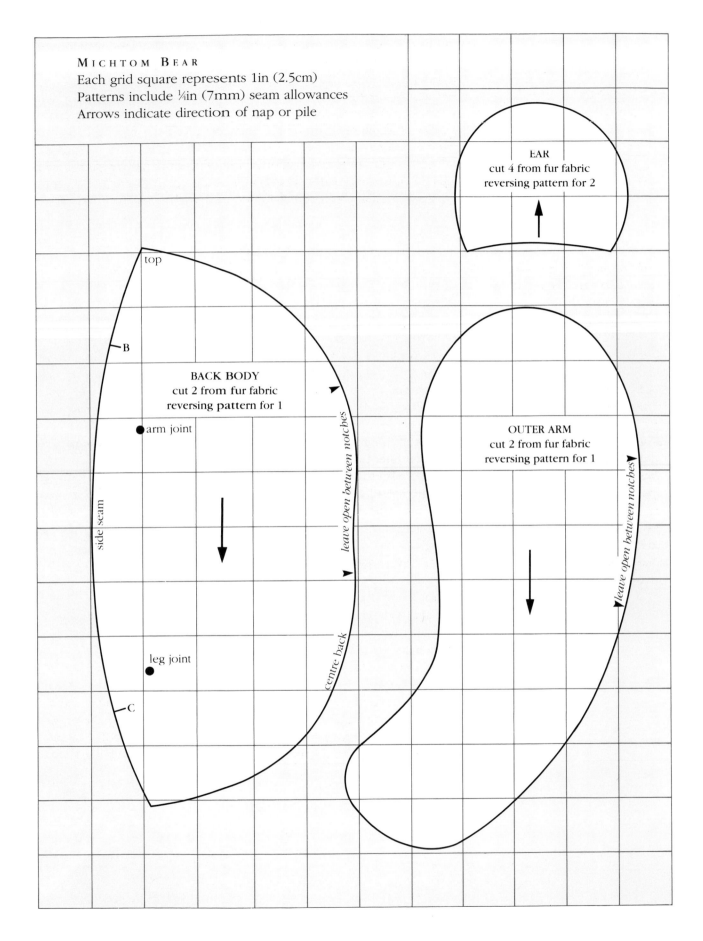

MICHTOM BEAR
Each grid square represents 1in (2.5cm)
Patterns include ¼in (7mm) seam allowances
Arrows indicate direction of nap or pile

EAR
cut 4 from fur fabric
reversing pattern for 2

top

B

BACK BODY
cut 2 from fur fabric
reversing pattern for 1

arm joint

side seam

leave open between notches

centre back

OUTER ARM
cut 2 from fur fabric
reversing pattern for 1

leave open between notches

leg joint

C

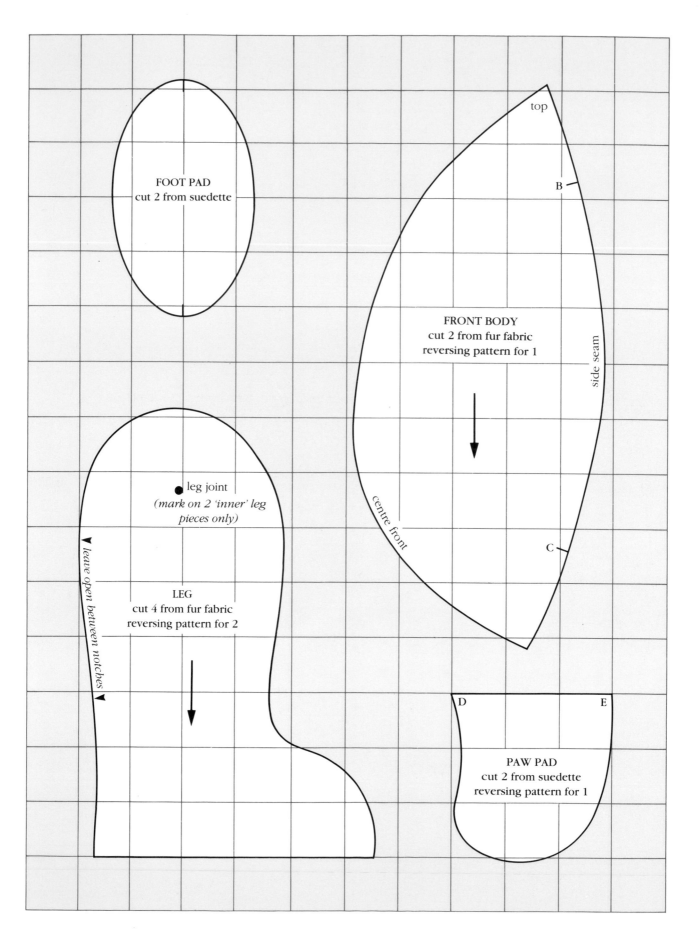

FOOT PAD
cut 2 from suedette

top

B

FRONT BODY
cut 2 from fur fabric
reversing pattern for 1

side seam

centre front

C

leg joint
*(mark on 2 'inner' leg
pieces only)*

leave open between notches

LEG
cut 4 from fur fabric
reversing pattern for 2

D          E

PAW PAD
cut 2 from suedette
reversing pattern for 1

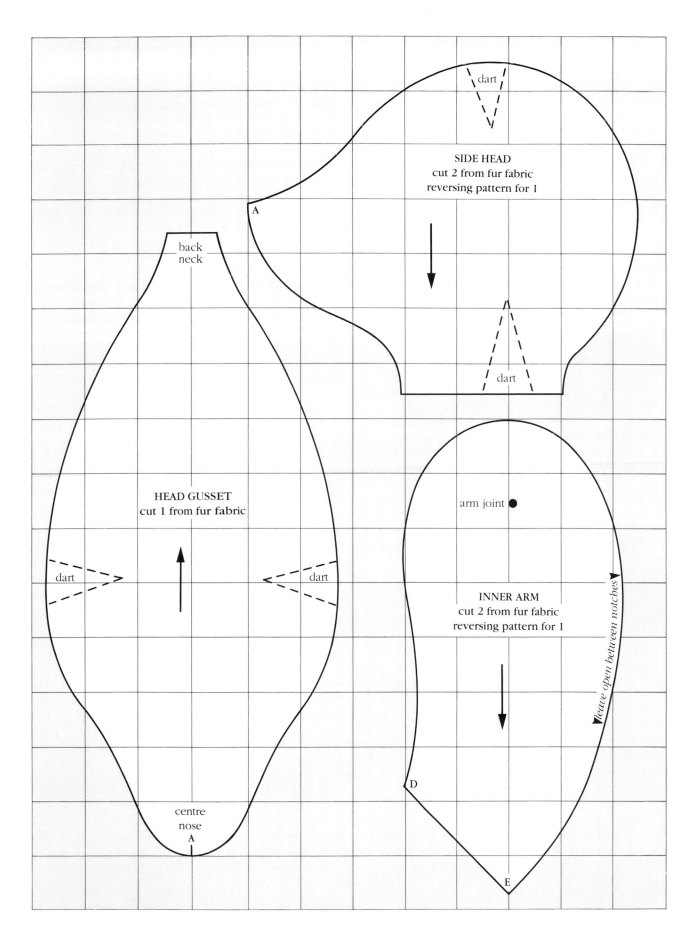

SIDE HEAD
cut 2 from fur fabric
reversing pattern for 1

dart

dart

A

back
neck

HEAD GUSSET
cut 1 from fur fabric

dart

dart

centre
nose
A

arm joint ●

INNER ARM
cut 2 from fur fabric
reversing pattern for 1

leave open between notches

D

E

# EARLY GERMAN BEAR

*The bear pictured here was inspired by early German bears. Made from honey-beige distressed pile mohair fabric, it is 14½in (37cm) tall and has pale beige suedette paw and foot pads.*

Although disabled from childhood by polio, German-born Margarete Steiff conquered her disability to become a world-renowned toy maker. And it is for the Steiff teddy bears that she is probably best known. Without doubt, the toy bears created by the Steiff factory in the early part of this century are the great-grandfathers of today's teddies.

History is still slightly confused over the origins of the Steiff bear, although it is commonly thought the toy was the brainchild of Margarete's nephew, Richard, who often sketched bears at Stuttgart Zoo.

It evidently took several years to persuade Margarete Steiff that bears with movable joints and plush fur were the toy of the future, but after setbacks and various modifications, the first Steiff bear, called Friend Petz, was completed in time for the Leipzig Toy Fair of 1903. Even then, it looked as though the bear was destined for the reject pile, as no one showed any particular interest. On the last day of the Fair, a leading New York toy importer approached the Steiff stand. It is said he was disappointed that there were no really new or exciting toys that year. Friend Petz was brought to his attention by Richard and so enthralled him that he placed an order for 3,000 bears then and there. The Steiff legend was born!

Over the few years following the Leipzig Toy Fair, bear production rose rapidly. By 1907 an amazing 974,000 bears were produced. Steiff led the bear market! Even today, this is remembered as the year of the bear.

Around 1914 the Steiff style began to change; the hump disappeared and the muzzle shortened and thickened. Bears in general took on a friendlier form. From 1920, the stuffing changed from wood wool to kapok and by 1921, glass eyes replaced boot buttons.

Classic Steiff bears can now be expected to fetch sums in excess of four figures when sold at auctions today. All bears manufactured by the company before 1910 are extremely valuable and the few with their growlers still working prove particularly desirable.

The record price for a bear at auction is held by the 1920s Steiff bear, "Happy," made in dual plush fabric. Originally purchased in Ireland, it had been with the same family for some time. It was bought for a staggering £55,000 ($81,000) by the chairman of a modern teddy bear manufacturer on behalf of a

*The Steiff button label above
is dated circa 1910.*

## Materials

*½yd (.45m) of 54in (137cm)
 wide honey-beige distressed
 pile mohair with ½in
 (12mm) pile
Small square of pale beige
 suedette
Tacking (basting) thread
Matching sewing thread
Matching heavy-duty thread
One 1⅜in (35mm)
 hardboard crown joint
Four 1in (25mm) hardboard
 crown joints
Small amount of "firm-fill"
 polyester filling (stuffing)
1lb (450 g) wood wool
Two ⅝in (16mm) amber and
 black glass boot button eyes
One skein black "soft cotton"
 and one skein terracotta
 "stranded cotton"
 embroidery thread*

friend. (By the time you read this, this record price for a teddy bear at auction might easily have been surpassed.)

It was as early as 1905 that the firm of Steiff protected its products by registering its now famous "button in the ear" trademark. Although other companies tried to imitate this, legal action prevented them from doing so.

This delightful bear has some of the characteristics of a Steiff creation of around 1904. It has a marked hump and long, slim, curved arms with claws embroidered in terracotta thread on its paw pads. Its nose is worked in satin stitch onto a thin, tapering muzzle and its rounded ears are set vertically across the head gusset seams. Instead of wooden boot buttons, it has amber glass eyes, set rather close together, and it is made in long pile distressed honey-beige mohair to provide a classic effect.

### MAKING THE EARLY GERMAN BEAR

Before starting to make the bear, carefully read the chapter on Classic Bear-making. Following the step-by-step instructions there, make the 9 templates, cut out the fabric pieces and assemble the bear, taking into consideration the special points below. Take care to keep your working surfaces as clean as possible at all times.

Unlike other bears in this book, those made from distressed pile mohair should not be brushed with a teasel brush, as this is likely to alter the characteristics of the fabric.

The claws are formed by embroidering four straight stitches on each of the bear's paw pads, using six strands of terracotta stranded cotton embroidery thread.

The eyes are placed just below the head gusset seam, so that their lower edges are 2in (5cm) from the tip of the muzzle.

The muzzle is trimmed back slightly unevenly, and a small amount of pile is cut away around the eyes to improve their appearance.

The ears should be set at the top of the head across the gusset seams and about 1½in (4cm) apart.

The nose is worked in horizontal satin stitches across the tip of the muzzle, using black soft cotton embroidery thread and forming a triangle. Using two strands of black soft cotton embroidery thread, work a ¼in (7mm) straight stitch downwards from the tip of the nose along the lower muzzle seam. Then using a single strand of the same thread, work a ½in (12mm) straight stitch upwards to either side to form the smiling mouth.

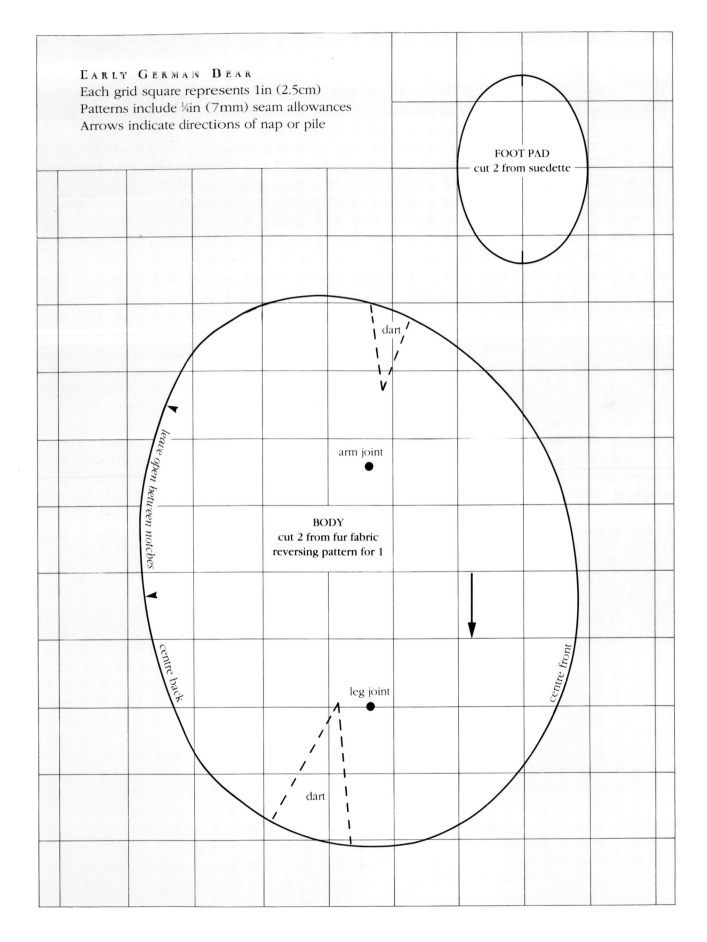

EARLY GERMAN BEAR
Each grid square represents 1in (2.5cm)
Patterns include ¼in (7mm) seam allowances
Arrows indicate directions of nap or pile

FOOT PAD
cut 2 from suedette

dart

leave open between notches

arm joint
●

BODY
cut 2 from fur fabric
reversing pattern for 1

centre back

centre front

leg joint
●

dart

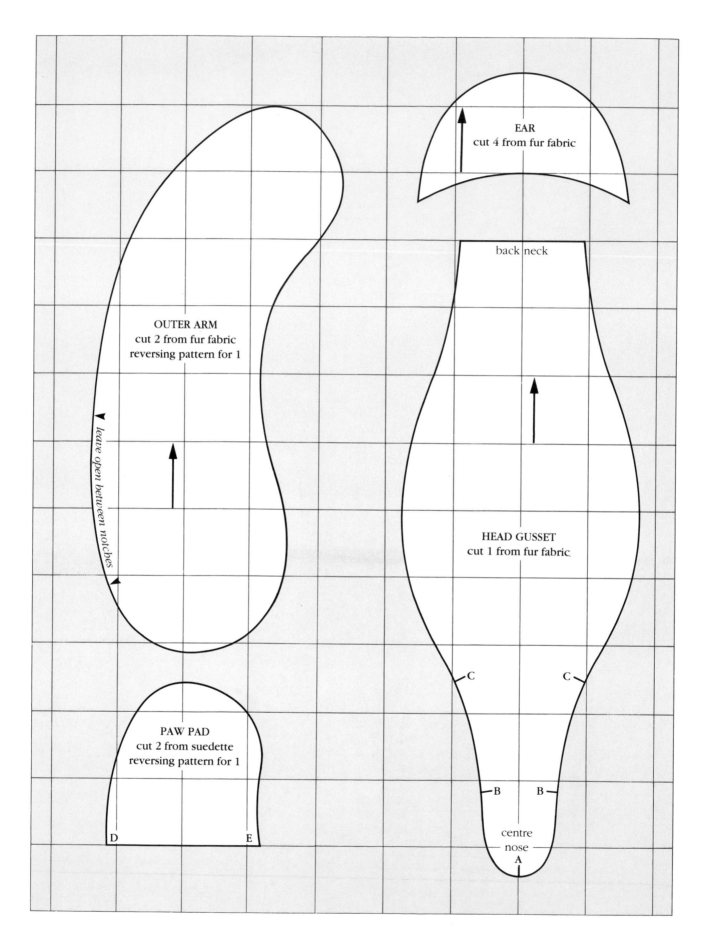

EAR
cut 4 from fur fabric

back neck

OUTER ARM
cut 2 from fur fabric
reversing pattern for 1

*leave open between notches*

HEAD GUSSET
cut 1 from fur fabric

C

C

PAW PAD
cut 2 from suedette
reversing pattern for 1

D

E

B

B

centre
nose

A

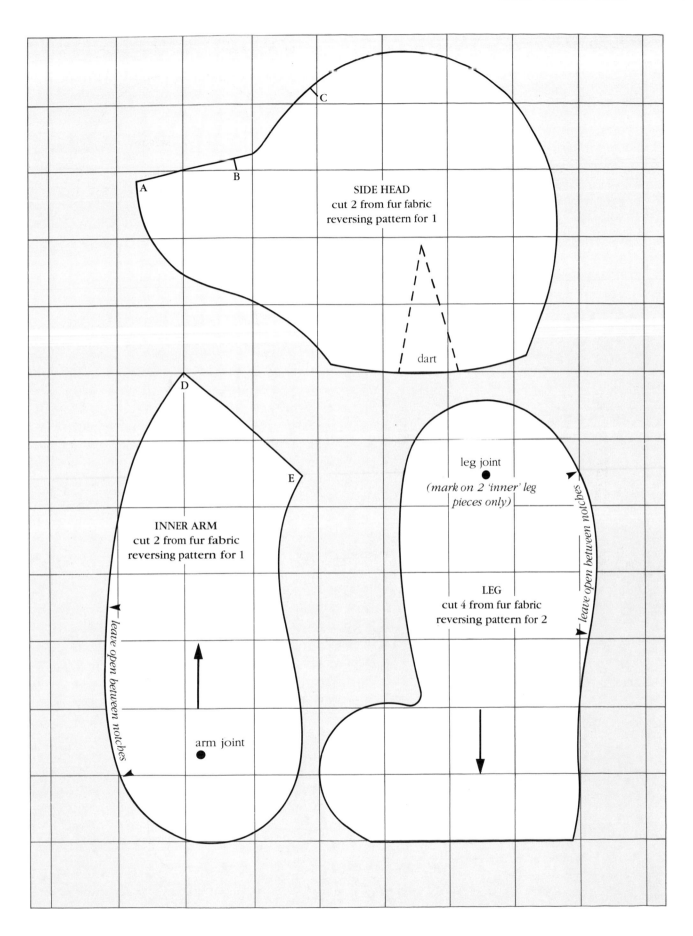

SIDE HEAD
cut 2 from fur fabric
reversing pattern for 1

dart

C

B

A

D

E

INNER ARM
cut 2 from fur fabric
reversing pattern for 1

leave open between notches

arm joint

leg joint
(mark on 2 'inner' leg
pieces only)

leave open between notches

LEG
cut 4 from fur fabric
reversing pattern for 2

# 1920s German Bear

Up until the outbreak of World War I in 1914, the basic teddy bear had changed little from its early beginnings. However, the war brought disruption to trading and production, and it wasn't until the turn of the decade that bears again began to fill the shelves.

By the 1920s, German bears were once again exported in large numbers. Factories such as Bing, Gebrüder Hermann, Gebrüder Sussenguth and, of course, Steiff, were all in evidence.

Bing bears, as they came to be known, were mechanical and often colorfully dressed. Gebrüder Sussenguth produced the rather ferocious Peter bears already discussed on page 30. Hermann bears, on the other hand, closely resembled the famous Steiff bears. In fact, the Hermann company was founded in 1907 specifically to make bears. It was only in later years that the company widened its range to include other toys.

However, by the 1920s, the German manufacturers were up against stiff competition from a growing number of toy companies in other countries manufacturing teddy bears for the first time.

In Britain, Chad Valley had made use of the war, which blocked German imports, to firmly establish itself as a soft toy manufacturer. Its teddy bears did not roll off the production line though until 1920.

Like Steiff bears, the Chad Valley ones bore a metal trade button quite often clipped to the ear.

Other major manufacturers included Dean's and J. K. Farnell in Britain and the Ideal Toy Company and Knickerbocker Toy Company in America.

By the 1920s, bears were evolving into a more modern design. Glass eyes were replacing boot buttons, the hump was beginning to lessen in size, the limbs began to shorten and the torso grew more rotund. In other words, the bears became more cuddly than they had been before. The stuffing for bears had also changed as they evolved.

Many bears manufactured in the 1920s were stuffed with a substance known as "Aerolite". This was the trade name for kapok, a natural fiber which can be mixed with wood wool or sawdust (and indeed it was) to create a softer feel.

One of the most famous bears from the early 1920s is surely Winnie the Pooh, a character created by A. A. Milne and almost certainly inspired

*This German bear (1910-20) is only 8in (20cm) tall.*

## Materials

*½yd (45cm) of 54in (137cm) wide gold crushed pile mohair (with ¾in (21mm) pile*

*Small square of tight beige suedette*

*Tacking (basting) thread*

*Matching sewing thread*

*Matching heavy-duty thread*

*One 3in (76mm) hardboard crown joint*

*Four 2in (50mm) hardboard crown joints*

*2lb (1kg) "firm-fill" polyester filling (stuffing)*

*Two ⅝in (17mm) black glass boot button eyes*

*One skein black 'pearl cotton' embroidery thread*

by a J. K. Farnell bear. However, the illustrations of Pooh, drawn by Ernest Shepard, are modeled upon a Steiff bear called Growler.

The other notable bear of the period is "Happy," a brown-tipped, beige, dual plush mohair bear from the Steiff factory. Happy was sold at auction in 1989 for a record sum of £55,000 ($81,000), making it the most expensive teddy bear in the world to date.

The bear featured here has large, narrow feet in the classic style and large round ears set wide apart. It has long, slim arms and light beige suedette foot and paw pads. Although toy bears were evolving at this time, German manufacturers, more than others, continued to make the traditional long-muzzled bears.

This bear has black glass boot button eyes and a black embroidered nose, but brown glass eyes and a brown embroidered nose and mouth could be substituted to achieve a closer resemblance to Happy. The famous bear's pads were made from a yellowish, beige felt; velveteen or suedette would make an acceptable substitute.

### MAKING THE 1920s GERMAN BEAR

Before starting to make the bear, carefully read the chapter on Classic Bear-making. Following the step-by-step instructions there, make the 9 templates, cut out the fabric pieces and assemble the bear, taking into consideration the special points below. Take care to keep your working surfaces as clean as possible at all times.

When working with extra long pile mohair, great care must be taken at the cutting stage. Use small, pointed and very sharp scissors, ensuring that only the backing fabric is cut. As each piece is finished, pull it away from the fabric carefully, separating the mohair strands as you do so.

As the pattern pieces are pinned and then tacked (basted) together, try using the flat of the pin or needle to push the pile inwards. This will help when the seams are machine stitched, preventing excessive amounts of pile being caught in the stitches.

The muzzle of this bear is left untrimmed. However, it may be advisable to trim away the pile in the area of the nose, before stitching. This will give a much neater effect and make working easier. Some pile may be trimmed from around the eyes if preferred.

The eyes are placed on the head gusset seam, so that their lower edges are 2½in (6.5cm) from the center of the tip of the nose.

The ears should be set about 2in (5cm) apart across the gusset seams and at a slight angle with the lower edges tilting forwards a little.

The nose is worked in vertical satin stitches across the seam at the end of the muzzle, forming a rectangle about ¾in (2cm) wide and ½in (12mm) deep. The bear has no embroidered mouth.

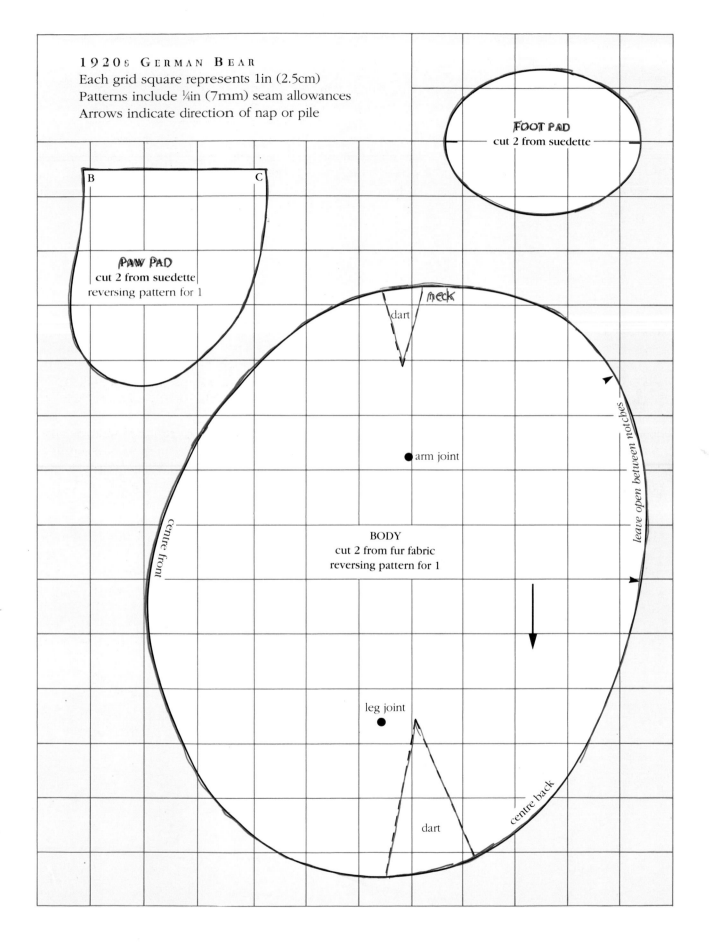

1920s GERMAN BEAR
Each grid square represents 1in (2.5cm)
Patterns include ¼in (7mm) seam allowances
Arrows indicate direction of nap or pile

FOOT PAD
cut 2 from suedette

B          C

PAW PAD
cut 2 from suedette
reversing pattern for 1

neck

dart

arm joint

centre front

leave open between notches

BODY
cut 2 from fur fabric
reversing pattern for 1

leg joint

dart

centre back

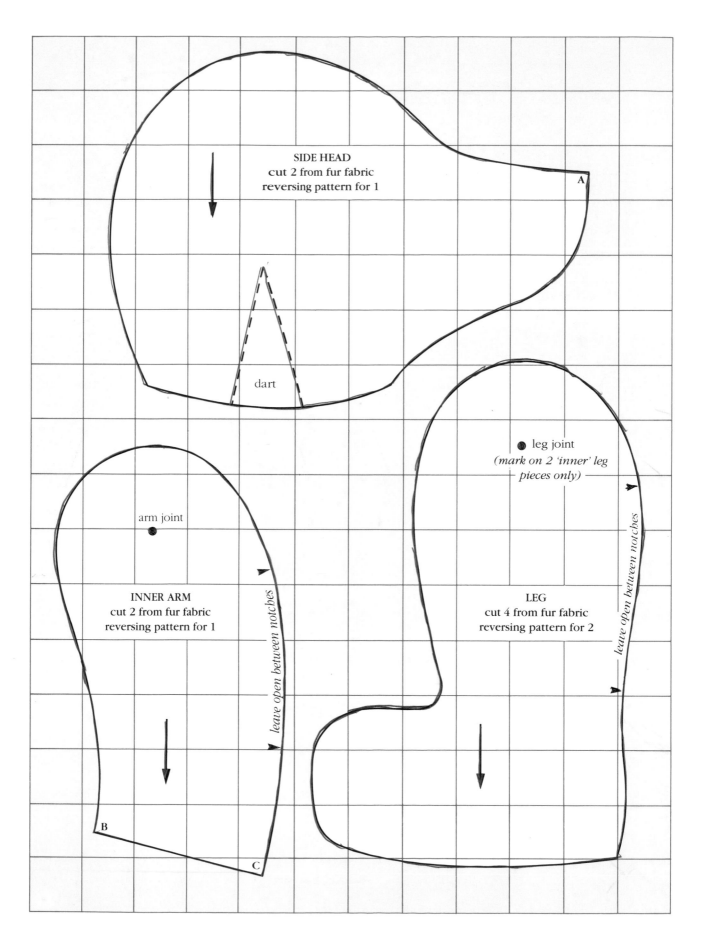

SIDE HEAD
cut 2 from fur fabric
reversing pattern for 1

A

dart

leg joint
(mark on 2 'inner' leg
pieces only)

arm joint

INNER ARM
cut 2 from fur fabric
reversing pattern for 1

LEG
cut 4 from fur fabric
reversing pattern for 2

*leave open between notches*

*leave open between notches*

B

C

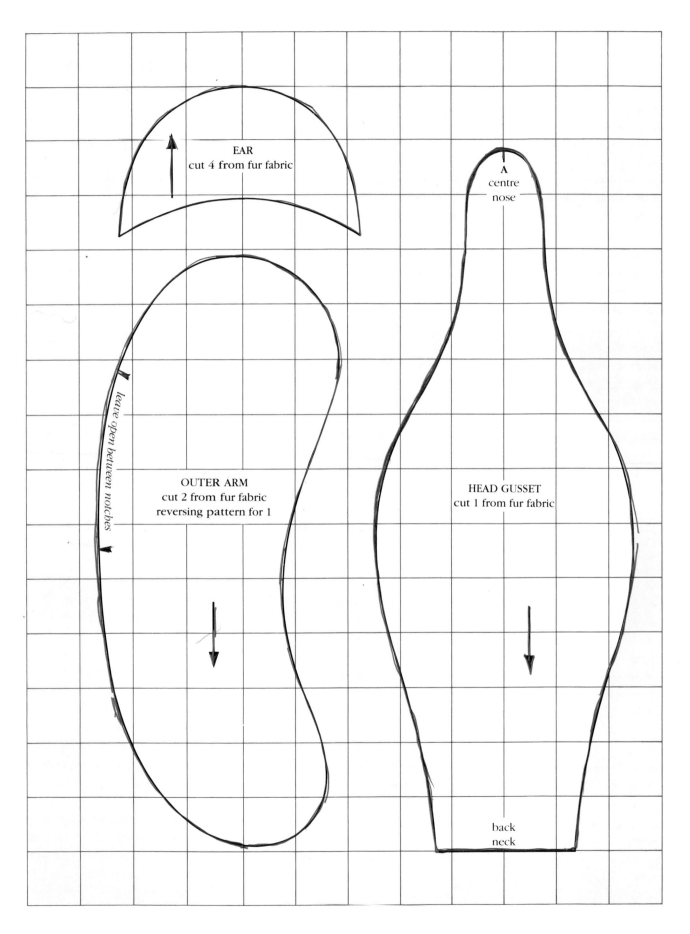

EAR
cut 4 from fur fabric

OUTER ARM
cut 2 from fur fabric
reversing pattern for 1

leave open between notches

A
centre
nose

HEAD GUSSET
cut 1 from fur fabric

back
neck

# MINIATURE BEAR

Once teddy bears had established themselves firmly in the toy trade, so various manifestations appeared. One of the most endearing and popular types was the tiny or miniature bear.

What defines a real miniature is often subject to conjecture. One of the early Steiff lines was a small bear of 9in (23cm) in height, but it is generally agreed that bears must be no taller than 7in (18cm) to be classed as miniature.

One of the principal manufacturers of tiny bears was Schreyer, a German company, often known more commonly as Schuco. Established in 1912, the company produced an unusual range of bears over the years. Its tiny stuffed bears were often made in various colors; the smallest one measured just over 2in (5cm) tall. Schuco also manufactured bears which could nod or shake their heads. These "Yes/No" teddy bears were also produced in miniature versions.

During the 1920s, scent bottles and lipstick cases came in the guise of little bears to put into a handbag or evening purse.

Miniature bears have the advantage that they can be popped into a pocket and carried around with their owner. Many people profess to having a miniature bear mascot which accompanies them everywhere. Small bears require a great deal of skill and patience to produce. Seams must be very accurately sewn and care must be taken when turning tiny sections, such as arms and legs. However, there is great satisfaction and pleasure in the final results, which have a distinctive charm. The obvious choice of fabric would be a short-piled mohair, but camel hair, cashmere or mohair cloth would be equally acceptable.

The bear featured here is jointed with the smallest commercially produced hardboard joints, but the joints for smaller bears can be made from two buttons, which can be pulled together using heavy duty thread. However, these joints will not be so readily movable as a crown joint. Take care when bending the split pin on some small joints, as they can be particularly unyielding. In some cases it may be best to substitute a longer pin, which can be curved over several times.

Some classic miniature bears were filled with sawdust, as wood wool would prove almost impossible to use.

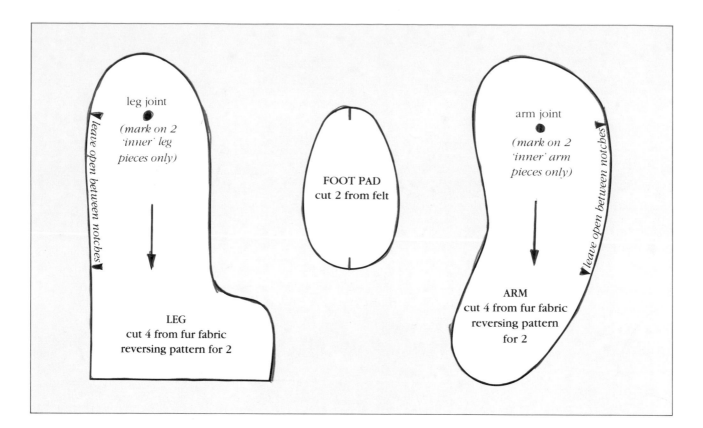

leg joint
● *(mark on 2 'inner' leg pieces only)*

*leave open between notches*

**LEG**
cut 4 from fur fabric
reversing pattern for 2

**FOOT PAD**
cut 2 from felt

arm joint
● *(mark on 2 'inner' arm pieces only)*

*leave open between notches*

**ARM**
cut 4 from fur fabric
reversing pattern
for 2

## Materials

*¼yd (25cm) of 54in (137cm) wide honeysuckle mohair with ⅜in (9mm) pile (this will be enough for several bears)*

*3in (7.5cm) square of cream-colored felt*

*Tacking (basting) thread*

*Matching sewing thread*

*Matching heavy-duty thread*

*Black heavy-duty thread*

*One 1in (25mm) hardboard crown joint*

*Four ¾in (18mm) hardboard crown joints*

*4oz (110 g) "firm-fill" polyester filling (stuffing)*

*Two small round black glass beads*

*One skein black "stranded cotton" embroidery thread*

### MAKING THE MINIATURE BEAR

Before starting to make the bear, carefully read the chapter on Classic Bear-making. Following the step-by-step instructions there, make the 7 templates, cut out the fabric pieces and assemble the bear, taking into consideration the special points below.

Great care must be taken when machine stitching such a small bear. Seam allowances should be kept to a minimum – about ³⁄₁₆in (5mm). Areas which need special attention such as the pads and the muzzle are best stitched by hand, using a doubled thread and a firm backstitch. Any points which are likely to be strained during stuffing should be hand stitched with a double row of stitches.

The position of the eyes will depend on the size and shape of the beads chosen. This bear has eyes placed just outside the head gusset about ¾in (18mm) from the tip of the nose. Bead eyes are applied using a similar technique to glass, except that they sit on the fur fabric and are not inserted through it. Heavy-duty black thread should be used. This should be taken from the position of the ear, through the head, to the point where the bead is to sit. Thread on the bead and settle it against the head, checking that the position is correct. Take a small stitch the width of the bead back into the head and take the needle across to the position of the second eye. Fasten this with another straight stitch and take the needle to the second ear position before finishing off.

The nose is worked in horizontal satin stitches using six strands of black stranded cotton and forming a small rectangle. From the center of the nose a ¼in (7mm) straight stitch is taken down the seamline and a smiling mouth is then made by taking a straight stitch to left and right upwards and outwards to each side.

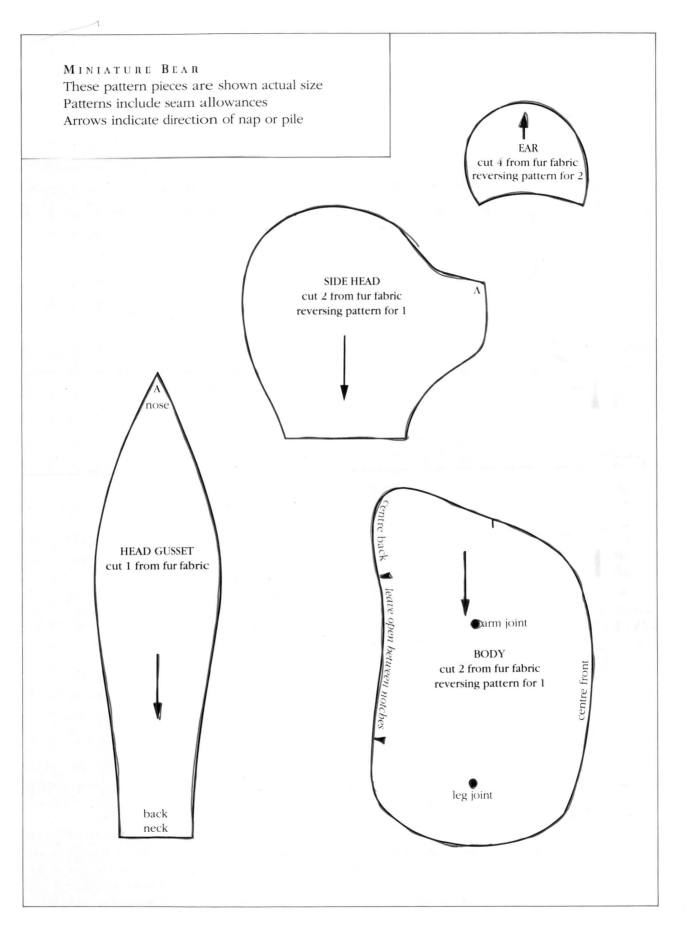

MINIATURE BEAR
These pattern pieces are shown actual size
Patterns include seam allowances
Arrows indicate direction of nap or pile

EAR
cut 4 from fur fabric
reversing pattern for 2

SIDE HEAD
cut 2 from fur fabric
reversing pattern for 1

A
nose

HEAD GUSSET
cut 1 from fur fabric

back
neck

Centre back

leave open between notches

arm joint

BODY
cut 2 from fur fabric
reversing pattern for 1

centre front

leg joint

# CLASSIC WHITE BEAR

The 1920s saw a great diversity in bear types, not least the colors and various kinds of fabrics used to make them. Shortages during the war years forced the manufacturers to experiment with a range of different materials and dyes, even though the most desirable and classic bears were still chosen from the range of mohair available.

White mohair bears are not perhaps as popular as their more usual honey-gold and brown cousins, but they do have a charm and appeal all their own.

One early white bear was produced by Steiff in the year 1921. This delightful bear was made from white plush and stood 15in (38cm) tall. It was of the classic shape although its legs were rather shorter than those of its predecessors. This white bear did not prove to be a huge success at the time and manufactured numbers were somewhat limited. This, of course, now makes white bears of this type extremely collectable and valuable.

Some years later, in the year 1927, Steiff manufactured a small white teddy bear called Petz. This bear is being produced again by Steiff as one in their successful replica range.

Apart from teddy bears, there have also been a large number of lookalike polar bears. In Britain, toy polar bears dating from the early 1950s were based on real life animals in the zoo. Two well known examples include Ivy and her son Brumas, polar bears then living at the London Zoo.

Early Australian bears were made in a variety of colors, including white. These white bears often had blue glass eyes, giving them an almost human expression.

Over the years, many firms across the world have produced white teddy bears. In more recent years, white teddies seem to have grown in popularity with many bear ranges including more than one white-fur variety.

Keeping needlework clean is important whatever the task. However, when working with white mohair, it is absolutely essential. Following these simple guidelines will enable you to keep your fabric in the best possible condition throughout the sewing process.

*This 15in (38in) bear is
probably a 1930s Chiltern.*

## Materials

*½yd (45cm) of 54in (137cm)
wide ivory mohair with ⅜in
(9mm) pile*
*Small square of ivory-colored
suedette*
*Tacking (basting) thread*
*Matching sewing thread*
*Matching heavy-duty thread*
*One 2in (50mm) hardboard
crown joint*
*Four 1⅜in (35mm)
hardboard crown joints*
*Small amount of "firm-fill"
polyester filling (stuffing)*
*1lb (450g) wood wool*
*Two ⁷⁄₁₆in (11mm) black glass
boot button eyes*
*One skein light terracotta
"stranded cotton"
embroidery thread*

Before beginning to cut out the fabric, lay it face downwards on a clean pillow case. Cut it out using sharp-pointed scissors, picking up the fabric away from the pillow case as you work. When all the pieces have been cut, these can then be stored away in the pillow case, which can also be used as a table or lap cover when work is actually in progress.

No matter how carefully you work, fur fabric will shed some pile during handling. This is particularly noticeable with white and other pastel colors, so a lap cover serves the dual purpose of keeping the fabric clean and preventing loose pile from covering your clothes.

The ivory bear featured here is similar in style to the bear produced in the Steiff factory during the 1920s. However, it has small black boot button eyes, giving it a somewhat quizzical expression. In the traditional manner its nose has been embroidered in a rectangle of vertical satin stitches using a terracotta embroidery thread. The same thread has been used to embroider claws which are stitched across the fur fabric onto the pad itself.

### MAKING THE CLASSIC WHITE BEAR

Before starting to make the bear, carefully read the chapter on Classic Bear-making. Following the step-by-step instructions there, make the 10 templates, cut out the fabric pieces and assemble the bear, taking into consideration the special points below. Take care to keep your working surfaces as clean as possible at all times.

When drawing around templates, it is absolutely essential to ensure that the inked markings will not transfer from the surface of the templates to the fabric and a sharp, soft lead pencil should be used to draw around each shape as lightly as possible.

Small black glass eyes have been used for the bear featured here, but you may like to try colored eyes, blue in particular, for a different expression. Larger eyes will give your bear a more wide-awake and innocent look.

The teddy bear's eyes here are placed just below the head gusset seam, so that their lower edges are 1¼in (3cm) from the center of the tip of the bear's muzzle.

The ears should be set so that they start at the gusset seam with the lower edges tilting backwards a little.

The nose is worked with six strands of stranded cotton in vertical satin stitches across the seam at the end of the muzzle, forming a rectangle about ¾in (2cm) wide and ½in (12mm) deep. Each side of the mouth is worked downwards from the center of the nose in two short stitches to form a slight curve.

Four claws have been embroidered on each pad using six strands of stranded cotton embroidery thread. Insert the needle through the paw at the seamline and take it to the position for working the first claw about ½in (12mm) away from the seam into the fur fabric. Pull the thread through until the tail lies within the paw itself and make a straight stitch across the seamline to ½in (12mm) across the pad. Take the needle back through the paw to the stitching position for the second claw and repeat the process until four claws have been made. Take the needle back through the paw to the seamline, pull firmly and cut the thread. The tail should then disappear into the paw, leaving a neat and tidy finish.

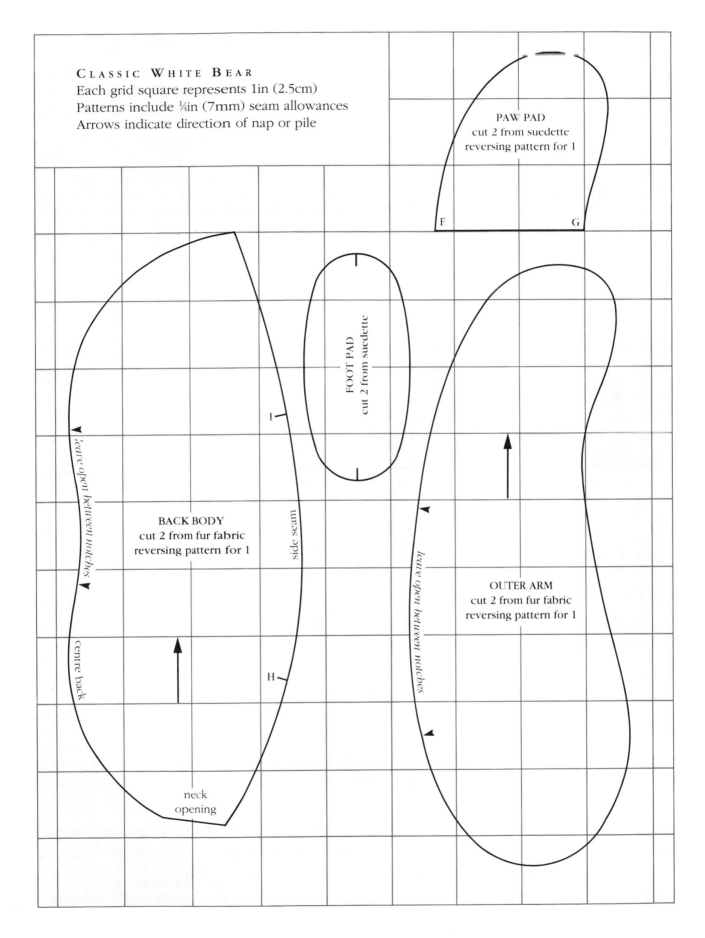

CLASSIC WHITE BEAR
Each grid square represents 1in (2.5cm)
Patterns include ¼in (7mm) seam allowances
Arrows indicate direction of nap or pile

PAW PAD
cut 2 from suedette
reversing pattern for 1

F          G

FOOT PAD
cut 2 from suedette

BACK BODY
cut 2 from fur fabric
reversing pattern for 1

side seam

leave open between notches

centre back

I

H

neck opening

OUTER ARM
cut 2 from fur fabric
reversing pattern for 1

leave open between notches

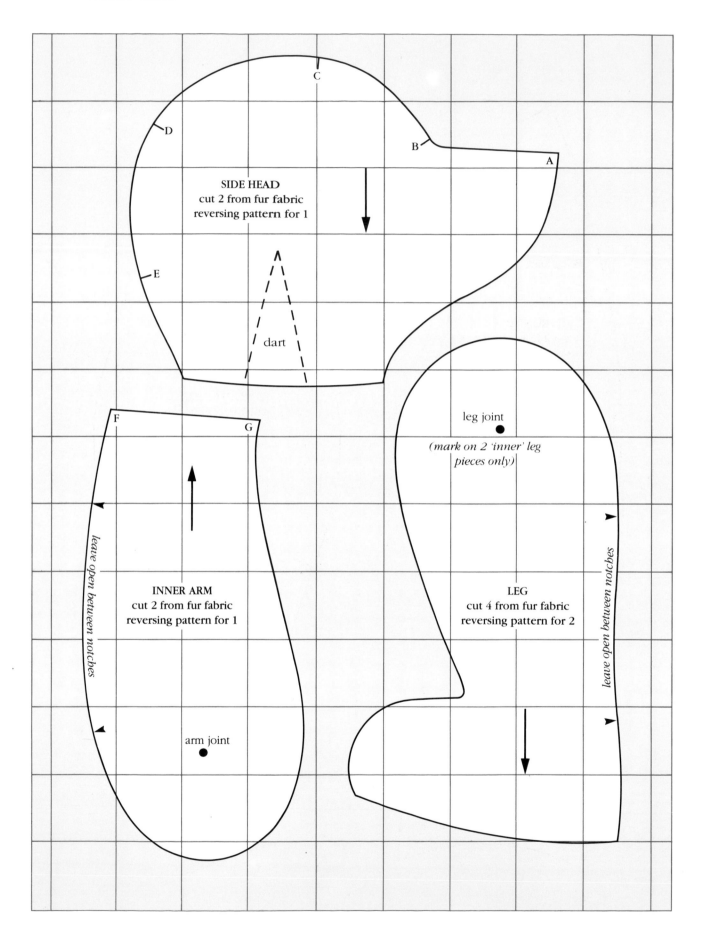

**SIDE HEAD**
cut 2 from fur fabric
reversing pattern for 1

C

D

B

A

E

dart

F

G

leg joint

*(mark on 2 'inner' leg
pieces only)*

**INNER ARM**
cut 2 from fur fabric
reversing pattern for 1

*leave open between notches*

arm joint

**LEG**
cut 4 from fur fabric
reversing pattern for 2

*leave open between notches*

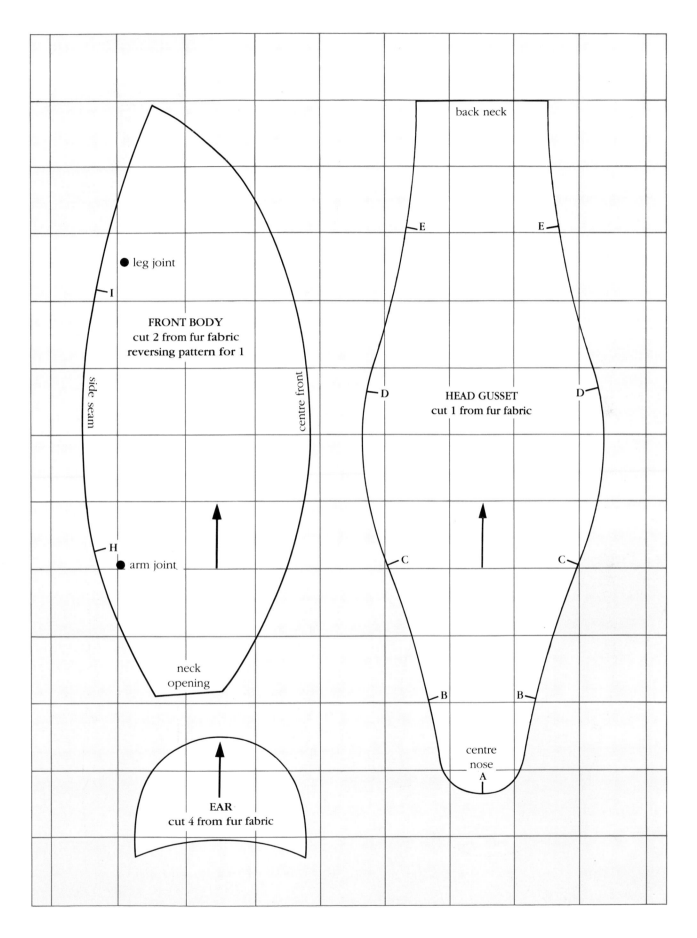

● leg joint

I

FRONT BODY
cut 2 from fur fabric
reversing pattern for 1

side seam

centre front

H
● arm joint

neck
opening

EAR
cut 4 from fur fabric

back neck

E                    E

D                    D

HEAD GUSSET
cut 1 from fur fabric

C                    C

B            B

centre
nose
A

# 1930s BEAR

As 1930 dawned, the British teddy bear industry saw the genesis of a new company, Merrythought. Founded by C. J. Rendel of Chad Valley and A. C Janisch of J. K. Farnell, Merrythought was established with the help of a mohair company – Holmes and Laxton – in Shropshire, central England. The shrewd mohair spinners were only too well aware of the growing threat from synthetic fibers to their industry; they saw teddy bear manufacturing as a way to survival.

Merrythought's trademark is a wishbone (merrythought is an old English term meaning wishbone) which was imprinted on a celluloid button and sewn to the ear or the shoulder of the bear. Later the bears were labelled on the undersides of their feet.

Alongside Dean's and Chad Valley, the Merrythought Company flourished.

English bears had a generally softer outline and rounder form than their German counterparts. By the 1930s their pads were being made from Rexine, a simulated leather fabric.

Other popular teddy bears of the day were those made for the department stores and mail order catalogues. As these were produced en masse, they never had a lasting, formal identification mark label like the Merrythought or Steiff bears, so it is now difficult to trace their origins. However, the Chiltern Company, founded in the 1920s, almost certainly made a substantial number of these bears. The department store and mail order bear came in a wide array of sizes and colors.

Merrythought produced a successful range of dressed bears called Bingie bears. These 1930s novelty bears often wore extravagant costumes. Their ears were lined with a new synthetic fabric called silk plush.

Although many of the teddy bear manufacturers thrived in the 1930s, J. K. Farnell sadly ceased production in 1934 due to a big fire which devastated the factory.

By the close of the decade, World War II had begun and although many manufacturers were still in production, teddies were being replaced in the factories by more essential items. Then homemade bears made from all manner of fabrics and oddments began to appear.

## Materials

*1yd (90cm) of 54in (137cm)
wide fawn distressed pile
mohair with ¾in (21mm)
pile*

*Small square of dark
chocolate brown velvet*

*Tacking (basting) thread*

*Matching heavy-duty sewing
thread*

*One 3in (76mm) hardboard
crown joint*

*Four 3½in (88mm)
hardboard crown joints*

*1lb (450 g) kapok*

*2¼lb (1kg) wood wool*

*Two ⅝in (15mm) amber and
black glass eyes*

*One large deep-voiced
growler (optional)*

*Scrap of calico or muslin for
growler (optional)*

*One skein black "stranded
cotton" embroidery thread*

*A 1930s Merrythought label.*

The bear featured on the cover of this book is an early Merrythought teddy, purchased in the 1930s. It is 28in (70cm) tall and is fitted with a growler, which, sadly, no longer works. Over the years it has given and received much love and its fur in places has worn very thin! This bear is a delightful example of the pleasure to be gained from bears of all shapes and sizes.

### MAKING THE 1930s BEAR

Before starting to make the bear, carefully read the chapter on Classic Bear-making. Following the step-by-step instructions there, make the 10 templates, cut out the fabric pieces and assemble the bear, taking into consideration the special points below. Take care to keep your working surfaces as clean as possible at all times.

As this bear is quite large, it is advisable to use heavy-duty thread for all machine stitched seams.

The center head gusset of this bear is in two sections. Cut these out as a pair, turning over the template to produce a "pair" of pattern pieces. Join the center seam before attaching the gusset to the side-of-head pieces in the usual manner.

Before turning the head right side out, trim the side head and center gusset seams around the muzzle. The head should then be stuffed and closed around the hardboard joint.

The leg templates are turned over along the back seamline to produce the pattern piece, so only two leg sections are cut. The stuffing opening in this case is on the front of the leg as there is no back seam.

As the distance from the ear position to the eye socket is too far to insert a bodkin, use a doubled, knotted length of heavy-duty thread, which should be inserted close to the final placing of the eye (about 2½in (6cm) from the nose tip along the side head gusset seam). Make a few very tiny oversewing (overcasting) stitches before bringing the bodkin out a little way from these. Enlarge the hole using a bodkin, thread on the eye loop and insert the eye. Take the bodkin across the muzzle to the approximate position of the second eye, pull the thread tightly and make a few more tiny oversewing (overcasting) stitches. Make a hole and insert the eye. Then take the bodkin to the tip of the nose, finishing off with oversewing (overcasting) stitches and snipping the tail thread closely. (These stitches will be covered by the embroidery stitches of the nose.)

The nose is a rectangle of vertical satin stitches measuring 1¼in (3cm) across and 1in (2.5cm) deep and is worked using six strands of stranded cotton. The edges are neatened with several horizontal straight stitches at the top and bottom.

The smiling mouth is formed from a few straight stitches, the horizontals of which are looped upwards slightly to form a smile.

An optional growler has been inserted in this bear. If you wish to include a voice, instructions can be found on page 27.

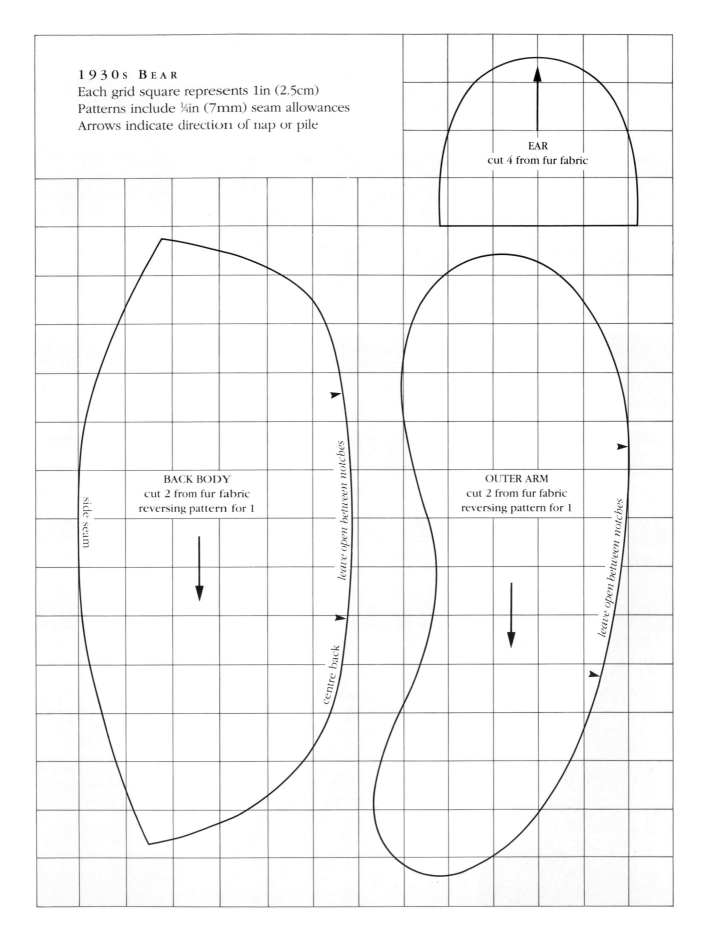

**1930s BEAR**
Each grid square represents 1in (2.5cm)
Patterns include ¼in (7mm) seam allowances
Arrows indicate direction of nap or pile

EAR
cut 4 from fur fabric

BACK BODY
cut 2 from fur fabric
reversing pattern for 1

side seam

leave open between notches

centre back

OUTER ARM
cut 2 from fur fabric
reversing pattern for 1

leave open between notches

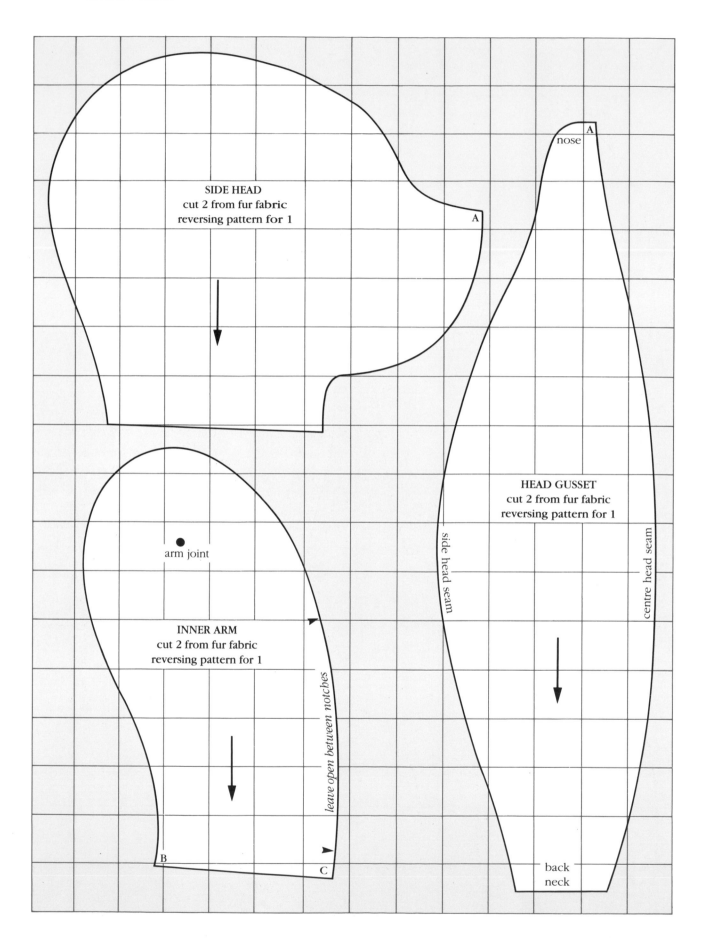

SIDE HEAD
cut 2 from fur fabric
reversing pattern for 1

A

nose

A

HEAD GUSSET
cut 2 from fur fabric
reversing pattern for 1

side head seam

centre head seam

arm joint

INNER ARM
cut 2 from fur fabric
reversing pattern for 1

leave open between notches

B

C

back
neck

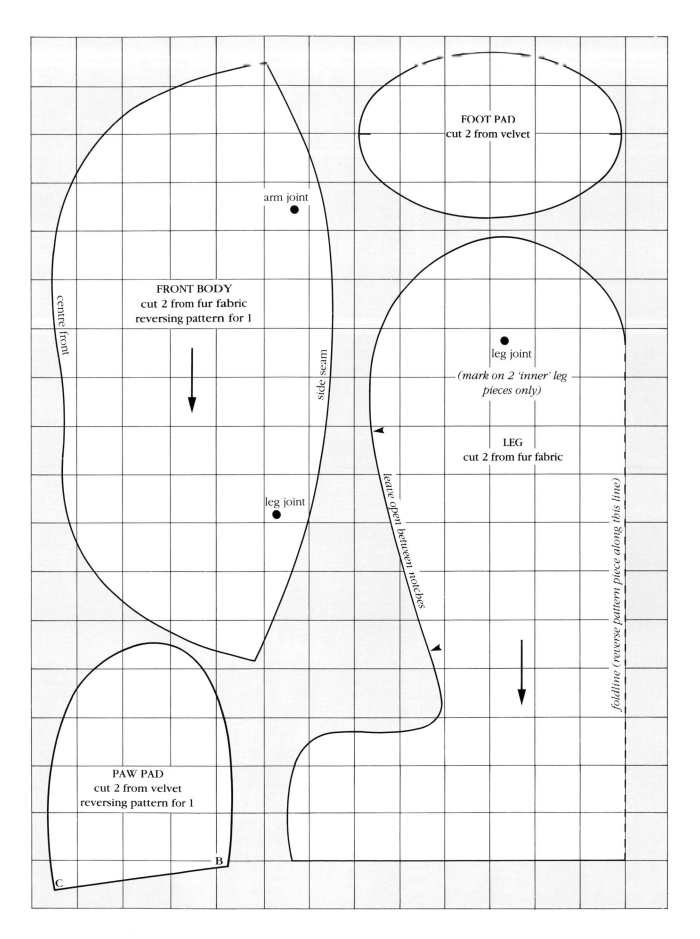

FOOT PAD
cut 2 from velvet

arm joint

FRONT BODY
cut 2 from fur fabric
reversing pattern for 1

centre front

side seam

leg joint

leg joint

(mark on 2 'inner' leg
pieces only)

LEG
cut 2 from fur fabric

leave open between notches

foldline (reverse pattern piece along this line)

PAW PAD
cut 2 from velvet
reversing pattern for 1

B

C

# FRENCH BEAR

*The bear pictured here was inspired by French bears. Made from honey-gold mohair pile fabric, it is 12in (31cm) tall and has dark beige suedette pads.*

Until World War I most bears sold in France, as in Britain, were imported from Germany. However, as the conflict continued, a small but nevertheless significant domestic industry set about manufacturing teddy bears.

Generally, French bears were not of such high quality as German models; fur was usually of a lower standard – being harsher and more bristly. It was also often a brasher, brighter gold. Later on, in the 1930s, many bears were made from an inferior artificial plush.

The most notable thing about the French teddy was its appearance. Being less substantial than its German counterpart, it tended to have much thinner arms and legs, as well as a shorter muzzle. Bodies were also often slimmer and straighter than other bears, especially if compared with quality Steiff or Hermann teddies.

Jointing on French teddies was also very different as a cruder exterior wire system was used which, when the fabric disintegrated, meant the bear really did fall to pieces. Eyes were usually clear glass, hand-painted on the back in black or brown. These were often held in place with glue or fastened individually by means of a wire loop.

As the French tended to favor dolls, teddy bear manufacturing never took off like it did in Britain, the United States, Germany or even Eastern Europe.

As French bears were generally constructed in an inferior way, few good bear examples from the early part of the century exist.

One noted French producer was M. Pintel Fils & Cie. Bears from this and similar factories can be identified by a trade button, rather like the famous Steiff mark, on the chest or ear.

The French are probably better known for their mechanical bears, some excellent examples of which still exist from around the 1920s.

Because of the French bears' rather slimmer shape, they make an interesting alternative to sew. This bear is made from a honey-gold mohair, although one of the bright new colors could be used as a substitute. The pads are dark beige suedette and the eyes are cheeky little boot buttons.

A little experience with making teddy bears will show that no two bears look exactly the same. The slightest variation in the positioning of the ears or eyes will produce a very different character from the

ones shown in the photographs in this book. One of the pleasures of making classic bears is that, as they are assembled, they take on their own particular personality. You will soon decide just how you like your bear to look.

Traditionally, bears have been given an inverted "Y" shaped mouth, but even within this guideline, there are endless variations of expression. Should the fur pile cause long stitches to shift position, hold them down with a few tiny straight anchoring stitches.

Most early bears have small eyes which are rather close-set. Placing eyes further apart will give a wide-eyed and innocent look. In general, teddy bears' eyes look best set low down on the head, not too far from the muzzle, but this again is a matter of preference. A rather vacant expression can be achieved by moving the eyes further towards the ears, spacing them widely apart.

## Materials

*¼yd (25cm) of 54in (137cm) wide honey-gold mohair with ⅜in (9mm) pile*
*Small square of dark beige suedette*
*Tacking (basting) thread*
*Matching sewing thread*
*Matching heavy-duty thread*
*One 2in (50mm) hardboard crown joint*
*Four 1⅜in (36mm) hardboard crown joints*
*Small amount of "firm-fill" polyester filling (stuffing)*
*1lb (450g) wood wool*
*Two ½in (12mm) black glass boot button eyes*
*One skein black "soft cotton" embroidery thread*

### MAKING THE FRENCH BEAR

Before starting to make the bear, carefully read the chapter on Classic Bear-making. Following the step-by-step instructions there, make the 10 templates, cut out the fabric pieces and assemble the bear, taking into consideration the special points below. Take care to keep your working surfaces as clean as possible at all times.

Stuff the muzzle firmly, using polyester filling (stuffing), to form a short, angular shape.

The eyes should be placed on the head seam, so that their lower edges are about 1¾in (4.5cm) from the tip of the muzzle.

The ears should be set vertically downwards from the head gusset seams on the sides of the head 1¾in (4.5cm) from the eye position. The top tip of each ear should just be touching the head gusset seam.

The nose is worked in horizontal satin stitches, following the tip of the head gusset seamlines and forming a blunt-ended triangle which finishes just below the point of the head gusset seam.

From the center of the lower edge of the nose, make a ½in (12mm) straight stitch downwards, following the lower seamline and using two strands of soft cotton thread. The mouth is then formed by making a ¾in (18mm) straight stitch from the center to the right, back to the center and a ¾in (18mm) straight stitch from the center to the left. The expression of your bear can be altered by varying the angle of these straight stitches. Upturned stitches will express a contented bear, while downturned stitches will portray a need to be cuddled!

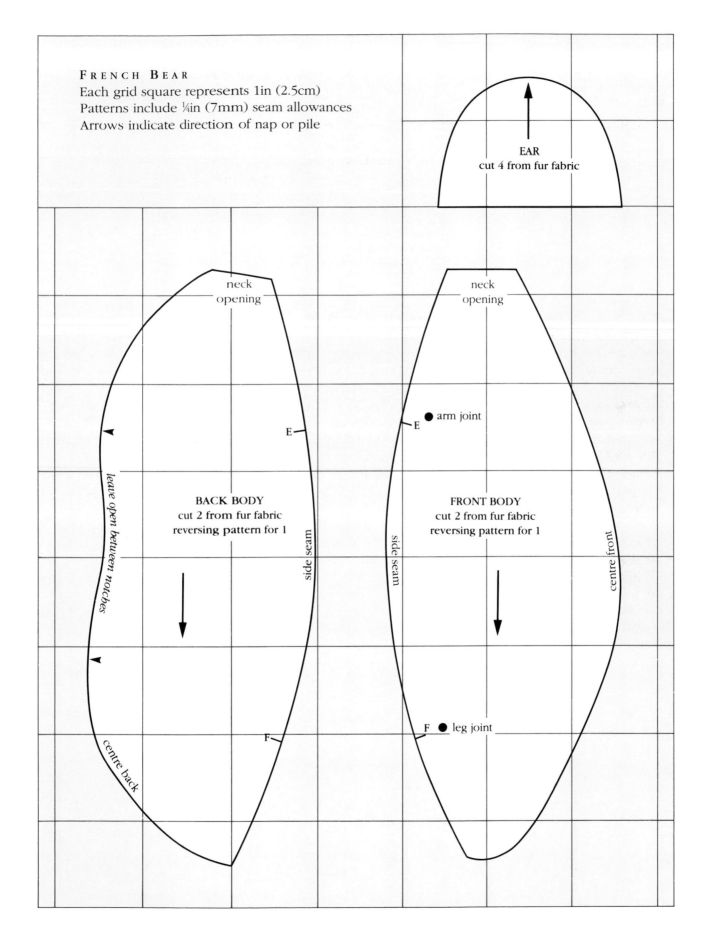

FRENCH BEAR
Each grid square represents 1in (2.5cm)
Patterns include ¼in (7mm) seam allowances
Arrows indicate direction of nap or pile

EAR
cut 4 from fur fabric

neck opening

neck opening

● arm joint

E

E

BACK BODY
cut 2 from fur fabric
reversing pattern for 1

FRONT BODY
cut 2 from fur fabric
reversing pattern for 1

leave open between notches

side seam

side seam

centre front

centre back

F

F ● leg joint

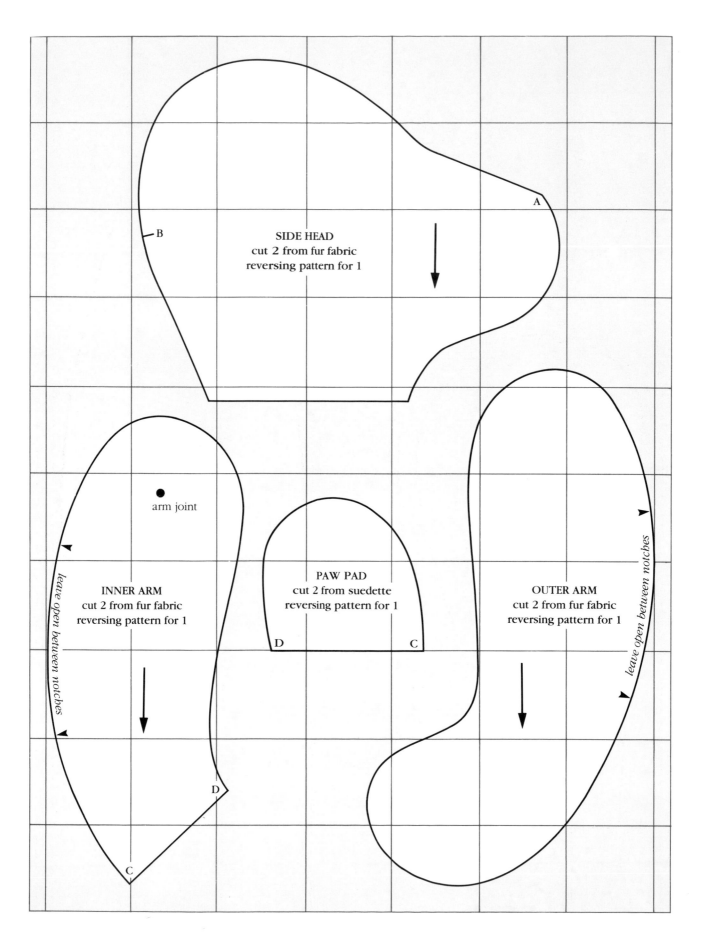

SIDE HEAD
cut 2 from fur fabric
reversing pattern for 1

A

B

arm joint

INNER ARM
cut 2 from fur fabric
reversing pattern for 1

PAW PAD
cut 2 from suedette
reversing pattern for 1

OUTER ARM
cut 2 from fur fabric
reversing pattern for 1

D        C

D

C

leave open between notches

leave open between notches

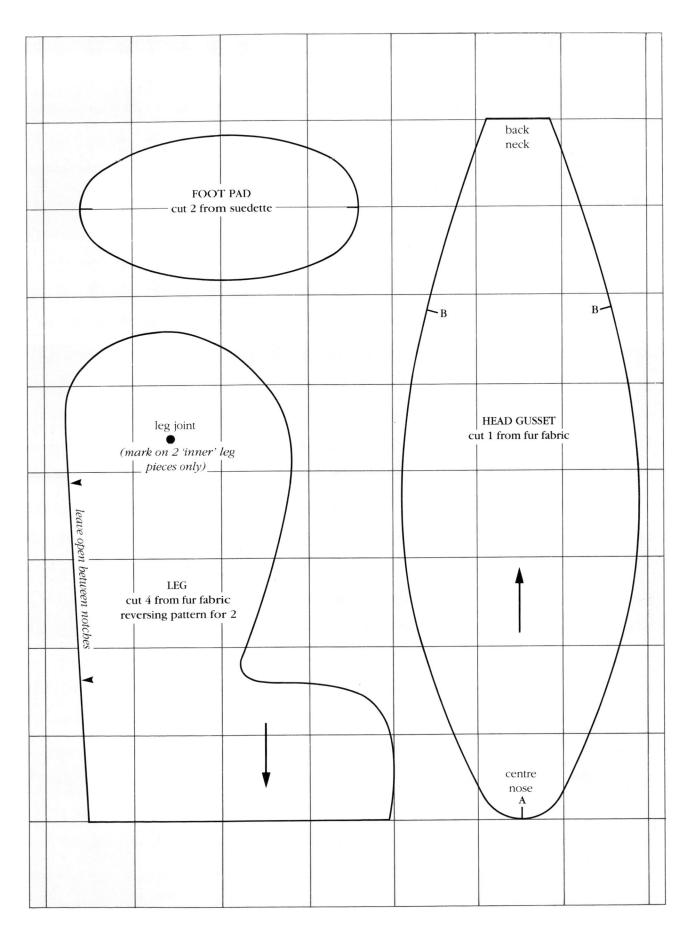

FOOT PAD
cut 2 from suedette

back
neck

B          B

HEAD GUSSET
cut 1 from fur fabric

leg joint
●
(mark on 2 'inner' leg
pieces only)

LEG
cut 4 from fur fabric
reversing pattern for 2

leave open between notches

centre
nose
A

# WARTIME BEAR

*The bear pictured here was inspired by a bear-style popular during World War II. Made from honey-gold mohair pile fabric, it is 14in (36cm) tall and has dark beige suedette pads.*

During World War II, imports were once again restricted. In the early part of the war, the domestic markets boomed. In Britain, firms such as Chad Valley, Chiltern and Merrythought took advantage of the lack of competition from the mainly German factories. But as the conflict dragged on, supplies for toy manufacture diminished, even though the best mohair fabrics were produced in Yorkshire. Many smaller manufacturers which had been formed to meet the demand for teddy bears over the previous fifteen or so years were forced to close down.

However, teddy bears continued to be made. As stocks on the shelves dwindled, publishers were quick to respond to the demands of needlewomen and produced instruction books for making a variety of soft toys. Patterns also appeared in women's magazines and newspapers. One publication stressed the therapeutic value of creative handiwork, recommending the satisfaction to be derived from producing a cuddly toy from the contents of a rag bag! Some of the more unlikely materials suggested for recycling were moth-eaten bathing suits, old undershirts and discarded hats. Old stockings and cotton fabrics were shredded to form the filling, while buttons and old leather gloves were recommended for creating the features.

Many much-loved bears exist from this time. Some were made from old blankets or coats. Others wore hand-knitted clothes. Because of the shortage of fur fabric, the bodies of some bears were made from clothing fabric while what little fur was available was saved for the head, paws and feet.

In other parts of the world, bears were being put together from equally unusual bits and pieces. Australia's small manufacturing industry turned out teddies made from sheepskin, a readily available material.

This bear is based on a style popular during World War II, but it has been made in a traditional short-pile mohair fabric. Its nose, however, has been cut from leather salvaged from a pair of soft leather gloves. The pattern could also be used to make a bear from an old cashmere or wool coat in line with the wartime "make do and mend" spirit.

As with all the patterns in this book, the materials used have been listed for your convenience and guidance, but with a little experience, a variety of different fabrics can be used with any of the patterns to produce bears with very different characteristics and expressions. Try taking the ear shape from one bear and the eye

position from another to achieve a variety of permutations. Or change an arm or body shape to produce your own individual friend. Before cutting the precious fabric, however, fit together the templates to build the basic bear shape. You will soon be able to judge quite accurately the finished effect of your bear by assessing the cardboard cut-outs.

## MAKING THE WARTIME BEAR

Before starting to make the bear, carefully read the chapter on Classic Bear-making. Following the step-by-step instructions there, make the 10 templates, cut out the fabric pieces and assemble the bear, taking into consideration the special points below. Take care to keep your working surfaces as clean as possible at all times.

The front and back leg sections on this particular bear are cut in one piece which is then folded over to form a single back seam. When cutting the legs out, cut two pieces, remembering to turn the pattern piece over and to reverse all the markings to form a "pair" of legs.

The feet are formed from separate crescent-shaped sections which are attached before the back seam is stitched. Do take care to match the notches correctly. The half moon should sit centrally along the lower straight edge of the leg, and should be eased slightly to fit. There will be a small space on either side of the leg section. This is to accommodate the seam allowance. Tack (baste) and machine stitch the foot in place, before closing the back seam. The foot pad can then be positioned in the usual way.

The four arm pieces are cut from a single pattern piece. Again do remember to draw two sections, before turning over the template to draw the second pair. The suedette pads are slip stitched into position (turning a tiny hem) when the arms are completed, but before they are attached to the body.

Position the eyes just wide of the head gusset seam about 1¼in (3cm) from the nose tip. The inner edge of the eyes should sit just on the seamline on each side of the head.

Stitch the inner third of each ear along the head gusset seam, starting about 1¾in (4.5cm) from the top of the eye and working towards the back of the head. When the back seam of the ear has been secured, twist the remaining two-thirds downwards vertically and stitch in place. Complete the front seam of the ear in the normal way.

The nose on this bear has been cut from a small scrap of glove leather. If this is not available, felt can be used. Trim away a little of the fur pile at the tip of the muzzle before attaching the nose using a matching thread and small straight stitches. The mouth has been embroidered with straight stitches, using six strands of brown stranded cotton. The center stitch following the muzzle seam and each of the two branches forming the mouth are all ¼in (7mm) long.

## Materials

¼yd (25cm) of 54in (137cm)
  wide honey-gold mohair
  with ⅜in (9mm) pile
Small square of dark beige
  suedette
Tacking (basting) thread
Matching sewing thread
Matching heavy-duty thread
One 1⅜in (36mm)
  hardboard crown joint
Four 1in (25mm) hardboard
  crown joints
Small amount of "firm-fill"
  polyester filling (stuffing)
1lb (450 g) wood wool
Two ½in (12mm) amber
  glass eyes
Small scrap of fine dark
  brown leather or felt
One skein dark brown
  "stranded cotton"
  embroidery thread

*A 12in (30cm) 1940s bear.*

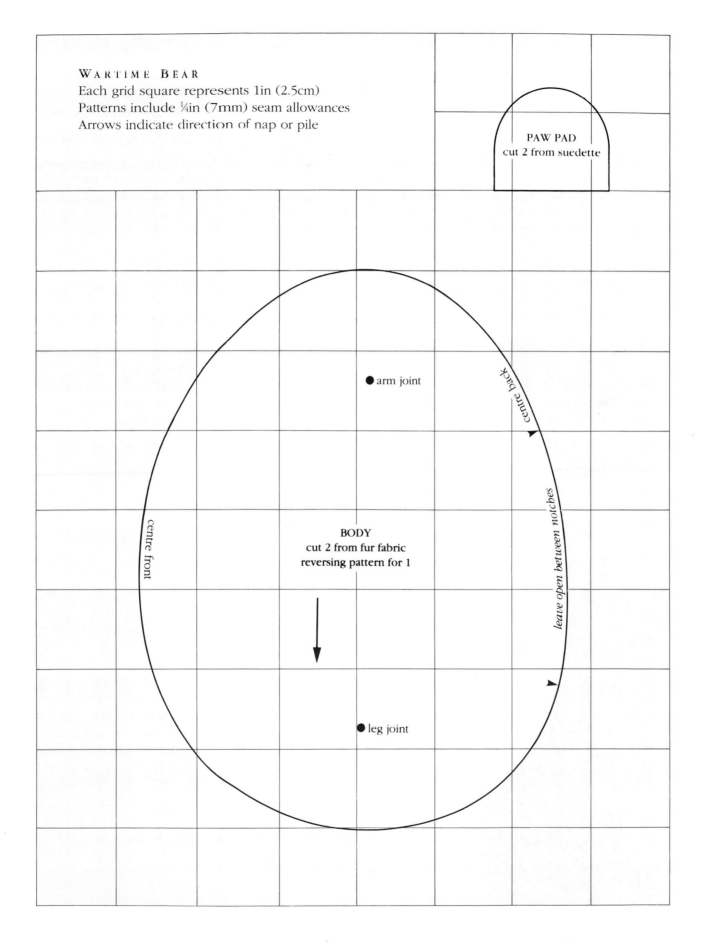

WARTIME BEAR
Each grid square represents 1in (2.5cm)
Patterns include ¼in (7mm) seam allowances
Arrows indicate direction of nap or pile

PAW PAD
cut 2 from suedette

arm joint

centre back

leave open between notches

centre front

BODY
cut 2 from fur fabric
reversing pattern for 1

leg joint

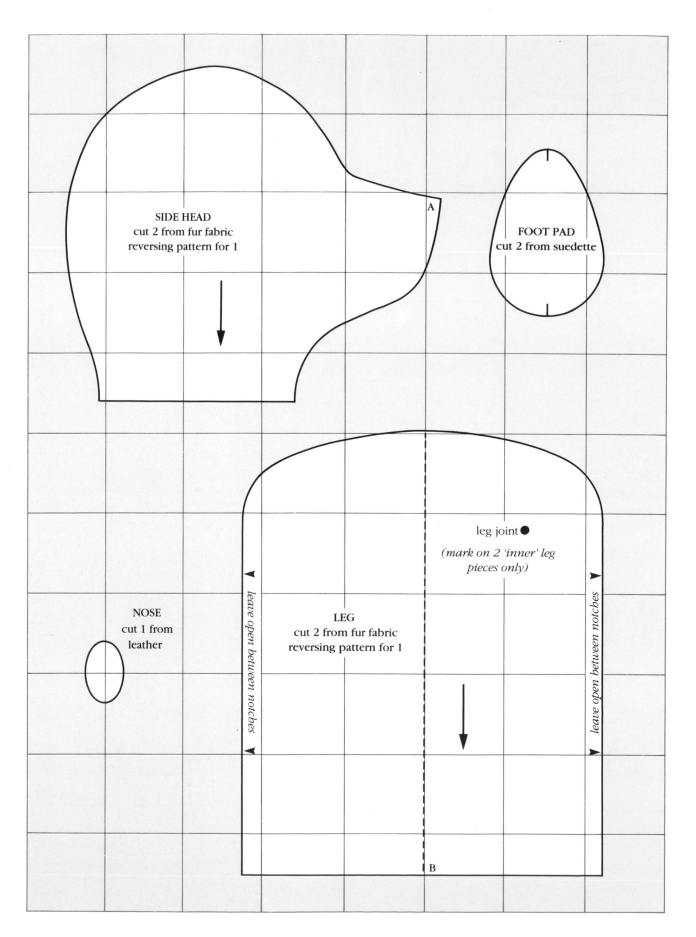

SIDE HEAD
cut 2 from fur fabric
reversing pattern for 1

A

FOOT PAD
cut 2 from suedette

leg joint ●

*(mark on 2 'inner' leg
pieces only)*

NOSE
cut 1 from
leather

LEG
cut 2 from fur fabric
reversing pattern for 1

*leave open between notches*

*leave open between notches*

B

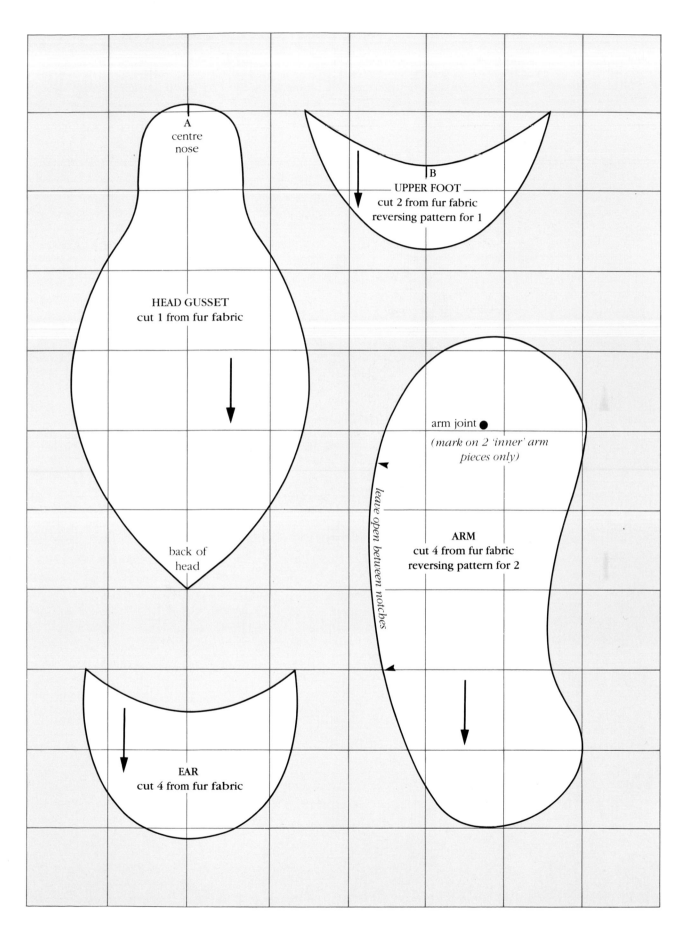

A
centre
nose

B
UPPER FOOT
cut 2 from fur fabric
reversing pattern for 1

HEAD GUSSET
cut 1 from fur fabric

arm joint ●
(mark on 2 'inner' arm
pieces only)

back of
head

*leave open between notches*

ARM
cut 4 from fur fabric
reversing pattern for 2

EAR
cut 4 from fur fabric

# AMERICAN BEAR

The years between the two world wars saw an unprecedented boom in the manufacture of teddy bears.

In America, production during this time thrived. One of the more successful companies was the Knickerbocker Toy Co. Inc. Originally founded in the early 1900s in New York, some of the bears from this manufacturer still survive in excellent condition.

The bear featured here is similar to the Knickerbocker bear in production around 1940. It has a typically large round head with a relatively flat, snubbed muzzle.

Bear shapes and features were continually evolving. Around this time, the body shape was changing quite dramatically. Gone was the hump; legs and arms became shorter and thicker and claws were often omitted. Stuffing was almost entirely kapok, giving a softer shape to the bear's physique. Although most bears' arms still displayed the distinctive curve of the earlier models, these new varieties were much more familiar to the teddy bears we know today.

The trademark of the Knickerbocker Toy Company at this time showed an inverted horseshoe containing the figure of a child. This could be seen on sew-in labels, usually placed in the front body seam or in the ear. Later labels were to proclaim the slogan "Animals of Distinction".

The Knickerbocker toy factory is still famous for its Smoky Bear characters, manufactured during the 1960s and 1970s. Smoky was used to promote the work of the Junior Forest rangers and the young owners were encouraged to enroll in this organization which aimed to prevent the outbreak of forest fires. Several toy companies, including The Ideal Toy Co., were also licensed to produce this popular bear, which was named after Smoky Joe Martin, an employee of the New York Fire Department in the 1920s.

Although the Knickerbocker bears, in common with most others of that time, were made from mohair fabric, this bear is made from synthetic knitted fabric and is, therefore, an ideal bear for a beginner to attempt. Synthetic fabric is relatively cheap, and so mistakes in cutting out are not so crucial, as with expensive mohair. Fabric with a knitted

backing does, however, need careful handling during the stuffing process as it may pull out of shape or distort. For this reason a light polyester filling has been used, and, as in the original bear, the arms and legs have been less firmly stuffed than is usual. Polyester filling is non-allergenic and conforms to toy safety standards. If this bear is to be made as a child's toy, plastic lock-in safety eyes must be used.

**Materials**

*½yd (45cm) of 54in (137cm) wide gold acrylic fur fabric*
*Small square of dark beige suedette*
*Tacking (basting) thread*
*Matching sewing thread*
*Matching heavy-duty thread*
*One 1⅜in (36mm) hardboard crown joint*
*Four 1in (25mm) hardboard crown joints*
*1lb (450 g) washable "firm-fill" polyester filling (stuffing)*
*Two ½in (12mm) amber and black glass eyes*
*One skein black "soft cotton" embroidery thread*

### MAKING THE AMERICAN BEAR

Before starting to make the bear, carefully read the chapter on Classic Bear-making. Following the step-by-step instructions there, make the 8 templates, cut out the fabric pieces and assemble the bear, taking into consideration the special points below. Take care to keep your working surfaces as clean as possible at all times.

On this bear four complete arm sections are cut out, making two pairs. These are then machine sewn together, leaving an opening between the notches for stuffing in the usual way.

The paw pads are formed from narrow ovals of dark beige suedette which are sewn in place after the side seams have been sewn, but before the arms are stuffed. The pads on the feet are large ovals, which are inserted in the usual manner.

The ears should be set at the center of the top of the head across the gusset seams and at a slight angle with the lower edges tilting backwards a little. They are slightly padded out with a small amount of polyester filling (stuffing).

The bear's muzzle should be clipped to a neat oval, finishing just below the eyes.

Amber glass eyes with black pupils have been used and the securing thread has been pulled firmly to cause a depression for each eye socket. The eyes are placed on the head gusset seam, so that their lower edges are 1⅜in (3.5cm) from the center of the tip of the nose.

The nose is worked in vertical satin stitches across the seam at the end of the muzzle, forming a horizontal oval about ⅞in (22mm) wide and ⅝in (16mm) deep.

The mouth is formed from three straight stitches in an inverted "Y" shape, using soft cotton embroidery thread.

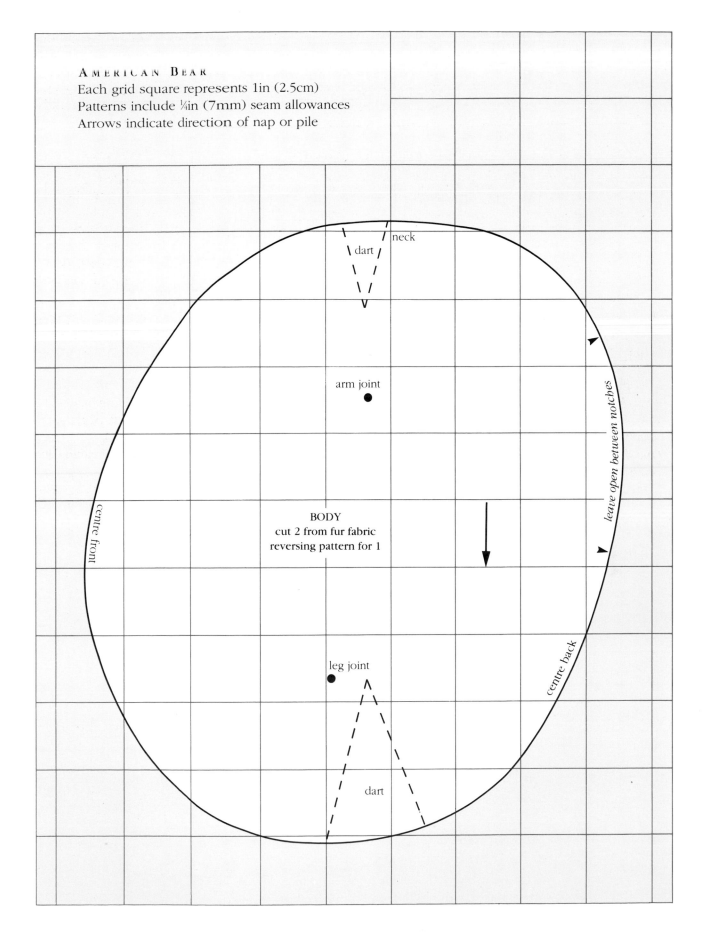

AMERICAN BEAR
Each grid square represents 1in (2.5cm)
Patterns include ¼in (7mm) seam allowances
Arrows indicate direction of nap or pile

neck

dart

arm joint

centre front

leave open between notches

BODY
cut 2 from fur fabric
reversing pattern for 1

leg joint

centre back

dart

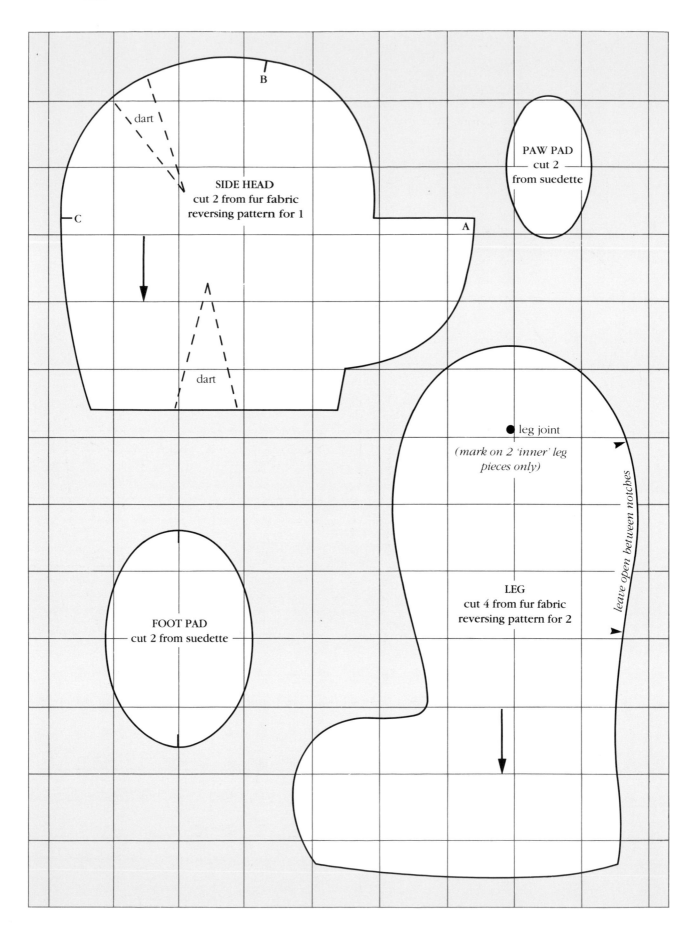

SIDE HEAD
cut 2 from fur fabric
reversing pattern for 1

dart

dart

B

C

A

PAW PAD
cut 2
from suedette

leg joint
(mark on 2 'inner' leg
pieces only)

LEG
cut 4 from fur fabric
reversing pattern for 2

leave open between notches

FOOT PAD
cut 2 from suedette

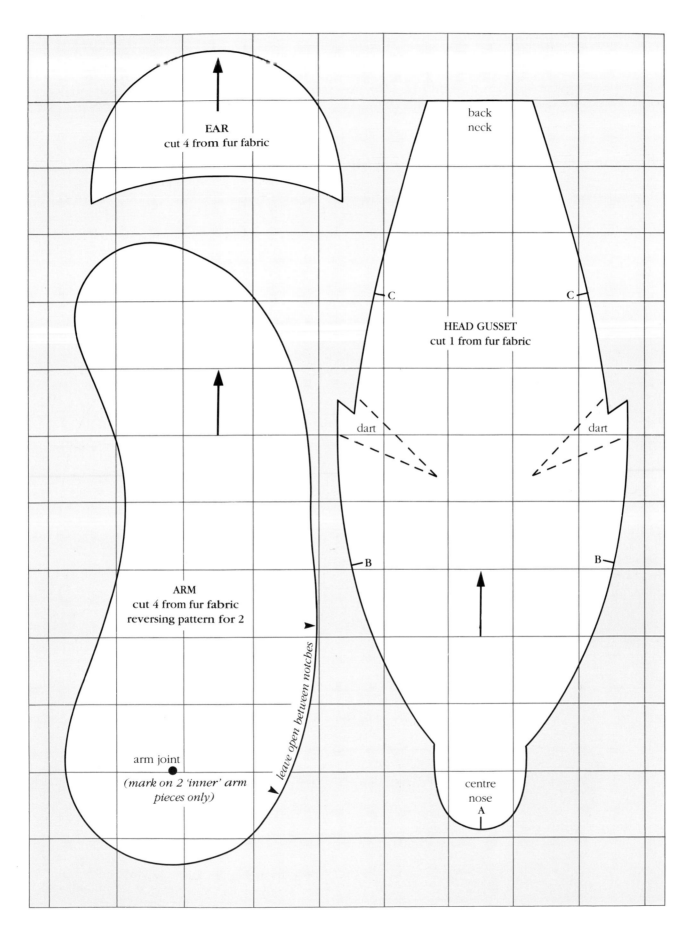

**EAR**
cut 4 from fur fabric

back
neck

C        C

**HEAD GUSSET**
cut 1 from fur fabric

dart        dart

B        B

**ARM**
cut 4 from fur fabric
reversing pattern for 2

*leave open between notches*

arm joint

*(mark on 2 'inner' arm
pieces only)*

centre
nose
A

# CHARACTER BEAR

Over the years, since the first teddy bears were developed, some of them have been characterized and thus immortalized in literature for everyone to enjoy.

As the teddy bear craze gained momentum at the beginning of the century, so teddy bears began to appear in print. *The Tale of Teddy Bright-Eyes* was published in Britain in 1909, teddies also appear in stories by Mrs Craddock in 1917. But it was not until the 1920s that two of the most famous bears of literature were born: Rupert and Winnie the Pooh.

Rupert Bear made his first appearance in Britain's *Daily Express* newspaper as a comic strip character. He was created by Mary Tourtel, a talented illustrator who was married to the paper's night editor. Rupert became an instant success and Mary Tourtel's stories set in the fictional world of Nutwood with a host of animal friends still delight children today the world over.

When Mary retired in 1935, Rupert's adventures were taken over by Alfred Bestall who continued to submit a daily comic strip for another 30 years. As Rupert's fame continued, his adventures could be followed in annuals, cartoons, jigsaw puzzles and even in a television series.

Four years after the arrival of Rupert, Winnie the Pooh was to enter the arena with the publication of *When We Were Very Young*. A. A. Milne based his Pooh stories on his son Christopher's teddy, bought at Harrods in London one birthday. The bear – probably of Farnell manufacture – was named Edward.

It is the E. H. Shepard illustrations of Pooh (inspired incidentally by a different teddy – a Steiff called Growler) that will be familiar to Pooh devotees all over the world.

The original Winnie the Pooh now lives in the New York Public Library on Fifth Avenue.

More recently, other teddy bears have found fame in newspapers, books and television. In France, Gros Nounours began his career in newspapers during the 1960s before finding real fame on the television in a series which ran for over 1,000 episodes.

Nounours' career runs parallel with the British glove puppet Sooty and the American cartoon bear, Yogi. And there are so many others: Paddington Bear, SuperTed and Carebears are known across the world.

The character bear to make here could sport a scarf in the Rupert Bear tradition. He wears tiny bells in its ears. It is made from honeysuckle-colored short-pile mohair and has paw and foot pads of light beige.

*This 11in (28cm) tall Winnie the Pooh bear was produced in a limited edition in 1993.*

## Materials

*½yd (45cm) of 54in (137cm)*
 *wide honeysuckle mohair*
 *with ⅜in (9mm) pile*
*Small square of light beige felt*
*Tacking (basting) thread*
*Matching sewing thread*
*Matching heavy-duty thread*
*One 1⅜in (36mm)*
 *hardboard crown joint*
*Four 1in (25mm) hardboard*
 *joints*
*Two ⁹⁄₁₆in (15mm) amber*
 *glass eyes*
*Small amount of "firm-fill"*
 *polyester filling (stuffing)*
*1lb (450 g) wood wool*
*One skein black "soft cotton"*
 *black embroidery thread*
*Two small bells (for ears)*

### MAKING THE CHARACTER BEAR

Before starting to make the bear, carefully read the chapter on Classic Bear-making. Following the step-by-step instructions there, make the 10 templates, cut out the fabric pieces and assemble the bear, taking into consideration the special points below. Take care to keep your working surfaces as clean as possible at all times.

A small bell has been placed in each ear before it is sewn in position. These will make the bear "tinkle" gently when it is shaken. The ears have been placed slightly to the back of the head, slightly overlapping the center head gusset on each side. The distance from the nose tip to the ear is about 4in (10cm).

The eyes are positioned just across the head gusset 2in (5cm) from the nose tip. They have been pulled in slightly to create an eye "socket" and the fur has been trimmed away to give a wide-eyed expression.

The heart-shaped nose is worked in vertical satin stitches using black soft cotton embroidery thread.

The mouth is formed as a large inverted "Y" following the muzzle seam. The first downwards stitch should measure about ½in (12mm) and each branch of the mouth ⅜in (1cm).

By following the pattern markings for placing the leg joints, the bear will have an endearing pigeon-toed appearance.

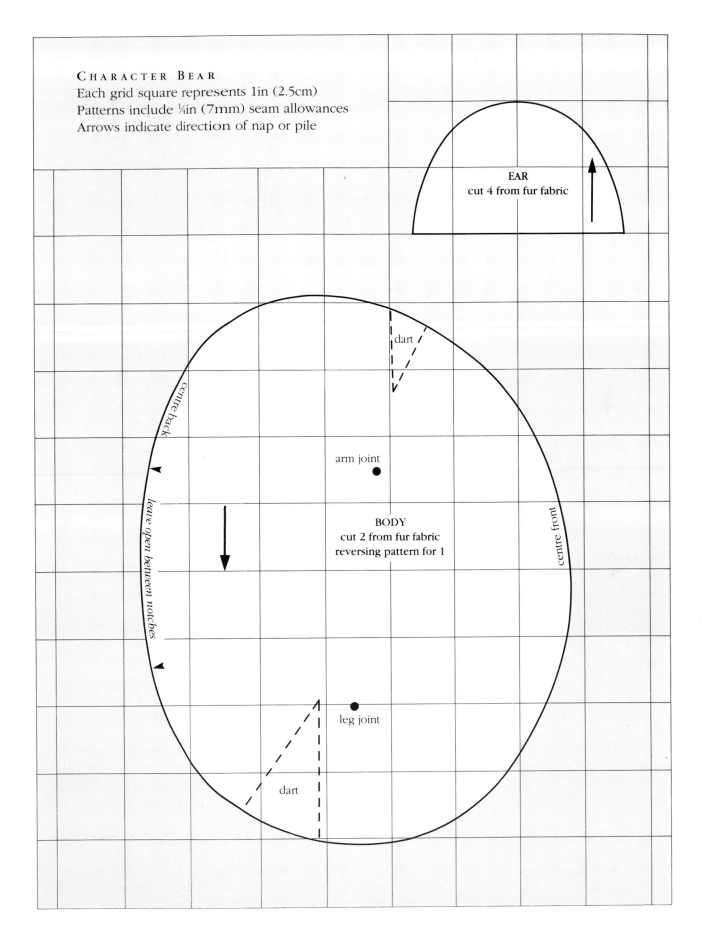

CHARACTER BEAR
Each grid square represents 1in (2.5cm)
Patterns include ¼in (7mm) seam allowances
Arrows indicate direction of nap or pile

EAR
cut 4 from fur fabric

dart

centre back

arm joint

leave open between notches

BODY
cut 2 from fur fabric
reversing pattern for 1

centre front

leg joint

dart

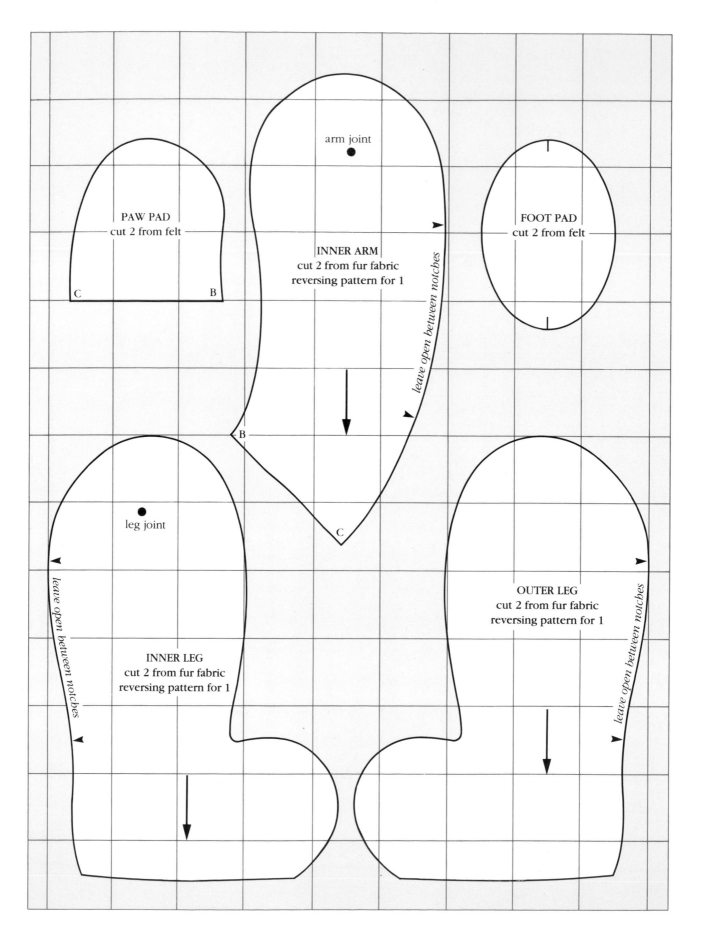

PAW PAD
cut 2 from felt

C          B

arm joint

INNER ARM
cut 2 from fur fabric
reversing pattern for 1

FOOT PAD
cut 2 from felt

*leave open between notches*

B

C

leg joint

OUTER LEG
cut 2 from fur fabric
reversing pattern for 1

*leave open between notches*

INNER LEG
cut 2 from fur fabric
reversing pattern for 1

*leave open between notches*

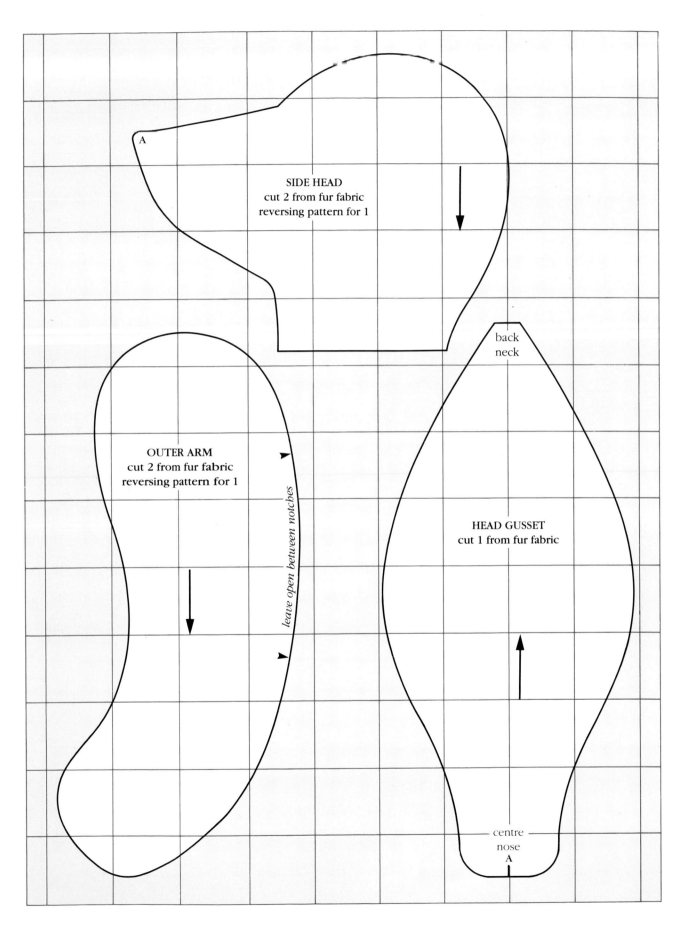

A

SIDE HEAD
cut 2 from fur fabric
reversing pattern for 1

back
neck

OUTER ARM
cut 2 from fur fabric
reversing pattern for 1

*leave open between notches*

HEAD GUSSET
cut 1 from fur fabric

centre
nose
A

# 1950s British Bear

*The bear pictured here was inspired by 1950s British bears. Made from gold fur fabric, it is 14in (36cm) tall and has dark chocolate brown pads.*

Some of the most famous and early British bears came from the Chad Valley toy factory which began trading in that name in 1919. The company's origins are even earlier and date back to well before the turn of the century. However, Chad Valley teddy bears were not in full-time production until 1920.

Over the years, many soft toys were manufactured under the Chad Valley name but the most impressive must have been a range of large teddy bears which measured up to 28in (71cm). Chad Valley's advertisements proudly proclaimed that these bears were produced exclusively of British materials and were available in fabrics such as brown long beaver and best golden fur – the cheapest teddy in the range was described as an upright golden.

By the time World War II had ended and rationing across many countries had begun to subside, the 1950s had been ushered in and with them a newer, brighter teddy. To begin with, its fur was probably of synthetic cotton-rayon rather than the more expensive mohair. Joints were cruder and several bear types had immovable limbs. The most important change in bears of this period was the introduction of the lock-in safety eyes, first patented by Wendy Boston for her washable bears of 1948.

Wendy Boston was one of the most renowned teddy bear producers of the 1950s. Her designs were usually unjointed and stuffed with kapok for a soft teddy.

Merrythought, of course, was another manufacturer of some note. During the 1950s, the company came up with the Cheeky bears range. These bears have broad faces, velvet noses and safety eyes.

It is also worth mentioning the Irish company, Gaeltarra Eireann or Tara Toys. This state-sponsored company began manufacturing bears shortly after World War II for export to Britain and the U.S., as well as the domestic market.

In Northern Ireland, the Pedigree factory was producing teddy bears by the end of the 1940s. Pedigree's other factory in Merton, known as the Triang works, was the other source of 1950s bears. Pedigree bears are very much the teddies of childhood – jointed limbs with brown velvet pads and glass eyes.

Lefray was the other British manufacturer of the day, producing traditional jointed gold and cinnamon bears with velvet pads.

Many bears from the 1920s onwards were stuffed with washed fleece. This makes a wonderful filling material, as it is hygienic, soft and easily worked. It is ideally suited for use with bears made from knitted fabrics, as it is less likely to distort the sewn shapes. Fleece should be used in the same way as kapok or polyester filling and can be bought from shops specializing in spinning requirements or by mail order from the suppliers listed on page 112.

## Materials

*½yd (45cm) of 54in (137cm) wide gold acrylic fur fabric*
*Small square of dark chocolate brown felt*
*Tacking (basting) thread*
*Matching sewing thread*
*Matching heavy-duty thread*
*One 1⅜in (36mm) hardboard crown joint*
*Four 1in (25mm) hardboard crown joints*
*1lb (450g) natural fleece or polyester filling (stuffing)*
*Two ½in (12mm) amber glass eyes*
*One skein black "pearl cotton" embroidery thread*

### MAKING THE 1950s BRITISH BEAR

Before starting to make the bear, carefully read the chapter on Classic Bear-making. Following the step-by-step instructions there, make the 8 templates, cut out the fabric pieces and assemble the bear, taking into consideration the special points below. Take care to keep your working surfaces as clean as possible at all times.

As the fabric used for this bear has a woven backing, great care must be taken when stitching and stuffing that it is not allowed to stretch and become misshapen. Tack (baste) all the seams carefully before machine stitching and do not over-stuff.

The felt front paws for this bear are stitched in position after the arms have been stuffed and closed. Use heavy-duty thread and tiny oversewing (overcasting) stitches to attach each paw, taking care to tease out any strands of pile which have been caught under the felt as you work.

The eyes are offset slightly from the head gusset seam, so that their lower edges are about ⅞in (22mm) from the center of the tip of the teddy bear's nose.

The ears should be set across the head gusset seams on top of the head, about 2in (5cm) apart. Do experiment with alternative positions, using "T" pins to anchor the bear's ears in place, until you are satisfied with the results.

Trim the fur around the nose tip slightly, before working a small triangular nose in horizontal satin stitches, following the seamline at the tip of the muzzle for guidance. The mouth is then formed as an inverted "T" from the tip of the triangle, using two strands of pearl cotton embroidery thread.

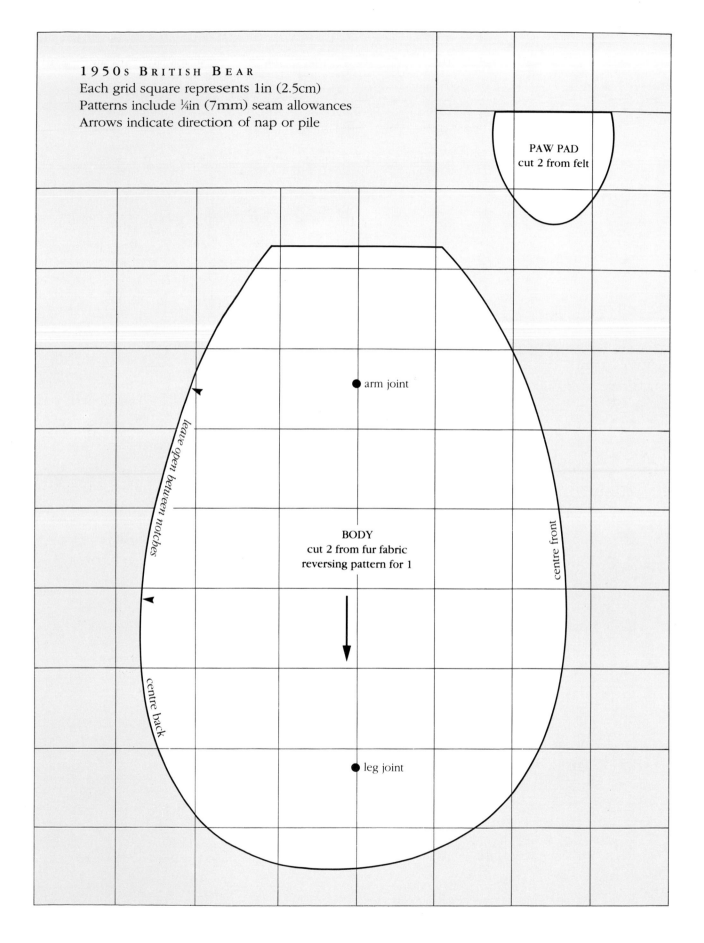

1950s BRITISH BEAR
Each grid square represents 1in (2.5cm)
Patterns include ¼in (7mm) seam allowances
Arrows indicate direction of nap or pile

PAW PAD
cut 2 from felt

arm joint

leave open between notches

centre front

BODY
cut 2 from fur fabric
reversing pattern for 1

centre back

leg joint

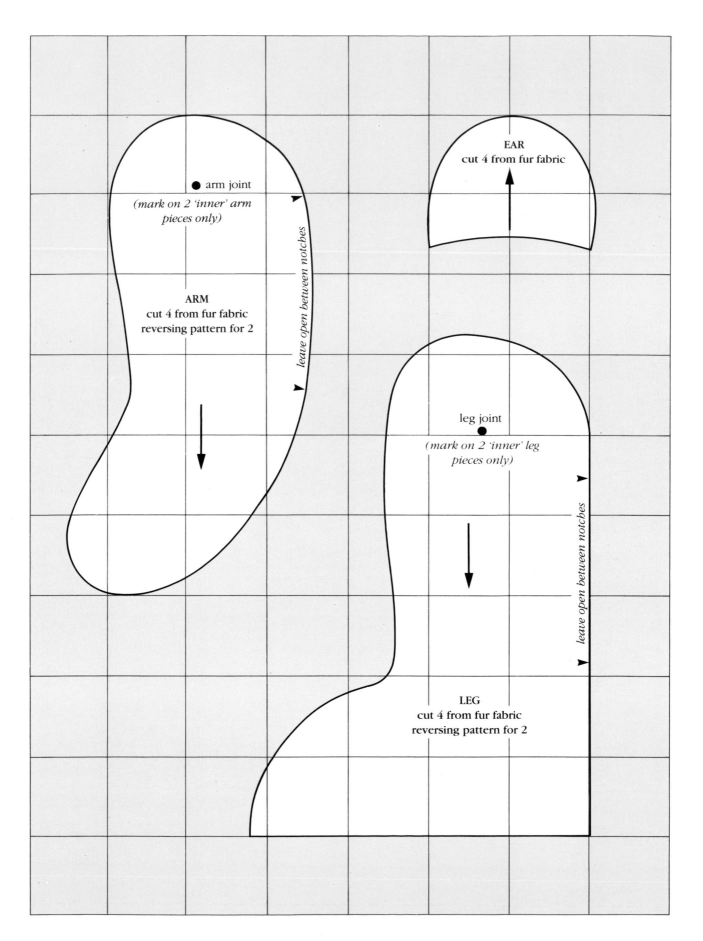

● arm joint

*(mark on 2 'inner' arm
pieces only)*

**ARM**
cut 4 from fur fabric
reversing pattern for 2

*leave open between notches*

**EAR**
cut 4 from fur fabric

● leg joint

*(mark on 2 'inner' leg
pieces only)*

*leave open between notches*

**LEG**
cut 4 from fur fabric
reversing pattern for 2

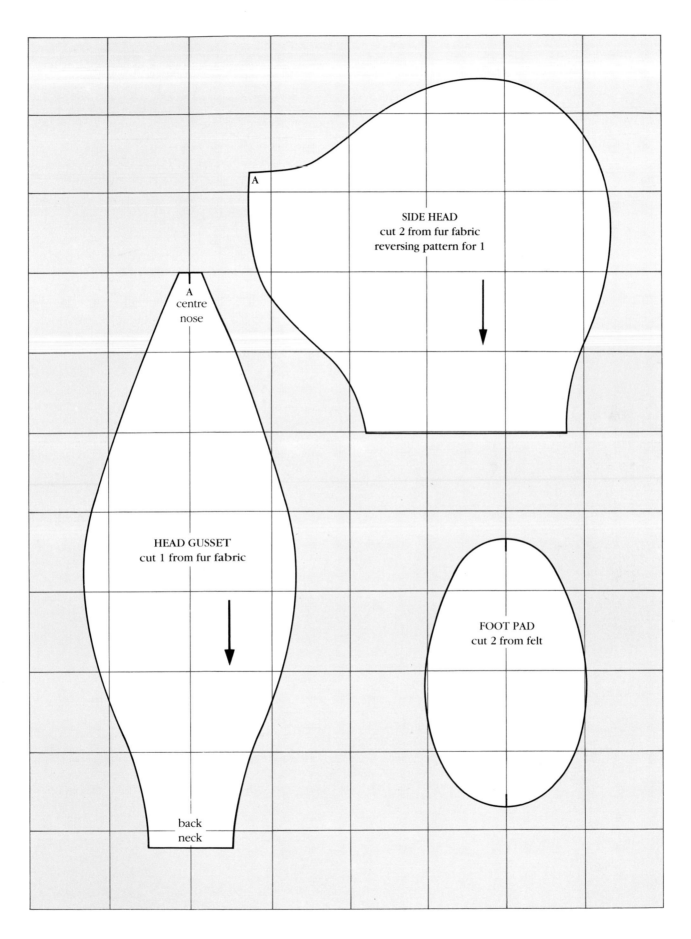

SIDE HEAD
cut 2 from fur fabric
reversing pattern for 1

A
centre
nose

A

HEAD GUSSET
cut 1 from fur fabric

back
neck

FOOT PAD
cut 2 from felt

# 1980s BEAR

*The bear pictured here was inspired by 1980s bears. Made from honeysuckle mohair pile fabric, it is 9½in (24cm) tall and has dark brown velvet pads.*

In all his ninety years of life, the teddy bear has never been more popular than he is now in the 1990s. Despite the coming of high technology and electronic gadgetry the traditional teddy bear still wins everyone's heart.

Teddy bears themselves have not escaped this new age, though. Teddy bears are now often equipped with hidden tape cassettes so that they can speak or play music.

Television has had a large influence on new characters: Rupert Bear and Winnie the Pooh have been around since the 1920s, but are still much watched. Toys of these characters are also produced in abundance. More recently, characters like Paddington Bear, the creation of author Michael Bond, SuperTed and Teddy Ruxpin have been viewed by millions.

However, many modern bears were not living up to the success of their ancestors. Cheaper exports from the Far East caused many toy manufacturers to close because they simply could not keep up with the competition. The Australian teddy bear industry, for example, died in the 1970s because of this economic pressure.

It was the traditional bear that many people sought, and companies like the Knickerbocker Toy Company and Steiff discovered that now was the time to bring the classic bears back. Since the early 1980s, Steiff has begun to produce replicas of the antique bears. The new bears still carry a Steiff button, larger than the original one, as well as a Steiff label. Firms like Dean's Co. Ltd. (Dean's Rag Book Co. Ltd.) began to market a range of reproduction jointed bears. The House of Nisbet introduced their Childhood Classics range of bears, Bully Bear being modeled on a bear from Peter Bull's collection (Peter Bull was an English actor, renowned for his love of bears).

Many other companies produced replica bears, often made with new materials which give a softer feel. Because classic bears are now so sought after and therefore very expensive, many teddy bear collectors are looking for replica bears as one way of assembling a range of classics without spending an absolute fortune.

Modern bears based on classic designs have certainly found a place in the market. Unlike replica

bears, these teddies have all the hallmarks of a well-designed, jointed bear, but are not strictly based on any previous model. These bears are often made from the finest materials and may even possess a range of accessories like scarves, hats or boots.

This 1980s bear is sporting a pair of tiny round spectacles, giving it a studious academic look. Equipped with a little knitted muffler in college or university colors, it would be an ideal gift for a student or graduate.

This small, rotund bear has dark brown velvet paws, which contrast nicely with its honeysuckle-colored fur. Alternatively, a light beige or mushroom fabric could be used.

## MAKING THE 1980S BEAR

Before starting to make up the bear, carefully read the chapter on Classic Bear-making. Following the step-by-step instructions there, make the 10 templates, cut out the fabric pieces and assemble the bear, taking into consideration the special points below. Seam allowances should be kept to a minimum – about ³⁄₁₆in (5mm).

The paw and foot pads for this bear have been cut from velvet. Use very small, even tacking (basting) stitches and pull out any trapped pile before machine stitching the paw pad to the inner arm section. Use the same technique to sew inner and outer arm sections together, leaving the tacking (basting) stitches in place if possible.

The foot pads are quite tricky to machine accurately, so it may be best to backstitch by hand over the tacking (basting) stitches using heavy-duty thread. The tacking (basting) stitches can then be left in, giving extra strength to the seam.

The eyes are placed on the head gusset seam, so that their lower edges are ³⁄₄in (2cm) from the nose tip.

The extra large ears should be set vertically on the head, the upper edge just touching the head gusset seam about 3in (8cm) from the tip of the nose.

Clip the fur back lightly around the muzzle before embroidering the nose, using short horizontal satin stitches to form a small rectangle. An inverted "T" then forms the mouth which is worked using six strands of the stranded embroidery thread.

## Materials

*¼yd (25cm) of 54in (137cm) wide honeysuckle mohair with ³⁄₈in (9mm) pile*

*Small square of dark brown velvet*

*Tacking (basting) thread*

*Matching sewing thread*

*Matching heavy-duty thread*

*One 1⅜in (36mm) hardboard crown joint*

*Four 1in (25mm) hardboard crown joints*

*8oz (230g) "firm-fill" polyester filling (stuffing)*

*Two ³⁄₈in (9mm) black boot button eyes*

*One skein black "stranded cotton" embroidery thread*

*Small pair of gold-rimmed glasses (optional)*

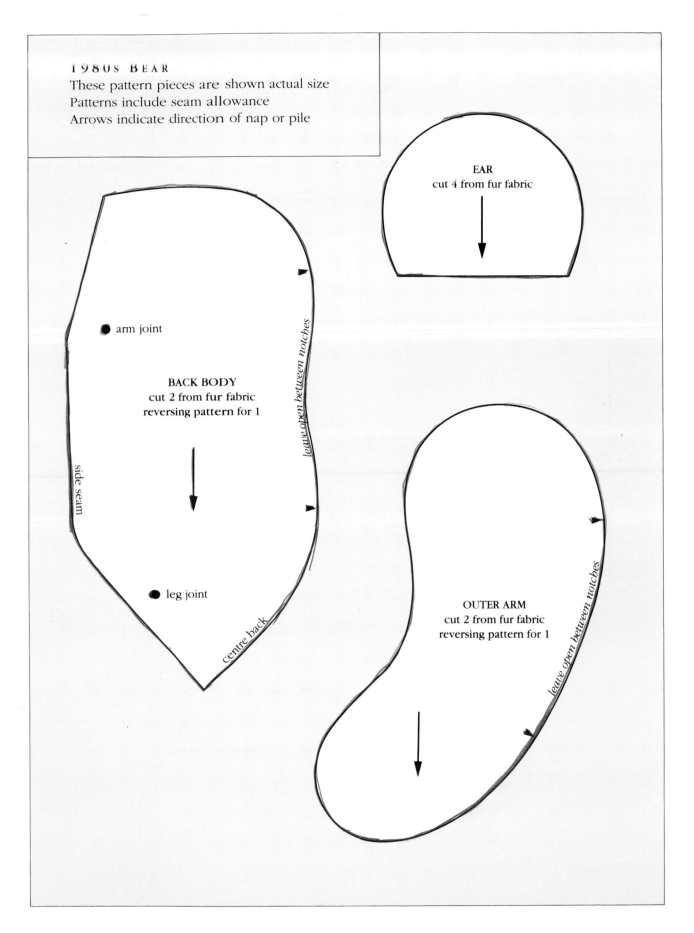

1980S BEAR
These pattern pieces are shown actual size
Patterns include seam allowance
Arrows indicate direction of nap or pile

EAR
cut 4 from fur fabric

arm joint

BACK BODY
cut 2 from fur fabric
reversing pattern for 1

leave open between notches

side seam

leg joint

centre back

OUTER ARM
cut 2 from fur fabric
reversing pattern for 1

leave open between notches

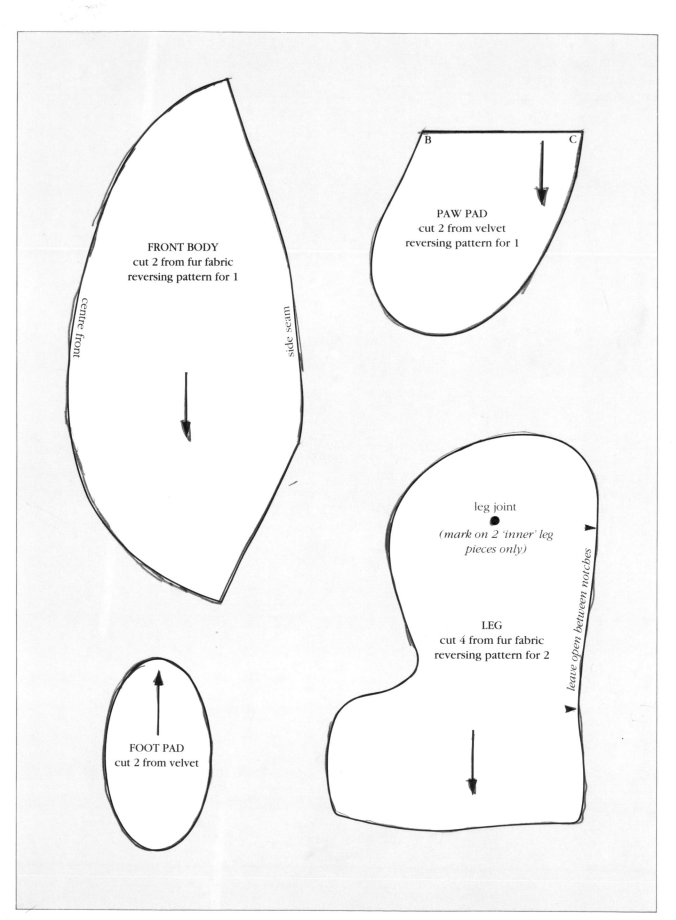

FRONT BODY
cut 2 from fur fabric
reversing pattern for 1

centre front

side seam

PAW PAD
cut 2 from velvet
reversing pattern for 1

B

C

leg joint
*(mark on 2 'inner' leg
pieces only)*

LEG
cut 4 from fur fabric
reversing pattern for 2

*leave open between notches*

FOOT PAD
cut 2 from velvet

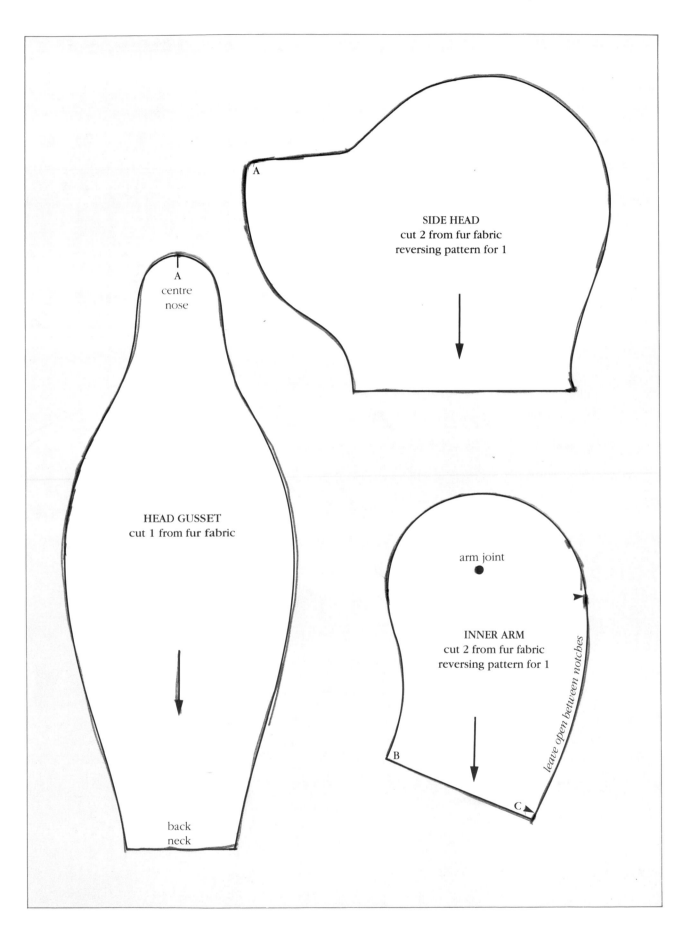

SIDE HEAD
cut 2 from fur fabric
reversing pattern for 1

A

centre
nose

HEAD GUSSET
cut 1 from fur fabric

back
neck

arm joint

INNER ARM
cut 2 from fur fabric
reversing pattern for 1

leave open between notches

B

C

# MODERN BEAR

Is there a typical modern bear? With so many varieties of teddy on the market, it is almost impossible to define.

In the 1970s, cheap toys from the Far East put many Western manufacturers out of business. Certainly, the Australian industry, which had experienced a notable resurgence in the 1950s, could not compete, and teddy bear manufacturers in the country were just about wiped out.

However, with the craving for nostalgia, the classic bear has – since the 1980s – made something of a revival. Today, many companies in various countries produce traditional style bears from the highest quality materials with "boot button" eyes and mohair fabric.

Traditional producers like Steiff and Merrythought quickly saw how this demand could be exploited and both companies now manufacture a successful line in replica bears – faithful reproductions of popular early teddy bears. These teddy bears are usually produced in a limited number and are made principally for the growing teddy bear collectors' market.

Teddy bear collecting in the United States and in Great Britain is experiencing something of a boom and interest is also strong in Germany and Japan. The widening availability of a large range of traditional mohair, cashmere and silk fabrics through mail order outlets and interest in teddy bear memorabilia has ensured that this interest should continue.

So great has been the revival of interest in classic teddy bears that many artists and craftsworkers have ventured into the field, producing distinctive bears, both classic and modern.

Generally, modern manufactured teddies display the most appealing characteristics from bears over a number of periods. However, the short, plump arms and legs give the modern bear a chubbier appearance. The modern bear's ears are also slightly padded to give the face an eager and inquiring look.

If you wish to experiment with your own style of bear, it is possible to adapt pieces from the various patterns in this book to create your own designs. By drawing the pattern shapes onto plain paper, it is possible to get an idea of how a finished bear might look by

*A 1990s Big Softies bear
called Marmaduke.*

## Materials

*½yd (45cm) of 54in (137cm)
  wide honey-beige distressed
  pile mohair with ½in
  (12mm) pile*
*Small square of pale beige
  suedette*
*Tacking (basting) thread*
*Matching sewing thread*
*Matching heavy-duty thread*
*One 2in (50mm) hardboard
  crown joint*
*Four 1⅜in (36mm)
  hardboard crown joints*
*Small amount of firm-fill
  polyester filling (stuffing)*
*1lb (500g) wood wool*
*Two ½in (12mm) black glass
  boot button eyes*
*One skein black "pearl
  cotton" embroidery thread*

assembling these paper templates. With a little practice it becomes quite easy to gauge accurately the effect achieved by substituting a different ear shape or a thinner or longer arm.

It is a good idea, until you are confident in your abilities, to cut your experimental bear from a cheaper fabric. An inexpensive acrylic fabric is useful for testing on, even though it is slightly stretchier. Any adaptations and alterations can be made on the prototype bear at little cost until you achieve the type of bear that appeals most. This can be great fun and the result is a unique and totally individual creation.

The modern bear here has a cuddly, round body and an unusual but endearing expression. It has been made from a honey-beige, long-pile mohair and just longs to be hugged! Mohair can be obtained in a range of dramatic colors, including royal blue, purple and red, and this modern bear could be made in any of these shades – the choice is yours.

### MAKING THE MODERN BEAR

Before starting to make the bear, carefully read the chapter on Classic Bear-making. Following the step-by-step instructions there, make the 10 templates, cut out the fabric pieces and assemble the bear, taking into consideration the special points below. Take care to keep your working surfaces as clean as possible at all times.

Fill the muzzle firmly with polyester filling (stuffing) before continuing to stuff the head with wood wool. Stuff the body very firmly using wood wool with some polyester stuffing, if necessary, taking care to pack out the upper back to form a definite hump on the bear.

The eyes are placed just below the head gusset seam, so that their lower edges are 1⅜in (3.5cm) from the tip of the muzzle.

Before attaching the ears, pad them out slightly using a tiny amount of polyester filling. Take care when sewing them in position that strands of the filling do not become entangled with the stitching. The ears should be set towards the back of the head across the gusset seams and about 2½in (6cm) apart.

The triangular nose is worked in horizontal satin stitches over the tip of the head gusset.

From the tip of the nose triangle, the thread is doubled and two vertical straight stitches about 1in (2.5cm) in length are made following the center seam of the lower muzzle. From the lower point of the straight stitches, still keeping the thread doubled, a smiling mouth is formed by stitching two straight stitches at an angle to left and right.

The fur pile around the nose and mouth can be trimmed away slightly, just to tidy up the muzzle if necessary.

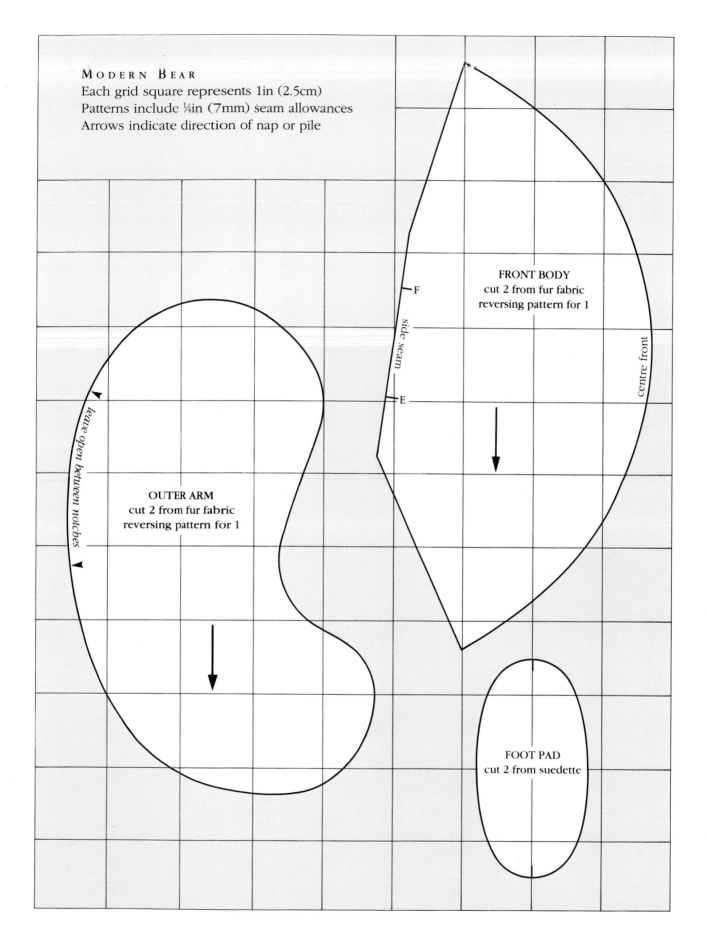

MODERN BEAR
Each grid square represents 1in (2.5cm)
Patterns include ¼in (7mm) seam allowances
Arrows indicate direction of nap or pile

FRONT BODY
cut 2 from fur fabric
reversing pattern for 1

F

*side seam*

E

*centre front*

OUTER ARM
cut 2 from fur fabric
reversing pattern for 1

*leave open between notches*

FOOT PAD
cut 2 from suedette

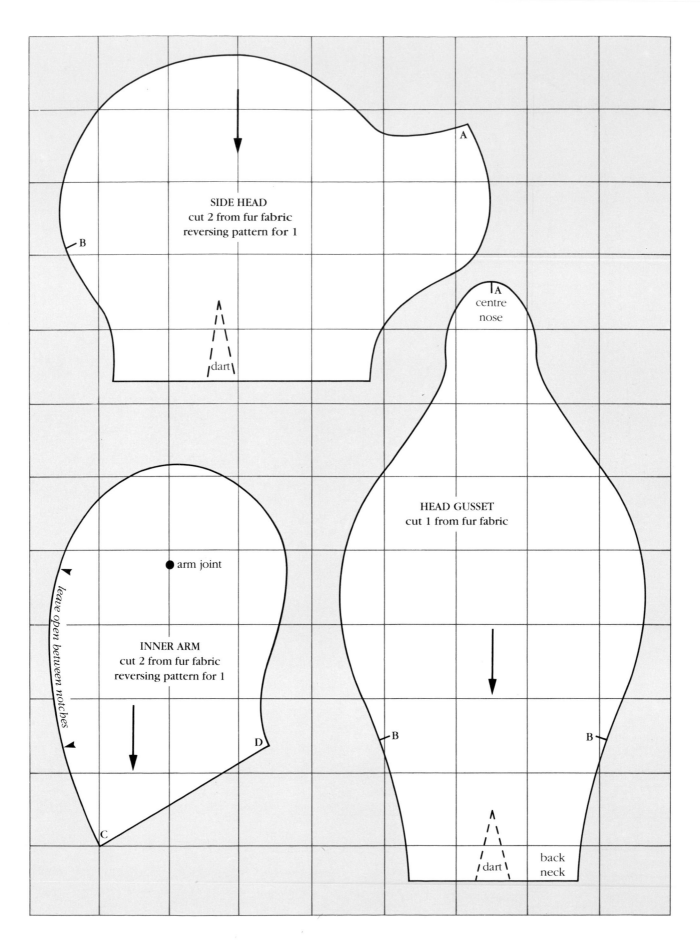

SIDE HEAD
cut 2 from fur fabric
reversing pattern for 1

A

B

dart

centre
nose

A

HEAD GUSSET
cut 1 from fur fabric

arm joint

INNER ARM
cut 2 from fur fabric
reversing pattern for 1

leave open between notches

D

C

B

B

dart

back
neck

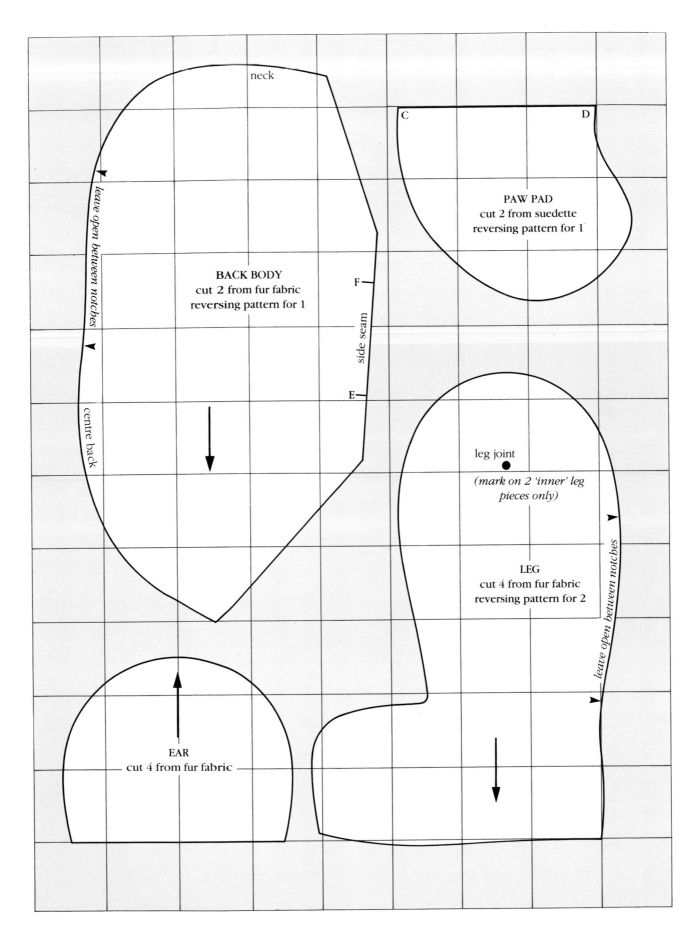

neck

**BACK BODY**
cut 2 from fur fabric
reversing pattern for 1

*leave open between notches*

centre back

F

side seam

E

**PAW PAD**
cut 2 from suedette
reversing pattern for 1

C          D

leg joint
●

*(mark on 2 'inner' leg
pieces only)*

**LEG**
cut 4 from fur fabric
reversing pattern for 2

*leave open between notches*

**EAR**
cut 4 from fur fabric

# USEFUL ADDRESSES

## Author
Julia Jones' Collectors' Bears,
PO Box 16, Swadlincote,
Derbyshire DE12 8ZZ, Great Britain.
*For specially commissioned bears. Also
after-dinner speaking engagements
and illustrated lectures.*

## Bear supplies
*For fabrics and/or bear components
and stuffings contact the following:*

Oakley Fabrics Ltd, 8 May Street,
Luton, Beds LU1 3QY, Great Britain.
Tel: 0582 424828. Fax: 0582 29362.
*(Mail order supplies worldwide)*

Nonsuch Soft Toys, 51 Dudley Close,
Tilehurst, Reading, Berkshire RG3 6JJ,
Great Britain. Tel: 0734 413006.
*(Mail order available)*

Bridon Bears of Cheltenham,
2 St Margaret's Terrace, Cheltenham,
Glos GL50 4DT, Great Britain.
Tel: 0242 513102.
*(Mail order available)*

Animal Crackers, 5824 Isleta,
Albuquerque, NM 87105-6628, USA.
Tel: (505) 873 2806.

Golden Fun, Box 10697-TBF, Golden,
CO 80401-0600, USA.

Carver's Eye Company, Dept 60,
PO Box 16692, Portland, OR 97216,
USA. Tel: (503) 666 5680.

Spare Bear Parts, PO Box 56F,
Interlochen, MI 49643, USA.
Tel: (616) 275 6993.
Fax: (616) 275 6230.

Bear Clawset, 27 Palermo Walk,
Long Beach, CA 90803, USA.
Tel: (310) 434 8077.

Good Bears of the World,
PO Box 13097, Toledo,
OH 43613, USA.
Tel: (419) 531 5356.

## Toy safety information
British Standards Institute,
Linford Wood, Milton Keynes,
MK14 6LE, Great Britain.
Tel: 0908 220022. Fax: 320 856.

## Publications
The Teddy Bear Times, Heritage Press,
Shelley House, 104 High Street,
Steyning, West Sussex BN4 3RD,
Great Britain.

The UK Teddy Bear Guide and Teddy
Bear Magazine, Hugglets, PO Box 290,
Brighton, West Sussex BN2 1DR,
Great Britain.

Teddy Bear and Friends Magazines,
Cumberland Publishing, Inc.,
900 Frederick Street, Cumberland,
Maryland 21502, USA.
Tel: (301) 759-5853.
Fax: (301) 759-9108.

## Teddy bear clubs
British Teddy Bear Association,
PO Box 290, Brighton, West Sussex
BN2 1DR, Great Britain.
Tel: 0273 697974.
Fax: 0273 62655.

Teddy Ecosse, The Wynd, Melrose,
Roxburghshire, Scotland TD6 9PA.

International League of Teddy Bear
Collectors Club, c/o 1023 Don Diablo,
Arcadia, California 91006, USA.
Tel: (818) 447 3809.

Teddy's Patch, Le Club des Amis de
l'Ours, 34 Rue Lieu de Santé, 76000
Rouen, France.
Tel: 35 88 96 00.

## Associations and guilds
British Toymakers Guild,
124 Walcot Street, Bath, Avon
BA1 5BG, Great Britain.
Tel: 0225 442440.

Teddy Bear Traders Association,
c/o Gerry Grey, The Old Bakery
Teddy Bear Shop, 38 Cambridge Street,
Wellingborough, Northants NN8 1DW,
Great Britain.
Tel: 0933 229191.
Fax: 0933 272466.

## Museums with bear collections
Bethnal Green Museum of Childhood,
Cambridge Heath Road, London
E2 9PA, Great Britain.
Tel: 081 981 1711.

The Bear Museum, 38 Dragon Street,
Petersfield, Hants GU31 4JJ, Great
Britain. Tel: 0730 265108.

Pollock's Toy Museum, 1 Scala Street,
London W1P 1LT, Great Britain.
Tel: 071 636 3452.

The Teddy Bear Museum, 19 Greenhill
Street, Stratford-upon-Avon CV37 6LF,
Great Britain. Tel: 0789 293160.

The Margaret Woodbury Strong
Museum, Rochester, New York, USA.

Margarete Steiff Museum, Giengen,
Germany.

Romy's Bazaar, 2 Badgery's Crescent,
Lawson 2783, Australia.

## Auctions
*Classic Bears are sometimes featured in
sales held by auctioneers Christies and
Sotheby's. For information contact
main offices in London or New York.*

PICTURE CREDITS
The Author would like to thank the
following for their immense help, both
practical and material, in the
researching and writing of this book:
Roy Pilkington of Oakley Fabrics;
Alastair McMinn and Donald McMillan
of Coats Patons Crafts; David Fish of
Tootal; Kath Mason of Mason Bears;
Bridon Bears of Cheltenham; David
and Susan Rixon of Nonsuch Bears
and Mr and Mrs Wharnsby of Good
Bears of the World.

Special thanks to Jon Stewart for the
photography and Kate Yeates of Anaya
Publishers, Alison Leach and Clare
Clements for their editorial and design
skills and finally to my brother and
sister-in-law, Roger and Pam Smith,
for their continuing encouragement
and support.

PICTURE CREDITS
The publishers would like to thank
The Bear Museum, Petersfild for use of
photos on pages 41, 50, 60, 66, 78 and
90; and The Teddy Bear Museum,
Stratford-upon-Avon for use of photos
on pages 1, 6 and 108.

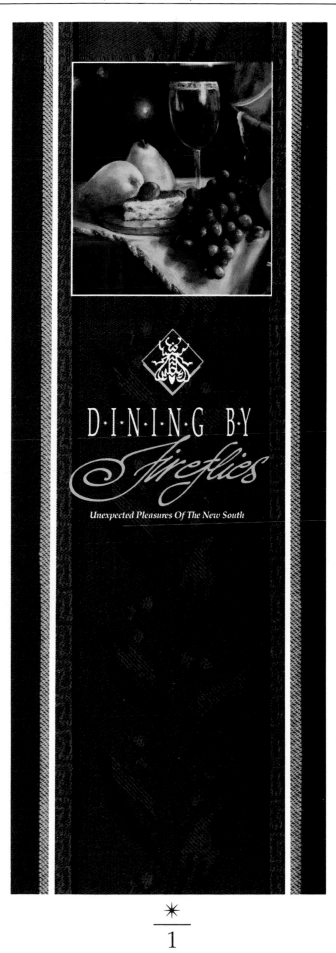

D·I·N·I·N·G B·Y

*Fireflies*

*Unexpected Pleasures Of The New South*

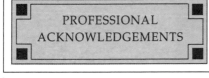

PROFESSIONAL
ACKNOWLEDGEMENTS

**Original Cover Artwork**
*T. Reitzel*

**Firefly Textile Design**
*Wesley Mancini*
Wesley Mancini Ltd

**Photography**
*Gerin Choiniere*
Gerin Choiniere Photography

**Food Styling**
*Penny Henry & Roger Overcash*
Foodworks, Inc.

**Art Illustration & Design**
*Ralph Van Dyke*
Delmar Printing & Publishing

**Wine Consultant**
*Chuck Richards*
Reid's Supermarket

***Dining By Fireflies:*** *Grilled Maple-Glazed Baby Back Ribs, p. 78; Cold Dilled New Potatoes with Carrots and Scallions, p. 80; Hot Cornbread Sticks, p. 79; Sweet-and-Sour Broccoli, Corn and Red Peppers in Tomato Cups, p. 80.*

# D·I·N·I·N·G  B·Y
## *Fireflies*

**Unexpected Pleasures Of The New South**

*There are threads of a single strand that often connect the past to the present and catching fireflies on a warm summer's evening is one of those.*

### THE JUNIOR LEAGUE OF CHARLOTTE

Published by:
The Junior League of Charlotte, Inc.

First Edition
First Printing, 30,000 copies, September, 1994
Second Printing, 10,000 copies, September, 1995

Printed by:
Delmar Printing & Publishing
Charlotte, North Carolina

Printed in the United States of America

ISBN 0-9613214-1-5

The Junior League of Charlotte is an organization of women committed to promoting voluntarism and to improving the community through the effective action and leadership of trained volunteers. Its purpose is exclusively educational and charitable.

For information on ordering additional copies of *Dining By Fireflies*, contact:

The Junior League of Charlotte, Inc.
ATTN: Cookbook
1332 Maryland Avenue
Charlotte, North Carolina 28209

Telephone  (800) 403-3463
         (704) 375-3463
       Fax  (704) 375-9730

Printed on Recycled Paper

The Junior League of Charlotte will be a
leading force in improving the lives of
children and families in this community.
*Vision Statement*

JLC Photographer: Debby Wallace

These children, with firefly-catching jars in hand, are from the United Cerebral Palsy
Children's Center (UCP) in Charlotte, North Carolina. UCP serves youngsters between the ages of 12 months and 5 years in a preschool setting. It is just one of the
projects of The Junior League of Charlotte.

Proceeds from the sale of *Dining By Fireflies* are returned to the community through the
projects of The Junior League of Charlotte, Inc.

# BRUNCHES, LUNCHES, AND PICNICS

# SIMPLE SUPPERS AND ELEGANT DINNERS

# HOLIDAY AND BUFFET ENTERTAINING

D·I·N·I·N·G BY

*fireflies*

*Unexpected Pleasures Of The New South*

# TABLE OF CONTENTS

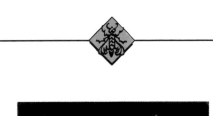

# BRUNCHES, LUNCHES AND PICNICS

*__Cut The Dijon!__ Country Pâté, p. 36; Melànge of Fresh Vegetables in French Tarragon Vinaigrette, p. 38.*

# Come Meet Your New Neighbors !

## *A Sunday Gathering For Ten*

THIS IS YOUR LIFE!
Join us to welcome new friends
and to learn unusual facts
about old friends that you thought
you already knew!

Brunch at Forrest and Nonie's
Sunday, June 8
12:30 p.m.

Let's make Mary-Richard
and Thomas Elliott
feel welcome in our neighborhood

R.S.V.P.
Call Nonie at 333-3456
to say you'll come and to
share an unusual fact about yourself

✳ In Charlotte, Southern hospitality and charm now complement a strong business prowess. This successful mix, blended with a booming economy and prolific arts community, brings new neighbors from throughout the nation.

✳ This Is Your Life . . . an adapted version of the old television program makes for a light-hearted opportunity for new-comers to get acquainted with the neighbors. The host compiles a list of unusual facts, one about each person attending the party. Each guest receives this list and a pencil upon arrival at the Sunday gathering.

✳ The object of the activity is to match each fact with the correct guest, thus encouraging conversation and min-gling. A prize can be given to the first guest who successfully completes the list. At the end of the party, present the new neighbors with a pretty address book with names, addresses, and phone numbers of the new friends met at this special Sunday gathering.

✳ The twentieth century Charlotte is a model of the "New South" to other cities on the go. With few natural resources, Charlotte has managed to become a city with major league sports, an international airport, and a top ranking banking industry, while maintaining a passion for voluntarism and community service. David Goldfield, professor at the University of North Carolina at Charlotte, describes Charlotte as "less a city than a phenomenon."

✳
10

## Come Meet Your New Neighbors !
( Serves 10 )

# MENU

NEW ORLEANS MILK PUNCH

OATMEAL RAISIN SCONES
WITH STRAWBERRY HONEY BUTTER
CARAMEL-PECAN
AND SOUR CREAM COFFEE CAKE

FRESH MUSHROOM, BACON, AND EGG PUFF

LAYERED FRUITS IN LEMON-PEAR SAUCE
WITH TOASTED ALMONDS
MAPLE CRUNCH COOKIES

*Wine suggestion:*
*Domaine De Pouy*
*Robert Kacher Selection*
*(A medium bodied white wine - consistently*
*rated as one of France's best wine values)*

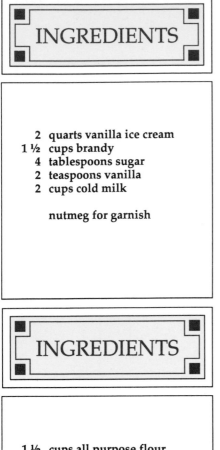

## INGREDIENTS

2 quarts vanilla ice cream
1 ½ cups brandy
4 tablespoons sugar
2 teaspoons vanilla
2 cups cold milk

nutmeg for garnish

# NEW ORLEANS MILK PUNCH

Place 1 quart ice cream in blender. Add ¾ cup brandy, 2 tablespoons sugar, and 1 teaspoon vanilla. Blend a few seconds until well mixed. Add 1 cup milk and blend 5 seconds longer. Pour into chilled julep cups or glasses. Sprinkle with nutmeg. Repeat the same process with remaining ingredients. *(This may be made several hours ahead of time and refrigerated.)*

**YIELD:** 12 drinks

*Milk punch is an all time favorite in Louisiana. It is a wonderful way to start a brunch and appropriate to serve anytime you would serve a Bloody Mary.*

*Fresh nutmeg adds a nice touch to this drink. An average nutmeg yields approximately three teaspoons when grated.*

## INGREDIENTS

1 ½ cups all purpose flour
1 ¼ cups quick cooking oats, uncooked
¼ cup brown sugar
1 tablespoon baking powder
½ teaspoon salt
⅔ cup butter, melted
½ cup milk
2 egg whites
1 teaspoon vanilla
½ cup raisins
⅓ cup pecans, chopped (optional)

**Strawberry Honey Butter (recipe follows)**

# OATMEAL RAISIN SCONES

Preheat oven to 425 degrees.

Combine flour, oats, sugar, baking powder, and salt in medium bowl. Add melted butter, milk, egg whites, and vanilla, stirring until dry ingredients become moist. Stir in raisins and pecans.

Place mixture on lightly-floured work surface and press out dough to about ¾-inch thickness. Cut into wedge shapes (or, using a cookie cutter, cut into desired shape). Bake on greased cookie sheet 12-15 minutes until golden brown. Serve with Strawberry Honey Butter.

**YIELD:** 8-12 scones

*For the holidays, add ½ cup dried cherries or cranberries, and a dash of cinnamon. Cut into Christmas tree shapes!*

*Scones, England's version of our biscuits, are traditionally served with butter, marmalade, and Devonshire clotted cream (heavy whipped cream can be substituted).*

*Oatmeal Raisin Scones, p. 12; Strawberry Honey Butter, this page.*

*New Orleans Milk Punch, p. 12; Maple Crunch Cookies, p. 17.*

# STRAWBERRY HONEY BUTTER

*Try Orange Honey Butter instead! Substitute 1 tablespoon of orange juice and grated rind of 1 orange for the strawberries.*

Purée strawberries in food processor or blender and strain through fine sieve. Place strawberries in medium saucepan along with honey, sugar, and lime juice. Boil mixture, stirring until thickened, approximately 3 minutes. Cool to room temperature.

Combine strawberry mixture and butter in medium bowl and let stand, covered, for 1 hour. Serve butter with scones, croissants, or rolls. (*Strawberry Honey Butter may be wrapped in wax paper and stored in refrigerator up to 2 days or frozen up to 2 months.*)

**YIELD:** Approximately 1 cup

## INGREDIENTS

1 pint strawberries, washed and hulled
3 tablespoons honey
1 teaspoon sugar
1 teaspoon fresh lime juice
¾ cup unsalted butter, slightly softened

## INGREDIENTS

**BATTER**

1 ½  cups sugar
1  cup butter, softened
2  eggs, beaten
1  teaspoon vanilla
2  cups all purpose flour
½  teaspoon baking soda
1  teaspoon baking powder
1  cup sour cream

**FILLING**

1 ½  teaspoons cinnamon
⅓  cup brown sugar, firmly packed
1  cup pecans, finely chopped (optional)

**CARAMEL TOPPING**

½  cup butter
6  tablespoons milk
¾  cup brown sugar, firmly packed
1  cup pecan pieces, finely chopped

# CARAMEL-PECAN AND SOUR CREAM COFFEE CAKE

Preheat oven to 350 degrees.

**FOR BATTER:**

Cream sugar and butter in large bowl. Add eggs and vanilla. Combine flour, baking soda, and baking powder in separate bowl. Alternately add flour mixture and sour cream to butter mixture. Beat until fluffy.

**FOR FILLING AND ASSEMBLY:**

Combine cinnamon, brown sugar, and pecans in small bowl.

Grease and flour 9 x 13-inch baking dish. Pour half of batter into pan and spread evenly. Sprinkle half of filling over batter. Pour and spread remaining batter and sprinkle with remaining filling. Bake 35 minutes. While cake is baking, prepare topping.

**FOR CARAMEL TOPPING:**

Melt butter in medium saucepan over moderate heat. Add milk, brown sugar, and pecans and stir 3-4 minutes.

When cake is done, remove from oven and pour caramel mixture over top, spreading evenly. Broil cake, watching carefully, until caramel topping begins to bubble, about 3 minutes. Let cake cool completely. (*Cake can be prepared 1 day ahead, covered, and stored in refrigerator.*) At time of serving, cut cake into squares and place on large platter.

**YIELD:** 2 dozen squares

*Layered Fruits in Lemon-Pear Sauce with Toasted Almonds, p. 16; Oatmeal Raisin Scones with Strawberry Honey Butter, pp. 12-13; Fresh Mushroom Bacon and Egg Puff, this page; Caramel-Pecan and Sour Cream Coffee Cake, p. 14.*

# FRESH MUSHROOM, BACON, AND EGG PUFF

*If you like curried dishes, add 2 teaspoons (or more) of curry powder.*

*Fresh mushrooms freeze well. Wash and dry them and place in a freezer bag, either sliced or unsliced, and freeze. Do not defrost when ready to use. They will taste fresh in any cooked dish.*

*(This must be made 1 day ahead.)*

Generously butter 9 x 13-inch baking dish. Arrange bread cubes in dish and sprinkle with cheese. Beat together next 6 ingredients in large bowl and pour evenly over cheese and bread. Sprinkle with bacon, mushrooms, and tomato. Cover and chill overnight.

Preheat oven to 325 degrees.

Bake casserole, uncovered, until set, about 1 hour. Tent with foil if top begins to get overly brown.

**SERVES:** 8 - 10

## INGREDIENTS

| | |
|---|---|
| 4 | cups day old white or french bread, cubed |
| 2 | cups shredded Cheddar cheese |
| 10 | eggs, lightly beaten |
| 4 | cups milk |
| 1 | teaspoon dry mustard |
| 1 | teaspoon salt |
| ¼ | teaspoon onion powder dash freshly ground pepper |
| 10 | slices cooked bacon, crumbled |
| ½ | cup fresh mushrooms, sliced |
| ½ | cup tomatoes, chopped |

✳
―――
15

## INGREDIENTS

- 29 ounces canned pear halves in heavy syrup
- 1 egg, beaten
- 2 tablespoons flour
- 1 teaspoon butter
- 2 teaspoons lemon juice
- 1 cup heavy cream, whipped
- 2 tablespoons powdered sugar
- 16 ounces canned pineapple chunks, drained
- 1 medium banana, sliced
- 1 pint strawberries, sliced
- 11 ounces canned mandarin oranges, drained
- 2 kiwi, chilled
- ¼ cup slivered almonds, toasted

# LAYERED FRUITS IN LEMON-PEAR SAUCE WITH TOASTED ALMONDS

Drain pears, reserving 1 cup syrup. Combine pear syrup, egg, and flour in medium saucepan. Cook over moderate heat until thickened. Stir in butter and lemon juice. Cool thoroughly. Fold in whipped cream sweetened with powdered sugar.

Cut 4 pear halves in half lengthwise and reserve. Dice remaining pears. Layer diced pears, pineapple, banana, strawberries, and oranges in large glass bowl. Spread cooled topping over all. Cover and chill overnight. Just before serving, peel and slice kiwi. Decorate layered fruit with reserved pear slices, kiwi, and almonds.

**SERVES:** 8-10

*Caramel-Pecan and Sour Cream Coffee Cake, p. 14.*

# MAPLE CRUNCH COOKIES

When buying pure maple syrup, be sure to read the labels since many contain large amounts of cane and little maple syrup. Finer grades of maple are light in color and contain more flavor than the darker grades.

Preheat oven to 375 degrees.

Sift together three times: flour, salt, soda, cloves, ginger, and cinnamon in medium bowl. Set aside.

Cream together maple syrup, shortening, and sugar in large bowl. Add egg and beat until fluffy. Add sifted ingredients and walnuts, blending well.

Drop by teaspoonsful onto ungreased cookie sheets and bake 10 minutes. While still warm, top with whole pecan or walnut, if desired.

**YIELD:** 5 dozen cookies

## INGREDIENTS

2 cups flour
½ teaspoon salt
1 teaspoon baking soda
¼ teaspoon ground cloves
½ teaspoon ground ginger
1 teaspoon cinnamon
¼ cup maple syrup
¾ cup shortening
1 cup sugar
1 egg
½ cup walnuts, finely chopped

whole pecans or walnuts for garnish (optional)

# Let's Catch Up !

## A Leisurely Lunch For Friends On The Run

Join us for a Leisurely Lunch at "Tara."
All of your worries will be
"Gone With The Wind."
So leave your hectic lives
in the foyer and strike the attitude,
"Frankly, I just don't give a damn."

Relax with the "O'Hara girls,"
Taylor Teague and Mason Smith,
on Tuesday, June 6
from 12:00 to 2:00 p.m.
5513 Topping Place

Forget the hoops and corsets.
Wear comfortable clothes.

R.S.V.P.  Taylor  345-5467
Mason  234-4356

✳ Women have always recognized the value of the camaraderie and support that comes from special friends and special times shared together. In the antebellum period, quilting was a popular form of socializing for women. A woman might invite as many as a dozen neighbors to help her complete a quilt in a day which otherwise could take her several weeks to complete on her own. They would usually arrive in the morning bearing thimbles, needles, and sometimes even snuff.

✳ For your women's lunch of the 1990's, give each one of your busy friends a little "surci" — an enchanting self-indulgence — to remember how treasured friendship truly is. Perhaps dried herbs or flowers from your garden, homemade sachets, a package of wildflower seeds, herbal teas wrapped in a pretty bow, freshly ground coffee, bouquet garni, or a small book of poetry — any of these would say, "I enjoyed catching up!"

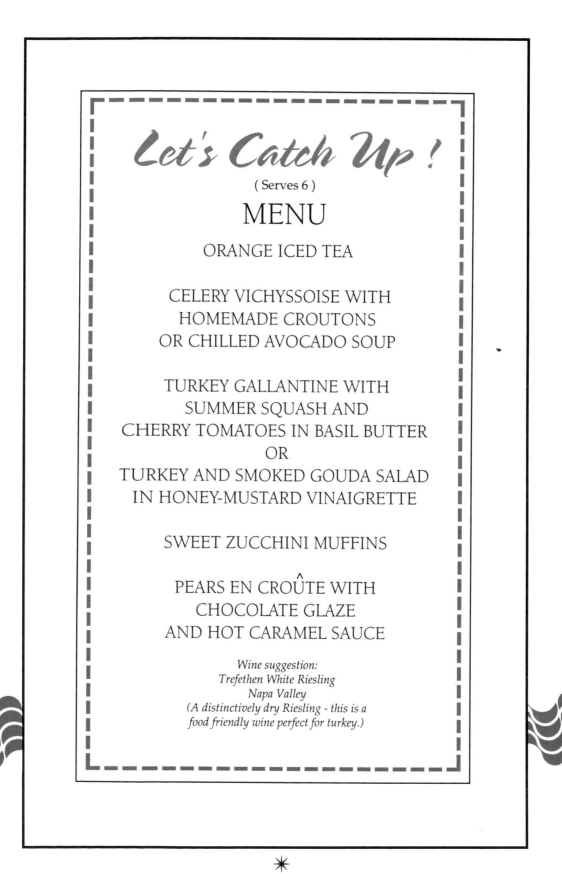

# *Let's Catch Up !*

( Serves 6 )

## MENU

ORANGE ICED TEA


CELERY VICHYSSOISE WITH
HOMEMADE CROUTONS
OR CHILLED AVOCADO SOUP


TURKEY GALLANTINE WITH
SUMMER SQUASH AND
CHERRY TOMATOES IN BASIL BUTTER
OR
TURKEY AND SMOKED GOUDA SALAD
IN HONEY-MUSTARD VINAIGRETTE


SWEET ZUCCHINI MUFFINS


PEARS EN CROÛTE WITH
CHOCOLATE GLAZE
AND HOT CARAMEL SAUCE

*Wine suggestion:*
*Trefethen White Riesling*
*Napa Valley*
*(A distinctively dry Riesling - this is a*
*food friendly wine perfect for turkey.)*

## INGREDIENTS

### STUFFING

16 ounces frozen sweet peas, thawed
2 tablespoons flour
3 tablespoons whole milk
2 eggs
6 green onions, chopped
3 tablespoons fresh parsley, chopped
½ teaspoon salt
¼ teaspoon pepper

### TURKEY

1 3-pound boneless turkey breast
½ pound cooked ham, cut into ⅜ inch strips
21 ½ ounces canned chicken broth
1 bay leaf
2 stalks celery, cut into 1 - inch pieces
2 large carrots, sliced
1 sweet onion, quartered

### WHITE ASPIC COATING

⅓ cup cold water
1 tablespoon vinegar
1 teaspoon granulated chicken bouillon
1 envelope unflavored gelatin
1 cup mayonnaise

  mixed lettuce leaves for garnish
  red pepper strips for garnish
  chive or green onion stems for garnish

# TURKEY GALLATINE

### FOR STUFFING:

Purée peas in food processor. Add remaining stuffing ingredients and process until smooth. Pour puréed mixture into top of double boiler. Cook over simmering water 10-15 minutes until thick. Remove from heat and cool.

### FOR TURKEY AND ASSEMBLY:

Lay turkey breast flat on waxed paper, skin side up. Slice away fat and skin. Turn breast over. From center of breast, slice horizontally through thickest part of each breast almost to outer edge. Open up and flip out each cut side to enlarge breast and create a more even thickness. Pound breast to ½-inch thickness. Spread half of pea mixture over turkey breast, leaving a 1-inch border all around. Lay ham strips lengthwise down breast and spread remaining pea mixture over ham. Fold in short sides of breast about an inch to make sides even.

Starting with long side, roll turkey breast, jelly roll style, over filling. Secure seam with toothpicks. Wrap breast in several layers of cheesecloth and tie ends with twine. Place turkey in large Dutch oven or fish poacher, seam side down. Add chicken broth and water to almost cover turkey. Add bay leaf, celery, carrots, and onion. Bring to boil, cover, reduce heat, and simmer one hour. Cool slightly in broth. Remove turkey and cool. Discard liquid and vegetables. Wrap turkey in plastic wrap and refrigerate 8 hours or overnight. *(Turkey can be prepared 1 day ahead up to this point.)*

*Skinless white-meat turkey breast is **the** leanest meat you can buy.*

### FOR WHITE ASPIC COATING:

Combine water, vinegar, and boullion in small saucepan. Sprinkle gelatin over mixture and let stand 5 minutes. Cook over low heat, stirring constantly, until gelatin dissolves. Remove from heat and whisk in mayonnaise until smooth.

Remove plastic wrap, cheesecloth, and toothpicks from turkey. Place turkey, seam side down, on wire rack and place rack in large roasting pan.

Spoon half of aspic coating over turkey. Refrigerate 5 minutes to set. Spoon remaining aspic over turkey. Refrigerate another 5 minutes to set. Transfer to serving platter and chill, covered loosely, until ready to serve. Garnish with mixed lettuce greens, red pepper strips, and chive or green onion stems.

**SERVES:** 6 - 8

*There is only one trick to successfully coating any food with aspic: the food must be very cold and the aspic gelatin must be cool but still liquid. This ensures that the aspic will set almost immediately.*

16 ounces yellow squash,
 thinly sliced
8 ounces cherry tomatoes,
 halved
2 tablespoons Basil Butter
 (recipe below)

**BASIL BUTTER**

1 shallot, minced
3 cloves garlic, minced
¾ cup fresh basil, minced
½ cup butter, softened
 freshly ground pepper
 to taste

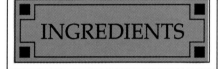

1 cup olive oil
2 cloves garlic
1 large turkey breast,
 cooked and julienned
8 ounces cheese tortellini,
 fresh or dried
1 green pepper, diced
3 stalks celery, diced
1 small red onion, thinly
 sliced
⅓ pound smoked Gouda
 cheese, julienned
2 tablespoons Dijon mustard
1 teaspoon dry mustard
¾ cup cider vinegar
¼ cup honey
3 ounces Canadian bacon or
 honey cured ham, thinly
 sliced and julienned

 lettuce leaves for garnish

# SUMMER SQUASH AND CHERRY TOMATOES IN BASIL BUTTER

Sauté squash and cherry tomatoes in 2 tablespoons basil butter in medium skillet until tender, approximately 10 minutes. Serve with extra basil butter on the side.

**FOR BASIL BUTTER:**

Place all ingredients in food processor and process until smooth. Refrigerate until solid.

**SERVES:** 6

*Basil, considered an imperial herb by ancient Greeks, has a flavor that is a cross between cloves and licorice. It can be grown inside during the winter months in a sunny window.*

*"A man taking basil from a woman will love her always."*
*Sir Thomas Moore*

# TURKEY AND SMOKED GOUDA SALAD IN HONEY-MUSTARD VINAIGRETTE

Heat 2 tablespoons olive oil in large skillet. Add garlic and sauté until brown. Remove garlic. Add turkey to hot oil and stir fry 3-4 minutes. Drain and set aside. Cook tortellini according to package directions. Drain and toss with 2 tablespoons olive oil. Cool.

Combine turkey, tortellini, green pepper, celery, onion, and Gouda cheese in large salad bowl.

Mix remaining olive oil with mustards, vinegar, and honey in small bowl. Pour over turkey-pasta mixture and toss well. Top with ham strips. Chill. Serve on bed of lettuce leaves. *(Can be prepared 1 day ahead, covered, and refrigerated.)*

**SERVES:** 6

*Turkey Gallantine, pp. 22-23;*
*Summer Squash and Cherry Tomatoes*
*in Basil Butter, p. 24; Sweet Zucchini*
*Muffins, this page.*

# SWEET
# ZUCCHINI MUFFINS

Preheat oven to 350 degrees. Grease muffin pans.

Sift together first four ingredients in medium bowl and set aside. Blend together oil, egg, vanilla, sugar, and salt in large bowl. Gradually add flour mixture and stir well. Add lemon or orange rind, pecans, and dates and mix well. Stir in grated zucchini. (Batter will be very stiff and thick.) Spoon into prepared muffin pans. Bake 25 minutes for small muffins, 30-35 minutes for medium to large muffins.

**YIELD:** 24 small or 15 medium to large muffins

## INGREDIENTS

1½ cups flour
½ teaspoon baking powder
¼ teaspoon baking soda
1 teaspoon ground cinnamon
½ cup vegetable oil
1 egg
1 teaspoon vanilla
1 cup sugar
½ teaspoon salt
1 teaspoon lemon or orange rind, grated
1 cup pecans, chopped
½ cup dates, chopped
1 small zucchini, grated

✳
25

# PEARS EN CROÛTE WITH CHOCOLATE GLAZE AND HOT CARAMEL SAUCE

*Amazingly easy, this dessert always receives applause!*

Preheat oven to 425 degrees.

Carefully peel pears leaving stems intact. Cut tops off just above thickest part of pear. Scoop out core, using small spoon or melon ball scooper. Do not break through bottom or sides of pears. Fill cavity with chocolate pieces and replace top.

Beat egg with water in small bowl.

On lightly-floured surface, roll out each pastry sheet to a 10 x 13-inch rectangle. Cut 6 squares from pastry, each about 3 ½ x 3 ½ inches. Reserve remaining pastry.

Place a pear in middle of each square and bring 4 corners together. Use remaining odd pieces to fully cover pear, exposing only stem. Press pieces together and brush pastry with egg mixture. *(Pears can be covered in plastic and refrigerated up to 24 hours.)*

Place pears on ungreased baking sheet and bake 15 minutes. Reduce temperature to 375 degrees and bake 5-8 minutes longer until pastry is puffed and golden brown.

Meanwhile, prepare chocolate glaze: melt chocolate over hot (not boiling) water in top of double boiler. Remove from heat and whisk in butter. Transfer chocolate mixture to clean, small heavy plastic bag.

To serve, spoon hot caramel sauce onto individual serving plates. Place pear on top of sauce. Snip a hole in one corner of plastic bag containing chocolate glaze. Drizzle glaze over each pear and serve immediately. Garnish with mint leaves.

**SERVES:** 6

## INGREDIENTS

6 medium ripe pears (Anjou are best)
  semisweet chocolate pieces
1 egg
1 tablespoon water
1 package (17.4 ounces) frozen puff pastry sheets, thawed
  flour

4 ounces semisweet chocolate pieces
3 tablespoons unsalted butter

  Purchased Caramel Sauce, heated
  mint leaves for garnish

# Pigs On A Blanket

## *An Outdoor Concert Picnic*

'Twas the night before Monday,
but the weekend's not over

We'll hear tunes to delight
as the sun slowly sets.

Let's be pigs on a blanket,
with a picnic galore.

Enjoy music at sunset
as our special guests.

Please join us at South Park
for a Concert Picnic

Sunday, June 21
6:00 p.m.

Ansley and Merrill Clark

Regrets
456-4323

B.Y.O.B.
(Bring your own blanket)

✳ Picnics should be festive!  Place all condiment jars in colorful cloth napkins.  Use a rubber band around the napkin at the top of the jar and allow the excess napkin to drape over.  And don't forget the citronella!

✳ If children will be coming along, let them run free while blowing these fabulous rainbow bubbles:

### Rainbow Bubbles
2 cups Joy dishwashing liquid
6 cups water
¾ cup Karo white corn syrup

Combine all ingredients and let sit 4 hours before using.

✳ Due to the mild weather in the Carolinas, outdoor concerts can be enjoyed from April through October and even longer for those residing at the coast.  Symphony orchestras delight outdoor concert goers with favorite show tune renditions, Pops, and light classics.  Beautiful Carolina parks provide the perfect setting for a picnic supper.

✳ As dusk falls on a summer picnic night, the air starts to sparkle with tiny bursts of light.  The fireflies have begun to flash their twinkling lamps.  They continue until the sun has truly set and heavy darkness settles down.  Then, except for a stay-up-late straggler or two, the fireflies turn off their lights and the lovely display is over for the evening.

# Pigs On A Blanket

( Serves 8 )

## MENU

STRAWBERRY-WATERMELON LEMONADE
SWEET POTATO CHIPS
WITH SESAME DIPPING SAUCE

PEANUT-CRUSTED PICNIC CHICKEN

ARTICHOKE-SHRIMP
PASTA SALAD
WITH SUNFLOWER SEEDS
SPICY BLACK BEAN AND CORN SALAD
OR
BROCCOLI FLORETS WITH BACON,
RAISINS, AND MUSHROOMS

CINNAMON PEAR TART

*Wine suggestion:*
*Trimbach-Pinot Blanc*
*White Alsace Wine*
*(A soft, fruity wine - excellent complement*
*to chicken or any picnic.)*

## INGREDIENTS

1   6-pound watermelon,
    seeded and cut into chunks
2   pints strawberries, hulled
½   cup sugar
12  ounces frozen lemonade
    concentrate, thawed
¾   cup fresh lemon juice

# STRAWBERRY-WATERMELON LEMONADE

Purée watermelon in food processor in batches until smooth. Strain through a sieve into large bowl or 2 quart pitcher. Process strawberries with sugar until smooth. Add strawberry purée, lemonade concentrate, and lemon juice to watermelon juice. Refrigerate.

**YIELD:**  8 drinks

*For adults only: two cups of vodka may be added to the lemonade.*

## INGREDIENTS

**SWEET POTATO CHIPS**

3   large sweet potatoes,
    peeled
    vegetable cooking spray
¼   teaspoon salt

**DIPPING SAUCE**

8   ounces water chestnuts,
    chopped fine
8   ounces sour cream
1   cup mayonnaise
1   clove garlic, minced
¼   cup fresh parsley, minced
2   tablespoons onion, minced
1   teaspoon soy sauce
½   teaspoon ground ginger
2   tablespoons sesame seeds,
    toasted

# SWEET POTATO CHIPS WITH SESAME DIPPING SAUCE

**FOR SWEET POTATO CHIPS:**

Preheat oven to 325 degrees.

Spray baking sheet with cooking spray. Slice sweet potatoes very thin and arrange in single layer on baking sheet.  Bake 15 minutes or until crisp.  Remove individual chips as they brown.  Drain on paper towels.  Sprinkle with salt.  Serve with Sesame Dipping Sauce.

**FOR DIPPING SAUCE:**

Combine all ingredients in medium bowl. Cover and chill overnight.

**YIELD:**  Approximately 5 dozen chips

*Did you know that sweet potatoes are virtually fat free and contain no more calories than white potatoes?*

*This dipping sauce is also a wonderful accompaniment to fresh vegetables.*

# PEANUT-CRUSTED PICNIC CHICKEN

Preheat oven to 350 degrees.

Combine first 6 ingredients and ⅔ cup flour in medium bowl. Place remaining 2 ⅓ cups flour and buttermilk in separate bowls. Dredge chicken in flour, dip in buttermilk, and roll in peanut mixture.

Bake chicken, covered tightly with foil, 45 minutes in greased, shallow baking dish. Carefully remove foil and bake another 20-25 minutes or until chicken is golden brown. Remove chicken from baking dish and cool. (Chicken will crisp as it cools.)

**SERVES:** 8

## INGREDIENTS

2 cups dry roasted peanuts, ground fine
⅔ cup yellow cornmeal
5 large cloves garlic, minced
2 tablespoons fresh ginger, minced
1 teaspoon pepper
2 tablespoons salt
3 cups flour
2 cups buttermilk
8 chicken breast halves

# ARTICHOKE-SHRIMP PASTA SALAD WITH SUNFLOWER SEEDS

Place artichoke hearts and shrimp in large bowl.

Combine vinegar, mustard, chives, egg yolk, and shallots in food processor or blender. Purée. Gradually add oils in a thin stream while machine is running. Season to taste with salt and pepper.

Add cooled pasta to shrimp and artichokes. Pour dressing mixture over pasta, shrimp, and artichokes and mix gently but thoroughly. Cover and refrigerate at least 3 hours. (*Can be made 1 day ahead up to this point.*) Stir in sunflower seeds just before serving.

**SERVES:** 8

## INGREDIENTS

9 ounces marinated artichoke hearts, quartered and drained
½-⅔ pound medium shrimp, cooked, peeled, and deveined
¼ cup red wine vinegar
2 tablespoons Dijon mustard
2 tablespoons fresh chives, chopped
1 egg yolk
1 tablespoon shallots, minced
½ cup olive oil
2 tablespoons vegetable oil
   salt to taste
   pepper to taste
½ pound medium seashell pasta, cooked, drained, and cooled
¼ cup sunflower seeds

*For a change from seafood, try substituting cooked chicken in the Artichoke-Shrimp Pasta Salad.*

*Sunflowers, indigenous to North and Central America, were brought to Europe by Spanish explorers. The sun-worshipping Aztecs of Peru were thought to have crowned their high priestesses with this dramatic flower.*

*Sunflower seeds are very high in protein and add a wonderful flavor to salads and breads.*

## INGREDIENTS

1 16-ounce can black beans, drained
4 ounces Monterey jack cheese, cubed
3 ears corn, cooked and cut from cob, or 8 ounces canned corn, drained
½ cup green onions, sliced (including green tops)
¾ cup celery, thinly sliced
1 red bell pepper, diced
¾ cup mild picante sauce
2 tablespoons olive oil
2 tablespoons lemon juice
1 teaspoon ground cumin
1 clove garlic, minced

# SPICY BLACK BEAN AND CORN SALAD

Combine beans, cheese, corn, green onions, celery, and red bell pepper in large bowl. Combine remaining ingredients in small bowl and mix well. Toss with bean mixture, cover, and chill. *(Can be made 1 day ahead of time.)* Serve with additional picante sauce.

**SERVES:** 8

*Also known as turtle beans, black beans play a significant role in Latin American, Caribbean, and Southwestern "TexMex" cuisine. Low in fat and cholesterol, they have also become an important part of today's diet. So have a second helping of the Spicy Black Bean and Corn Salad.*

## INGREDIENTS

**SALAD**

1 bunch broccoli, cut into small florets
½ cup red onion, sliced
1 cup fresh mushrooms, sliced
1 cup raisins
6 slices bacon, cooked

**DRESSING**

1 egg
1 egg yolk
½ cup sugar
½ teaspoon dry mustard
1 teaspoon cornstarch
¼ cup water
¼ cup white vinegar
½ teaspoon salt
2 tablespoons unsalted butter, sliced
½ cup mayonnaise

# BROCCOLI FLORETS WITH BACON, RAISINS, AND MUSHROOMS

**FOR SALAD:**

Place all salad ingredients in large bowl. Refrigerate. *(Salad may be prepared early in day but add dressing just before serving.)*

**FOR DRESSING:**

Whisk first 5 ingredients in small bowl. Bring next 3 ingredients to boil in medium saucepan. Add bowl mixture to pan and cook over moderate-high heat 1 minute or until thick. (Be careful not to overcook or egg will turn brown). Remove from heat and add sliced butter and mayonnaise. Mix thoroughly. Cover and refrigerate several hours.

To serve, pour dressing over broccoli mixture and toss gently but thoroughly.

**SERVES:** 8

*This salad always gets rave reviews!*

*To ensure uniformity when slicing fresh mushrooms, use an egg slicer.*

# CINNAMON PEAR TART

**INGREDIENTS**

**FOR CRUST:**

Mix flour, grated lemon peel, and butter in medium bowl until mixture resembles small, pea-sized pieces. Add just enough water for mixture to hold together when pressed between fingers. Roll into ball and wrap in plastic. Let rest in refrigerator at least 30 minutes.

Preheat oven to 375 degrees.

Roll out crust large enough to cover a 9 ½- or 10-inch tart pan. Press crust into pan. Trim edges.

**FOR FILLING AND ASSEMBLY:**

Combine first 5 filling ingredients in medium bowl. Layer fruit closely together in spiral pattern in crust-prepared tart pan. Brush with melted butter.

Bake 30-45 minutes or until golden and crisp. Remove from oven and brush with currant jelly. Let cool 10 minutes. (*Can be prepared 1 day ahead and refrigerated.*)

Serve warm, cold, or at room temperature with whipped cream.

**SERVES:** 8

**CRUST**

1 ½  cups all purpose flour
¼  teaspoon lemon peel, grated
12  tablespoons butter, room temperature and sliced
1-2  tablespoons water

**FILLING**

4-5  firm pears, peeled and thinly sliced
pinch cinnamon
pinch nutmeg
2  teaspoons lemon juice
2-3  tablespoons sugar
1-2  tablespoons butter, melted

⅓  cup red currant jelly, melted
whipped cream

# Cut The Dijon !

## A Taste Of Europe In The Blue Ridge Mountains

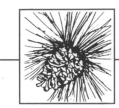

Listen, good people, and you shall hear,
the mountains are calling, "Come near, come here!"
So join us next Saturday in the crisp clean air.
Share feast and fun with deer and bear!

(Well, even if the animals can't make the picnic,
we hope you can!)

Saturday, April 24
Hosted by Clifford and Sterling Branstrom

Meet at our home at 11:00 a.m. for an
afternoon of fun,
food, and adventure!

✳ In the heart of the Blue Ridge Mountains lies Black Mountain, one of the most popular picnicking spots in North Carolina. Once believed to be a holy ground by the Cherokee Indians, it was called Grey Eagle.

✳ The spiritual nature of the mountain still exists today as Black Mountain has the largest concentration of religious conference centers in the world! Get in touch with your own spirit and those of friends in one of the most magical places in the Carolinas!

✳ Skiing, rafting, biking, and even rock hounding are just a few of the mountain outdoor activities for the more stout of heart. If you desire a panoramic view, we suggest traversing the swinging bridge of Grandfather Mountain.

✳ The Blue Ridge Parkway, unsurpassed as the most beautiful highway in the United States, has no commercial traffic, no stop signs, no stop lights, and no billboards. Picnic here for a memory of a lifetime!

✳ The Biltmore Estate in Asheville is one of the most breathtaking attractions North Carolina has to offer. The grandeur and serene beauty of the house and gardens strikes you from the outside but once inside, it becomes hard to believe that this 250-room architectural feat was completed in just five years.

✳ Open to the public, the estate includes, in addition to the incredible mansion, a large dairy and winery. Don't miss it!

# Cut The Dijon !

( Serves 4 -6)

## MENU

COUNTRY PÂTÉ WITH HIGH HAMPTON
HONEY-MUSTARD ESSENCE
MELÁNGE OF FRESH VEGETABLES
IN FRENCH TARRAGON VINAIGRETTE

BLUEBERRY PRESERVE
AND LEMON TARTLETS

*Wine suggestion:*
*Biltmore Estate*
*American Chardonnay Sur-Lies*
*(Fermented Sur-Lies ["on the skins"], this full bodied*
*dry Chardonnay is an excellent example*
*of our fine Southern wines.)*

## INGREDIENTS

2 pounds chicken livers
2 teaspoons Tellicherry pepper
¼ teaspoon sage
¼ teaspoon cayenne
¼ teaspoon ground thyme
1 teaspoon coriander seeds
10 bay leaves
6 cloves garlic, minced
1 cup dry white wine
1 cup Cognac or brandy
1 ½ pounds pork sausage
1 loaf stale french bread
½ cup heavy cream
grated zest of 2 oranges
3 cups chopped pecans
salt to taste
1 pound bacon, sliced thin
1 pound baked ham, cubed
bay leaves for garnish

**High Hampton Honey-Mustard Essence (recipe follows)**

# COUNTRY PÂTÉ WITH HIGH HAMPTON HONEY-MUSTARD ESSENCE

*(Make 1 or more days ahead.)*

Soak livers, spices, wine, and Cognac or brandy in bowl overnight in refrigerator, covered. Process all in food processor. Scrape into large bowl.

Sauté sausage until browned. Drain off fat and process in food processor until chopped fine but not creamed. Add to liver mixture.

Process bread and cream together in processor. Add to mixture. Stir orange zest and half of pecans into mixture. Season with salt to taste.

Preheat oven to 350 degrees.

Arrange bacon slices across bottom and sides of three 9 x 4-inch loaf pans leaving 2 inch overhang. Pack pâté mixture into pans, adding ham cubes randomly throughout. Fold ends of bacon over top. Cover each pan with aluminum foil.

Place three small loaf pans in large baking pan 1 inch deep. Add hot water to large pan to come half way up sides of small pans. Bake 1 ½ hours. Remove to rack and let cool 30 minutes. Place small boards or weights on top of pâtés. Leave overnight in refrigerator. Unmold pâtés from pans. When ready to serve, coat with reserved pecans. (Pat chopped pecans on all sides and top of pâté loaves.) Garnish with bay leaves. Serve with High Hampton Honey-Mustard Essence.

**YIELD:** Three 9 x 4-inch loaf pans.

*Tellicherry pepper is one of the finest varieties of black pepper. It may be found in the gourmet section of some supermarkets and most specialty markets. If unavailable, freshly ground black pepper can be substituted.*

*Extra pâtés can be wrapped in foil and frozen.*

*Country Pâté, p. 36; Melànge of Fresh Vegetables in French Tarragon Vinaigrette, p. 38.*

# HIGH HAMPTON
# HONEY-MUSTARD
# ESSENCE

Mix dry mustard with beer to medium
texture (not too soupy but not too thick).
Add honey and Cognac. Mix well and store
in airtight jar at room temperature for 3
days. (This makes the essence.) When
needed, mix 1 part essence with 3 parts
mayonnaise or whipping cream.

### INGREDIENTS

4 ounces dry mustard
6 ounces beer
3 tablespoons honey
1 ½ ounces Cognac
     mayonnaise or whipping
     cream, beaten until thick

## INGREDIENTS

### VEGETABLES

½ bunch broccoli, cut into small florets
1 large carrot, sliced into thin circles
1 yellow bell pepper, cut into thin strips
1 pint cherry tomatoes, halved and stems removed
1 can or jar white asparagus tips, drained
   fresh baby dill sprigs for garnish (optional)

### VINAIGRETTE

1 teaspoon salt
1 teaspoon sugar
½ teaspoon dry mustard
½ teaspoon celery salt
1 teaspoon Worcestershire sauce
1 clove garlic, mashed
1 cup olive oil
¼ cup tarragon vinegar
½ teaspoon pepper

# MELÀNGE OF FRESH VEGETABLES IN FRENCH TARRAGON VINAIGRETTE

**FOR VEGETABLES:**

Blanch broccoli in medium saucepan until bright green but still crisp, about 2 minutes. Cool. Combine broccoli with remaining vegetables. Cover and chill 1 hour or overnight. At time of serving, gently toss with French Tarragon Vinaigrette. Garnish with baby dill sprigs, if desired.

**FOR VINAIGRETTE:**

Combine all ingredients in small jar. Shake well. Refrigerate at least 2 hours or up to 2 days. Shake just before serving.

**Serves:** 4

*Always plunge blanched vegetables into ice water to halt cooking and retain crispness and color.*

*White asparagus is favored in Europe over the green variety favored in the United States. European white asparagus is a thicker variety that is planted in a deep trench. As the stalks grow, soil is mounded over them so they are never exposed to sunlight and are, therefore, unable to turn green.*

*Country Pâté, p. 36; Melànge of Fresh Vegetables in French Tarragon Vinaigrette, this page.*

*A pretty touch for tarts is to top them with a pastry "bow." Using excess pastry dough or a commercial refrigerated pie crust, cut 3 x ½-inch strips. Pinch together to form 2 loops of the bow and 2 streamers. Bake bows on cookie sheet 10-12 minutes at 425 degrees. When cool, place on top of tarts.*

# BLUEBERRY PRESERVE AND LEMON TARTLETS

Preheat oven to 325 degrees.

Spread a thin layer of preserves on bottom of tartlet shells or pie shell. Mix remaining ingredients together in medium bowl and pour on top of preserves until three-quarters full. Bake 40 minutes. When cool, dust with powdered sugar.

**YIELD:** 8 tartlets or 1 pie

## INGREDIENTS

1   jar blueberry preserves
8   tartlet shells or 1 pie
    shell
4   eggs
2   cups sugar
    juice of 2 lemons
    grated peel of 1 lemon

    powdered sugar for garnish

# MARCH MADNESS!

## *Hearty Fare Before The Game !*

Come show your team spirit with other alums. Enjoy hearty fare as we cheer our team on!

Meet at the "Sports Arena" of Bailey and Russell Barnhardt
4405 Selwyn Avenue
Saturday, March 13
11:00 a.m.

✳ The Atlantic Coast Conference (ACC) basketball tournament is one of the most popular sporting events in the Carolinas. North Carolina is home to four ACC college basketball teams — Duke University, Wake Forest University, The University of North Carolina at Chapel Hill, and North Carolina State University. With so many alumni in the area, pre-game parties are a great way to show team spirit.

✳ Table decor at a festive event before the big game could consist of pom poms, pennants, buttons, sports cards, mini basketballs, or team hats. Take a high top tennis shoe and place a glass in the opening. Tie the shoelaces to secure the glass, fill with water, and add flowers. For party favors, guests might receive a small bag of chocolate basketballs tied with colored ribbons of each sports fan's favorite team. This, of course, would work for football season as well.

✳ Charlotte's NBA team, the Hornets, burst on the sports scene in 1988. A brand new beautiful coliseum and chic purple and teal uniforms, created by clothing designer Alexander Julian, provided the backdrop for Hornet hysteria to sweep through the Queen City.

✳ The Carolina Panthers, Charlotte's NFL franchise awarded in 1993, brings professional football to the Carolinas for the first time.

# MARCH MADNESS!

( Serves 6 )

## MENU

**VARIETY OF BEERS**

**CRUNCHY SPICED WALNUTS**
**SPINACH QUESADILLAS WITH GRILLED SWEET POTATO**
**AND FOUR-PEPPER SALSA**

**VEGETABLE-BRAISED VEAL WITH LEMON ZEST**
**AND GARLIC OVER HOT FETTUCINE**
**OR**
**CLASSIC BOEUF BOURGUIGNONNE**
**OVER RICE PILAF WITH SLICED ALMONDS**

**MIXED GREENS WITH CITRUS VINAIGRETTE**
**GOLDEN BUTTER YEAST ROLLS**

**PEPPERMINT RIBBON PIE WITH FUDGE SAUCE**

*If you wish to serve:*
*White Wine - Macon-Lugny*
*(Choose from any of the better producers*
*of this fine French Burgundy - dry and crisp.)*

*Red Wine - Chateau de La Chaize*
*(This fragrant/fruity wine is best*
*served cool, not cold.)*

## INGREDIENTS

    6  cups water
    4  cups walnut halves
    ½  cup sugar
    1  teaspoon cinnamon
       salad oil
       salt to taste

# CRUNCHY SPICED WALNUTS

Heat water to boiling in large saucepan. Add walnuts and bring to boil. Pour walnuts into colander and rinse under hot water; drain.

Wash and dry saucepan. Combine sugar and cinnamon in large bowl. Gently toss walnuts with sugar mixture, using rubber spatula until sugar is dissolved.

Meanwhile, in same saucepan, over moderate heat, add about 1 inch salad oil and heat to 350 degrees on deep fat thermometer.

With slotted spoon, add half of walnuts to oil. Fry 5 minutes or until golden, stirring often and watching carefully not to burn. With slotted spoon, remove walnuts and place in sieve over bowl to drain. Sprinkle lightly with salt. Toss carefully to keep walnuts from sticking together. Cool on wax paper. Fry remaining walnuts in the same manner.

**YIELD:** 4 cups

*Store walnuts in a tightly covered container up to three weeks or freeze up to six months. These make a wonderful hostess gift or truly great addition to almost any salad. Just use directly from the freezer!*

# SPINACH QUESADILLAS

### FOR SPINACH MIXTURE:

Melt butter in large skillet and lightly sauté spinach and mushrooms. Stir in spices. Set aside. Drain if necessary.

### FOR QUESADILLAS:

Preheat oven to 375 degrees.

Place 5 tortillas on cookie sheet. Top with cream cheese, spinach mixture, and jack cheese. Place tortilla on top. Bake 7 minutes. (Tortillas should be crispy around edges with cheese melted.) Cut into quarters. Serve hot with sour cream and Grilled Sweet Potato and Four-Pepper Salsa.

**YIELD:** 20 quesadilla quarters

*Cilantro and cumin, known as "the Mexican spices," can be used interchangeably. For best results, buy these spices fresh.*

## INGREDIENTS

**SPINACH MIXTURE**

| | |
|---|---|
| ½ | tablespoon butter |
| 10 | ounces frozen chopped spinach, thawed and drained |
| ¼ | pound fresh mushrooms, sliced |
| | pinch nutmeg |
| | pinch cayenne pepper |

**QUESADILLAS**

| | |
|---|---|
| 10 | large flour tortillas |
| 8 | ounces cream cheese, softened |
| 10 | ounces Monterey jack cheese, shredded |
| | sour cream |

Grilled Sweet Potato and Four-Pepper Salsa (recipe follows)

# GRILLED SWEET POTATO AND FOUR-PEPPER SALSA

Preheat oven to 375 degrees.

Bake sweet potatoes until medium soft, approximately 40 minutes to an hour. Let cool, peel, and slice. On a grill or grill top stove, grill sweet potato slices and all peppers on both sides until lightly charred. Remove. Dice (or chop) sweet potato slices and pepper slices into small pieces.

Combine potato slices and peppers with onion, garlic, and cilantro in medium bowl. Toss with vinegars and oil. Add salt and pepper to taste. *(Cover and refrigerate several hours or overnight.)* Stir before serving.

**YIELD:** Approximately 2 cups

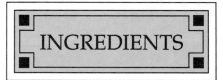

## INGREDIENTS

| | |
|---|---|
| 2 | large sweet potatoes, peeled and sliced ¼-inch thick |
| 1 | large green bell pepper, sliced into ½-inch strips |
| 1 | large yellow bell pepper, sliced into ½-inch strips |
| 1 | large red bell pepper, sliced into ½-inch strips |
| 1 | jalapeno pepper, seeded and halved (wear gloves) |
| 1 | medium red onion, diced |
| 4 | cloves garlic, minced |
| ¼ | cup fresh cilantro, chopped |
| ⅛ | cup balsamic vinegar |
| 2 | teaspoons red wine vinegar |
| ½ | cup extra virgin olive oil |
| | salt and pepper to taste |

## INGREDIENTS

3 pounds veal stew meat
3 tablespoons flour
¼ teaspoon salt
¼ teaspoon pepper
5 tablespoons olive oil
1 cup onions, chopped
½ cup carrots, chopped
⅓ cup celery, chopped
2 cups dry white wine
3 large cloves garlic,
    minced
1 3-inch strip lemon peel
2 14-ounce cans Italian Plum
    tomatoes, undrained
¼ cup fresh parsley, chopped
1 teaspoon thyme
1 teaspoon basil
1 bay leaf

1 ½ pounds cooked fettucine,
    drained and buttered

1 tablespoon fresh chopped
    parsley, for garnish

# VEGETABLE-BRAISED VEAL WITH LEMON ZEST AND GARLIC OVER HOT FETTUCINE

Pat veal dry. Mix flour, salt, and pepper in large flat dish. Coat veal in flour mixture. Heat 2 tablespoons olive oil in large skillet over moderate heat. Add veal, 7-8 pieces at a time, and brown lightly. Transfer veal to Dutch oven as it is finished. Add remaining oil as needed and cook remaining veal.

Reduce heat under skillet slightly. Add onions, carrots, and celery. Cook until onions are translucent, about 3 minutes. Add wine, garlic, and lemon peel. Cook 10 minutes, scraping brown bits from pan. Put in Dutch oven. Add remaining ingredients to Dutch oven. Simmer, covered, 1 ½ hours. Simmer uncovered to thicken.

Serve over hot fettucine pasta. Garnish with parsley.

**SERVES:** 6-8

*The "zest" or "peel" of lemon and other citrus is the outer skin only. Use a vegetable peeler or zester to peel or scrape off the top surface. Avoid the bitter white pith underneath.*

# CLASSIC BOEUF BOURGUIGNONNE

Preheat oven to 250 degrees.

Place first 5 ingredients in Dutch oven. Mix remaining ingredients in large bowl and pour over meat and vegetables. Bake 4-5 hours, stirring occasionally. (Keeping a lid on the Dutch oven will help meat to stay tender but make sure pot is left slightly ajar so "broth" does not become too watery.) Serve over Rice Pilaf with Sliced Almonds.

**SERVES:** 6

## INGREDIENTS

- 3 pounds beef stew meat, cubed
- 2 stalks celery, sliced
- 2 large carrots, sliced
- 2 white or yellow onions, quartered
- 1 pound fresh mushrooms, sliced
- 4 tablespoons tapioca pearls, soaked in water and drained
- 12 ounces tomato sauce
- 12 ounces Burgundy wine
- 1 teaspoon salt
- 1 teaspoon pepper

Rice Pilaf with Sliced Almonds (recipe follows)

# RICE PILAF WITH SLICED ALMONDS

Preheat oven to 375 degrees.

Add butter to medium skillet. Sauté rice and onion until golden. Pour mixture into 2-quart baking dish and cover with chicken stock. Add almonds and stir. Cover and bake 30 minutes or until rice is tender and broth is absorbed.

**SERVES:** 6

## INGREDIENTS

- 3 tablespoons butter
- 1 ½ cups uncooked rice
- 1 medium onion, finely chopped
- 2 ½ cups chicken stock
- ½ cup blanched almonds, sliced

### INGREDIENTS

**SALAD**

2 pounds mixed lettuce greens, including spinach
2 medium red onions, peeled
4 hard-boiled egg whites (reserve yolks for vinaigrette)
½ pound bacon, cooked and crumbled (reserve 1 tablespoon bacon fat for vinaigrette)

**VINAIGRETTE**

1 tablespoon bacon fat
4 hard-boiled egg yolks
1 cup olive oil
2 cloves garlic
2 tablespoons coarse-grain mustard
4 tablespoons frozen orange juice concentrate
½ cup flat-leaf parsley
½ cup cider vinegar
1 teaspoon freshly ground black pepper
1 teaspoon salt

# MIXED GREENS WITH CITRUS VINAIGRETTE

**FOR SALAD:**

Wash and dry greens and place in large bowl. Cut onion in half crosswise and slice as thinly as possible lengthwise (to form semi-circles). Sprinkle onion over greens. Add chopped egg whites and crumbled bacon to greens and cover.

At time of serving, mix enough vinaigrette with greens to coat thoroughly and toss.

**FOR VINAIGRETTE:**

*(This should be made 1 day ahead, refrigerated, and brought back to room temperature before tossing with salad.)*

Place reserved bacon fat and cooked egg yolks in blender. Add remaining vinaigrette ingredients to blender. Purée until smooth.

**SERVES:** 6-8

*Thin the vinaigrette with more oil if necessary to keep it light.*

*The vinaigrette may also be heated just before tossing with the greens for a hot salad dressing.*

### INGREDIENTS

1 ⅔ cups warm water
2 teaspoons salt
5 tablespoons sugar
3 packages active dry yeast
¼ cup vegetable oil
4 cups flour
½ cup dry milk
4 tablespoons butter, melted

# GOLDEN YEAST ROLLS

Combine warm water, salt, and sugar in large bowl. Add yeast, stirring enough to moisten. Let rest 10 minutes or until mixture begins to bubble. Add oil, flour, and milk. Mix and beat thoroughly. Roll out onto floured surface. Cut with any size biscuit cutter. Place on greased cookie sheet. Lightly brush tops with melted butter and let rise 1 ½ hours.

Preheat oven to 450 degrees.

Bake 10 minutes or until golden brown.

**YIELD:** 36 rolls

*For visual interest and a more complex taste, sprinkle the freshly-baked crust with sesame seeds, poppy seeds, caraway seeds, sunflower seeds, or finely minced garlic, onion, basil, or parsley.*

# PEPPERMINT RIBBON PIE WITH FUDGE SAUCE

## INGREDIENTS

**FOR FUDGE SAUCE:**

Melt butter and chocolate in medium saucepan. Stir in sugar, milk, and vanilla. Cook slowly, stirring mixture until cooked. Cool.

**FOR ASSEMBLY:**

Spread 1 pint softened ice cream in cooled pie shell. Cover with half of cooled fudge sauce. Freeze until firm. Repeat layer of ice cream and sauce. Freeze. *(Can be prepared several days ahead up to this point.)*

**FOR MERINGUE:**

Preheat oven to 500 degrees.

Beat egg whites, vanilla, and cream of tartar in large bowl until soft peaks form. Gradually add sugar, beating until stiff peaks form. Fold in crushed candy.

Spread meringue over pie, sealing edges. Place on cookie sheet and bake 3-5 minutes until golden.

**SERVES:** 6

*Feel free to omit peppermint candy and use any of your favorite ice cream flavors!*

**FUDGE SAUCE**

- 2 tablespoons butter
- 2 ounces unsweetened chocolate squares
- 1 cup sugar
- 6 ounces evaporated milk
- 1 teaspoon vanilla

**ASSEMBLY**

- 1 quart peppermint ice cream, softened
- 1 9" pie shell, baked and cooled

**MERINGUE**

- 3 egg whites
- ½ teaspoon vanilla
- ¼ teaspoon cream of tarter
- 4 tablespoons sugar
- 3 tablespoons peppermint candy, crushed

# The DAFFODILS *Are Up !*
## *A Sunday Celebration*

Spring is here!
Let's spread the good cheer!
Celebrate the daffodils
and brunch will appear!

Sunday, April 20
12 noon
Poppy and Blair Austin

✳ As warm spring days emerge after a cold winter, Charlotte neighborhoods come to life with an array of enchanting flowers. Daffodils, lilies, and azaleas are a few of these colorful delights.

✳ The Daffodil, introduced to America by colonists, is a timeless symbol of spring. Early Greek poets wrote of its beauty, and the ancient Chinese treasured it as a sign of life. There are an estimated 50 wild forms growing throughout the country.

✳ For an early spring Sunday celebration, fill your table with brightly colored daffodils or lilies in clay pots. Gather small treasures of springtime — porcelain bunnies, squirrels, and birds — to nestle among the clay pots and freshly cut branch leaves. If you have any whimsical children's china, this is your chance to use them as enchanting serving dishes.

✳ This menu would work beautifully for a Sunday christening or even a baby shower. For table decorations, place any silver baby items you have kept from your childhood or your children's (such as baby cups, teething rings, rattles, etc.) around the table, along with stuffed bears, china dolls, and even a lace baby bonnet or two.

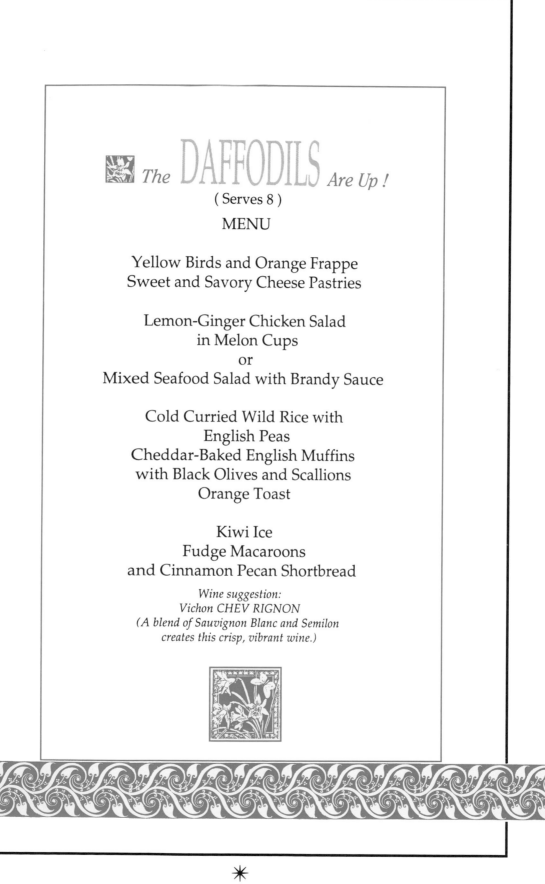

The **DAFFODILS** *Are Up !*

( Serves 8 )

MENU

Yellow Birds and Orange Frappe
Sweet and Savory Cheese Pastries

Lemon-Ginger Chicken Salad
in Melon Cups
or
Mixed Seafood Salad with Brandy Sauce

Cold Curried Wild Rice with
English Peas
Cheddar-Baked English Muffins
with Black Olives and Scallions
Orange Toast

Kiwi Ice
Fudge Macaroons
and Cinnamon Pecan Shortbread

*Wine suggestion:*
*Vichon CHEV RIGNON*
*(A blend of Sauvignon Blanc and Semilon*
*creates this crisp, vibrant wine.)*

## INGREDIENTS

8 ounces crème de banana
   liqueur
8 ounces light rum
2 ounces lemon juice
4 ounces unsweetened
   pineapple juice
4 ounces orange juice

# YELLOW BIRDS

Combine all ingredients in large pitcher.
Chill.  Serve over crushed ice in pretty
punch or julep cups.

**YIELD:**  8-10 drinks

*Delicious and smooth, Yellow
Birds do pack a powerful
punch. You may want to add
more orange juice to taste or
water.*

## INGREDIENTS

12 ounces frozen orange juice
   concentrate
20 ice cubes
 2 teaspoons vanilla
 2 cups milk
 2 cups water
½ cup sugar

# ORANGE FRAPPE

Combine all ingredients in blender.  Cover
and blend until smooth consistency.  Make
in batches if necessary.

**YIELD:**  8-10 drinks

# SWEET AND SAVORY CHEESE PASTRIES

*Dates could be called the candy that grows on trees. They are composed of one-half sugar. There are more than 100 varieties of dates grown in California, and they are a wonderful source of vitamins A and B, calcium, and iron.*

Preheat oven to 400 degrees.

Cream butter and cheese in medium bowl until smooth. Combine flour, cayenne pepper, and salt in small bowl. Add to cheese mixture along with water and stir until all dry ingredients are moistened. Roll dough to ⅛-inch thickness on lightly-floured surface and cut into 2-inch squares.

Cut a slit in each date and fill with pecan half. Place the filled date in the center of each pastry square. Encase the date in the cheese pastry, overlapping slightly, and press gently to seal. Place pastry on greased cookie sheet and bake 15 minutes or until lightly browned.

**YIELD:** 3 dozen

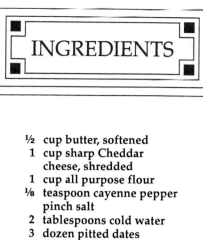

## INGREDIENTS

½ cup butter, softened
1 cup sharp Cheddar cheese, shredded
1 cup all purpose flour
⅛ teaspoon cayenne pepper
 pinch salt
2 tablespoons cold water
3 dozen pitted dates
3 dozen pecan halves

# LEMON-GINGER CHICKEN SALAD IN MELON CUPS

Combine first seven ingredients in medium bowl. Add chicken, grapes, and celery. Toss to coat well. Cover and chill at least 2 hours before serving. *(Can be made 1 day ahead up to this point.)* Serve salad in melon quarters and sprinkle with toasted slivered almonds.

**SERVES:** 8

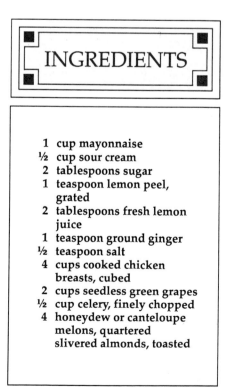

## INGREDIENTS

1 cup mayonnaise
½ cup sour cream
2 tablespoons sugar
1 teaspoon lemon peel, grated
2 tablespoons fresh lemon juice
1 teaspoon ground ginger
½ teaspoon salt
4 cups cooked chicken breasts, cubed
2 cups seedless green grapes
½ cup celery, finely chopped
4 honeydew or canteloupe melons, quartered
 slivered almonds, toasted

## INGREDIENTS

4 whole lobster, cooked

or

1 pound lobster meat,
  cooked and chopped
1 pound shrimp, cooked
  and peeled
1 pound scallops, cooked

Mixed Salad Greens

BRANDY SAUCE

3 teaspoons fine herbs
2 teaspoons vinegar
1 cup mayonnaise
2 tablespoons chili sauce
3 teaspoons onion, minced
2 tablespoons celery, minced
2 tablespoons brandy
  salt to taste
  dash cayenne

# MIXED SEAFOOD SALAD WITH BRANDY SAUCE

For whole lobster, cut cooked lobster in half and loosen tail meat from shell. Reserve 8 clean lobster halves. Place lobster meat back in shell. Arrange salad greens on 8 plates and top with filled lobster shells. Drizzle Brandy Sauce over all.

For mixed seafood, arrange rows of seafood on salad greens and drizzle Brandy Sauce over all.

Pass additional sauce at the table.

**FOR BRANDY SAUCE:**

Soak fine herbs in vinegar. Combine mayonnaise, chili sauce, onion, celery, brandy, salt, and cayenne in medium bowl. Add vinegar mixture to mayonnaise mixture and blend. Cover and chill until ready to use.

**SERVES:** 8

*The "fine herbs" used in the Brandy sauce recipe should be a combination of chervil, parsley, tarragon, and chives in dried form, often found in classic French cooking.*

# COLD CURRIED WILD RICE WITH ENGLISH PEAS

*You will find that curry powders, which are dried chilies ground with a variety of spices, will range in taste from brand to brand. A note of caution: they should never be too harsh.*

Combine rice, ¼ teaspoon curry powder, peas, and onions in large bowl. Set aside. Combine vegetable oil, soy sauce, cider vinegar, 1 teaspoon curry powder, sugar, and salt in small bowl. Add to rice mixture and mix well. Cover and chill 2 - 3 hours or overnight. Garnish with additional peas and red pepper or pimento strips. *(May be made 1 day ahead.)*

**SERVES:** 8

## INGREDIENTS

1 cup long grain wild rice, cooked and drained
1 ¼ teaspoons curry powder
1 cup frozen English peas, thawed
¼ cup onion, diced
½ cup vegetable oil
3 tablespoons soy sauce
2 tablespoons cider vinegar
½ teaspoon sugar
¼ teaspoon salt

English peas for garnish
red bell pepper or pimento strips for garnish

# CHEDDAR-BAKED ENGLISH MUFFINS WITH BLACK OLIVES AND SCALLIONS

Preheat oven to 450 degrees.

Combine all ingredients, except English muffins, in medium bowl. *(Can be prepared 1 day ahead up to this point, covered, and refrigerated.)* Spread mixture on English muffins and bake 10 minutes.

**SERVES:** 8

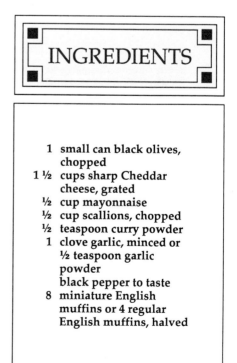

## INGREDIENTS

1 small can black olives, chopped
1 ½ cups sharp Cheddar cheese, grated
½ cup mayonnaise
½ cup scallions, chopped
½ teaspoon curry powder
1 clove garlic, minced or ½ teaspoon garlic powder
black pepper to taste
8 miniature English muffins or 4 regular English muffins, halved

**INGREDIENTS**

½ cup butter, softened
½ cup sugar
1 ½ tablespoons orange rind, grated
1 loaf Pepperidge Farm Thin White Bread, crusts trimmed

# ORANGE TOAST

Preheat oven to 325 degrees.

Combine butter, sugar, and orange rind. Spread evenly on trimmed bread. Cut into thirds. Bake 15 - 20 minutes or until lightly browned

**YIELD:** Appproximately 60 sticks

**INGREDIENTS**

4 kiwi, peeled and cubed
2 cups unsweetened apple juice
1 tablespoon lemon juice
½ teaspoon orange rind, grated
8 orange slices for garnish

# KIWI ICE

Combine kiwi, apple juice, and lemon juice in food processor or blender. Process until smooth. Stir in orange rind. Pour mixture into an 8-inch square baking pan and freeze until almost firm. Spoon mixture into medium bowl and beat with an electric mixer until fluffy. Let stand at room temperature 10 minutes before serving. Spoon into 8 dessert bowls and garnish with orange slices.

**SERVES:** 8

*Buy Kiwi that are firm and ripen them in a paper bag or a covered bowl at room temperature. They will keep in the refrigerator for up to two weeks once ripened.*

# FUDGE MACAROONS

Melt chocolate in top of double boiler and stir in oil. (Or combine chocolate and oil in large bowl and melt together in microwave.) Stir in sugar. Beat in eggs one at a time. Add vanilla, flour, and baking powder. Chill mixture.

Preheat oven to 375 degrees.

Form mixture into small balls and roll in powdered sugar. Place on greased cookie sheet and bake 12-15 minutes.

**YIELD:** 4-5 dozen

## INGREDIENTS

- 4 ounces unsweetened chocolate
- ½ cup vegetable oil
- 2 cups sugar
- 4 eggs
- 2 teaspoons vanilla
- 2 cups flour
- 2 teaspoons baking powder
  powdered sugar

# CINNAMON PECAN SHORTBREAD

Preheat oven to 300 degrees.

Combine all ingredients, except egg white and pecans, in large bowl. Blend until smooth. Press into 10 x 16-inch greased pan. Brush top with egg white. Sprinkle pecans over dough and press down slightly. Bake for 30 minutes. Remove from oven and cut into small squares while hot. Leave in pan until cooled.

**YIELD:** 4 dozen squares

## INGREDIENTS

- 1 cup butter, softened
- 1 cup sugar
- 1 teaspoon vanilla
- 1 egg, separated
- 2 cups flour
- ½ teaspoon cinnamon
- ¼ teaspoon salt
- 1 cup chopped pecans

# This Old House

## *Renovated And Ready For Revelry !*

You came over and helped
when we needed you so.
Tore out kitchen cabinets;
made hardwood floors glow.
The painting you did,
awards it will win!
Our brand new old house
sparkles outside and in.

It's time to say thank you
for all that you've done.
Join us for brunch. No work and all fun!

Saturday, May 15
11:00 a.m.
Margueritte and C. Mitchell Austin

* All of us, at one point or another in our lives, take on a house in need of repairs. Celebrate with friends when it's done or, better yet, invite them over to help paint and promise them a great meal in return.

* Sponge painting is easy! Buy a natural sponge from your local craft or paint store. Pour a small amount of paint (latex is best) into an aluminum pie pan or plastic coated paper plate, dip wet sponge in paint, and then gently dab off excess paint onto newspaper. Now you're ready for the wall!

* Lightly dab the wall with the sponge. Work in large sections to avoid uniformity. If you cannot find a natural sponge, try newspaper. Roll paper and crinkle as you go. Place in paint, dab off excess, and, in a rolling motion, blot on the wall in vertical rows.

* For a table cloth, try spattering paint on an old white sheet or sponge painting a pretty design.

* For table decor, scatter hammers and nails, paint brushes, wrenches, a measuring tape, and ruler about the table. Fill paint cans with flowers of the season.

# This Old House

( Serves 6 )

## MENU

STRAWBERRY SPARKLERS
CAROLINA SHRIMP
PEANUT BUTTER BREADSTICKS

QUAIL STUFFED WITH JALAPEÑO PEPPERS
GRITS SOUFFLÉ WITH CARAMELIZED ONIONS
AND ROASTED RED PEPPERS
SWEET POTATO BISCUITS
APPLES AND PEARS SAUTÉED IN BRANDY BUTTER

LEMON CAKETOP MOUSSE

*Wine suggestion:*
*Morgan Chardonnay*
*from the Monterey Peninsula*
*(Attention to detail makes this*
*one of the finest from California.)*

**INGREDIENTS**

2 ½ cups freshly squeezed
    orange juice, chilled
10 ounces frozen strawberries,
    partially thawed
1 bottle dry champagne,
    chilled
    whole strawberries for
    garnish

# STRAWBERRY SPARKLERS

Process orange juice and strawberries in blender or food processor until smooth. Pour into pitcher and refrigerate. Just before serving, add champagne and stir gently. Garnish each glass with a whole strawberry.

**YIELD:** 6 - 8 drinks

*Connoisseurs of champagne will tell you that only French champagnes are "true" champagnes. The California labels are considered to be sparkling wines.*

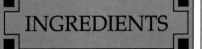

**INGREDIENTS**

1 pound medium shrimp,
    cooked, shelled, and
    deveined
1 large sweet onion, thinly
    sliced
2 teaspoons sugar
2 teaspoons salt
2 tablespoons Worcestershire
    sauce
1 tablespoon peppercorns
¼ cup catsup
½ cup cider vinegar
½ cup light salad oil
½ teaspoon dry mustard
2-3 bay leaves
2-3 dashes Tabasco sauce

    fresh dill for garnish
    fresh parsley for garnish

# CAROLINA SHRIMP

Layer shrimp and onions in deep glass container. Mix remaining ingredients, except fresh dill and parsley, and pour over shrimp and onions. Cover and refrigerate for at least 10 - 12 hours. Drain. Garnish shrimp with fresh dill and parsley. Serve with toothpicks. *(May be prepared 1 day ahead.)*

**SERVES:** 6

*To purchase the freshest shrimp, avoid those that are more than one color or appear to have a glossy sheen.*

# PEANUT BUTTER BREADSTICKS

*Peanut butter was invented by George Washington Carver, a plant scientist at Tuskeegee Institute in Alabama. He worked with Booker T. Washington, who was president of the institute at the time.*

## INGREDIENTS

- 1 loaf whole wheat sliced bread, frozen
- 13 ounces creamy peanut butter
- ½ cup vegetable oil
- 2 tablespoons sugar

Preheat oven to 300 degrees.

Trim crusts from slices. Save crusts. Cut each slice in half horizontally or crosswise. Make stick-like shapes by cutting each half into 4 pieces vertically. Bake sticks and crusts on ungreased cookie sheet 45 - 60 minutes until lightly browned or toasted. Place toasted crusts in a sealed plastic bag and crush with rolling pin. Place crushed crusts in medium bowl.

Heat peanut butter, oil, and sugar in top of double boiler, stirring frequently. Dip breadsticks, a few at a time, into mixture. Roll dipped sticks in crushed crumbs to coat all sides.

On wax paper or foil, place sticks on narrow edge to dry. *(May be stored in airtight container up to 1 week or frozen up to 2 months.)*

**YIELD:** 160

**INGREDIENTS**

2-3 tablespoons vegetable oil
2-3 tablespoons butter
12 whole quail
    salt
    freshly ground pepper
12 pieces country baked ham,
    cut into biscuit thin slices
    (optional)
½ cup Madeira wine
12 whole jalapeño peppers

# QUAIL STUFFED WITH JALAPEÑO PEPPERS

Preheat oven to 350 degrees.

Heat oil and butter in large skillet over high heat until hot. Season quail with salt and pepper. Add quail to skillet and quickly brown on all sides. Remove quail from skillet and wrap each in a piece of country ham, if desired. Stuff a whole jalapeño pepper into the cavity of each quail.

Place quail in 9 x 13-inch baking dish. Pour Madeira over quail, cover, and bake 30 minutes. Transfer quail to serving platter. Reduce liquid in baking dish by half over high heat, stirring about 10 minutes. Pour sauce over quail and serve immediately.

**SERVES:** 6

*You may also use 6 cornish game hens instead of quail as a variation for this rich and pungent dish.*

*Quail Stuffed with Jalapeño Peppers, this page; Grits Soufflé with Caramelized Onions and Roasted Red Peppers, p. 61; Apples and Pears Sautéed in Brandy Butter, p. 63; Sweet Potato Biscuits, p. 62.*

# GRITS SOUFFLÉ WITH CARAMELIZED ONIONS AND ROASTED RED PEPPERS

## INGREDIENTS

**GRITS**

| | |
|---|---|
| 4 | cups milk |
| 1 | cup quick-cooking grits |
| ½ | cup butter |
| ½ | teaspoon salt |
| ⅛ | teaspoon cayenne pepper |
| 3 | cups grated smoked Gouda or Cheddar cheese |
| 3 | eggs, well-beaten |

**CARAMELIZED ONIONS**

| | |
|---|---|
| 4 | tablespoons olive oil |
| 5 | large onions, peeled and sliced thinly |
| 2 | tablespoons sugar |

**ROASTED PEPPERS**

| | |
|---|---|
| 3 | whole red peppers |

*Grits are still a staple for much of the South, served alongside bacon and eggs as a breakfast dish or instead of rice or potatoes as an accompaniment to grilled poultry or game or as a terrific supper complement to shrimp. They are also wonderful by themselves anytime!*

*When working with red peppers, dip your hands in a mixture of water and vinegar to avoid stains.*

**FOR GRITS:**

Preheat oven to 350 degrees.

Bring milk to boil in large saucepan and stir in grits. Reduce heat and continue to stir until mixture thickens, 3 - 4 minutes. Remove from heat. Stir in other ingredients, except eggs. Beat in eggs with whisk. Pour into well-buttered 2 ½ quart casserole or soufflé dish. Bake uncovered 1 hour or until well-puffed and golden brown.

**FOR CARAMELIZED ONIONS:**

Add oil to large skillet and sauté onions until golden brown. Sprinkle on sugar and continue to sauté until onions are well browned and crisp. Place on paper towel to remove excess oil and set aside until ready to serve.

**FOR ROASTED PEPPERS:**

Preheat oven to 500 degrees.

Place red peppers on ungreased baking sheet. Bake 25 minutes. Place in heavy duty ziplock bag or paper bag. Close and let steam 10 minutes. Remove from bag and peel all skin from peppers. Remove stems, seeds, and ribs from inside peppers. Slice peppers into thin slices.

At time of serving, arrange caramelized onions and roasted red peppers over hot grits. Serve immediately.

**SERVES:** 6

*Quail Stuffed with Jalapeño Peppers, p. 60.*

## INGREDIENTS

¾ cup sweet potatoes, cooked
   and mashed
½ cup butter, melted
1 ¼ cups all purpose flour
4 teaspoons baking powder
1 tablespoon sugar
1 teaspoon salt

# SWEET POTATO BISCUITS

Preheat oven to 425 degrees.

Place potatoes and ¼ cup melted butter in large bowl and beat with electric mixer until smooth. Measure and sift dry ingredients in separate bowl. Add dry ingredients to potato mixture. Mix gently with spoon to incorporate dry ingredients. Do not overmix.

Roll out dough on well-floured surface and cut into biscuits with 1½-2 inch cutter. Bake on greased cookie sheet 12-15 minutes until golden brown. Remove from oven and brush with remaining melted butter.

**YIELD:** 2 dozen

*True sweet potatoes are only in season March through September. Yams are sold as a substitute during the remaining months, although they are lighter in color, not as sweet tasting, and more grainy in texture.*

*Grits Soufflé with Caramelized Onions and Roasted Red Peppers, p. 61; Sweet Potato Biscuits, this page; Apples and Pears Sautéed in Brandy Butter, p. 63.*

# APPLES AND PEARS SAUTÉED IN BRANDY BUTTER

*This is also a heavenly dessert served warm over ice cream.*

Sauté apples and pears in large heavy skillet with butter and brown sugar. Simmer until apples and pears are soft. Add brandy, simmer 1 minute more, and serve while still warm.

**SERVES:** 6

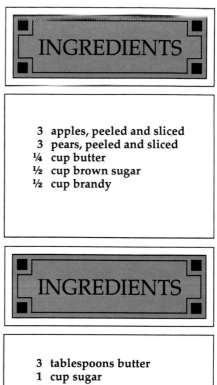

**INGREDIENTS**

| | |
|---|---|
| 3 | apples, peeled and sliced |
| 3 | pears, peeled and sliced |
| ¼ | cup butter |
| ½ | cup brown sugar |
| ½ | cup brandy |

# LEMON CAKETOP MOUSSE

*This dessert is a light but flavorful finish to any fine meal.*

Preheat oven to 325 degrees.

Grease 9 x 5-inch loaf pan. Cream butter and sugar in large bowl until light and fluffy. Add egg yolks, one at a time, and beat well. Add lemon juice, lemon peel, and salt. Add flour and mix well. Incorporate milk and almond extract into mixture.

In another large bowl, beat egg whites until stiff peaks form. Gently fold egg whites into yolk mixture. Pour into prepared loaf pan. Fill 9 x 13-inch pan with hot tap water to create a "water bath". Place loaf pan into water bath. Carefully place into oven. Bake 40 minutes. Turn oven up to 390 degrees and lightly brown top 5-10 minutes more. Chill dessert in refrigerator at least 1 hour. *(This can be made ahead up to 3 days.)*

To serve, dust dessert plate with powdered sugar. Cut a 2-inch slice of dessert loaf and gently remove to plate with spatula. Garnish with seasonal fresh fruit.

**SERVES:** 6

**INGREDIENTS**

| | |
|---|---|
| 3 | tablespoons butter |
| 1 | cup sugar |
| 4 | egg yolks |
| ⅓ | cup fresh lemon juice |
| 2 | teaspoons lemon peel, grated |
| ¼ | teaspoon salt |
| 3 | tablespoons all purpose flour |
| 1 | cup milk |
| ¼ | teaspoon almond extract |
| 4 | egg whites |

Powdered sugar for garnish
Fresh fruit for garnish

# MEN AT WORK:

## *A Mother's Day Potluck*

It's Mother's Day and the Fathers are doing the cooking! Come for a Potluck Brunch on Sunday, May 8 at 12:30 p.m. The enclosed recipe is for the husband of the household to prepare and bring along!

R.S.V.P.
Elizabeth and Spencer Harris
1300 Cherokee Road
327-0820

NO LEFT TURN

✳ Let the husbands prepare the Mother's Day feast with these easy, do-ahead recipes. How do they get the idea? Perhaps one wife conveniently leaves our cookbook open to this page on her husband's dresser a week or two in advance. Or she sends the recipes to the other wives, along with their invitation to brunch, and instructs them to let their husbands do the cooking!

✳ As for the table, each husband should definitely bring a flowering plant or fragrant bouquet to present to his wife at the end of the meal.

✳ Julia Ward Howe, who wrote the lyrics for "Battle Hymn of the Republic," was the first person to recommend Mother's Day as a national event, honoring mothers and promoting peace. It was her efforts which eventually led to the designation of the second Sunday in May as Mother's Day.

✳ Two of the Carolinas' most famous "men at work" are Orville and Wilbur Wright, who made transportation history with a 59-second air flight, on December 17, 1905 at Kitty Hawk, North Carolina. A National Memorial now marks the spot on the beautiful sandy shores of the Outer Banks of North Carolina which became the birthplace of the aviation age.

✳ Even today, the area is abundant with many varieties of wild birds, including hawks, sea gulls, and eagles. It was by observing the flight of these birds that the Wright brothers were able to perfect their flying machine.

# MEN AT WORK:

( Serves 8 )

MENU

PITCHERS OF BLOODY MARYS
AND PINEAPPLE RUM SUNRISES
POTTED SHRIMP AND CRACKERS
MYRTLE BEACH PICKLED OYSTERS
WITH TANGY SEAFOOD SAUCE

ORANGE-HONEY MUSTARD BISCUITS WITH HAM
OR
BACON, EGG, AND CHEDDAR-
TOPPED ENGLISH MUFFINS

AMBROSIA FRUIT KABOBS
FRESH DILLED GREEN BEANS

CHOCOLATE-BOURBON PECAN PIE

*Wine Suggestion:*
*De Loach White Zinfandel*
*(Serve this slightly chilled.)*

**INGREDIENTS**

2 ½ cans (45 ounces each)
    tomato juice
3 large lemons, juice and
    rind
3 tablespoons salt
3 tablespoons cracked
    pepper
3 tablespoons Worcestershire
    sauce
2 teaspoons Tabasco sauce
2 tablespoons prepared
    horseradish sauce
1 tablespoon dill weed
1 large onion, peeled and slit
12 ounces vodka

celery sticks for garnish

# BLOODY MARYS

*(This should be made 1 day ahead.)*

Mix all ingredients, except vodka, in a gallon jug. Refrigerate overnight. Just prior to serving, remove onion and lemon rind and add vodka. Serve in tall glasses over cracked ice with celery sticks for garnish.

**YIELD:** 16 drinks

*Bloody Marys were named after a queen of England. She was the daughter of Henry VIII and his first wife, Catherine of Aragon. Mary was a Catholic and did not care for the new Church of England created by her father (in part, so that he could divorce her mother). During her reign, she reinstated Catholicism as the official religion of England and bloody revolt followed!*

**INGREDIENTS**

4 cups pineapple juice
2 cups fresh orange juice
½ cup light or dark rum
⅓ cup amaretto
⅓ cup brandy
    dash Grenadine syrup

# PINEAPPLE RUM SUNRISES

*(This should be made several hours ahead.)*

Combine all ingredients, except Grenadine, in large pitcher. Mix well and chill.

At time of serving, place ice cubes in 8 tall glasses. Pour juice mixture over ice. Add a dash of Grenadine, stir, and serve.

**YIELD:** 8 drinks

# POTTED SHRIMP

*(This should be made 1 day ahead.)*

Combine all ingredients in a 3-4 cup crockery pot or container. Chill overnight. Serve with an assortment of crackers.

**SERVES:** 8

*Tabasco sauce, a hot pepper sauce named after a region in Mexico, is powdered chile peppers mixed with salt, pepper, and vinegar.
It keeps indefinitely stored in the refrigerator.*

## INGREDIENTS

16 ounces cream cheese, room temperature
½ cup butter, softened
2 tablespoons onion, minced
4 cups Bay shrimp, cooked and mashed
¼ teaspoon garlic salt
2 tablespoons lemon juice
2 tablespoons chili sauce
2 dashes Tabasco sauce

# MYRTLE BEACH PICKLED OYSTERS WITH TANGY SEAFOOD SAUCE

*(Both the pickled oysters and the sauce should be made 1 day ahead.)*

**FOR PICKLED OYSTERS:**

Remove oysters from liquid and wash. Put oyster liquid in pan and add washed oysters. Add vinegar, salt, and spices. Bring to boil, turn down heat, and simmer until oysters curl. Remove oysters and put in medium bowl. Return liquid to boiling and immediately remove from heat. Allow to cool slightly and then pour over oysters. Cover and refrigerate overnight. Drain and serve with crackers and Tangy Seafood Sauce.

**FOR TANGY SEAFOOD SAUCE:**

Mix all ingredients together, cover, and let stand in refrigerator overnight to blend flavors.

**SERVES:** 8

*Remember these hints when purchasing oysters: buy only in months that have "R's" in them (the winter months), and select ocean area, not gulf area, oysters.*

## INGREDIENTS

**PICKLED OYSTERS**

2 pints oysters
¼ cup vinegar
salt to taste
pinch allspice
6 whole cloves
pinch stick yellow mace
cayenne pepper to taste

**SEAFOOD SAUCE**

1 cup chili sauce
1 teaspoon lemon juice
½ teaspoon Worcestershire sauce
prepared horseradish sauce to taste

**BISCUITS**

    2   cups all purpose flour,
        sifted
    4   teaspoons baking powder
    ½   teaspoon salt
    ½   teaspoon cream of tartar
    2   teaspoons sugar
    ½   cup butter
    ⅔   cup milk
    1   tablespoon fresh parsley,
        finely minced

**MUSTARD**

    ½   cup Dijon mustard
    3   tablespoons mayonnaise
    ¼   cup honey
    2   tablespoons orange juice

   16   slices thin country-baked
        ham

# ORANGE-HONEY MUSTARD BISCUITS WITH HAM

**FOR BISCUITS:**

Preheat oven to 450 degrees.

Sift dry ingredients into large bowl. Cut in butter until coarse crumb consistency. Add milk and stir gently with fork until dough comes together. Turn dough onto lightly-floured surface. Sprinkle with parsley and roll into ½-inch thick rectangle. Cut dough straight down (no twisting) into 16 rounds using 2-inch cutter dipped in flour. Bake on ungreased baking sheet until golden, 10-12 minutes.

To serve, split biscuits in half horizontally. Spread halves with Orange-Honey Mustard. Top each bottom with ham slices. Cover with top half.

**FOR MUSTARD:**

Blend all ingredients in small bowl and refrigerate to set flavors.

**SERVES:** 8

# BACON, EGG, AND CHEDDAR-TOPPED ENGLISH MUFFINS

## INGREDIENTS

Mix eggs, cheese, onion, and bacon in large bowl. Add Worcestershire or soy sauce, mustard, Tabasco sauce, pepper, garlic powder, and mayonnaise. Consistency should be like chicken salad. (*This can be prepared ahead up to this point and stored, covered, in refrigerator up to 2 weeks.*)

At time of serving, preheat broiler. Spoon mixture onto English muffin halves and sprinkle with Parmesan cheese. Brown under broiler until hot and bubbly.

**SERVES:** 8

1 dozen eggs, hard boiled and diced
1 pound sharp Cheddar cheese, grated
1 small to medium onion, diced
½ pound bacon, fried, drained, and crumbled
Worcestershire or soy sauce to taste
1 tablespoon spicy mustard
Tabasco sauce to taste
freshly ground black pepper to taste
garlic powder to taste
mayonnaise to taste
Parmesan cheese to taste
8 English muffins, split

## INGREDIENTS

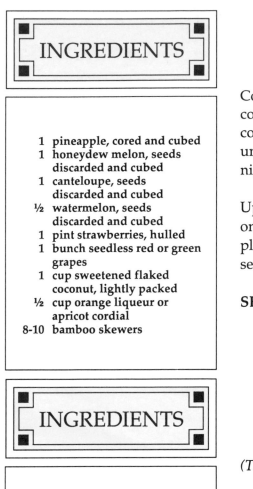

1 pineapple, cored and cubed
1 honeydew melon, seeds discarded and cubed
1 canteloupe, seeds discarded and cubed
½ watermelon, seeds discarded and cubed
1 pint strawberries, hulled
1 bunch seedless red or green grapes
1 cup sweetened flaked coconut, lightly packed
½ cup orange liqueur or apricot cordial
8-10 bamboo skewers

# AMBROSIA FRUIT KABOBS

Combine fruits in large bowl. Sprinkle coconut and orange liqueur or apricot cordial over fruits. Toss mixture gently until combined well. Cover and chill overnight or until ready to thread on skewers.

Up to 2 hours before serving, thread fruits on bamboo skewers and arrange on serving platter. Refrigerate, covered, until ready to serve.

**SERVES:** 8

## INGREDIENTS

1 ½ pounds fresh green beans
½ cup olive oil
¾ cup green onions, minced
3 tablespoons fresh dill weed, minced or 1 tablespoon dried dill weed
2 tablespoons sugar
2 tablespoons lemon juice
2 tablespoons Dijon mustard
1 tablespoon fresh parsely, chopped
1 tablespoon cider vinegar pinch of salt pinch of coarsely ground pepper
⅓ cup radishes, diced
⅓ cup walnuts, chopped

# FRESH DILLED GREEN BEANS

*(This should be prepared 1 day ahead.)*

Remove strings from green beans and wash thoroughly. Cut beans into 1 ½ inch pieces. Cook green beans, covered, in a small amount of boiling water 6-8 minutes or until just crisp and tender. Drain beans and set aside to cool.

Combine next 10 ingredients in a jar, cover tightly, and shake jar vigorously. Pour over beans and toss well. Cover and refrigerate overnight. Just before serving, stir in radishes and walnuts.

**SERVES:** 8

# CHOCOLATE-BOURBON PECAN PIE

Preheat oven to 350 degrees.

Let pastry shells reach room temperature. Combine remaining ingredients, except whipped cream, in large bowl, adding them one at time and stirring after each addition. Pour into pastry shells and bake until firm, approximately 45-50 minutes. Top with whipped cream just before serving.

**YIELD:** 2 pies or 16 tarts

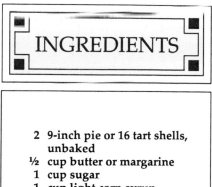

## INGREDIENTS

- 2 9-inch pie or 16 tart shells, unbaked
- ½ cup butter or margarine
- 1 cup sugar
- 1 cup light corn syrup
- 4 eggs, beaten
- 3 tablespoons bourbon
- 6 ounces semisweet chocolate chips
- 1 ½ cups pecans, chopped whipped cream, sweetened to taste

*My 12th Annual 29th Birthday Dinner:*
*Walnut Stilton Salad, p. 133.*

# SIMPLE SUPPERS
# AND ELEGANT DINNERS

# D·I·N·I·N·G BY *Fireflies*
## Summer In The South

Join Us
To Recapture
The Sweet Magic Of
Summer Nights
And Childhood Dreams

Sunday, July 18th 7:00 p.m.
Sharon and Bob Abbott

Buffet Dinner

Firefly Catching Attire
Jars Provided!

✳ When you think of fireflies, the image of something fairy-like or mystical comes to mind. While not really knowing how these beetles have come to be, you do not care but just enjoy their existence.

✳ That is the way it is when you have good friends who are truly friends. You do not question their motives. Instead, you enjoy their company and the pleasure of their presence at your table.

✳ To capture the enchantment of fireflies at your next dinner, scatter gold stars across the table, decorate with celestial objects you may have, and place adhesive stars on your goblets and candles.

✳ For placecards, fill small glass jars with glitter, tie a gold ribbon around the neck, and write your guest's name across the lid!

✳ Do you know where to find "The Firefly Capital of The World?" Entomologist Dr. James Lloyd searched the Southeast where fireflies are most prevalent and Southern traditions associated with fireflies reflect the blissful days of youth and the importance of nature.

✳ Six communities were finalists, but the interest in Boone, North Carolina and Boone's effort to organize a firefly festival made it a clear winner. The festival is usually held in June with a jug band contest, a firefly hunt for children to enjoy, a firefly costume contest, and a street dance.

# D·I·N·I·N·G  B·Y
## *Fireflies*
( Serves 8 )

## MENU

Sun-kissed Citrus Bourbon Slushes

Parmesan Pita Crisps and Icy Prawns with
a Trio of Celestial Dipping Sauces

Grilled Maple-Glazed Baby Back Ribs
Hot Cornbread Sticks
Cold Dilled New Potatoes
with Carrots and Scallions
Sweet-and-Sour Broccoli, Corn,
and Red Peppers in Tomato Cups

Moonlit Blueberry Pie with
Almond Crème Chantilly

*Wine suggestion:*
*Georges DuBoeuf Morgan*
*(This red wine is light on the palate*
*with a refreshing fruity finish -*
*serve cool.)*

**INGREDIENTS**

2 tea bags
7 ½ cups water
12 ounces frozen orange juice concentrate
12 ounces frozen lemonade concentrate
6 ounces frozen limeade concentrate
2 cups bourbon

# SUN-KISSED CITRUS BOURBON SLUSHES

Steep tea bags 5 minutes in 1 cup of the water, brought to a boil. Discard tea bags. Add remaining ingredients. Pour into freezer container and freeze until slushy, about 2-4 hours. Remove from freezer and pour into glass pitcher for "pour your own" drinks.

**YIELD:** 16-18 drinks

*These are just as good served over ice. Double recipe and freeze any "leftovers" for your next party.*

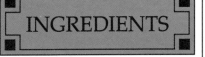

**INGREDIENTS**

4 6-inch pita rounds
6 tablespoons olive oil
1 teaspoon dried whole oregano
1 teaspoon garlic powder
½ cup Parmesan cheese, grated
1½ tablespoons sesame seeds

# PARMESAN PITA CRISPS

Preheat oven to 425 degrees.

Separate each pita round into two circles. Cut each circle into 6 wedges. Place wedges, rough side up, onto ungreased baking sheet.

Combine oil, oregano, and garlic powder in small bowl. Stir well. Brush lightly onto wedges. Combine Parmesan cheese and sesame seeds in small bowl. Sprinkle on top. Bake 10 minutes or until lightly browned. Cool. Store in airtight container.

**YIELD:** 4 dozen crackers

*The sesame seed, dating back to around 3000 B.C., was the first recorded seasoning.*

*Because sesame seeds are high in oil content, they should be stored in the refrigerator or freezer.*

*Sun-Kissed Citrus Bourbon Slushes, p. 76; Parmesan Pita Crisps, p. 76; Icy Prawns with Trio of Celestial Dipping Sauces, this page.*

# ICY PRAWNS

*Although technically, shrimp are saltwater shellfish and prawns are found in freshwater, most seafood markets and restaurants use the term "prawns" for the jumbo-sized shrimp.*

Add shrimp to large pot of boiling salted water. Reduce heat at once and simmer 2-4 minutes or until pink. Remove from heat. Drain and run under cool water to prevent from further cooking. Serve on ice surrounded by dipping sauces.

**SERVES:** 8

1 pound jumbo shrimp, peeled (leaving tail intact) and deveined

# TRIO OF CELESTIAL DIPPING SAUCES

### PESTO DIPPING SAUCE

1 cup parsley leaves, loosely packed
¼-½ cup fresh basil leaves or 1 tablespoon dried basil
¼ cup Parmesan cheese, grated
2 large cloves garlic, minced
1 cup mayonnaise

pine nuts for garnish

Process all ingredients, except pine nuts, in food processor or blender and purée until smooth. Place in airtight container. *(Cover and refrigerate up to 3 days.)* At time of serving, garnish with pine nuts.

**YIELD:** 1 cup

### FIERY TOMATO-ONION DIPPING SAUCE

3 large tomatoes, peeled, seeded, and finely chopped
2 fresh green chilies, minced, or
1 7-ounce can diced green chilies
1 small onion, minced
1 tablespoon fresh cilantro, minced
1 tablespoon olive oil
1 tablespoon fresh lime juice
1 teaspoon salt or to taste
¼ teaspoon pepper or to taste
pinch of sugar

Combine all ingredients in food processor and blend just until finely chopped, approximately 2-3 pulses. (Do not overprocess — ingredients will turn to liquid.) Cover and refrigerate.

**YIELD:** about 1 cup

### PEANUT CURRY DIPPING SAUCE

8 ounces cream cheese, softened
½ cup sour cream
1 tablespoon curry powder or more to taste
1 small clove garlic, minced
½ teaspoon salt
½ cup peanuts, finely chopped
2 slices bacon, cooked and crumbled
2 green onions, finely chopped

Combine first 5 ingredients in medium bowl until smooth. Stir in peanuts and bacon. *(Refrigerate, covered, up to 3 days.)* Let come to room temperature before serving. Garnish with green onions.

**YIELD:** about 1½ cups

## INGREDIENTS

1½ cups pure maple syrup
1½ cups apple cider vinegar
1 cup peanut, sunflower, or
   vegetable oil
½ cup molasses
½ cup soy sauce
3 tablespoons prepared
   sweet mustard
2 tablespoons juniper
   berries, crushed (optional)

4 racks baby back pork or
   beef ribs, cracked along
   backbone

# GRILLED MAPLE-GLAZED BABY BACK RIBS

Combine all ingredients, except ribs, in medium bowl and blend well.

Quickly rinse ribs under cold running water and pat dry with paper towels. Place in shallow glass or plastic container. Pour marinade over and turn to coat thoroughly. Cover and refrigerate at least 12 hours, turning ribs occasionally. Return to room temperature before cooking.

Preheat oven to 300 degrees.

Remove ribs from container, reserving marinade. Place ribs in large pan and bake for 50 minutes. Prepare covered grill for moderate direct-heat cooking.

Strain marinade into medium saucepan. Bring to boil and simmer on moderate heat for 1 hour or until marinade is reduced to about 2 ½ cups. (This will be used to glaze ribs while cooking on grill.)

When fire is ready, brush grill rack with oil. Place ribs on rack and cover grill. Brush ribs frequently with reduced marinade, turning until meat is tender and glazed, approximately 30 minutes. Slice ribs into individual portions and serve piping hot.

**SERVES:** 8

*For extra flavor, soak 3 cups of hickory-flavored wood chips in water and add to the fire before cooking.*

*Juniper berries can be found in the dried spice section of most supermarkets. They have the flavor and aroma of gin!*

*The making of molasses is a ritual which takes place each fall in the mountains of North Carolina. Molasses originates from the liquid of stripped sorghum cane which is then cooked over a wood fire. It is said that making molasses is an all-day affair enjoyed by families and neighbors alike.*

*Sweet-and-Sour Broccoli, Corn, and Red Peppers in Tomato Cups, p. 80; Grilled Maple-Glazed Baby Back Ribs, p. 78; Cold Dilled New Potatoes with Carrots and Scallions, p. 80; Hot Cornbread Sticks, this page.*

*Barbecue can be a difficult word to define. In the Northeast, it is used as a verb, as in "We're going to barbecue." This means "to cook on a grill outside." In the South and much of the rest of the nation, barbecue is a noun. It's meat and it's sauce and it's delicious but from there the definitions vary. Pork or beef? Pulled, shredded, or chopped meat? Cooked over an open pit or closed? "Wet" marinated meat or "dry" spice-rubbed meat?*

*And what about the sauces? The Carolinas alone boast four distinct styles of barbecue sauce:*

*Eastern style sauce is found on the North Carolina coast. It's vinegar based with red pepper and salt for extra flavor.*

*Further west in the Piedmont region, catsup is added to the mix for a darker red sauce. This is probably the most well known barbecue sauce for it can also be found in the Mid-West.*

*In the western part of North Carolina and Georgia and Florida, barbecue sauce becomes sweeter with the addition of brown sugar and more catsup.*

*South Carolina is the home of the mustard-based sauce. The same basic ingredients are used, but mustard is added instead of catsup for a rich golden sauce.*

*There are numerous variations on these four basic sauces, but no matter how you slice, pull, or shred it, barbecue is a distinctly delicious Southern tradition.*

# HOT CORNBREAD STICKS

Preheat oven to 350 degrees.

Combine dry ingredients in large bowl and mix well. Combine remaining ingredients in medium bowl and mix well. Add liquid mixture to dry ingredients, stirring until smooth. Pour into greased cornbread stick pans or 9 x 5 x 3-inch loaf pan.

Bake 20-25 minutes for sticks or 55 minutes for loaf or until toothpick inserted in center comes out clean. Cool in pan 10 minutes and invert on wire rack. Serve warm or cool completely. *(Can be frozen several months and reheated in microwave.)*

**SERVES:** 8

## INGREDIENTS

| | |
|---|---|
| 1½ | cups cornmeal |
| 1 | cup all purpose flour |
| ½ | cup sugar |
| 1 | tablespoon baking powder |
| ½ | teaspoon salt |
| 1½ | cups half-and-half |
| ⅓ | cup shortening, melted |
| 2 | eggs, beaten |
| ¼ | cup butter, melted |

# COLD DILLED NEW POTATOES WITH CARROTS AND SCALLIONS

**INGREDIENTS**

14  small new potatoes, scrubbed clean
6  hard-cooked eggs, peeled and quartered
1  medium carrot, peeled and grated
2  medium scallions, thinly sliced
3  tablespoons fresh dill, chopped, or 1 tablespoon dried
2  tablespoons fresh parsley, chopped
1  tablespoon caraway seeds
½  teaspoon salt
½  teaspoon freshly ground black pepper
¾  cup sour cream
¾  cup mayonnaise

Bring water to boil in medium saucepan. Add potatoes and cook until just tender, 20-25 minutes. Drain, cool, and cut in half. Combine potatoes, eggs, carrot, and scallions in large bowl. Add dill, parsley, caraway seeds, salt, and pepper and gently toss to combine. Fold in sour cream and mayonnaise. Refrigerate salad several hours. *(Can be prepared 1 day ahead.)*

**SERVES:** 8

*New potatoes are young potatoes that have a thin, red skin and a less starchy flavor.*

# SWEET-AND-SOUR BROCCOLI, CORN, AND RED PEPPERS IN TOMATO CUPS

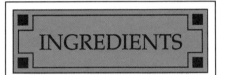

**INGREDIENTS**

1  cup olive oil
2  pounds broccoli, cut into ¾ inch pieces
2  cups fresh corn kernels or frozen, thawed
2  large red bell peppers, seeded and chopped
4  tablespoons white wine vinegar
4  tablespoons sugar
6  tablespoons lemon juice
½  teaspoon cinnamon
½  teaspoon pepper
½  cup raisins
½  cup pine nuts, toasted
4  medium tomatoes

Add oil to large skillet and cook broccoli over moderate heat until tender, approximately 12-15 minutes. Stir in corn, red peppers, vinegar, sugar, lemon juice, cinnamon, and pepper and simmer the mixture 5 minutes. Add raisins and pine nuts and simmer 2-3 minutes longer, until mixture thickens slightly. Remove from heat. Cover and refrigerate until chilled, approximately 2 hours. *(Can be prepared 1 day ahead up to this point.)*

Cut tomatoes in half and scoop out seeds, discarding pulp. Turn over and drain on paper towels. Cover and refrigerate. Just before serving, stuff tomatoes with sweet-and-sour broccoli mixture.

**SERVES:** 8

*Pine nuts, or pignoli, have a high fat content so it is best to keep them refrigerated or frozen to avoid turning rancid.*

*Pine nuts burn easily. When toasting, always watch the pan or toaster oven.*

# MOONLIT BLUEBERRY PIE WITH ALMOND CRÈME CHANTILLY

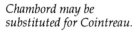

*Chambord may be substituted for Cointreau.*

### FOR PIE:

Combine 1 cup blueberries, sugar, and water in blender and purée until smooth. Pour mixture into medium saucepan and add dissolved cornstarch. Heat until thickened, stirring frequently. Stir in butter and Cointreau. Add almonds and remaining blueberries, stirring gently to combine. Pour into baked pie shell and chill.

### FOR CRÈME CHANTILLY:

Combine cream, sugar, and almond extract in chilled small bowl and whip until stiff peaks form. Just before serving, spread on top of chilled pie.

**SERVES:** 8

## INGREDIENTS

**PIE**

- 4 cups fresh blueberries, washed
- ¾ cup sugar
- ½ cup water
- 2 tablespoons cornstarch, dissolved in 2 tablespoons water
- 1 9-inch deep dish pie shell, baked
- 1 tablespoon butter
- 4 tablespoons Cointreau liqueur
- ¼ cup slivered almonds, toasted

**CRÈME CHANTILLY**

- 1 cup heavy cream, whipped
- 2 tablespoons sugar
- ¼ teaspoon almond extract

# Company's Coming

*They're Expecting
Fried Chicken And Grits
And I'm From New Jersey!*

**Hey Ya'll!**
I'm not from these parts, but I'm a quick learner,
So drop on by for a Southern Supper
that'll make you forget I was ever a Damn Yankee!
Sunday, August 8
6:30 p.m.
Carol Barrier
17 Poplar Street

Regrets 332-8178

✳ Everyone wants to come visit once you've moved to the South! "Company's Coming" provides the updated Southern spread to impress all those Northern guests or newly-made Southern friends! Better yet, cook these Southern delights no matter where you live!

✳ Southerners have always been known for their love of tradition. Recipes and treasures are handed down from generation to generation. Pull out your grandmother's linen tablecloth and set the table with your favorite heirloom silver and serving pieces. Don't be afraid to mix old and new chinas and crystal. Magnolia leaves or blossoms make a wonderful centerpiece for a Southern table any time of year.

✳ Newcomers quickly adapt to the delights of Southern living in North Carolina, the "Tar Heel" state. The phrase "Tar Heel" was coined by a North Carolina soldier during the Civil War. Apparently, North Carolina troops were abandoned by their supporting column yet went on to fight to victory on a Virginia battlefield. The soldier from the North Carolina ranks was heard to quip that next time, North Carolina might try putting a little "tar" on its supporting column's "heels" so that they might stick better during the fight.

# Company's Coming
(Serves 6)

## MENU

Southern Almond Tea
Black-eyed Pea Cakes with Fresh Salsa

Copper Pennies Salad

Country Ham
in Brown Sugar-Mustard Glaze
Burgundy Baked Bananas
Fried Green Tomatos

Virginia Spoon Bread

Southern Pound Cake or
Sundrop Pound Cake

*Wine suggestion:*
*Carmenet Old Vines Colombard*
*(A unique wine with a near "cult" following-*
*-it is completely dry with floral aromas.)*

3 cups boiling water
5 tea bags
1¼ cups sugar
½ cup lemon juice or to taste
½ teaspoon almond extract
1 teaspoon vanilla

**BLACK-EYED PEA CAKES**

2 cups dried black-eyed peas, soaked overnight
1 large onion, chopped
1 cup dry breadcrumbs
2 large eggs
1 bunch fresh cilantro, chopped
1 teaspoon cayenne pepper
2 cups cornmeal
2 tablespoons butter or oil
  salt to taste
  pepper to taste
  sour cream

**FRESH SALSA**

4 medium ripe tomatoes, diced
1 medium red bell pepper, finely diced
1 medium yellow bell pepper, finely diced
1 medium green bell pepper, finely diced
1 medium red onion, finely diced
1 bunch fresh cilantro, chopped
¼ cup lime juice
¼ cup olive oil
1 tablespoon garlic, minced
  salt and pepper to taste

# SOUTHERN ALMOND TEA

Pour boiling water over tea bags in gallon pitcher. Steep 10 minutes and discard tea bags. Add sugar and stir. Add additional water and ice to make almost 1 gallon. Stir in lemon juice, almond extract, and vanilla. Serve immediately over ice or cool to room temperature and refrigerate. *(May be prepared 1 day ahead.)*

**SERVES:** 6

# BLACK-EYED PEA CAKES WITH FRESH SALSA

**FOR CAKES:**

Boil peas and onion in salted water until tender. Drain and let cool. Mash peas and onion in large bowl. Add next four ingredients and mix well. Shape into 12 3-ounce cakes. Roll in cornmeal and sauté in butter or oil until very crisp on the outside. Season with salt and pepper. Serve with sour cream and fresh salsa.

**FOR SALSA:**

Mix all ingredients together in large bowl and let marinate at least 1 hour. Spoon over pea cakes.

**YIELD:** 12 cakes

*Black-eyed peas originated in India, traveled to the West Indies, and could be found in Florida in the 18th century. They have gradually made their way north but not too far! Black-eyed peas don't grow well in chilly climates and have, therefore, remained a Southern tradition.*

# COPPER PENNIES SALAD

Clean carrots and slice into ¼-inch rounds. Boil carrots in medium saucepan of water until slightly tender. Drain and cool. Alternate layers of carrots, bell pepper, and onion in 1 quart casserole dish. Mix remaining ingredients in small bowl and pour over vegetables. Let marinate in refrigerator at least 8 hours or overnight. *(Can be made 2 days ahead.)*

**SERVES:** 6

### INGREDIENTS

| | |
|---|---|
| 1 | pound carrots |
| ½ | medium green bell pepper, diced |
| ½ | medium onion, diced |
| ¼ | cup salad oil |
| ½ | cup sugar |
| ¼ | cup plus 1 tablespoon vinegar |
| ½ | can tomato soup |
| ½ | teaspoon dry mustard |
| ½ | teaspoon Worcestershire sauce |

# COUNTRY HAM IN BROWN SUGAR-MUSTARD GLAZE

Wash ham and place in large roasting pan, skin side up. Pour tea, molasses, and Coca-Cola over ham and marinate overnight in refrigerator. Drain marinade and return ham to pan.

Preheat oven to 350 degrees.

Pour water over ham. Bake, covered, until small bone near shank moves easily, about 4 hours. Remove ham from oven and let cool. Carefully slice away ham skin with sharp knife.

Combine catsup, mustard, and brown sugar. Spread glaze over ham and return to oven. Continue baking 30 minutes, basting frequently with beer.

**SERVES:** 6-8 (with leftovers)

### INGREDIENTS

| | |
|---|---|
| 12-14 | pound Smithfield or country-style ham |
| 2 | quarts weak tea |
| 12 | ounces black molasses |
| 32 | ounces Coca-Cola |
| 2 | quarts water |
| 1 | cup brown sugar, firmly packed |
| 1 | cup tomato catsup |
| 3 | tablespoons prepared mustard |
| 12 | ounces bottled beer |

*The phrase "Bringing home the bacon" came from 12th century England. At the time, if any man could vow on a Bible in the church at Dunmow that he had not fought with his wife for a year and a day, he was presented with a side of bacon for his achievement.*

*Smithfield and other country-style hams are usually made from the hind legs of fresh corn-or peanut-fed hogs. They are salted, smoked, and aged in a procedure that takes from 6-12 months.*

*This particular country ham recipe is taken directly from the 1942 edition of **Old North State Cookbook**, the first cookbook ever published by the Junior League of Charlotte.*

**INGREDIENTS**

6 large ripe bananas, peeled
3 tablespoons shortening
3 tablespoons dark brown
   sugar
2 tablespoons butter,
   cut into bits
⅓-½ cup red wine
   (dry Burgundy is best)

# BURGUNDY
# BAKED BANANAS

Preheat oven to 325 degrees.

Cut bananas in half crosswise and then slice in half lengthwise. Add shortening to medium skillet and sauté bananas on moderate-high heat 2 minutes. Transfer to paper towels and drain. In 8 x 8 inch buttered baking dish, arrange bananas in layers with brown sugar and butter bits. Cover bananas with wine. Bake 1 hour.

**SERVES:** 6

**INGREDIENTS**

6 slices bacon
4 green tomatoes
   salt to taste
   pepper to taste
⅓ cup cornmeal

# FRIED
# GREEN TOMATOES

Fry bacon until crisp, reserving drippings. Cut tomatoes into slices ⅛ inch thick. Season with salt and pepper. Dredge in cornmeal. In reserved bacon drippings, fry tomatoes until golden brown. Crumble bacon and sprinkle over tomatoes.

**SERVES:** 6

*Season the tomatoes with a teaspoon of dried rosemary to add a herbaceous taste to this classic southern dish.*

**INGREDIENTS**

2 cups cold milk
3 large eggs
1 cup water
1½ teaspoons salt
2 tablespoons butter
1½ cups yellow cornmeal
1 teaspoon sugar
1 teaspoon baking powder

# VIRGINIA
# SPOON BREAD

Mix milk and eggs together in medium bowl and set aside. Bring water, salt, and butter to boil.

Stir cornmeal and sugar together in small bowl. Slowly add cornmeal mixture to boiling water while constantly whisking. Bring to simmer and remove from heat. Whisk in milk and egg mixture. Add baking powder. Pour mixture into buttered 2-quart soufflé or casserole dish. Bake 40 minutes until puffed and golden brown.

**SERVES:** 6

*Spoonbread may have gotten its name from an Indian porridge called "suppawn" or "suppone" or perhaps because it is often eaten with a spoon. It is usually very soft, not like a bread at all, but more like a soufflé.*

# SOUTHERN POUND CAKE

Preheat oven to 325 degrees.

Using electric mixer, beat butter, cream cheese, and sugar in large mixing bowl until fluffy. Add eggs, one at a time, with mixer continuing to run. Add vanilla and almond extract.

Combine salt and flour in small bowl. Gradually add flour to batter. Beat until smooth. Pour into greased and floured bundt or tube pan. Bake 1 hour 20 minutes. Let cool 10 minutes and remove from pan. Dust with powdered sugar when completely cool. *(May be stored 5-7 days or frozen if wrapped well.)*

**YIELD:** 1 cake

**INGREDIENTS**

1½  cups butter, room temperature
8  ounces cream cheese, room temperature
3  cups sugar
6  eggs
1  teaspoon vanilla
1  teaspoon almond extract
   pinch salt
3  cups cake flour, sifted twice before measuring
¼  cup powdered sugar, sifted

# SUNDROP POUND CAKE

Preheat oven to 325 degrees.

Cream butter, shortening, and sugar in large bowl. Add eggs one at a time. Stir in flour slowly. Add vanilla, lemon, and Sundrop. Stir well. Pour into buttered and floured bundt pan. Bake 1 hour 20 minutes.

**YIELD:** 1 cake

*Sundrop is a soft drink that is produced in Gastonia, North Carolina and distributed from Charlotte. It is similar in taste to Mello Yellow and Mountain Dew, which may be substituted.*

**INGREDIENTS**

1  cup butter, softened
½  cup vegetable shortening
3  cups sugar
5  large eggs
3½  cups flour, sifted
1½  teaspoons vanilla
½  teaspoon lemon extract
7  ounces Sundrop soft drink

# It Can't Still Be February!

## A Hands-on Asian Dinner

Groundhog says:
If his shadow he pops up and sees,
There's six more weeks of winter's freeze.
Confusious says:
Slip off your shoes and ignore the cold,
Enjoy good friends, both new and old!
Please come to an
Authentic Asian Dinner
from chopping to chopsticks
at the home of
Tish and Chandler Guthery
Saturday, February 2
7:00 p.m.
(forks and spoons
available for the
timid but hungry)

✳ Food and the ritual of eating play a central role in the philosophy of Chinese life. To the Chinese, it is not only what is eaten that is important, but how it is made and the atmosphere which prevails during eating and preparation. From the first cut of a vegetable to the actual consumption, there is a process of bonding between family and friends.

✳ What better way to enjoy an otherwise dreary winter evening than to share in a meal from beginning to end — mincing garlic and ginger with kitchen conversation and finally relaxing over tea and good fortunes!

✳ Set your Asian dinner table with chopsticks, of course, inexpensively purchased from an oriental market or even from your favorite local restaurant.

✳ Fill Chinese takeout boxes with fortune cookies for party favors or set out one or two on a buffet table to serve with dessert. By the way, fortune cookies are an American creation!

✳ And any oriental objects can be turned into serving pieces for your meal — jars, boxes, or porcelain pieces can hold flowers, cookies or dessert spoons. Tie napkins with silk tassels purchased at local fabric shops.

✳ Fireflies are not just indigenous to the Southern United States. In Japan, many people keep busy during May and June catching and selling fireflies which are then put into little cages and used to decorate restaurants and gardens.

# It Can't Still Be February!
### (Serves 8)

## MENU

Sesame Lamb Wontons with Two Sauces
Thai Chicken with Roasted Peanuts
in Lettuce Cups

Oriental Cucumber Salad
or
Korean Spinach Salad

Five -Flavored Shrimp with Snow Peas
Beef Mandarin
Mu Shu Pork with Mandarin Pancakes
or Sweet Potatoes, Pork,
and Broccoli in Ginger Sauce

Lemon Mousse in Orange Cups
with Almond Cookies
Purchased Fortune Cookies

*Wine suggestion:*
*Trimbach Gewurztraminer*
*(Goes well with any Thai dish -*
*richly fragrant with a lightly spicy finish.)*

## INGREDIENTS

1 pound ground lamb
1 teaspoon sesame oil
½ teaspoon sugar
½ teaspoon salt
½ teaspoon pepper
½ cup water chestnuts, chopped
½ cup mushrooms, chopped
3 green onions, sliced
2 tablespoons fresh ginger, minced
4 teaspoons soy sauce
1 tablespoon dry sherry

1 pound wonton wrappers
1 egg, beaten
   oil for frying

   Purchased Sweet and Sour Sauce
   Purchased Chinese Hot Mustard

# SESAME LAMB WONTONS WITH TWO SAUCES

Combine lamb with all remaining ingredients in large bowl, except wonton wrappers, egg, and oil. *(Can be prepared 1 day ahead up to this point and refrigerated, covered.)*

Assemble wontons by placing 1 heaping teaspoon of filling in center of wonton wrapper. Fold in half, crosswise, to form a triangle, pressing to seal edges. Moisten bottom corners with beaten egg and bring corners toward each other, pinching them together. Repeat until all wrappers are filled.

Heat 1 inch oil until hot in electric skillet or large regular skillet. Fry wontons in hot oil in batches 3-5 minutes, turning once, until golden brown. Drain on paper towels. *(While best if served immediately, wontons may be fried several hours ahead and refrigerated. To reheat, place on shallow baking sheet and bake at 375 degrees 5-7 minutes until hot.)*

Serve with purchased Sweet and Sour Sauce and Chinese Hot Mustard for dipping.

**YIELD:** 50

*May substitute chicken or pork for the lamb.*

*Have your guests pitch in and make the wontons!*

*Use the kitchen table as a "work" surface covered with wax paper. Give each of your guests a number of wonton wrappers and let them fill the wontons with the lamb mixture.*

*Fry the wontons as they are assembled and serve them hot while guests are working.*

*Sesame Lamb Wontons with Two Sauces, p. 90; Thai Chicken
with Roasted Peanuts in Lettuce Cups, p. 92.*

# THAI CHICKEN WITH ROASTED PEANUTS IN LETTUCE CUPS

## INGREDIENTS

1 tablespoon olive oil
2 cloves garlic, minced
1 pound boneless, skinless chicken breasts
½ cup chicken broth
½ cup whole salted dry roasted peanuts
2 tablespoons Thai fish sauce
2 tablespoons soy sauce
4 tablespoons fresh lime juice
1 can water chestnuts, finely minced
1 medium red onion, finely minced
3 green onions, finely diced
3 tablespoons fresh ginger, minced
1 teaspoon crushed red pepper flakes

1 head iceberg, green leaf, or red leaf lettuce

Add oil to small skillet and sauté garlic until golden brown, about 1-2 minutes. Remove from heat and set aside.

Finely mince chicken breasts either with knife or in food processor. Heat chicken broth in large skillet over moderate heat 1 minute. Add chicken and stir 3-5 minutes, until cooked and broth is nearly evaporated. Remove from heat. Stir in garlic and remaining ingredients, except lettuce. *(Can be prepared 2 days ahead, covered, and refrigerated. However, omit roasted peanuts. Reheat just before serving and add peanuts.)*

To serve, carefully separate lettuce into leaves. Mound chicken mixture in center of large platter. Arrange lettuce leaves in a circle around chicken. Have each guest spoon the chicken mixture onto a lettuce leaf and fold the leaf over to eat.

**SERVES:** 8

*Thai fish sauce, which is found in the speciality section of most supermarkets or Asian markets, is essential to the flavoring of this outstanding dish!*

*Thai Chicken also tastes great over rice.*

# ORIENTAL CUCUMBER SALAD

Peel cucumbers and cut lengthwise in two. With small spoon, scrape out seeds from each half, leaving hollow, boat-like shells. Chop into small pieces.

Combine remaining ingredients in medium bowl and mix well. Add cucumbers and toss to coat. Allow to chill at least 3 hours. (*May be prepared 1 day ahead.*) Serve very cold.

**SERVES:** 8

## INGREDIENTS

2 medium cucumbers
2 tablespoons white vinegar
2 tablespoons soy sauce
1 teaspoon sugar
1 tablespoon sesame oil
  salt to taste
  pepper to taste

# KOREAN SPINACH SALAD

(*Must be prepared several hours ahead.*)

If using fresh spinach, wash thoroughly and remove large stems. Blanche in boiling water, immediately drain, and cool with cold water. Squeeze out all water and form into a ball. Slice several times. Place in medium bowl. (If using frozen spinach, defrost and remove large stems. Squeeze out all water and form into a ball. Follow directions for fresh spinach.)

Mix soy sauce, vinegar, and sesame oil in small bowl. Pour over spinach, tossing well. Marinate in refrigerator several hours. Near serving time, sauté sesame seeds in small skillet over moderate heat until golden brown. With mortar and pestle, mash seeds to release flavor. Let cool.

To serve, add sesame seeds to spinach and toss well. Garnish with chopped pimento or roasted red peppers.

**SERVES:** 8

## INGREDIENTS

 2 pounds fresh spinach, or
20 ounces frozen leaf spinach
 3 tablespoons soy sauce
 3 tablespoons vinegar
 2 tablespoons sesame oil
 2 tablespoons sesame seeds

  chopped pimento or
  roasted red peppers for
  garnish

**INGREDIENTS**

3 cloves garlic, finely minced
½ teaspoon fresh ginger,
   finely minced

3 tablespoons tomato sauce
   or purée
2 tablespoons dry sherry
1 tablespoon oyster sauce
1 tablespoon soy sauce
1 teaspoon red wine vinegar
1 teaspoon sesame oil
½ teaspoon sugar

2 tablespoons cornstarch
¼ cup warm water

2 tablespoons oil
1 pound medium shrimp,
   shelled and deveined
¼ pound snow peas
3 green onions, cut into
   3-inch pieces

**INGREDIENTS**

2 pounds London broil,
   cut 2½ inches thick
1 cup olive oil
⅓ cup red wine vinegar
¼ cup honey
1 tablespoon soy sauce
¼ cup Triple Sec or
   orange-flavored liqueur
1-2 sliced oranges for garnish

# FIVE-FLAVORED SHRIMP WITH SNOW PEAS

Combine garlic and ginger in small bowl; set aside. Combine tomato sauce or purée, sherry, oyster sauce, soy sauce, vinegar, sesame oil, and sugar in medium bowl; set aside. Mix cornstarch and water in small bowl; set aside.

Heat wok to very high; add 1 tablespoon oil and shrimp. Stir-fry until shrimp are translucent. Remove shrimp. Add another tablespoon oil to wok along with snow peas, onions, and garlic/ginger mixture. Stir-fry several seconds or until onions turn bright green. Pour in tomato sauce mixture, and return shrimp to wok. Stir in cornstarch mixture to thicken. Serve immediately.

**SERVES:** 8 as part of multi-course meal.

# BEEF MANDARIN

Trim any visible fat from meat. Pierce top and bottom of meat with sharp cooking fork and place in shallow 2-quart dish or ziplock bag. Whisk all remaining ingredients, except orange slices, in medium bowl. Pour marinade over meat. Cover and refrigerate several hours or overnight, turning occasionally. One hour before cooking, drain and reserve marinade.

Prepare grill. When ready, place meat on greased grill and sear 1 minute on each side. Raise grill and cook until meat reaches desired degree of doneness, about 45 minutes for rare. Turn occasionally and baste with reserved marinade.

To serve, slice meat thinly on the diagonal. Garnish with orange slices.

**SERVES:** 8 as part of multi-course meal.

*Oyster sauce, available in bottles, jars, and cans in the speciality section of most supermarkets and Asian markets, is a dark brown liquid popularly used in Cantonese cooking to heighten the flavor of meats and vegetables. It will keep indefinitely in the refrigerator.*

*The marinade for Beef Mandarin is also superb for pork tenderloin.*

※

*u Shu Pork in Mandarin Pancake, p. 96; Five-Flavored Shrimp*
*h Snow Peas, p. 94; Korean Spinach Salad, p. 93.*

## INGREDIENTS

6 green onions, finely
shredded into 2-inch pieces
1 tablespoon ginger, minced
2 cloves garlic, minced

3½ tablespoons soy sauce
2 tablespoons water
2 tablespoons dry sherry
or rice wine
1 teaspoon sugar
2 tablespoons cornstarch
1 pound lean pork loin, cut
into matchstick shreds

4 tablespoons oil
4 eggs, lightly beaten

½ cup bamboo shoots,
shredded
2 cups cabbage, shredded
1 cup carrots, shredded
½ cup (1 package) dried black
mushrooms, soaked in
warm water 30 minutes,
drained, and chopped
½ cup plus 2 tablespoons
Hoisin sauce

16 Mandarin Pancakes (recipe
follows) or small flour tortillas,
warmed

## INGREDIENTS

2 cups flour
½ teaspoon salt
1 cup boiling water
¼ cup sesame oil

# MU SHU PORK

Combine green onions, ginger, and garlic in small bowl; set aside. Combine 2 tablespoons soy sauce, water, sherry or rice wine, sugar, and cornstarch in medium bowl. Add pork loin and set aside. Heat 2 tablespoons oil in wok or large skillet over moderate heat. Add eggs and cook just until set. Remove to cutting board and cut into thin strips. Set aside.

Wipe wok or skillet clean. Heat remaining oil over moderate heat. Add garlic mixture and stir-fry 1 minute. Add pork mixture and stir-fry until tender, about 2 minutes. Add remaining vegetables and stir-fry 2 minutes longer. Add egg strips, remaining 1½ tablespoons soy sauce, and 2 tablespoons Hoisin sauce. Cook until nearly all liquid has evaporated. Taste for seasoning and transfer to serving platter.

Serve with warm Mandarin Pancakes or flour tortillas. For each serving, spread a pancake or tortilla with Hoisin sauce, top with some of the Mu Shu Pork mixture, and roll pancake or tortilla around filling.

**SERVES:** 8 as part of multi-course meal

# MANDARIN PANCAKES

Combine flour and salt in large bowl. Add boiling water. Mix to form ball. Place dough ball on flour-dusted work surface and knead briefly. Cover with inverted bowl until cool, about 5 minutes.

Roll dough into rope about 1½ inches in diameter. Cut rope into 16 pieces. Flatten two pieces of dough into 3-inch disks. Cover remaining dough with a towel to keep moist. With basting brush, place small

*Also known as cloud ears, tree ears, wood ears, and black fungus, dried black mushrooms are available in most Asian or gourmet sections of supermarkets. Fresh white mushrooms may be substituted.*

*Pork (and any meat) is easier to cut while partially frozen.*

*Packaged Mu Shu Shells, available in Asian markets, may also be used in place of Mandarin Pancakes or flour tortillas.*

amount of sesame oil on one disk.  Place second disk on top and press together.  Roll out 2-layered disk into 6-inch circle.

Heat small skillet over moderate heat.  Add pancake disk, cook for 3 minutes, turn over, and cook 1 additional minute.  (Pancake should be dry to the touch but not brown.) Remove from pan and gently pull apart the 2 pancakes.  Wrap in aluminium foil and place in 200 degree oven to keep warm while making remaining pancakes in same manner.

*(The pancakes may be made 1 day ahead, wrapped in plastic wrap, and refrigerated or frozen up to 1 month before reheating.)*

**YIELD:** 16 pancakes

*Lemon Mousse in Orange Cups, p. 99; Beef Mandarin, p. 94; Korean Spinach Salad, p. 93; Mu Shu Pork, p. 96, Five-Flavored Shrimp with Snow Peas, p. 94; Sesame Lamb Wontons, p. 90; Thai Chicken with Roasted Peanuts in Lettuce Cups, p. 92.*

## INGREDIENTS

- 1 **tablespoon cornstarch**
- 3 **tablespoons soy sauce**
- 2 **tablespoons sherry**
- 1 **tablespoon ginger, minced**
- 4 **scallions, cut in 1-inch pieces (including green tops)**
- 2 **cloves garlic, minced**
- 1 **tablespoon oil**
- 1 **pound pork tenderloin, partially frozen and sliced thin**
- 1 **sweet potato, peeled and julienned**
- 1 **green bell pepper, cut into 1-inch pieces**
- 2 **cups broccoli florets**

  **steamed rice**

# SWEET POTATOES, PORK, AND BROCCOLI IN GINGER SAUCE

Combine corn starch, soy sauce, sherry, and ginger in small bowl; set aside. Sauté white parts of scallions and garlic in oil over moderate-high heat in wok or large skillet. Add pork and cook 4-5 minutes or until pork is done. Remove pork and set aside.

Add sweet potato, bell pepper, and broccoli. Cover wok or skillet and steam until broccoli is crunchy-tender, about two minutes. Return pork to wok. Stir soy sauce mixture and add to wok. Stir until sauce thickens. Add green parts of scallions; stir to combine. Serve immediately over rice.

**SERVES:** 8 as part of multi-course meal.

*To mince fresh ginger easily, first peel the outer layer with a knife or vegetable peeler. Then cut into narrow strips and mince, rocking the blade across the ginger strips.*

*One tablespoon of fresh ginger equals one-half teaspoon of powdered or ground ginger.*

# LEMON MOUSSE IN ORANGE CUPS

Combine lemon juice, orange juice, water, sugar, flour, salt, egg yolks, and lemon peel in top of double boiler. Cook over moderate heat, stirring frequently, until thickened. Remove from heat. When cool, gently fold in whipped cream. Spoon into orange halves. Chill several hours or overnight. Garnish with additional grated lemon peel and a lemon or orange peel twist. (*May be prepared 1 day ahead.*)

**SERVES:** 8

## INGREDIENTS

5 tablespoons lemon juice
¾ cup orange juice
⅔ cup water
1 cup sugar
4 tablespoons flour
¼ teaspoon salt
5 egg yolks
1 teaspoon lemon peel, grated
2 cups whipping cream, whipped
4 oranges, halved and hollowed out

grated lemon peel for garnish
lemon or orange peel twists for garnish

# ALMOND COOKIES

Preheat oven to 350 degrees.

*It is the shortening which gives these rich almond cookies their tender crispness.*

Combine shortening and sugar in large bowl. Beat until smooth. Add egg, ground almonds, and almond extract; set aside. Sift together flour, baking powder, and salt in medium bowl. Add to egg mixture. Dough will be stiff.

Shape dough into 36 balls. Place 2 inches apart on greased baking sheet. Press almond half into each ball, flattening slightly to a 2-inch cookie.

Beat yolk with water; lightly brush over each cookie. Bake 20 minutes or until golden brown. (*May be stored in airtight container 3 days.*)

**YIELD:** 36 cookies

## INGREDIENTS

1 cup shortening
1 cup sugar
1 egg, beaten
½ cup blanched almonds, ground
1 teaspoon almond extract
2½ cups flour
1½ teaspoons baking powder
½ teaspoon salt
36 blanched almond halves
1 egg yolk
1 tablespoon water

# Saturday Night Sommelier
## *A Wine Tasting Party*

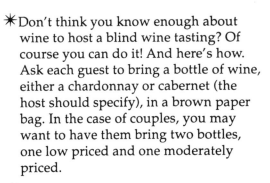

CHÂTEAU LAFITE·ROTHSCHILD
1817

IT'S A
WINE TASTING!

*Chardonnary for a poultry dinner.*
*For pasta, Zinfandel is a winner.*
*Perhaps a Sauvignon Blanc for the fish*
*or a fruitier blush for that sweeter dish.*
*What goes with what? Which tastes divine?*
*Come help us decide and sip some wine!*

*Saturday, September 2*
*7:30 p.m.*

*Carrington and Ralph Olmstead*
*You provide the wine (2 bottles of*
*Chardonnay in paper bags).*
*We'll provide the dinner!*

✳ Don't think you know enough about wine to host a blind wine tasting? Of course you can do it! And here's how. Ask each guest to bring a bottle of wine, either a chardonnay or cabernet (the host should specify), in a brown paper bag. In the case of couples, you may want to have them bring two bottles, one low priced and one moderately priced.

✳ During the cocktail hour, guests are to taste the wines (left in paper bags), scoring them with the light-hearted rating scale suggested below or a similar version:

### WINE RATING SYSTEM

10 = Ooh, I feel like I'm in France.
 8 = Far out. This must be California.
 6 = This must be something I can afford.
 4 = Ooh, I feel like I'm in Spartanburg (or any small city that doesn't produce wine)
 2 = Screw top, right?

| Reds: | | Whites: | |
|---|---|---|---|
| 1. | 6. | 1. | 6. |
| 2. | 7. | 2. | 7. |
| 3. | 8. | 3. | 8. |
| 4. | 9. | 4. | 9. |
| 5. | 10. | 5. | 10. |

✳ Before dinner, the rating scores are tallied and the wines unveiled. Guests will enjoy the surprising results of this festive event.

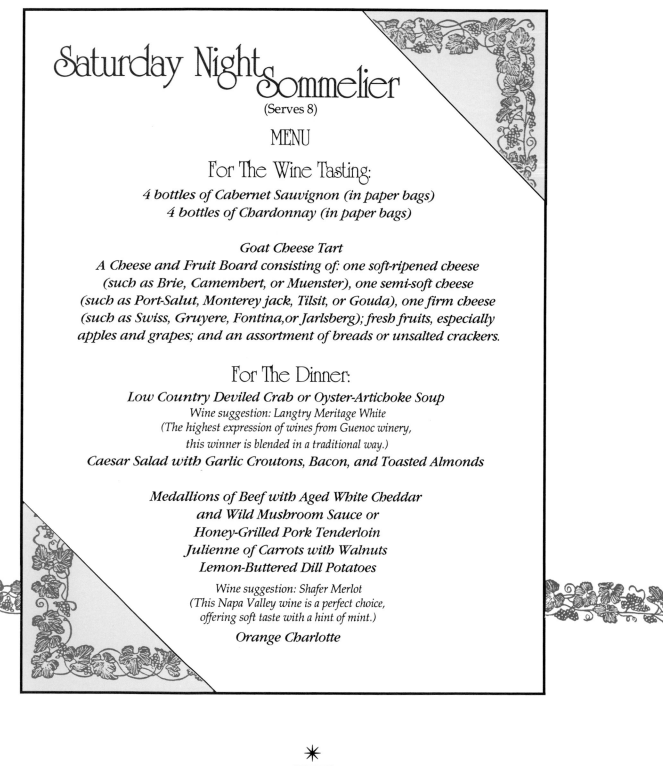

# Saturday Night Sommelier

(Serves 8)

## MENU

### For The Wine Tasting:

*4 bottles of Cabernet Sauvignon (in paper bags)*
*4 bottles of Chardonnay (in paper bags)*

*Goat Cheese Tart*
*A Cheese and Fruit Board consisting of: one soft-ripened cheese*
*(such as Brie, Camembert, or Muenster), one semi-soft cheese*
*(such as Port-Salut, Monterey jack, Tilsit, or Gouda), one firm cheese*
*(such as Swiss, Gruyere, Fontina,or Jarlsberg); fresh fruits, especially*
*apples and grapes; and an assortment of breads or unsalted crackers.*

### For The Dinner:

*Low Country Deviled Crab or Oyster-Artichoke Soup*
*Wine suggestion: Langtry Meritage White*
*(The highest expression of wines from Guenoc winery,*
*this winner is blended in a traditional way.)*
*Caesar Salad with Garlic Croutons, Bacon, and Toasted Almonds*

*Medallions of Beef with Aged White Cheddar*
*and Wild Mushroom Sauce or*
*Honey-Grilled Pork Tenderloin*
*Julienne of Carrots with Walnuts*
*Lemon-Buttered Dill Potatoes*

*Wine suggestion: Shafer Merlot*
*(This Napa Valley wine is a perfect choice,*
*offering soft taste with a hint of mint.)*
*Orange Charlotte*

**INGREDIENTS**

1 unbaked (folded) pie shell
2-3 shallots, peeled
9-11 ounces goat cheese
1 clove garlic
¼ cup fresh dill
1 cup heavy cream
3 eggs
white pepper to taste

# GOAT CHEESE TART

Preheat oven to 350 degrees.

Transfer pie shell to quiche or tart pan.

Purée remaining ingredients in blender or food processor. Pour mixture into unbaked pie shell, leaving ½ inch unfilled. Bake 45 minutes or until golden and puffy.

Serve warm or at room temperature.

**SERVES:** 8

*For extra color, a layer of roasted red peppers can be placed in the pie shell before adding the goat cheese filling.*

*Any leftover filling may be baked in a small loaf pan alongside the tart for a cook's treat!*

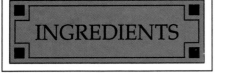

**INGREDIENTS**

3 slices bacon
1 stalk celery, diced
¼ red bell pepper, diced
1 small onion, diced
1 pound fresh lump
   crabmeat, picked over well
½ cup mayonnaise
¼ cup catsup
1 tablespoon prepared
   mustard
2 eggs, beaten
3 dashes hot sauce
1 cup butter cracker or bread
   crumbs, finely crushed

paprika for garnish
lemon wedges for garnish
parsley for garnish

# LOW COUNTRY DEVILED CRAB

Preheat oven to 350 degrees.

Fry bacon in large skillet until crisp, reserving 2 teaspoons bacon fat. Crumble bacon and set aside. Sauté celery, bell pepper, and onion in reserved fat. Remove from heat and combine with crab and bacon in large bowl. Add mayonnaise, catsup, prepared mustard, eggs, and hot sauce. Mix well.

Place ½ cup mixture in crab shells, scallop shells, or individual ramekins. Top with cracker crumbs. *(Can be prepared ahead up to this point, covered, and refrigerated or frozen.)*

Before baking, sprinkle with paprika. Bake 30-40 minutes. Garnish with lemon slices and parsley before serving.

**SERVES:** 8

*"Low country" refers to the lush region around Charleston, South Carolina, known for its gracious plantations, ancient live oaks, and outstanding cuisine.*

# OYSTER-ARTICHOKE SOUP

*This deliciously rich soup serves 8 as a soup course or 4 as a main course.*

Place oysters and liquid in large saucepan. Simmer on low heat until edges of oysters begin to curl. Remove oysters and chop.

Combine butter with oyster liquid and heat. Add onions and sauté 3-5 minutes. Stir in mushrooms. As mushrooms darken, sprinkle in flour and cook 3 more minutes.

Slowly add milk, stirring constantly. As milk begins to simmer, add chopped oysters, artichoke hearts, lemon juice, garlic powder, hot sauce, salt, and pepper. DO NOT LET BOIL. *(Can be prepared 1 day ahead up to this point and refrigerated. Gently reheat on low before continuing.)*

Just before serving, mix egg yolks with ½ cup soup mixture in small bowl. Combine with rest of soup and heat just until hot. Sprinkle with nutmeg for garnish.

**SERVES:** 8

## INGREDIENTS

| | |
|---|---|
| 3 | dozen oysters with liquid |
| ¼ | cup butter |
| ½ | cup green onions, chopped |
| ½ | pound mushrooms, sliced |
| 2 | tablespoons flour |
| 2 | cups milk |
| 1 | 4½ ounce jar marinated artichoke hearts, drained and chopped |
| 2 | tablespoons lemon juice |
| ½ | teaspoon garlic powder |
| 2 | dashes hot sauce |
| | salt to taste |
| | pepper to taste |
| 2 | egg yolks, beaten |
| | nutmeg for garnish |

## INGREDIENTS

½ pound bacon, diced
2 heads Romaine lettuce
2 eggs
1 clove garlic
1 cup fresh Parmesan cheese, grated
½ cup olive oil
1 tablespoon white wine vinegar
⅓-½ cup fresh lemon juice
2 tablespoons white wine
1 tablespoon dried basil
2 teaspoons Dijon mustard
½ teaspoon Worcestershire sauce
black pepper to taste
1 cup Garlic Croutons (recipe follows)
½ cup slivered almonds, toasted

**Garlic Croutons (recipe follows)**

# CAESAR SALAD WITH GARLIC CROUTONS, BACON, AND TOASTED SLIVERED ALMONDS

Fry bacon until crisp in large skillet, reserving 2 tablespoons bacon fat for garlic croutons. Drain bacon on paper towels; set aside. Wash Romaine lettuce leaves carefully; pat dry with paper towel. Cut leaves into bite-sized pieces; refrigerate in large salad bowl.

To coddle eggs, place eggs in small saucepan with enough water to cover. Bring water to boil over high heat. Immediately remove pan from heat and allow eggs to sit covered, in hot water for 1 ½ - 2 minutes. Remove eggs and place in cold water.

Add garlic, Parmesan cheese, and coddled eggs to blender or food processor. Mix until just blended. Slowly add oil in a stream while blending. Add remaining ingredients, except bacon, croutons, lettuce, and slivered almonds, and blend well. Refrigerate in jar until ready to serve.

At time of serving, shake dressing and pour enough over lettuce leaves to coat thoroughly; toss gently. Sprinkle with Garlic Croutons, bacon, and slivered almonds; toss again. Serve immediately.

**SERVES:** 8

*Said to have been created in the 1920's by a hotel chef in Baja, California, the Caesar salad is a beloved classic. Add grilled chicken strips, steak, or shrimp and you have a meal in itself.*

*Coddled eggs are soft-cooked eggs traditionally used in Caesar salads. The egg is quickly broken into the blender or bowl as directed in the recipe and any remains scooped out with a spoon.*

# GARLIC CROUTONS

Preheat oven to 300 degrees.

Remove crusts from bread and cut slices into ½-inch cubes. Melt bacon fat, butter, and oil in large skillet over moderate heat. Add garlic and stir briefly. Add bread cubes and stir quickly to coat.

Remove bread cubes from skillet and spread in single layer on baking sheet. Bake 25-30 minutes or until golden brown and crisp. Cool. *(Can be stored in airtight container up to 1 week.)*

**YIELD:** 2 cups

*Once you've made your own croutons, store-bought will never taste the same.*

### INGREDIENTS

8  slices stale white bread, or
6  slices stale french bread
2  tablespoons bacon fat
2  tablespoons butter
2  tablespoons olive oil
1  clove garlic, minced

# FAVORITE WINES

| Name | Grape Variety | Taste Description | Vintage | Price |
|---|---|---|---|---|
| *Robert Mondavi* | *Cabernet Sauvignon* | *dry, full-bodied; great with hearty food* | *1990* | *$18.00* |
| | | | | |
| | | | | |
| | | | | |
| | | | | |
| | | | | |
| | | | | |
| | | | | |
| | | | | |
| | | | | |
| | | | | |
| | | | | |
| | | | | |
| | | | | |

## INGREDIENTS

1    pound beef bones, cut into small pieces by butcher
10   tablespoons peanut oil
8    large white mushrooms, cleaned and thinly sliced
4    large shallots, chopped
2    cloves garlic, chopped
4    sprigs fresh thyme, ends clipped off and stems discarded
4    cups chicken stock
2    cups heavy cream

2    cups white Cheddar cheese, grated

2    tablespoons unsalted butter
3-4   cups wild mushrooms, sliced thinly into julienne strips

     salt to taste
     pepper to taste
     juice of 1 lemon

8    1-inch filet mignons, sliced to ½-inch thickness for total of 16 medallions

# MEDALLIONS OF BEEF WITH AGED WHITE CHEDDAR & WILD MUSHROOM SAUCE

Preheat oven to 400 degrees.

Place beef bones on baking sheet and roast in oven 12-15 minutes or until brown. (Be careful not to burn or blacken.)

Heat 2 tablespoons peanut oil in large saucepan over moderate heat. Add white mushrooms and sauté 1 minute. Add shallots and garlic; sauté 1 minute longer. Add browned bones, thyme, and chicken stock. Bring to boil, lower heat, and simmer 20 minutes. Add cream and return liquid to boil. Lower heat and simmer 15 minutes or until liquid is reduced by about one-quarter, or thick enough to coat the back of a spoon.

Remove bones from sauce. Pour sauce into blender along with cheese. Process until smooth. Strain and keep warm.

Melt butter in large skillet over moderate heat. Add wild mushrooms and sauté 2 minutes; season lightly with salt and pepper. Fold sautéed mushrooms into sauce. Adjust seasoning with salt and lemon juice. *(Sauce can be prepared up to 2 hours ahead and gently reheated.)*

Heat remaining 8 tablespoons oil in large skillet over moderate heat. Season filets with salt, pepper, and lemon and quickly sauté 3 minutes on each side. (Do not crowd pan.) Remove from pan and keep warm.

To serve, ladle Cheddar-mushroom sauce on bottom of each warmed dinner plate. Place two medallions of beef on top of sauce. Pass remaining sauce at table.

**SERVES:** 8

*If bones are hard to find, simply add 1-2 beef bouillon cubes to the chicken stock.*

*Until recently, wild mushrooms were available in the United States only to specialists who knew how to forage for them in the deep forests. The following varieties are now commercially cultivated and commonly found in most supermarkets: chantrelles, morels, shitake, porcini, enokitake, and oyster mushrooms.*

# HONEY-GRILLED PORK TENDERLOIN

## INGREDIENTS

2 1-pound pork tenderloins
⅓ cup soy sauce
½ teaspoon ground ginger
5 cloves garlic, halved
2 tablespoons brown sugar
3 tablespoons honey
3 tablespoons dark sesame oil

Trim fat from tenderloins. Butterfly tenderloins by making a lengthwise cut in each, cutting to within ¼ inch of other side. Place in large ziplock plastic bag.

Combine soy sauce, ginger, and garlic in small bowl. Pour over tenderloins. Seal and refrigerate at least 3 hours. Turn occasionally. *(May be marinated in refrigerator overnight.)*

Remove tenderloins and discard marinade. Combine brown sugar, honey, and oil in small saucepan. Cook over low heat, stirring constantly until sugar dissolves.

Prepare grill; coals should be moderately hot. Place tenderloins on greased rack and brush with honey mixture. Grill 20 minutes, turning once and basting frequently, until meat thermometer inserted at the thickest point reads 160 degrees. Slice and serve immediately.

**SERVES:** 8

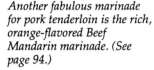

*Another fabulous marinade for pork tenderloin is the rich, orange-flavored Beef Mandarin marinade. (See page 94.)*

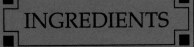

3  pounds carrots
1  cup water
½  teaspoon salt
2  tablespoons green onions
   (including tops), sliced
½  cup butter, softened
1  tablespoon honey
7  ounces walnuts, broken
   salt to taste
   pepper to taste

# JULIENNE OF CARROTS WITH WALNUTS

Scrape carrots and remove ends. Cut carrots into julienne strips, about 2-3 inches long. Combine water and salt in large saucepan and heat to boil. Add carrots and onions. Cover and return to boil. Reduce heat and simmer until tender, about 25 minutes. Drain carrots and toss with butter, honey, and walnuts. *(May be prepared up to 2 days ahead, refrigerated, and reheated.)*

**SERVES:** 8

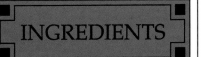

4  large potatoes, baked
8  tablespoons butter, melted
⅓  cup sour cream
2  tablespoons fresh dill,
   finely chopped
4  teaspoons fresh lemon
   juice
½  teaspoon garlic salt
1  tablespoon onion, finely
   minced
   salt to taste
   freshly ground pepper to
   taste
   paprika for garnish

# LEMON-BUTTERED DILL POTATOES

Preheat oven to 350 degrees.

Cut each baked potato in half lengthwise and scoop out pulp, leaving skin as a shell. Mix potato pulp with 5 tablespoons melted butter and remaining ingredients, except paprika, in large bowl. Beat with mixer until smooth. Put mixture back into potato shells. Brush with remaining 3 tablespoons melted butter. Sprinkle with paprika. *(May be prepared ahead up to this point and refrigerated several hours or overnight.)* Bake 15-20 minutes or until lightly browned.

**SERVES:** 8

# ORANGE CHARLOTTE

*(Best if prepared 1 day ahead.)*

Soak gelatin in ⅓ cup cold water until soft. Bring remaining ⅓ cup water to boil in medium saucepan and add gelatin mixture. Stir in sugar until dissolved. Cool slightly. Add juices. Place in refrigerator until mixture begins to congeal slightly.

Meanwhile, whip 1 pint cream in medium bowl until soft peaks form. Remove gelatin mixture from refrigerator and whip in large bowl. Fold whipped cream into gelatin. Add orange and lemon zests.

Line bottom and sides of 9- or 10-inch springform pan with lady fingers. Pour mixture into pan. Chill until firm. Remove sides to serve. Additional sweetened whipped cream may be used to garnish. Top with sprig of mint and several orange sections for color.

**SERVES:** 8

*Once the sides of the springform pan are removed, wrap a pretty ribbon around the Orange Charlotte and tie in a bow. This will help to keep the cake together and make a lovely presentation for serving.*

## INGREDIENTS

|   |   |
|---|---|
| 2 | packages unflavored gelatin |
| ⅔ | cup water |
| 1 | cup sugar |
| 1 ¼ | cups fresh orange juice |
| 4 | tablespoons lemon juice |
| 1 | pint whipping cream rind of 1 orange, finely grated peel of 1 lemon, finely grated |
| 2 | packages lady fingers, split open lengthwise |

sweetened whipped cream for garnish
mint sprig for garnish
orange sections for garnish

# Life's A Beach:

## A Seafood Supper For Inlanders

By the sea, by the sea,
by the beautiful . . .
well, we may not be able to hear
the ocean,
but we can taste it!

Join us for a seafood seaside
(uh... poolside) supper.
Saturday, July 9
7:30 p.m.
Dee Dee and Palmer McCorkle
9 Queens Road

Regrets
377-0886

✳ Did you know that in the South, every-one goes "to the beach," in the North, everyone goes "to the shore" or "to the cape," and in the West, everyone goes "to the ocean?"

✳ Although you may not be able to transport your dinner party to the beach, you can create the ambiance of the shore for your "inlander" guests. Scallop shells gathered along the tides can be used as placecards for your table. Scatter sand around a centerpiece decor of driftwood, shells, dried seaweed, and other beach treasures. You can almost feel the sea breeze!

✳ Residents of the Carolinas know that nothing relieves stress like a summer afternoon nap in a Pawleys Island hammock. Pawleys Island is the oldest resort along the South Carolina coast.

✳ Designed by a riverboat pilot in the late 1800's, the hammock is woven of 1,000 feet of cotton rope, without knots, to insure perfect comfort and coolness.

✳ In addition to Pawleys Island, we'll let you in on a little secret. Board a passenger ferry at Southport and delight in a 15-minute ride across inland waters to Bald Head Island, the southernmost point along North Carolina's coast. Once on the island enjoying fourteen miles of un-spoiled beaches, you will feel a world apart from the traffic and crowds that you left behind. Vacation here and you will find yourself returning year after year (but only tell your closest friends about this secret spot)!

# Life's A Beach:
## (Serves 8)

# MENU

*Peach Fuzz Buzzes*
*Grilled Scallops in Lime Marinade*
*or Cape Fear Crab Cakes*
*With Lemon Dill Sauce*

*Cold Strawberry Soup*

*Salmon Wellington With Spinach Pâté*
*And Shrimp Sauce*
*Asparagus With Herbed Vinaigrette*
*Red Pepper Popovers*

*Iced Coffee Soufflé*

*Wine suggestion:*
*Newton Chardonnay*
*(One of the best from Napa, this is*
*a rich Chardonnay with layers of fruit flavor.)*

## INGREDIENTS

4 **medium, ripe peaches**
6 **ounces frozen pink
  lemonade concentrate**
6 **ounces rum**
4 **ounces vodka
  ice**

# PEACH FUZZ BUZZES

Cut up peaches, leaving on peel. Place in blender. Add lemonade, rum, and vodka. Add ice and blend until thick and smooth.

**YIELD:** 8 drinks

*While peaches come in many varieties, all are either categorized as Clingstone or Freestone. In Clingstone peaches, the fruit clings to the pit, whereas the fruit of the Freestone peaches separates easily from the pit.*

*Peach Fuzz Buzzes, this page; Grilled Scallops in Lime Marinade, p. 113.*

# GRILLED
# SCALLOPS
# IN LIME MARINADE

Combine lime juice, salt, soy sauce, oregano, pepper, and Tabasco in large bowl. Add scallops and marinate in refrigerator 30 minutes to 1 hour.

Spray metal skewers with cooking spray. Drain scallops and reserve liquid. Wrap each scallop in partially cooked bacon and thread onto skewers. Leave room between scallops.

Grill on moderate-high heat or broil in oven. Turn skewers often and baste with reserved marinade. Cook 4-5 minutes. Scallops should be slightly springy to the touch.

Scallops can be arranged on a platter and passed as an appetizer or served on individual plates as a first course.

**SERVES:** 8

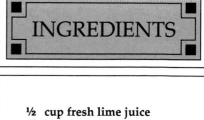

## INGREDIENTS

½ cup fresh lime juice
1 teaspoon salt
1 tablespoon soy sauce
1 teaspoon dried oregano
1 teaspoon cracked black peppercorns
3-6 drops Tabasco sauce
3 pounds fresh sea scallops
½ pound thinly sliced bacon, partially cooked

*Sea scallops can become quite large in diameter, sometimes 2-3 inches. The mid-sized scallops will work best for wrapping and threading onto skewers.*

*Although shellfish is thought to be high in cholesterol, most varieties, e.g., crab, scallops, mussels, clams, and lobster, are actually a little lower in cholesterol than poultry or beef.*

## INGREDIENTS

### CRAB CAKES

- 3 tablespoons butter
- 1 green onion, finely chopped
- 1 clove garlic, pressed
- 2 tablespoons red bell pepper, finely chopped cayenne pepper to taste
- 3 tablespoons heavy cream
- 1 tablespoon Dijon mustard
- 1 egg, beaten
- 1 teaspoon fresh basil, minced
- 1 teaspoon fresh parsley, minced
- 1 cup bread crumbs
- 1 pound fresh lump crabmeat, picked over and cleaned
- ¼ cup Parmesan cheese
- 2 tablespoons oil

### LEMON DILL SAUCE

- ¾ cup mayonnaise
- ½ cup buttermilk
- 2 tablespoons fresh dill, chopped
- 1 tablespoon parsley, minced
- 2 teaspoons fresh lemon juice
- 1 tablespoon lemon peel, grated
- 1 clove garlic, pressed

- 6 cups fresh strawberries, hulled and washed
- 2 cups orange juice
- ¼ cup Grand Marnier liqueur
- 1 cup sour cream or plain yogurt

# CAPE FEAR CRAB CAKES WITH LEMON DILL SAUCE

### FOR CRAB CAKES:

Melt 1 tablespoon butter in large skillet and sauté onion, garlic, and red pepper until wilted (about 2 minutes). Add cayenne, cream, and Dijon mustard. Cool slightly. Add beaten egg, basil, parsley, ½ cup bread crumbs, and crabmeat. Mix lightly. Mold into 16 2-inch wide patties.

Combine ½ cup remaining bread crumbs and cheese in shallow dish. Roll patties in crumb and cheese mixture. Chill at least 1 hour. *(Can be made early in day.)*

Combine oil and remaining 2 tablespoons butter over moderate heat in large skillet. Sauté crab cakes 3 minutes on each side. Serve with Lemon Dill Sauce.

### FOR LEMON DILL SAUCE:

Combine all ingredients in medium bowl. Chill until mixture thickens.

**SERVES:** 8

# COLD STRAWBERRY SOUP

Purée all but 12 strawberries in blender or food processor. Transfer strawberry purée to large pitcher. Whisk in remaining ingredients until well blended. Cover and refrigerate at least 6 hours or overnight. *(Can be made 1 day ahead.)*

Serve in chilled, shallow soup bowls. Slice reserved strawberries lengthwise in ¼-inch slices. Carefully lay 3-5 slices on top of each serving, making a "star" pattern.

**SERVES:** 8

*This is one of the best crab cake recipes you'll ever find!*

*When selecting lump crabmeat for cakes, backfin meat is preferred over claw meat because it is lighter in color and makes for a more attractive presentation.*

*This soup is unexpected and refreshing as a first course in summer or light dessert course with cookies anytime.*

*Using large, shallow soup bowls helps the strawberries to stay "afloat."*

*Cape Fear Crab Cakes with Lemon Dill Sauce, p. 114; Cold Strawberry Soup, p. 114.*

## INGREDIENTS

### SALMON

4-5 pound salmon fillet
2 carrots
1 onion, quartered
2 stalks celery
1 lemon, sliced
  salt to taste
  black pepper to taste
1 cup dry white wine

### SPINACH PÂTÉ

1 ½ pounds fresh spinach
2 tablespoons butter
1 pound fresh mushrooms, sliced
8-10 green onions, sliced
2 cups sour cream
  chopped fresh dill to taste
  juice of 1 lemon
  salt to taste
  pepper to taste

### ASSEMBLY

1 box frozen puff pastry, thawed

### SHRIMP SAUCE

4 tablespoons butter
½ pound fresh shrimp, peeled and deveined
2 tablespoons onion, minced
½ cup vermouth
2 tablespoons flour
2 cups half-and-half
½ cup sour cream
  chopped fresh dill to taste
  salt to taste
  pepper to taste
  dash of lemon juice (optional)

# SALMON WELLINGTON WITH SPINACH PÂTÉ AND SHRIMP SAUCE

## FOR SALMON:

Preheat oven to 375 degrees.

Line roasting pan with large piece of heavy duty aluminum foil. Center fish on foil. Add vegetables, lemon slices, salt, and pepper. Pour wine over all. Bring edges of foil together and seal to form packet. Bake 30 minutes to 1 hour or until fish is opaque. (Time will vary according to thickness of fish fillet.) Remove from oven and cool. Discard vegetables and lemon slices. Remove skin from fish and discard. Set fish aside. *(Can be prepared 1 day ahead up to this point and refrigerated. Bring fish to room temperature before proceeding with recipe.)*

## FOR SPINACH PÂTÉ:

Wash spinach and remove stems. Steam until wilted, drain and reserve. Melt butter in medium skillet and sauté mushrooms and onions. Set aside. Combine all remaining pâté ingredients in food processor. Add spinach and mushroom mixture and purée until smooth.

## FOR ASSEMBLY:

Preheat oven to 375 degrees.

Place large rectangle of thawed puff pastry on large greased baking sheet. (If pastry is not large enough to hold fish, it may be enlarged slightly by using a lightly-floured rolling pin.) Place chilled salmon on puff pastry and top with spinach pâté. Cover

*This is as easy as it is elegant and mouth-wateringly delicious.*

*The spinach pâté also makes an excellent spread for crackers or vegetables served as an appetizer during the cocktail hour.*

salmon with remaining sheet of puff pastry. Pinch edges to seal and score top of pastry in criss-cross pattern. Bake until pastry is brown and spinach is heated through. Slice and serve with Shrimp Sauce.

**FOR SHRIMP SAUCE:**

Melt 2 tablespoons butter in medium skillet and sauté shrimp and onion. Add vermouth and set aside.

Melt remaining 2 tablespoons butter in medium saucepan over moderate heat and stir in flour. Gradually add half-and-half, stirring until thickened. Add sour cream, reserved shrimp mixture, and remaining ingredients. Reduce to low and heat thoroughly. *(Can be prepared early in day and gently reheated just before serving.)*

**SERVES:** 8

*The shrimp sauce may be served over any other baked or poached fish for an easy but elegant entrée.*

## INGREDIENTS

3-4 **pounds fresh asparagus, trimmed**
2 **eggs, hard boiled and chopped (optional)**
½ **cup pine nuts, toasted (optional)**
8 **red pepper strips, blanched**

### VINAIGRETTE

2 **tablespoons red wine vinegar**
½-1 **teaspoon salt**
1 **tablespoon Dijon mustard**
¼ **cup olive oil**
¼ **cup vegetable oil**
3 **tablespoons maple syrup**
2 **teaspoons dried tarragon**

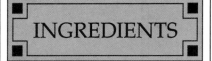

## INGREDIENTS

6 **large eggs**
3 **cups milk**
2 **tablespoons vegetable oil**
1 **teaspoon salt**
3 **cups all purpose flour**
2 **tablespoons chives, minced**
2 **tablespoons parsley, minced**
2 **tablespoons red bell pepper, finely minced**

# ASPARAGUS WITH HERBED VINAIGRETTE

Steam asparagus until bright green and barely tender.  Rinse immediately in cold water to stop cooking process.  Drain and pat dry.  Arrange on large platter and refrigerate, covered, at least 1 hour or overnight.

Just before serving, spoon vinaigrette over asparagus.  Sprinkle chopped eggs and pine nuts on top for garnish, or wrap individual asparagus bundles with a thin red pepper strip.

### FOR VINAIGRETTE:

Mix vinegar, salt, and mustard in glass jar.  Add oils, maple syrup, and tarragon.  Shake vigorously.  Refrigerate, covered, at least 1 hour. *(Can be refrigerated up to 3 days.)*

**SERVES:** 8

# RED PEPPER POPOVERS

Preheat oven to 425 degrees.  Grease 6 popover pan cups.

Process eggs, milk, oil, and salt in blender at high speed.  Add flour and process at low speed until smooth.  Scrape down sides of blender as needed.  Do not overblend.  Stir in herbs and red pepper.  Pour batter into prepared pans, dividing evenly. Bake 15 minutes. Reduce oven temperature to 375 degrees.  Bake 45 minutes longer.  Serve warm.

**YIELD:** 6 popovers (recipe doubles easily)

*When purchasing fresh asparagus, the smaller, thinner stalks retain the most flavor while steamed.  Be sure water is boiling before placing stalks into the steamer and handle them gently, as the tips break easily after cooking.*

*Red bell peppers are typically sweeter in taste than the more common green ones.  There are over 800 varieties of peppers, ranging in color, flavor, texture, and size.*

# ICED COFFEE SOUFFLÉ

*Salmon Wellington with Spinich Pâté and Shrimp Sauce, pp. 116-117; Asparagus with Herbed Vinaigrette, p. 118; Red Pepper Popovers, p. 118.*

Combine gelatin, ½ cup sugar, salt, and instant coffee in a 2 ½-quart saucepan. Beat egg yolks with milk in medium bowl. Add to mixture in saucepan. Cook and stir over moderate heat about 12-15 minutes or until mixture thickens. Remove from heat. Add almond extract. Chill, stirring occasionally, until mixture mounds slightly when dropped from a spoon.

Form 2-inch collar on soufflé dish by binding a strip of aluminum foil around top edge. Beat egg whites in large bowl until stiff. Add remaining ½ cup sugar. Beat until very stiff. Fold beaten egg whites into chilled gelatin mixture. Whip cream until soft peaks form and fold into gelatin mixture. Spoon into soufflé dish. Chill until firm. Remove collar. Garnish with toasted almonds. *(Can be made 1 day ahead and refrigerated.)*

**SERVES:** 8

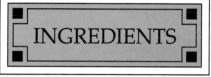

## INGREDIENTS

2 envelopes unflavored gelatin
1 cup sugar
¼ teaspoon salt
4 tablespoons instant coffee
4 eggs, separated
2 ½ cups milk
1 teaspoon almond extract
2 cups heavy cream

1 cup toasted almonds for garnish

*
119

# New Beginnings

## First Dinner Date Since The Divorce

*Come enjoy an evening that promises to recapture the "New Beginning" feeling.*

*Please join me for a Romantic Dinner and Fabulous Company*

*Debi's house
Saturday,
February 23
7:00 p.m.*

✳ "New beginnings" may take on many different forms throughout a person's life, whether it be divorce, marriage, children leaving home for the first time, or, even much more cause for celebration, children leaving home for the second time! Along with a healthy serving of romance, this menu is designed to reward and pamper someone for making it through an emotional time in life.

✳ Set the mood with lots of candles. Arrange different size candle sticks on the table with different height candles. Make the setting cozy, perhaps a small skirted table in front of the fire. Place fragrant flowers, such as roses, hyacinth, or gardenia, around the candles and let the romance begin.

✳ Fact and fantasy are joined to create the romantic legend of Blowing Rock, North Carolina. Legend has it that a down-hearted lover, a Cherokee brave, threw himself over the edge of this great rock. When his saddened amour, a Chickasaw maiden, begged the Great Spirit for his return, the brave was blown back up to the top of the rock with the next gust of wind — a legendary "new beginning!"

✳ Stimulate conversation at that first "new beginning" dinner date by telling your guest about the flashing lights of fireflies. The lights are used as mating signals. It takes approximately 400 firefly lights to equal the light of one candle.

# New Beginnings

(Serves 2)

## MENU

Campari Aperitifs
Escargot In Mushroom Caps

Carrot Vichyssoise
or High Tide Ginger Scallops on Spinach Bed

Baked Chèvre Salad with Red Grape Clusters

Lobster Sautéed In Wine and Lime Sauce Over Rice
Stir-Fried Mixed Vegetables

Flaming Bananas with Brandy and Butter
over French Vanilla Ice Cream
or Assorted Berries with Cognac Crème Anglaise
and Cinnamon Puff Hearts

Lemon-Rimmed Irish Coffee

Wine suggestion:
Robert Mondavi Chardonnay
(Showing the enhancement of French oak, this classic white wine
lends itself to lobster. For that extra special evening, try the Reserve.)

## INGREDIENTS

2 jiggers Campari
2 sugar cubes (optional)
champagne

## INGREDIENTS

6 tablespoons butter,
    softened
1 ½ teaspoons shallots, minced
1 large clove garlic, mashed
1 tablespoon fresh parsley,
    chopped
    salt to taste
    pepper to taste
6 medium mushroom caps,
    brushed clean
6 escargot, drained and
    rinsed well

4 crusty French rolls

## INGREDIENTS

1 leek
¼ cup onion, chopped
1 tablespoon butter
1 cup carrots, thinly sliced
1 large potato, peeled and
    sliced
1 cup chicken broth
½ teaspoon salt
½ cup milk
½ cup half-and-half

chopped chives for garnish

# CAMPARI APERITIFS

Chill two champagne glasses. Place 1 jigger of Campari and a sugar cube (if desired) into each glass. Fill with champagne and stir to combine.

**YIELD:** 2 drinks

# ESCARGOT IN MUSHROOM CAPS

Preheat oven to 400 degrees.

Combine butter, shallots, garlic, parsley, salt, and pepper in small bowl. Mix well. Put a dab of butter mixture inside each mushroom cap. Top with an escargot and add another dab of butter mixture. Place mushroom caps in ramekin or oven-proof dish. Add any extra butter mixture. Bake 10 minutes or until butter mixture is bubbly and mushroom caps can be easily pierced. Serve piping hot with French rolls.

**SERVES:** 2

# CARROT VICHYSSOISE

Wash leek and remove green stems. Slice white part and combine with onion. Melt butter in large saucepan and add leek and onion. Cook until lightly golden brown and translucent. Add carrots, potato, broth, and salt. Bring to boil. Reduce heat and simmer 35 minutes.

Purée mixture in blender or food processor. Return mixture to heat and add milk. Bring

*Look for vineyard snails or petit-gris. These are considered superior to any other escargot. You can find these canned in gourmet shops and some grocery stores. Remember to rinse them repeatedly before baking.*

*When buying domestic mushroom caps, also known as button mushrooms, look for those that have tightly closed caps. The mushrooms are past their prime if any gills are showing.*

*Look for a small to medium, unblemished leek and clean thoroughly — it has a tendency to get rather sandy in its multi-layered leaves.*

*Emperor Nero was said to have eaten leeks several days a month to clear his voice.*

to boil and remove from heat immediately. Add half-and-half, stirring thoroughly, and refrigerate overnight. Serve chilled, topped with chives. *(Can be made 2 days ahead and refrigerated.)*

**SERVES:** 2-4

# HIGH TIDE GINGER SCALLOPS ON SPINACH BED

**INGREDIENTS**

7-8 tablespoons butter
6 jumbo sea scallops
1 8-ounce package button mushrooms, quartered
1 tablespoon fresh ginger, grated
1 can water chestnuts, drained and sliced
   juice of 1-2 lemons
1 package fresh spinach leaves, rinsed and dried
   olive oil

chopped green onions for garnish

Melt 2 tablespoons butter in large skillet over moderate-high heat. Add scallops and cook until slightly firm to touch while remaining milky white. Remove scallops from skillet.

Sauté mushrooms in 1-2 tablespoons butter in same skillet. Add ginger and water chestnuts. Reduce liquid by half. Add juice of 1 lemon or to taste. Remove from heat and quickly stir in 3-4 tablespoons chilled butter. (This will allow sauce to thicken.) Return scallops to skillet and heat thoroughly.

In large bowl, sprinkle spinach with remaining lemon juice and drizzle with olive oil. Cover with wax paper and microwave on high for approximately 1 minute (or sauté on high heat in large skillet to wilt). Arrange wilted spinach leaves on each plate. Top with scallops and sauce. Garnish with green onions.

**SERVES:** 2

*This appetizer can easily become an entrée by increasing the number of scallops and serving them over Basmati rice with spinach. Plan for a third to a quarter of a pound per person.*

**INGREDIENTS**

2 tablespoons brown sugar
2 tablespoons unsalted butter
2 ripe bananas, peeled and halved lengthwise
1 tablespoon lemon juice
   dash cinnamon
   dash nutmeg
¼ cup brandy, warmed

2 scoops French vanilla ice cream

**INGREDIENTS**

2 cups assorted berries

**CRÈME ANGLAISE**

2 cups milk
1 teaspoon vanilla
4 egg yolks
4 tablespoons sugar
4 tablespoons Cognac (or liqueur of choice)

**Cinnamon Puff Hearts (recipe follows)**

# FLAMING BANANAS WITH BRANDY AND BUTTER

Melt brown sugar and butter in chafing dish or oval pan. Add bananas and sauté until tender, about 2-3 minutes. Add lemon juice, cinnamon, and nutmeg. Pour brandy over bananas and carefully ignite liquid. Spoon liquid over bananas and shake pan until flame goes out. Serve over ice cream.

**SERVES: 2**

*The Flaming Bananas are great served with frozen vanilla yogurt too!*

# ASSORTED BERRIES WITH COGNAC CRÈME ANGLAISE

Divide mixed berries between two crystal goblets. Spoon Cognac Crème Anglaise over top. Serve with Cinnamon Puff Hearts.

**FOR CRÈME ANGLAISE:**

Bring milk to boil in small saucepan. Set aside. Combine vanilla, yolks, and sugar in top of double boiler and beat until thickened and pale lemon-colored. Slowly add hot milk to egg yolk mixture, stirring until mixture thickens, about 8 minutes. Remove and strain into small bowl through fine sieve. Mix in Cognac. Cover with plastic wrap to prevent skin from forming and chill. *(Crème Anglaise can be prepared up to 2 days ahead.)*

**SERVES: 2**

*If Cognac is not available, choose one of the following to suit your taste:*

*Crème de Menthe
Hazelnut Liqueur
Grand Marnier
Kahlua*

# CINNAMON PUFF HEARTS

Preheat oven to 350 degrees.

Roll pastry out on lightly-floured surface to 11 x 14-inch rectangle. Cut out approximately 16 hearts using a 3- or 4-inch heart-shaped cookie cutter. Carefully transfer to cookie sheet. Combine sugar and spices in small bowl. Sprinkle over hearts. Bake cookies until puffed and golden, approximately 15 minutes. Transfer to rack and cool. *(Can be stored in airtight container several days.)*

**YIELD:** 16

## INGREDIENTS

1   sheet frozen puff pastry, thawed
2   tablespoons sugar
½   teaspoon ground cinnamon
¼   teaspoon ground nutmeg

*If nothing else warms up your guest's heart, this Irish coffee is guaranteed to do the job!*

*Traditional Irish coffee does call for brown sugar in the bottom of the glass but does not use the lemon and white sugar frosting on the rim.*

# LEMON-RIMMED IRISH COFFEE

Rub cut lemon on rims of two wine or Irish coffee glasses. Place sugar in flat dish and submerge rim in sugar to coat. In bottom of each glass add 1 teaspoon brown sugar and 1 jigger Irish whiskey. Add coffee within 1 inch of rim. Add dollop of whipped cream. Do not stir.

**SERVES:** 2

## INGREDIENTS

1   lemon, cut in half
¼   cup sugar
2   teaspoons brown sugar
2   jiggers Irish whiskey (no substitute)
2   cups hot black coffee
2   tablespoons sweetened whipped cream

# My 12th Annual 29th Birthday Dinner

## *Saavy And Chic : Black Tie For Eight*

I'ts Emma's 29th Birthday--
12th Annual, 29th Birthday,that is.
Who's counting? Who cares!
Join us to celebrate, once again,
at Emma's 29th Birthday Bash.
Saturday, March 10
7:30 p.m.
333 Maryland Avenue

Black Tie

Regrets
Whitley
234-0987

✳ This birthday celebration is an evening not soon to forget! Surround a beautiful flowered centerpiece with gold and silver helium-filled balloons. Anchor balloons inside sand-filled bags wrapped in metallic paper or secure them around gaily-colored wrapped "packages" placed about the table. Napkins and the stems of glasses can be tied with ribbon bows to match the table packages.

✳ Strew silver and gold or colored confetti and streamers about each place at the table. Twinkle tiny white lights all around the room. And for a special touch, use small silver frames as placecards. These can go home with each guest as a remembrance.

✳ And for the quintessential "12th Annual 29th Birthday Dinner" celebration — have it catered!

✳ The ultimate dining room for serving something savvy and chic could arguably be found in the 21,740 square foot mansion in the heart of Charlotte, purchased by J.B. "Buck" Duke in 1919, who soon tripled its size.

✳ Mr. Duke's second wife, having toured Italy, decided to erect an enormous fountain on the grounds. The fountain became a major tourist attraction, spraying from 50 to 150 feet of water into the air. Although the fountain was later removed, many Charlotteans remember driving by to see it on a Sunday afternoon.

✳ Currently, the Duke Mansion is the private home of a Charlotte family.

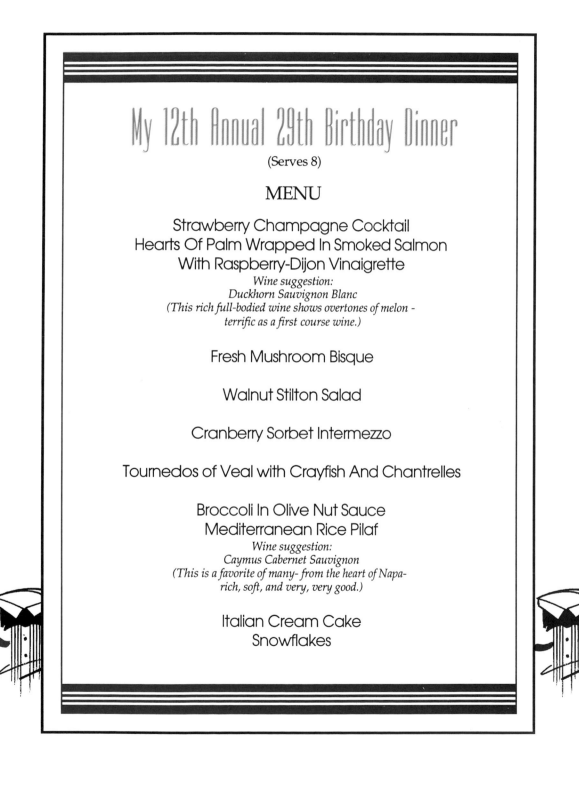

# My 12th Annual 29th Birthday Dinner

(Serves 8)

## MENU

Strawberry Champagne Cocktail
Hearts Of Palm Wrapped In Smoked Salmon
With Raspberry-Dijon Vinaigrette

*Wine suggestion:*
*Duckhorn Sauvignon Blanc*
*(This rich full-bodied wine shows overtones of melon -*
*terrific as a first course wine.)*

Fresh Mushroom Bisque

Walnut Stilton Salad

Cranberry Sorbet Intermezzo

Tournedos of Veal with Crayfish And Chantrelles

Broccoli In Olive Nut Sauce
Mediterranean Rice Pilaf

*Wine suggestion:*
*Caymus Cabernet Sauvignon*
*(This is a favorite of many- from the heart of Napa-*
*rich, soft, and very, very good.)*

Italian Cream Cake
Snowflakes

# STRAWBERRY CHAMPAGNE COCKTAIL

1 bottle domestic
champagne, chilled
aromatic bitters
lump sugar
whole strawberries for
garnish

Place one lump of sugar into each champagne glass. Shake 5 to 6 drops of bitters onto the sugar. Add one whole, hulled strawberry. Fill each glass with icy, cold champagne.

**YIELD:** 6-8 glasses

# HEARTS OF PALM WRAPPED IN SMOKED SALMON WITH RASPBERRY-DIJON VINAIGRETTE

1 14-ounce can hearts of
palm, refrigerated
½ pound smoked salmon,
cut into thin strips

VINAIGRETTE:

2 tablespoons raspberry
vinegar
1 tablespoon lemon juice
1 tablespoon Dijon mustard
½ teaspoon salt
¼ teaspoon dried tarragon
½ cup olive oil

lettuce leaves or parsley for
garnish

Drain hearts of palm and cut lengthwise into halves or thirds to make uniform long sticks. Wrap smoked salmon around hearts of palm sticks. Arrange in serving dish or on platter in spoke wheel fashion and refrigerate, covered, for several hours or overnight. Just before serving, spoon vinaigrette generously over top. Garnish with lettuce leaves or parsley, if desired.

**FOR VINAIGRETTE:**

Combine all ingredients in jar. Shake well and refrigerate. *(Can be prepared up to 3 days ahead of serving.)*

**SERVES:** 8-10

*If you prefer, wrap the hearts of palm in prosciutto ham instead of smoked salmon.*

*...rawberry Champagne Cocktail, p. 130; Hearts of Palm wrapped in ...noked Salmon with Raspberry-Dijon Vinaigrette, p. 130.*

*Walnut Stilton Salad, p. 133.*

# FRESH MUSHROOM BISQUE

Heat oil in large saucepan. Add celery and onion. Cook until soft. Add flour and cook about 3 minutes. Do not brown. Add boiling chicken stock all at once and whisk. Cook until thick. Slowly add warm milk, salt, nutmeg, white pepper, and tarragon. Reduce heat and stir occasionally.

Melt margarine in heavy skillet and cook sliced mushrooms until tender. Add mushrooms to soup mixture. Before serving, add sherry if desired. Garnish with parsley and almond flakes.

**SERVES:** 8

## INGREDIENTS

2 tablespoons corn oil
¼ cup celery, minced
¼ cup onion, minced
2½ tablespoons flour
1 cup homemade or canned chicken stock, boiling
1½ cups lowfat or whole milk, warmed
½ teaspoon salt
⅛ teaspoon ground nutmeg
¼ teaspoon white pepper
½ teaspoon tarragon
4 teaspoons margarine
2 cups fresh mushrooms, thinly sliced
2 tablespoons sherry (optional)

½ cup minced parsley for garnish
2 tablespoons toasted almond flakes for garnish

# WALNUT STILTON SALAD

Wash and dry lettuce. Tear into bite-sized pieces. Mix lettuce and walnuts in large bowl. Crumble cheese in small bowl. Pour vinaigrette over salad and toss. Sprinkle crumbled cheese on top.

**FOR VINAIGRETTE:**

Mix all ingredients in jar and shake well. *(May be prepared 2 days ahead, covered, and refrigerated.)*

**SERVES:** 8

## INGREDIENTS

3 heads Boston bibb lettuce
¾ cup walnuts, coarsely chopped
4-6 ounces Stilton cheese

**VINAIGRETTE:**

¼ cup red wine vinegar
¾ cup olive oil
1 tablespoon onion, finely chopped
1 teaspoon Dijon mustard
2 tablespoons water
1 tablespoon parsley, chopped
1 teaspoon basil
½ teaspoon oregano
½ teaspoon garlic powder
salt to taste
pepper to taste

## INGREDIENTS

12 ounces frozen cranberry
    raspberry juice
16 ounces jellied cranberry
    sauce
½ cup orange juice
½ cup grapefruit juice
½ cup Sprite or Wink

fresh raspberries for
garnish
fresh mint leaves for
garnish

# CRANBERRY
# SORBET INTERMEZZO

Combine all ingredients, except garnishes, in blender. Mix thoroughly. Pour into 9 x 11-inch glass baking dish. Cover with foil and freeze until almost solid (about 6 hours or overnight). Beat partially frozen mixture with electric mixer until creamy. Put in small bowl, cover tightly, and freeze until serving time. Place 1 scoop, per person, in small sherbert cup or bowl; garnish with raspberries and mint leaves.

**SERVES:** 8

*The "intermezzo" course is a refreshing interlude meant to cleanse the palate before the entrée is served.*

# TOURNEDOS OF VEAL WITH CRAYFISH AND CHANTRELLES

*This Tournedos of Veal recipe may sound complicated but it is actually quite easy to prepare and outstanding by any standard.*

---

*Chantrelles are full-flavored, large, wild mushrooms with a wavy cap and thick stem. If not available fresh, look for them dried (reconstitute according to package directions) or substitute large button mushrooms.*

Debone veal chops. Trim silverskin away and wrap each around ribeye muscle. Secure with toothpick or string. Refrigerate, covered.

Melt 1½ tablespoons butter in large skillet and add Chantrelles. Sauté over high heat. Add salt, pepper, garlic, and parsley. Cover to release water from mushrooms and then uncover to let moisture evaporate. Transfer mixture to large bowl and set aside. Wipe skillet clean.

Add 1 tablespoon butter to medium skillet and sauté onion and carrot over moderate heat. Add crayfish or shrimp. Increase heat to high and sauté 1-2 minutes. Add brandy and reduce heat. Cook 8 minutes. Add to Chantrelle mixture in large bowl.

Melt remaining butter in cleaned skillet over moderate heat. Salt and pepper each side of veal chops and pan fry about 4 minutes on each side. Press down to heat. Remove veal and keep warm.

Deglaze veal pan with stock, removing excess butter. Add cream and cook on moderate-high heat a few minutes. Strain sauce into large skillet. Add veal and Chantrelle/crayfish mixture. Heat through. Sprinkle with tarragon, if desired.

**SERVES: 8**

## INGREDIENTS

| | |
|---:|---|
| 8 | thick veal rib chops |
| 4 | tablespoons unsalted butter |
| 1 | pound Chantrelle mushrooms, cleaned salt to taste pepper to taste |
| 1 | clove garlic, pressed |
| 1 | tablespoon parsley, chopped |
| 1 | onion, finely chopped |
| 1 | carrot, chopped |
| 16 | crayfish or shrimp, peeled and deveined |
| ½ | ounce brandy or cognac |
| ⅓ | cup veal or other meat stock |
| ½ | cup heavy cream |
| 1 | tablespoon tarragon (optional) |

*Broccoli in Olive Nut Sauce, p. 137; Tournedos of Veal with Crayfish and Chantrelles, p. 135; Mediterranean Rice Pilaf, p. 137.*

# BROCCOLI
# IN OLIVE NUT SAUCE

Melt butter in small skillet. Sauté almonds, lemon juice, garlic, and olives in butter. Let stand 1 hour to blend flavors. *(May be refrigerated overnight.)*

Steam broccoli until tender and place in serving dish. Reheat Olive Nut Sauce and pour over broccoli. Serve immediately.

**SERVES:** 8

## INGREDIENTS

¼ pound butter
½ cup slivered almonds
3 tablespoons lemon juice
2 cloves garlic, crushed
¼ cup ripe olives, sliced
1 teaspoon lemon pepper
3 pounds fresh broccoli, trimmed

# MEDITERRANEAN
# RICE PILAF

*This is also a wonderful complement to shish kabobs, especially those using chunks of lamb or pork.*

Bring stock to boil in 1-quart saucepan. Combine remaining ingredients in medium saucepan. Pour in stock. Cover and cook over low heat 20 minutes or until all liquid is absorbed and rice is tender.

**SERVES:** 8

## INGREDIENTS

3 cups chicken stock
1 ½ cups white long grain rice, uncooked
4 tablespoons vegetable oil
⅔ cup seedless golden raisins
½ teaspoon turmeric
½ teaspoon curry powder
3 tablespoons soy sauce

## INGREDIENTS

**CAKE**

- 2 cups sugar
- ½ cup vegetable shortening
- 5 egg yolks
- 2 cups flour
- 1 cup buttermilk
- 1 small can shredded coconut
- 1 cup nuts chopped
- 1 teaspoon baking soda
- 5 egg whites, beaten until stiff

**ICING**

- 11 ounces cream cheese, softened
- 6 tablespoons butter, softened
- 1 teaspoon vanilla
- 1 ½ cups powdered sugar, sifted

  coconut for garnish

# ITALIAN CREAM CAKE

**FOR CAKE:**

Preheat oven to 350 degrees.

Cream sugar and shortening in large bowl. Add egg yolks. Alternately add flour and milk. Stir in coconut, nuts, and baking soda. Fold in egg whites. Blend.

Grease and flour three 9-inch round cake pans. Pour batter into pans. Bake 18-20 minutes. Let cool 10 minutes before removing from pans. Let cake cool completely before icing.

**FOR ICING:**

Beat cream cheese and butter in medium bowl. Add vanilla and stir. Add powdered sugar until mixture is thick but spreadable. Layer icing between layers of cake and top cake with remaining icing. Sprinkle with additional coconut, if desired.

**SERVES:** 8

*Try a garnish of colorful confetti coconut:*

*Combine water and different food colorings in several bowls. Add coconut and soak until it absorbs intensity of color desired. Drain and blot dry on paper towels.*

*...lian Cream Cake, p. 138;*
*...owflakes, this page.*

# SNOWFLAKES

Mix all ingredients in large pitcher. Pour over ice and serve.

**SERVES:** 8

## INGREDIENTS

8 ounces Hazelnut liqueur
4 ounces vodka
16 ounces whole milk

# The Tax Man Cometh:

## *A Champagne Dinner On A Beer Budget*

We Can't Promise You Champagne,
We Can't Promise You Caviar,
For As We All Knoweth,
The Tax Man Just Cometh!

But Join Us For Dinner,
Whether Rich Or Poor,
Good Company! Good Commiseration!
That We Can Assure!

Saturday the 16th of April

At the humble abode of
Linda and Jack Prewitt

✴ When? The day after April 15th of course. Bleary-eyed (we saw you racing to the post office at 11:45 p.m.) and broke?! Well, you may as well commiserate with friends — cheaply!

✴ For table decor, how about using IRS Forms taped together as a "placemat" with each guest's name written on the top line. Tie napkins with thick rubber bands and strew fake money across the table along with adding machine tape, calculators, yellow pads, and even a few pencils with the erasers chewed off!

✴ Although after April 15th some of us may be "mint-less" with respect to the green kind, Charlotteans will still have their "Mint." In 1936, the Mint Museum of Art, the first art museum in North Carolina, opened in Charlotte. Originally, it had been built as a branch of the U.S. Mint in Philadelphia to handle gold shipments from Carolina mines until the outbreak of the Civil War.

# The Tax Man Cometh:

## MENU
(Serves 6)

Faux Champagne
Counterfeit Caviar`a la South

*Wine suggestion:*
*Napa Valley*
*Sauvignon Blanc*

Avocado and Citrus Salad
with Rose Vinaigrette
*or*
Gorgonzola and Pecan Crunch Salad
with Hazelnut Vinaigrette

*Wine suggestion:*
*California*
*Monterey County*
*Chardonnay*

Lime-Grilled Chicken
with Black Bean Sauce
Summer Squash Shells With Bacon,
Onions, and Tomatillos
Green Chive Rice

Latticed Raspberry Crostada with
Cornmeal Lemon Crust
*or*
Rum Raisin Butterscotch
Phyllo Cheesecake

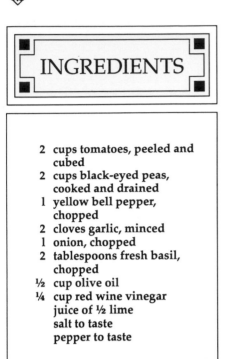

**INGREDIENTS**

2 cups tomatoes, peeled and cubed
2 cups black-eyed peas, cooked and drained
1 yellow bell pepper, chopped
2 cloves garlic, minced
1 onion, chopped
2 tablespoons fresh basil, chopped
½ cup olive oil
¼ cup red wine vinegar
 juice of ½ lime
 salt to taste
 pepper to taste

# COUNTERFEIT CAVIAR À LA SOUTH

Combine all ingredients.  Let sit 4 hours or overnight. Serve with favorite corn chips. *(Can be made 1 day ahead and refrigerated.)*

**SERVES:**  8

*Historically said to have magic powers, fresh garlic can be minced in a large quantity in the food processor and stored in oil (airtight) in the refrigerator up to 3 months.*

**INGREDIENTS**

**SALAD**

2 heads Bibb lettuce
3 large oranges, peeled and sectioned
3 large grapefruit, peeled and sectioned
1 ripe avocado, peeled and thinly sliced

**ROSE VINAIGRETTE**

¼ cup raspberry vinegar
¼ cup sugar
1 cup light olive oil
 freshly ground black pepper to taste

# AVOCADO AND CITRUS SALAD WITH ROSE VINAIGRETTE

**FOR SALAD:**

Divide lettuce evenly among six salad plates. Arrange orange and grapefruit sections in pinwheel design on top of each salad.  Drizzle with Rose Vinaigrette and garnish with avocado slices. *(Oranges and grapefruit may be prepared ahead and kept refrigerated until ready to serve.)*

**FOR ROSE VINAIGRETTE:**

Combine all ingredients in glass jar and shake well.

**SERVES:**  6

*An easy way to section fresh oranges without the white membrane is to cover the unpeeled oranges with boiling water and let stand for five minutes before peeling.*

*Vinegar derives its name from the French word "vinaigre" which means sour wine. However, vinegar can be made from anything that ferments.  Grains, beers, fruits, molasses, and cider make excellent vinegars.*

*Raspberry vinegar has a mild, sweet flavor and adds a lovely pink rose tint to salad dressings.*

# GORGONZOLA AND PECAN CRUNCH SALAD WITH HAZELNUT VINAIGRETTE

## FOR SALAD:

Wash and dry mixed lettuces. Tear into bite-sized pieces. Set aside. Combine a handful of lettuces with 1 ounce Gorgonzola cheese per person and place on individual salad plates. To serve, sprinkle Pecan Crunch on each salad and drizzle with Hazelnut Vinaigrette.

## FOR PECAN CRUNCH:

Sauté all ingredients in small saucepan until sugar caramelizes. Place pecan mixture in small paper bag to cool. Shake occasionally to break up pieces. *(Can be stored in airtight container up to 1 week or frozen up to 1 month.)*

## FOR HAZELNUT VINAIGRETTE:

Combine all ingredients, except oils, in medium bowl. Whisk in oils. *(Can be refrigerated up to 2 days.)*

**SERVES:** 6

## INGREDIENTS

### SALAD

- 7 cups mixed lettuces (e.g., red leaf, green leaf, bibb, butter)
- 6 ounces Gorgonzola cheese, crumbled

### PECAN CRUNCH

- ⅔ cup pecans, chopped
- 2 tablespoons butter
- 1 tablespoon sugar
- ½ teaspoon salt
  freshly ground black pepper to taste
- ¼ teaspoon cayenne pepper

### HAZELNUT VINAIGRETTE

- 1 teaspoon Dijon mustard
- 1 teaspoon orange zest, grated
- 2 teaspoons honey
- 2 tablespoons red wine vinegar
- 4 tablespoons orange juice
- ¼ cup hazelnut oil
- ¼ cup light olive oil

*In most salads, a variety of different types of lettuces can be substituted for iceberg. They have similar caloric content and nutritional value, offering a contrast in color, texture, and flavor.*

*Triple the pecan crunch recipe and freeze the unused portion. Take directly from the freezer and sprinkle on green leaf or vegetable salads.*

## INGREDIENTS

**CHICKEN**

- 6 boneless, skinless chicken breasts
- 4 ½ tablespoons fresh lime juice
- 3 tablespoons vegetable oil
- ¼ teaspoon cayenne pepper
- 6 medium cloves garlic, crushed

**BLACK BEAN SAUCE**

- 1 cup canned black beans, drained
- ½ cup unsweetened orange juice
- 2 tablespoons balsamic vinegar
- ¼ teaspoon salt
- ⅛ teaspoon black pepper
- 2 medium cloves garlic, crushed

**TOPPING**

- 3 cups water
- ½ cup red bell pepper, chopped
- 1 purple onion, coarsely chopped

  chopped fresh cilantro for garnish

# LIME-GRILLED CHICKEN WITH BLACK BEAN SAUCE

**FOR CHICKEN:**

Wash and dry chicken and place in ziplock bag. Combine next 4 ingredients in small bowl and blend thoroughly. Pour over chicken and marinate 8 hours or overnight. Grill chicken over moderate heat until no longer pink inside, basting with marinade.

To serve, spoon Black Bean Sauce onto platter and top with grilled chicken. Place Bell Pepper and Onion Topping over chicken and garnish with cilantro.

**FOR BLACK BEAN SAUCE:**

Combine all ingredients in food processor and process until smooth. Place in small saucepan and cook over moderate heat to thoroughly combine flavors (at least 30 minutes). *(Can be made 1 day ahead, refrigerated, and reheated prior to serving.)*

**FOR BELL PEPPER AND ONION TOPPING:**

Bring water to boil in medium saucepan. Add red pepper and onions and blanche 30 seconds. Drain and immediately plunge into ice water to stop cooking process. Set aside. *(Can be made 1 day ahead and refrigerated. Bring to room temperature or gently reheat before serving.)*

**SERVES:** 6

*True or False: The skin should be removed from chicken **before** baking or grilling rather than after in order to eliminate the most fat.*

*The answer is False! A study published in 1991 reported that skinning before cooking made no significant difference with respect to fat content.*

*Balsamic vinegar is very strong, pungent, and expensive. So use it sparingly!*

*A special product of Modena, Italy, it is made from reduced grape juice and then aged for years. For a flavorful pasta salad dressing, combine one-half distilled and one-half balsamic vinegar.*

# SUMMER SQUASH SHELLS WITH BACON, ONIONS, AND TOMATILLOS

Preheat oven to 350 degrees.

Steam squash. Let partially cool. Cut in half lengthwise. Scoop out pulp and place in medium bowl. Set shells aside. Add onions, tomatillos, cheese, and bacon to squash pulp and blend. Fill squash shells with pulp mixture and place in 9 x 13-inch baking dish. Sprinkle with bread crumbs and drizzle with melted butter. Bake 25-30 minutes. *(Shells can be stuffed and refrigerated overnight before baking.)*

**SERVES:** 6

*When shelling out the inside of the squash, lightly salt and press with paper towels. This will help to remove excess water to insure squash does not become soggy.*

*Tomatillos, popular in Latin American cooking, resemble small, firm green tomatoes encased in a papery husk. Their flavor is tart like a lemon or apple.*

*If fresh tomatillos are not available, canned tomatillos may be used (found in the Mexican section of most supermarkets) or one large tomato may be substituted.*

## INGREDIENTS

6 medium yellow squash, ends trimmed
½ cup green onions, chopped
3 small tomatillos, husked and chopped
¾ cup Monterey jack cheese, grated
5 slices bacon, cooked and crumbled
¾ cup bread crumbs
2-3 tablespoons butter, melted

# GREEN CHIVE RICE

Melt butter in large saucepan over moderate heat and sauté onion until softened. Add rice and cook 1 minute. Add chicken broth and orange juice and bring to boil. Cover, reduce heat, and simmer 10 minutes. Finely chop green beans in food processor. Add to rice mixture. Cover and simmer 7-10 minutes or until rice is tender and all liquid has been absorbed. Stir in chives, salt, and freshly ground pepper to taste. Serve immediately.

**SERVES:** 6

*The ritual of throwing rice at newly weds can be traced back to ancient Rome. It means, "Go forth and multiply."*

*When purchasing fresh chives, look for those with medium green ends. Dark green ends may indicate that they are over ripe.*

## INGREDIENTS

3 tablespoons butter
2 tablespoons onion, finely chopped
1 cup long grain white rice, uncooked
14 ½ ounces chicken broth
¼ cup orange juice
½ pound fresh green beans, trimmed
2 tablespoons fresh chives, chopped
½ teaspoon salt
freshly ground pepper

## INGREDIENTS

### RASPBERRY FILLING

3 cups fresh or frozen raspberries
½ cup turbinado or brown sugar
⅛ teaspoon ground cinnamon

### CORNMEAL LEMON CRUST

2 cups all purpose wheat flour
⅓ cup yellow cornmeal
1 teaspoon baking powder
½ teaspoon salt
½ cup turbinado or brown sugar
¾ cup chilled margarine, cut into small pieces
2 teaspoons lemon peel, finely grated
1 egg, lightly beaten
1 egg yolk, lightly beaten

powdered sugar for garnish

# LATTICED RASPBERRY CROSTADA WITH CORNMEAL LEMON CRUST

**FOR FILLING:**

Combine raspberries, sugar, and cinnamon in medium saucepan. Cover and bring to boil. Simmer 20 minutes, stirring occasionally, until mixture thickens. Transfer to small container and refrigerate.

**FOR CRUST:**

Preheat oven to 350 degrees.

Toss flour, cornmeal, baking powder, salt, and sugar in large bowl. Cut in margarine until mixture is crumbly, using pastry blender or 2 knives. Stir in lemon peel. Add egg and egg yolk and mix with fork. Sprinkle ⅔ of crumb mixture on bottom of 9-inch round tart pan with removable sides. Spoon in chilled berry mixture. Pat remaining crumb mixture into a square on floured surface. Cut into 9 even strips. Roll strips into ½-inch widths. Criss-cross strips over berry mixture, lattice fashion. Press ends against inside of crust. Bake 45-50 minutes or until golden brown. Cool 10 minutes on wire rack.

Dust with powdered sugar before serving.

**SERVES:** 8

*Blueberries or blackberries may be substituted for the raspberries.*

*The coarse, golden-colored crystals known as turbinado sugar have the rich flavor of molasses found in brown sugar. When using raw sugar, it should feel soft in consistency rather than hardened in the package to indicate a fresh product.*

# RUM RAISIN BUTTERSCOTCH PHYLLO CHEESECAKE

**FOR CRUST:**

Soak raisins in rum overnight. Cream butter and sugar in medium bowl until light and fluffy. Beat in egg. Gradually mix in flour. Cover and chill 2 hours.

Preheat oven to 325 degrees.

Grease and flour bottom and sides of 10-inch springform pan. Roll refrigerated dough out on lightly-floured surface to ¼- to ⅛- inch thickness. Cut out a 10-inch circle and fit into bottom of prepared pan. Brush each phyllo sheet with melted butter. Arrange sheets, buttered side up, over dough in pinwheel pattern, draping ends over sides of pan so that inside of pan is completely covered. Drain raisins and sprinkle over phyllo.

**FOR FILLING:**

Beat cream cheese in large bowl until smooth. Add sugar and flour and mix until smooth. Beat in eggs and yolk one at a time. Add whipping cream and stir just to incorporate. Pour into crust. Fold overhanging phyllo over filling, forming a jagged crown.

Bake cake until firm, about 70 minutes. Cool completely.

**FOR SAUCE:**

Melt butter in heavy, medium saucepan. Stir in sugar, cream, and corn syrup. Increase heat and bring to boil. Remove sauce from heat and add vanilla. Blend well. Place cake on large platter. Drizzle sauce over top. *(Sauce can be made ahead and reheated just before serving.)*

**SERVES:** 8

*Although delicate, phyllo dough (also spelled Filo) is actually very easy to work with if package directions are followed for handling. You will not regret using phyllo in this unusual cheesecake recipe when guests rave over the crisp, flaky crust and rich filling.*

**CRUST**

- ½ cup raisins
- 3 tablespoons dark rum
- ½ cup butter
- ⅓ cup sugar
- 1 egg
- 1 ½ cups all-purpose flour
- 10 sheets phyllo dough
- ¼ cup butter, melted

**FILLING**

- 32 ounces cream cheese, softened
- ½ cup sugar
- 2 tablespoons all-purpose flour
- 4 eggs, room temperature
- 1 egg yolk, room temperature
- ½ cup whipping cream

**SAUCE**

- 5 tablespoons butter
- 1 cup light brown sugar, firmly packed
- ⅓ cup whipping cream
- 2 tablespoons dark corn syrup
- 1 teaspoon vanilla

# Saturday Night At The Movies

## *Videos And Vittles For Six!*

Tickets please . . . .
to the All Favorites Film Festival
Exclusive Screening: Saturday, March 26
7:00 p.m.
Bring a video of your best-loved movie.
Tissues, popcorn, and dinner provided.

Regrets only
Sidney and Warren Webster
546-8079

✳ When North Carolinians sit down for a "Saturday Night at the Movies," chances are the video they are watching was filmed in their home state. North Carolina is the second largest film making state in the country after California. Blockbusters such as *The Fugitive*, *Dirty Dancing*, *Teenage Mutant Ninja Turtles*, and *Last of the Mohicans* were filmed in various locations here.

✳ For your own "Saturday Night At the Movies," ask friends to pick out and bring their favorite videos while you provide the food and the screen. Offer individual bags of peanut butter popcorn and white chocolate candy for munching during the movies.

✳ For dinner, set the table to include pictures of Hollywood stars, cut out from magazines and put in frames that can also be used as placecards. Match up the stars to the names of your "look-alike" guests. Cut strips of camera film to form napkin rings or place napkins in plastic sunglasses which can be worn during dinner and taken home as a party favor.

✳ North Carolina's appeal to film makers includes its mild 4-season climate and its variety of scenic and architectural locations.

✳ Other movies made here include the classic *Where the Lilies Bloom*, the off-beat *Blue Velvet*, the cult classic *Evil Dead II*, and the romantically funny *Bull Durham*.

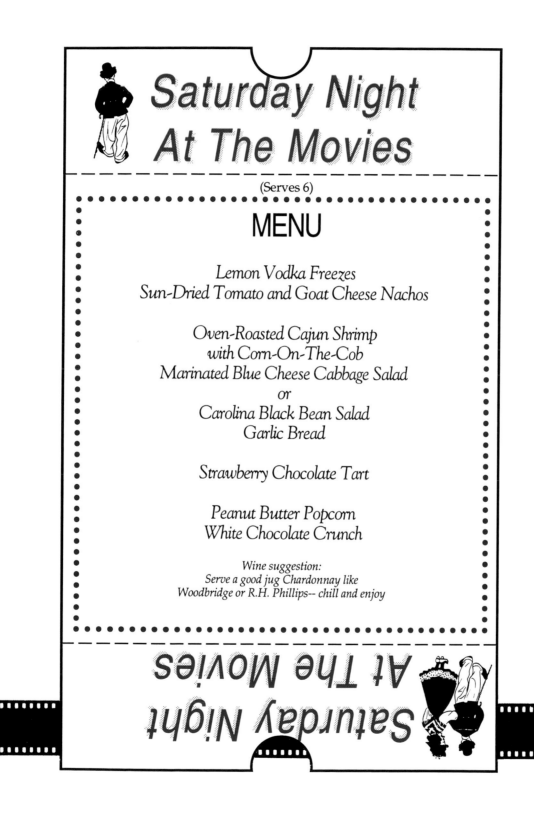

# Saturday Night At The Movies

(Serves 6)

## MENU

*Lemon Vodka Freezes*
*Sun-Dried Tomato and Goat Cheese Nachos*

*Oven-Roasted Cajun Shrimp*
*with Corn-On-The-Cob*
*Marinated Blue Cheese Cabbage Salad*
*or*
*Carolina Black Bean Salad*
*Garlic Bread*

*Strawberry Chocolate Tart*

*Peanut Butter Popcorn*
*White Chocolate Crunch*

*Wine suggestion:*
*Serve a good jug Chardonnay like*
*Woodbridge or R.H. Phillips-- chill and enjoy*

Saturday Night At The Movies

## INGREDIENTS

2 liter bottle 7-up
12 ounces frozen lemonade concentrate, thawed
1 pint vodka

## INGREDIENTS

4 ounces goat cheese
4 ounces sun-dried tomatoes, packed in olive oil, drained, and chopped
1 clove garlic, minced
⅛ teaspoon fresh black pepper
2 tablespoons fresh cilantro, chopped
8 ounces blue corn chips

cilantro sprigs for garnish

# LEMON VODKA FREEZES

Combine all ingredients in freezer container, stir, and freeze overnight. When ready to serve, stir again, and pour into pitcher.

**YIELD:** 16 drinks

# SUN-DRIED TOMATO AND GOAT CHEESE NACHOS

Preheat oven to 300 degrees.

Crumble goat cheese and toss with sun-dried tomatoes, garlic, pepper, and cilantro. Sprinkle on top of blue corn chips and bake 20 minutes until cheese is warmed through (cheese will not melt). Garnish with cilantro sprigs and serve immediately.

**SERVES:** 6

*Goat cheese, also known as chèvre (French for goat), is popular in many cuisines today, contributing its tangy flavor to salads, pizza, soufflés, and even nachos!*

*For variation, Feta cheese may be substituted in this recipe.*

*Packaged sun-dried tomatoes may be used instead of oil-packed. Simply reconstitute them according to package directions, soak them in olive oil several minutes, and then drain.*

*Oven-Roasted Cajun Shrimp with Corn-on-the-Cob, this page; Marinated Blue Cheese Cabbage Salad, p. 152.*

# OVEN-ROASTED CAJUN SHRIMP WITH CORN-ON-THE-COB

*This shrimp is authentic New Orleans style. It is also very messy so be sure to have plenty of paper napkins on hand. Cloth towels, dampened and warmed, are even better for cleaning sticky fingers, and the finger bowl has never really gone out of style.*

Preheat oven to 500 degrees.

Boil corn in water 5 minutes. Drain and cut ears in half. Place fresh shrimp and corn into large 4-inch deep roasting pan. Cut butter into 1-inch slices, placing on top of shrimp and corn. Combine remaining ingredients in small bowl and pour over shrimp and corn. Top with lemon slices. Bake 8-10 minutes or until shrimp turn pink, basting and turning shrimp often.

**SERVES:** 8

## INGREDIENTS

| | |
|---|---|
| 8 | ears corn |
| 4-5 | pounds large shrimp, unpeeled |
| 1 | cup butter |
| ¼ | cup olive oil |
| ¼ | cup Worcestershire sauce |
| ¼ | cup soy sauce |
| 2 | teaspoons salt |
| 2 | teaspoons pepper |
| 2 | cloves garlic, minced |
| 2 | tablespoons dried oregano |
| | cayenne pepper to taste |
| ½ | teaspoon Tabasco sauce or to taste |
| 4 | lemons, sliced |

## INGREDIENTS

1 medium head cabbage, shredded
4 green onions, chopped
1 cup mayonnaise
1 tablespoon horseradish
4 ounces blue cheese, crumbled
½ cup sour cream
2-3 tablespoons fresh lemon juice
salt to taste
pepper to taste
½ red bell pepper, sliced into thin strips
½ green bell pepper, sliced into thin strips

## INGREDIENTS

2 15-ounce cans whole hominy, drained
2 15-ounce cans black-eyed peas, drained
2 15-ounce cans black beans, drained
1 onion, chopped
2 ripe tomatoes, chopped
1 cup parsley, chopped
1 green bell pepper, chopped
1 yellow bell pepper, chopped
1 red bell pepper, chopped
1 16-ounce jar thick and chunky salsa
1 cup olive oil
½ cup vinegar
1 tablespoon Tabasco sauce
salt to taste
pepper to taste

# MARINATED BLUE CHEESE CABBAGE SALAD

Combine all ingredients, except red and green bell pepper strips, in large bowl. Cover and chill at least 2 hours or overnight. Just before serving, garnish with bell pepper strips. *(Can be made 1 day ahead.)*

**SERVES:** 6-8

# CAROLINA BLACK BEAN SALAD

*(This should be made 24 hours ahead.)*

Combine all ingredients in large bowl. Marinate 24 hours.

Adjust seasonings before serving.

**SERVES:** 8

*Hot Garlic Bread will round out this meal beautifully:*

*Garlic Bread*

6 *slices Italian bread*
3 *teaspoons fresh garlic, chopped*
*dash dried oregano*
*dash freshly ground pepper*
1 *tablespoon fresh parsley, chopped*
6 *tablespoons olive oil*

*Preheat broiler.*

*Place slices of bread in shallow baking pan. Spread each slice with chopped garlic, sprinkle with seasonings, and drizzle with olive oil. Place under broiler until bread is brown.*

*SERVES: 6*

*Hominy is dried field corn. Southern cooks use whole canned hominy, found in supermarkets, to flavor scrambled eggs, puddings, and casseroles. Mexican cooks use it to make tortillas, tamales, and masa (corn dough).*

*Did you know that canned beans are basically just as nutritious as the dried beans which you cook yourself?*

# STRAWBERRY CHOCOLATE TART

*This dessert is simply scrumptious.*

### FOR CRUST:

Combine all ingredients and work together to form dough ball. Cover with plastic wrap and chill for at least two hours. *(Dough can be stored in refrigerator up to 3 weeks.)*

Preheat oven to 375 degrees.

Pat dough into buttered and floured 10-inch tart shell, building up sides. Prick well. Bake 20 minutes or until crust is light brown. Let cool. *(The tart shell can be baked 1 day ahead of time, but the tart must be assembled the day of use.)*

### FOR FILLING:

Melt chocolate over double boiler. Whisk in melted butter and Kirsch. Add sugar and water and whisk until smooth. Pour into cooled tart shell.

While chocolate is still warm, place berries, tip up, on shell, working in a circular pattern from outside to inside until surface is covered.

### FOR GLAZE:

Whisk jelly and Kirsch together over medium heat until smooth. Brush warm glaze generously over all berries. Refrigerate at least 2 hours. Remove 1 hour before serving. Garnish with fresh mint sprigs.

**SERVES:** 8

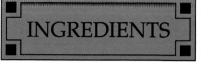

## INGREDIENTS

**CRUST**

- ½ cup sugar
- 1 ½ cups flour
- 1 cup butter, softened

**CHOCOLATE FILLING**

- 1 cup semisweet chocolate pieces
- 2 tablespoons butter, melted
- ¼ cup Kirsch liqueur
- ¼ cup powdered sugar
- 1 tablespoon water

- 2 pints strawberries, washed and stemmed

**GLAZE**

- ¼ cup red currant jelly
- 1 ½ tablespoons Kirsch liqueur

  mint sprigs for garnish

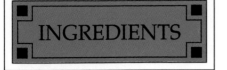

## PEANUT BUTTER POPCORN

½ cup butter
¼ cup creamy peanut butter
2 cups raisins
4 quarts popcorn
  salt to taste

Melt butter with peanut butter in small saucepan. Stir in raisins. Pour over popcorn and toss lightly. Add salt to taste.

**YIELD:** 4 ½ quarts

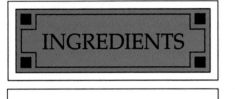

## WHITE CHOCOLATE CRUNCH

1 ½ pounds white chocolate
6 cups Rice Chex cereal
3 cups Cheerios cereal
2 cups pretzel sticks
2 cups cashews
12 ounces plain M&M's

Melt white chocolate over double boiler or in microwave. Mix together remaining dry ingredients in large bowl. Place dry ingredients in 2 flat baking pans. Pour chocolate over dry mixture and let harden in cool place. Break into bite-sized pieces and store in airtight container. *(Can be made 3 days ahead.)*

**SERVES:** 8

*You might want to double the recipe. No one can eat just one handful of this marvelous munchie!*

*Strawberry Chocolate Tart, p. 153; Peanut Butter Popcorn, p. 154; White Chocolate Crunch, p. 154.*

# Mom, I'm Coming Home!

## Please Fix All My Favorites

We got your report card --
you did quite well.
Of your accomplishments,
we love to tell.
No matter what happens,
you'll always be
that special little boy
to Dad and me.
your favorites are cooking
so come home soon.
Bring all your laundry;
we're preparing your room.

Next weekend at Mom's

Just call (collect)
to say you're coming.
Can't wait!

* "Mom, I'm Coming Home." It's a welcome phrase that those of us with out-of-town college students love to hear. A great way to say "We're proud of you," is with that special college student's favorite dishes. They're sure to evoke memories of happy times and the joy of family fellowship.

* North and South Carolina are blessed with an abundance of some of the nation's finest colleges and universities. For example, Davidson College in Davidson, North Carolina, was founded in 1837 as an institution to educate Southern men. Today, Davidson's enrollment is over 1500 men and women.

* Salem College in Winston-Salem was established in 1766 in the historic village of Salem. It was started by the Moravians who held a strong belief in the education of women — an innovative view for this time in American history.

* The University of North Carolina (UNC) - Chapel Hill is the oldest public university in the nation and is now part of a 16 campus system which includes the Queen City's own UNC at Charlotte, which enrolls nearly 16,000 students.

* And, of course, everyone has heard of Duke!

## *Mom, I'm Coming Home!*
(Serves 6)

## MENU

Heirloom Meat Loaf
Fresh Green Beans
with Cucumber Topping
Silver Queen Corn Pudding
Peanut Butter Ice Cream Pie
with Hot Fudge Sauce

*Wine selection:*
*French Beaujolais*
*(This light, refreshing red wine should be served cool.)*

or
Wrightsville Beach Grilled Fish
Squash, Onion, and Sweet Pepper Kabobs
Fettucine Alfredo
or Risotto alla Milanese
Fresh Peach Cobbler
with Cinnamon Ice Cream

*Wine selection:*
*Fetzer "Barrel Select" Chardonnay*
*(A consistent medal winner year after year –*
*this wine is an excellent value.)*

or
Breakfast For Dinner!
Apple-Puffed Pancake
or Fruit-Stuffed French Toast
Fried Sausages or Crispy Bacon

Giant Chocolate Chip Cookie Pizza

## INGREDIENTS

**MEAT LOAF**

- 1 pound ground chuck
- ⅓ pound lean ground pork
- ¾ cup saltine crackers, finely crushed
- ½ medium onion, grated
- 1 teaspoon salt
- ¼ teaspoon black pepper
- 4 ounces tomato sauce
- 4 ounces whole milk
- 1 egg, beaten
- 1 teaspoon Worcestershire sauce
- ¼ teaspoon Tabasco sauce
- 1 teaspoon baking powder
  salt to taste
  pepper to taste
  bacon strips

**TOMATO SAUCE**

- 4 ounces tomato sauce
- 1 tablespoon prepared mustard
- 1 tablespoon brown sugar
- 1 tablespoon fresh lemon juice
- 1 tablespoon white vinegar
- 1 teaspoon salt
- ½ cup water

# HEIRLOOM MEAT LOAF

**FOR MEAT LOAF:**

Preheat oven to 350 degrees.

Mix all ingredients, except bacon, in large bowl. Place in greased loaf pan and cover with bacon strips. Bake loaf 1½ hours, basting with tomato sauce after first 15 minutes of baking. Continue basting every 30 minutes until all sauce is used. Remove bacon strips prior to serving.

**FOR TOMATO SAUCE:**

Whisk all ingredients in small bowl.

**SERVES:** 6

*This is one of the best meat loaf recipes around.*

*For an extra fine meat loaf, ask your butcher to triple grind the ground chuck and ground pork together.*

*Some people say that leftover meat loaf sandwiches are even better than the dinner meal! Just remember that it's easier to slice the loaf when cold.*

# FRESH GREEN BEANS WITH CUCUMBER TOPPING

**FOR GREEN BEANS:**

Wash beans and trim ends. Snap into 2-inch pieces. In medium saucepan, add enough water to partially cover beans. Add chopped onion and seasonings. Cover and simmer 30 minutes or until tender. Drain and place in serving dish. Pour cucumber topping over beans and serve.

**FOR CUCUMBER TOPPING:**

Combine cucumber and onion in small bowl. Add seasonings and dressing. Mix well. (*Make 4-8 hours ahead and refrigerate.*)

**SERVES:** 6

*Some Southerners, especially with old family recipes like this one, may cook their vegetables anywhere from 30 minutes to an hour. If you prefer crisp green beans, steam them 3-5 minutes.*

*To preserve the vitamin content and enhance the taste, try sautéeing the green beans in a small amount of oil before adding liquid to them.*

## INGREDIENTS

**GREEN BEANS**

- 1 pound fresh green beans
- 1 large Vidalia or sweet onion, chopped
- 2 chicken boullion cubes
- ¼ teaspoon sugar
  fresh dill to taste
  chopped fresh parsley to taste
  salt to taste

**CUCUMBER TOPPING**

- 2 large cucumbers, chopped
- 1 large Vidalia or sweet onion, chopped
  fresh dill to taste
  chopped fresh parsley to taste
- ½ cup Italian dressing

# SILVER QUEEN CORN PUDDING

Preheat oven to 300 degrees.

Grate corn on corn scraper or cut kernels from cob with sharp knife (but be sure to go over cob several times with knife). Combine corn with melted butter in large bowl. Beat eggs and fold into corn. Add remaining ingredients and pour into 2-quart casserole dish. (*Can be made 1 day ahead up to this point and refrigerated.*) Place in pan of water and bake 1 hour 15 minutes or until set in center. (*Can be baked 1 day ahead and re-heated.*)

**SERVES:** 6

*Silver Queen corn is a sweet white corn grown in the Carolinas.*

*Remember these easy tips to tell if corn is fresh: the butt end should be moist and white, not dry or brownish. Look at the small, narrow leaves that protrude near the top of the ear. These will become brittle and shrivel if corn is not fresh.*

*Never cook corn in salted water. This will toughen the kernels. Instead, add a couple of tablespoons of milk to the water to enhance the sweet flavor.*

## INGREDIENTS

- 8 ears fresh white corn, husks and silk removed
- ½ cup butter, melted
- 5 eggs
- 1 pint half-and-half
- ½ tablespoon sugar
  salt to taste
  pepper to taste

## INGREDIENTS

**CRUST**

⅓ cup creamy peanut butter
½ cup light corn syrup
2 cups Rice Krispies cereal

**PIE**

2 pints ice cream (vanilla or chocolate), softened

**HOT FUDGE SAUCE**

1 cup sugar
3 tablespoons cocoa
1 tablespoon dark corn syrup
½ cup milk

1 tablespoon butter
½ teaspoon salt
½ teaspoon vanilla
¾ cup nuts, chopped (optional)

# PEANUT BUTTER ICE CREAM PIE WITH HOT FUDGE SAUCE

**FOR CRUST:**

Blend peanut butter with corn syrup. Add Rice Krispies and stir until evenly coated. Press mixture into 8-inch pie pan to form a crust. Refrigerate 1 hour.

**FOR PIE:**

Fill peanut butter crust with softened ice cream. Re-freeze to harden. *(Can be made ahead and placed in freezer up to 1 week.)* Just prior to serving, spoon hot fudge over each piece of pie.

**FOR HOT FUDGE SAUCE:**

Combine sugar, cocoa, corn syrup, and milk in medium saucepan and bring to boil. Add butter, salt, vanilla, and nuts, stirring constantly. Serve hot.

**SERVES:** 6

# WRIGHTSVILLE BEACH GRILLED FISH

*Wrightsville Beach is a charming "family" beach frequented by Carolinians who treasure miles of sandy shoreline and few high-rise condominiums or hotels. It is located near Wilmington, North Carolina, which was once a major seaport and where the U.S.S. North Carolina is still docked.*

Combine all ingredients, except fish, in small bowl. Mix well. Pour over fresh fish and allow to marinate 4-24 hours in refrigerator. When ready to grill, remove fish from marinade. Grill until fish flakes with fork, about 10 minutes cooking time for each inch of thickness.

**SERVES:** 6

### INGREDIENTS

2 tablespoons fresh lemon or orange juice
¼ cup olive oil
2 tablespoons sesame oil (optional)
1 teaspoon salt
¼ teaspoon freshly ground pepper
½ teaspoon ground ginger
1 clove garlic, chopped
2 teaspoons soy sauce
2 pounds fresh orange roughy, grouper, or swordfish

# SQUASH, ONION, AND SWEET PEPPER KABOBS

*Fresh or dried basil, oregano, tarragon, or parsley are excellent herbs to combine with olive oil for basting grilled vegetables or fish.*

Thread squash, onion, and pepper pieces alternately on skewers. *(May be made ahead up to this point and refrigerated.)* Place skewers on platter and drizzle lightly with olive oil. Sprinkle generously with pepper and seasoned salt (or seasonings of your choice). Grill on preheated grill (moderate-high) approximately 6-8 minutes per side or until vegetables are tender. Baste with olive oil and seasonings.

**SERVES:** 6

### INGREDIENTS

1 pound small yellow squash, sliced into ¾-inch slices
1 onion, quartered
3 small red bell peppers, cut into 1-inch squares
⅓ cup olive oil
   freshly ground pepper to taste
   seasoned salt to taste
6 wooden or metal skewers

## INGREDIENTS

½ cup unsalted butter
1 cup cream
1 cup sour cream
1 pound fettucine, cooked and drained
1 cup freshly grated Parmesan cheese
½ cup fresh chives, finely chopped
   salt to taste
   freshly ground pepper to taste

# FETTUCINE ALFREDO

Melt butter in medium saucepan over low heat; add cream. Stir sour cream in container until smooth; add to butter and cream mixture. Heat until very hot but do not allow to boil. Add pasta, cheese, chives, salt, and pepper. Serve immediately in heated serving bowl.

**SERVES:** 6

## INGREDIENTS

8 tablespoons butter
1 medium onion, finely chopped
1 cup white wine
2 cups Arborio rice
1 teaspoon salt
¼ teaspoon freshly ground pepper
¼ teaspoon saffron (optional)
4-5 cups chicken broth
1 cup freshly grated Parmesan cheese or to taste

# RISOTTO ALLA MILANESE

Melt 5 tablespoons butter in 4-quart saucepan over moderate heat. Add chopped onion and cook until transparent. Add wine and cook over high heat until evaporated. Add rice and season with salt and pepper. Stir in saffron, if desired, and 2 cups of chicken broth. Cook until almost all liquid has evaporated; gradually add remaining broth. Reduce heat and continue to cook, uncovered, stirring frequently, 20-25 minutes. Add remaining butter and Parmesan cheese to taste. Serve immediately.

**SERVES:** 6

*Before adding saffron to this dish, pour about 1 tablespoon of hot (not boiling) water over the saffron and mix. This will enhance the flavor and color.*

*Three tablespoons of fresh lemon juice is a zesty substitution if saffron is not on hand.*

*Risotto is best if made with short-grain Italian Arborio rice, which has a distinctive creamy texture without being mushy. The key to success with Arborio is stirring the rice continuously as the liquid is absorbed.*

*White rice may be substituted for the Arborio rice.*

# FRESH PEACH COBBLER WITH CINNAMON ICE CREAM

*An amazingly easy way to peel peaches is to submerge them in boiling water (off the heat) and let them stand 3 minutes before draining. Peel skin with a firm downward pull.*

*For cinnamon ice cream, start with your favorite variety of vanilla ice cream. Allow to soften and stir in ground cinnamon to taste. Refreeze until firm.*

Combine flour and salt in food processor. Add frozen butter (in pieces) and shortening. Process in short bursts until mixture is consistency of small peas. Add ice water and continue to process until dough begins to form a ball. *(Dough can be made ahead, wrapped in wax paper, and refrigerated 1 day.)*

Preheat oven to 450 degrees.

Roll out dough into large circle, dusting with flour as necessary. Lightly grease 2-quart baking dish. Place dough over dish and gently conform to sides, allowing excess to hang over. Place sliced peaches in dish, cover with sugar, and dot with 3 tablespoons butter. Fold excess dough back over peaches. Place in oven, adjust temperature to 425 degrees, and bake 45 minutes. Cool and serve with cinnamon ice cream.

**SERVES:** 6

## INGREDIENTS

1 ½ cups flour
¼ teaspoon salt
5 tablespoons butter, frozen
½ cup shortening, frozen
5 tablespoons ice water
4-5 cups fresh peaches, peeled and sliced
¾ cup sugar
3 tablespoons butter

cinnamon ice cream (see sidebar)

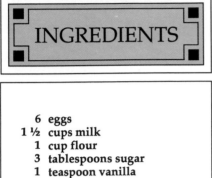

## INGREDIENTS

6 eggs
1 ½ cups milk
1 cup flour
3 tablespoons sugar
1 teaspoon vanilla
½ teaspoon salt
½ teaspoon cinnamon
½ cup butter
3 Granny Smith apples, peeled and sliced thin
2-3 tablespoons brown sugar

warm maple syrup

# APPLE-PUFFED PANCAKE

Preheat oven to 425 degrees.

Blend eggs, milk, flour, sugar, vanilla, salt, and cinnamon in large bowl. Batter may remain lumpy. Add butter to 12-inch quiche pan or 9 x 13-inch baking dish and melt in oven. Add apple slices to heated pan and return to oven until butter sizzles (do not let butter burn). Remove from oven and immediately pour batter over apples. Sprinkle with brown sugar. Bake in center of oven 20 minutes or until puffed and brown on top. Serve with warm maple syrup.

**SERVES:** 6

*Sausage patties or links, Canadian bacon slices, or crisp bacon strips should accompany this recipe.*

*To pan fry bacon, remember to start with a cold, heavy skillet and cook slowly over low heat. A lid that fits inside the skillet to cover the bacon will avoid spattering and keep the edges from curling.*

*To microwave bacon, overlap strips on a paper towel-lined baking dish. Microwave on 100% power 1 minute for each slice of bacon up to 6 slices. Add 30 seconds for each additional slice. Bacon will become crisp as it stands.*

For a child away at school, send a Giant Chocolate Chip Cookie Pizza as a "care package" during exams or anytime. Mail the cookie in a cardboard pizza box purchased from your child's favorite pizzeria. Guaranteed to make him or her the most popular student in the dorm!

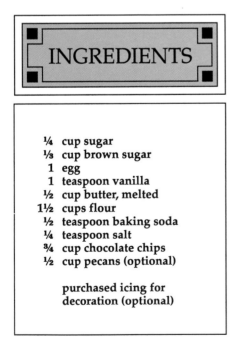

## INGREDIENTS

¼ cup sugar
⅓ cup brown sugar
1 egg
1 teaspoon vanilla
½ cup butter, melted
1 ½ cups flour
½ teaspoon baking soda
¼ teaspoon salt
¾ cup chocolate chips
½ cup pecans (optional)

purchased icing for decoration (optional)

# GIANT CHOCOLATE CHIP COOKIE PIZZA

Preheat oven to 350 degrees.

Combine first 4 ingredients in large bowl. Add melted butter and beat well with mixer. Add next 3 ingredients and mix well. Stir in chocolate chips and pecans, if desired.

Spread with greased hand into greased 12-inch disposable aluminium pizza pan. Bake 15-18 minutes. Allow to cool and then, if desired, decorate with purchased icing for your favorite occasion.

*For the beloved dog of the family!*

*BOW WOW*
*DOG BISCUITS*

2 ½ cups whole wheat flour
½ cup wheat germ
½ cup powdered milk
½ teaspoon salt
½ teaspoon garlic powder
1 teaspoon brown sugar
½ cup margarine, softened
1 egg, beaten
2 tablespoons beef or
  chicken broth
½ cup ice water
  crumbled bacon or
  cheese, optional

*Preheat oven to 350 degrees.*

*Combine first 6 ingredients in large bowl. Cut in margarine until mixture becomes crumbly. Add egg, broth, and water and mix well. Add bacon or cheese, if desired. Add additional ice water, if needed, to form ball.*

*On floured surface, roll out or pat dough to ½-inch thickness. Cut with cookie cutter (preferably bone shaped). Place on cookie sheet lined with foil and lightly oiled.*

*Bake 30 minutes or until dark brown and hard at edges.*

*YIELD: 25-30 small biscuits*

# FRUIT-STUFFED FRENCH TOAST

Place buttered bread slices in lightly-greased baking dish. Scoop out just the center of each slice of bread, forming a well.

## FOR FRUIT STUFFING:

Combine powdered sugar, cream cheese, vanilla, rum or rum extract, and fruit preserves in small bowl. Mix well. Divide fruit mixture evenly into well of each bread slice.

## FOR BATTER:

Combine eggs, buttermilk, vanilla, and powdered sugar in medium bowl. Pour mixture over bread slices. *(Allow to set overnight in refrigerator up to this point.)*

Preheat oven to 350 degrees.

Bake French toast 45 minutes. Garnish each plate with fresh fruit and serve with warm maple syrup.

**SERVES:** 6

**INGREDIENTS**

1  small loaf French bread,
   sliced thick and buttered

**FRUIT STUFFING**

⅓  cup powdered sugar
4  ounces cream cheese
½  teaspoon vanilla
1  tablespoon rum, or
1  teaspoon rum extract
1  tablespoon fruit preserves

**BATTER:**

4  eggs
1 ½  cups buttermilk
½  teaspoon vanilla
2  teaspoons powdered sugar

   fresh fruit for garnish
   warm maple syrup

# The GOURMETS Are Coming !
# The GOURMETS Are Coming !
## Supper Club Dinner For Eight

CALLING ALL
PAMPERED PALATES!
The Sunday Night Supper Club
Presents Its Fourth Annual
"Gathering of the Gourmets"
Sunday, March 27th, 7:30 p.m.
Lois and Brooks Hoak
6382 Richardson Drive
Regrets: 365-8842

⁂ Gourmet societies, which continue to grow in epidemic proportions, join groups of people who enjoy sharing fine food together. Each group, however, is distinctive in its formation.

⁂ Beth Tartan, a North Carolinian who wrote the charming *Instant Gourmet and How to Form a Gourmet Society*, relates that one gourmet society may decide to have two kinds of meals, informal mini-dinners and black tie dinners. Another society may decide to put on ethnic meals after research on a given country. Yet another group may meet to cook only three or four weekends a year, planning meals and wines in exquisite detail. An entirely different society may adhere to firm rules, including no flowers on the table to interfere with the bouquet of the wine.

⁂ Tartan offers a few suggestions for forming (or joining) a society:

Select the group carefully. "The cult of gourmets, like marriage, is not to be entered into lightly."

Make up your group of people with similar degrees of appreciation. One group may enjoy only spaghetti and chianti. Another group might start with spaghetti but intend to eventually make their own pasta.

Six people are enough; 12 is a good number.

After the meal, do a critique of it.

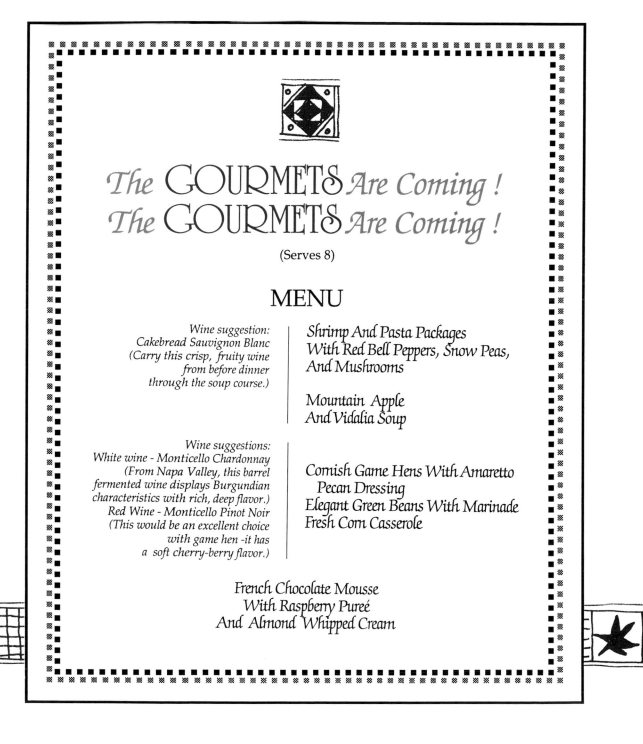

# The GOURMETS Are Coming !
# The GOURMETS Are Coming !

(Serves 8)

## MENU

*Wine suggestion:*
*Cakebread Sauvignon Blanc*
*(Carry this crisp, fruity wine*
*from before dinner*
*through the soup course.)*

Shrimp And Pasta Packages
With Red Bell Peppers, Snow Peas,
And Mushrooms

Mountain Apple
And Vidalia Soup

*Wine suggestions:*
*White wine - Monticello Chardonnay*
*(From Napa Valley, this barrel*
*fermented wine displays Burgundian*
*characteristics with rich, deep flavor.)*
*Red Wine - Monticello Pinot Noir*
*(This would be an excellent choice*
*with game hen -it has*
*a soft cherry-berry flavor.)*

Cornish Game Hens With Amaretto
Pecan Dressing
Elegant Green Beans With Marinade
Fresh Corn Casserole

French Chocolate Mousse
With Raspberry Pureé
And Almond Whipped Cream

## INGREDIENTS

| | |
|---|---|
| 1 | pound angel hair pasta, cooked and drained |
| 48 | medium shrimp, cooked and peeled |
| 1 | cup butter |
| 1 | red bell pepper, finely chopped |
| ½ | pound mushrooms, sliced |
| ½ | cup green onions, diced |
| ½ | cup fresh parsley, chopped |
| 3 | tablespoons soy sauce |
| 2 | teaspoons Worcestershire sauce |
| 2 | teaspoons garlic salt |
| ½ | teaspoon powdered ginger dash Tabasco |
| 10 | ounces chicken broth |
| 15 | fresh snow peas, cut lengthwise into slivers |

# SHRIMP AND PASTA PACKAGES WITH RED BELL PEPPERS, SNOW PEAS, AND MUSHROOMS

Preheat oven to 350 degrees.

Cut 8 squares of aluminum foil, approximately 12 x 12 inches. Divide pasta evenly among squares, mounding it in center. Place 6 shrimp on top of each mound of pasta.

Melt butter over moderate heat in large skillet and add all remaining ingredients, except chicken broth and snow peas. Stir 2 minutes. Add chicken broth and stir another 3 minutes. Divide mixture evenly and pour over each pasta portion. Top with slivered snow peas. With each foil square, bring two opposite sides together over top and fold down until almost touching shrimp. Seal the two open ends, forming a square package. *(Can be made 1 day ahead up to this point, refrigerated, and brought to room temperature before baking.)*

Put packages on large baking sheet and bake 20 minutes. Remove from oven and place on individual plates. Prior to serving, cut an X in top of foil and lift edges away.

**SERVES:** 8

*These delightful hors d'oeuvres should be served in their foil packages during the wine or cocktail hour. They are also marvelous as a first course.*

# MOUNTAIN APPLE AND VIDALIA SOUP

## INGREDIENTS

Combine beef stock and apple cider in large stock pot. Bring to light boil. Add bay leaf, thyme, black pepper, and salt. Simmer 1 hour.

Melt butter in medium skillet and sauté onions until soft. Add sugar and continue cooking onions until brown. Deglaze skillet with sherry and add mixture to beef stock. Simmer another hour.

To serve, ladle soup into oven safe soup bowls and top each bowl with croutons, grated Parmesan cheese, and slice of Gruyère cheese. Broil 1-2 minutes or until cheese melts and browns. Garnish with diced apples before serving.

**SERVES:** 8

- 1 quart beef stock
- 12 ounces apple cider
- 1 bay leaf
- ½ teaspoon thyme
- 1 teaspoon coarsely ground black pepper
- ½ teaspoon salt
- 2 tablespoons butter
- 1 pound Vidalia onions, thinly sliced
- ½ teaspoon sugar
- ⅓ cup dry sherry
  garlic croutons
  Parmesan cheese, freshly grated
  Gruyère cheese, thinly sliced

- ⅔ cup red apple, finely diced and chilled, for garnish

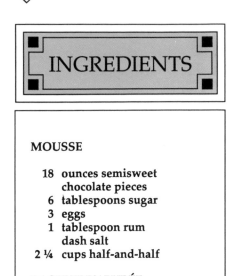

## INGREDIENTS

**MOUSSE**

| | |
|---|---|
| 18 | ounces semisweet chocolate pieces |
| 6 | tablespoons sugar |
| 3 | eggs |
| 1 | tablespoon rum |
| | dash salt |
| 2 ¼ | cups half-and-half |

**RASPBERRY PURÉE**

| | |
|---|---|
| 1 | pint fresh raspberries |
| ½ | cup sugar |
| ½ | cup water |
| 2 | tablespoons Grand Marnier |

**WHIPPED CREAM**

| | |
|---|---|
| 1 | cup heavy cream |
| 2 | tablespoons sugar or to taste |
| ½ - 1 | teaspoon almond extract |

# FRENCH CHOCOLATE MOUSSE WITH RASPBERRY PURÉE AND ALMOND WHIPPED CREAM

**FOR MOUSSE:**

Place all ingredients, except half-and-half, in blender. Scald half-and-half and add, while hot, to blender. Blend on high 1 minute. Pat down any bubbles with rubber spatula and let mixture stand for several minutes. Carefully pour into glass serving bowl. Refrigerate, covered, at least three hours or overnight. (*May be prepared 2 days ahead and refrigerated.*)

To serve, place healthy dollop of chocolate mousse on each plate. Pass Raspberry Purée and Almond Whipped Cream separately.

**FOR RASPBERRY PURÉE:**

Bring all ingredients to boil in medium saucepan. Purée in blender or food processor and strain through fine sieve. Pour into small serving dish and refrigerate, covered, several hours or overnight. (*May be prepared 2 days ahead and refrigerated.*)

**FOR ALMOND WHIPPED CREAM:**

Whip cream until stiff peaks form. Add sugar to taste. Stir in almond extract. Spoon into serving dish. (*May be prepared several hours ahead, covered, and refrigerated; at serving time rewhip lightly if necessary.*)

**SERVES:** 8

*This velvety rich chocolate mousse takes but minutes to prepare and is always a winner. It is perfect for the host or hostess to serve from the dining room table. Or, it may also be poured into 8 pot de crème cups or individual soufflé dishes.*

If you're not a "gourmet" but have a group of good friends who simply enjoy being together, a "supper club," popular in the South, may be for you. Either the hostess prepares the entire dinner or, even more fun, assigns dishes for a potluck feast.

So start a supper club. Whether it meets once a month or once a year, it's guaranteed to be a delightful evening for everyone.

# The Kids Are Back In School !

## *Rejoice Over Dinner With Friends*

Parents Rejoice

Com Celebrate!

I'ts A Bak 2 Scool Party!

U R Invited to
Irene and Starke Throckmorton's
September 9 at 7:00 p.m.

Regrets
5 4 3 - 6 7 8 9
Wear your children's school colors

✳When the children head back to school, not only is it time to rejoice over a sumptuous meal with friends, but perhaps, as well, it's time for the grown-ups to head off for a few days of "fall break."

✳A favorite spot for Carolinians, especially those with a penchant for the links, is Pinehurst. Pinehurst, North Carolina is known to many golfers as the "Heaven of Golf." Even British golf writer Henry Longhurst has compared it favorably with Old St. Andrews in Scotland. Pinehurst Country Club boasts five golf courses designed by Donald Ross, with the legendary number two course being one of the most challenging and beautiful courses in the world.

✳In addition, Pinehurst can boast that it was called home for a time by "Little Sure Shot," Annie Oakley. She and her husband gave exhibitions and shooting lessons after her world-renowned prowess as a sharpshooter began to wane in 1915. When Annie came to Pinehurst, she was 55 but she could still plug brass dollars with a rifle as fast as her husband could throw them in the air!

✳Table decorations for your "Kids Are Back In School" dinner could include flash cards, crayons, and red apples scattered about; a lunch box filled with fall flowers; napkins tied with kids' shoelaces; and childishly scrawled placecards.

# The Kids Are Back In School !

( Serves 6 )

## MENU

Blinis and Caviar
*Wine suggestion:*
*Roederer Estate Sparkling Wine*
*(A wonderful example of California bubbly -*
*toasty - creamy - rich.)*

Tomato-Orange Soup

Spinach and Pear Salad
with Sugared Dates and Pecans
*Wine Suggestion:*
*Sancerre*
*(A delicate, crisp French white wine-*
*excellent with salads; choose from any of*
*the better producers, such as Thomas.)*

Seasoned Pork Roast with Mushroom Sauce
Baked Acorn Squash
Wild Rice Medley with Toasted Pine Nuts,
Dried Apricots, and Golden Raisins
Cool-Rise Whole Wheat Bread
or Bakery-Fresh Cloverleaf  Rolls
*Wine suggestion:*
*Robert Mondavi Pinot Noir (One of the best.)*

Apple Cranberry Tart
Rum-Buttered Lemonade
with Cinnamon Sticks

## INGREDIENTS

1 ¾  cups milk
1  package active dry yeast
¼  cup warm water
½  teaspoon sugar
¼  cup buckwheat flour
1  cup all purpose flour
2  eggs, separated
¼  teaspoon salt
1 ½  tablespoons sour cream
1 ½  tablespoons melted butter

Garnishes:

    caviar
    melted butter
    sour cream
    chopped hard-boiled egg
    chopped onion
    lemon wedges

# BLINIS AND CAVIAR

Scald milk and cool to warm.

Place yeast in water and add sugar. Let sit 5 minutes and then stir to dissolve yeast.

Combine 1 cup milk, yeast mixture, both flours, egg yolks, salt, sour cream, and melted butter in medium bowl. Mix thoroughly. Beat egg whites until stiff and gently fold into batter. Allow to rest 30 minutes. Stir in remaining ¾ cup milk.

Lightly grease large skillet. Fry blinis over moderate-high heat, using 3 tablespoons of batter for each. Cook until golden and turn. Keep blinis, covered, in 200 degree oven until serving time.

To serve blinis, place garnishes in individual dishes with tiny spoons. Have guests roll up warm blinis with favorite garnishes inside.

**SERVES:** 6

*The 3 best known kinds of sturgeon caviar are Beluga, Osetra, and Sevruga. Beluga, the highest prized caviar, comes from the Caspian Sea, bordering Russia and Iran.*

*Serving good sturgeon caviar is out of the question for most budgets. Inexpensive lumpfish can be used but the taste will be compromised. We have good reviews of the golden caviar from the Great Lakes whitefish. It is reasonably priced and native to the United States.*

*Tomato-Orange Soup, p. 177.*

# TOMATO-ORANGE SOUP

Cut tomatoes in half and squeeze to remove seeds. Combine tomatoes with next 8 ingredients in large saucepan and bring to boil. Stir in salt and simmer on low heat 1 hour. Do not purée. Strain through sieve into large bowl. Rinse saucepan, return to heat, and melt butter. Stir in flour and add strained soup. Simmer 5-10 minutes to thicken. Add sugar to taste. *(Soup may be refrigerated up to 2 days or frozen up to 2 months.)*

When ready to serve, stir in cream and blend well. Garnish each serving with chopped tomato, orange peel strips, and tarragon sprigs. Can be served hot or cold.

**SERVES:** 6

*Canned tomatoes can be substituted if fresh tomatoes are not in season.*

## INGREDIENTS

2 pounds fresh tomatoes
1 medium carrot, thinly sliced
1 medium onion, thinly sliced
1 bay leaf
½ lemon, thinly sliced with rind removed
1 large orange, thinly sliced with rind removed
5 peppercorns
4 cups chicken stock
1 cup fresh orange juice
salt to taste
3 tablespoons butter
3 tablespoons flour
sugar to taste
¾ cup whipping cream

chopped tomato, orange peel strips, and tarragon sprigs for garnish

# SPINACH AND PEAR SALAD WITH SUGARED DATES AND PECANS

Combine spinach, pears, dates, and pecans in large bowl. Toss with dressing. Add salt and pepper to taste.

**FOR SALAD DRESSING:**

Mix all ingredients in jar and refrigerate. *(May be prepared 2 days ahead.)*

**SERVES:** 6

*Try adding an edible flower or two to your salad greens for a colorful presentation. Be sure to choose flowers grown without pesticides or chemicals. Nasturtiums, chive blossoms, and pansies (all easily grown at home) make beautiful garnishes.*

## INGREDIENTS

1 pound fresh spinach, washed and trimmed
2 pears, sliced
½ cup sugared dates, chopped
¾ cup pecans, chopped

**SALAD DRESSING**

¼ cup fresh orange juice
¼ cup wine vinegar
½ cup salad oil
1 tablespoon brown sugar
1 teaspoon garlic salt
½ teaspoon curry powder
salt to taste
pepper to taste

## INGREDIENTS

### PORK ROAST

    2  teaspoons fresh rosemary,
       crushed
    1  teaspoon black
       peppercorns, crushed
    ½  teaspoon Szechuan
       peppercorns (optional)
  1 ½  teaspoons dried leaf sage
    ¾  teaspoon thyme
    1  teaspoon kosher salt
    ½  teaspoon coriander seed
    1  teaspoon minced garlic
    4  pound pork loin roast,
       rolled and tied

### MUSHROOM SAUCE

    2  tablespoons olive oil
    3  cloves garlic, minced
    1  shallot, sliced
    1  pound mushrooms, cut in
       quarters (discard stems)
    1  cup dry sherry or Madeira
    1  cup chicken stock
    1  tablespoon soy sauce
    2  teaspoons cornstarch
       dissolved in 1 tablespoon
       water
       salt to taste
       pepper to taste

## INGREDIENTS

    3  acorn squash
    1  onion, sliced
    1  teaspoon olive oil
    1  teaspoon butter, melted
       cinnamon to taste
       salt to taste
       pepper to taste

# SEASONED PORK ROAST WITH MUSHROOM SAUCE

### FOR PORK ROAST:

Preheat oven to 425 degrees.

Mix all spices together in small bowl. Coat roast with spices, patting to keep on meat. Insert meat thermometer and place roast on rack in shallow baking pan. Bake 30 minutes. Turn temperature down to 350 degrees and continue to bake until center temperature registers 165 degrees, about 25 minutes per pound. Slice and serve with Mushroom Sauce.

### FOR MUSHROOM SAUCE:

Heat oil in medium skillet. Sauté garlic and shallot 1 minute. Add mushrooms and sauté 4-5 minutes or until tender. Add sherry and simmer until most of liquid evaporates. Add chicken stock and soy sauce. Bring to boil. Stir in cornstarch mixture and simmer 2-3 minutes. Season with salt and pepper, if desired.

**SERVES:** 6

# BAKED ACORN SQUASH

Preheat oven to 350 degrees.

Slice squash in half crosswise and remove seeds. Slice into rings, leaving on skin. Arrange in 9 x 13-inch baking dish and layer onion on top. Mix olive oil and butter and drizzle over squash. Sprinkle with cinnamon, salt, and pepper to taste. Bake 45 minutes. Baste with juices before serving.

**SERVES:** 6

*Other wonderful seasonings to use with pork are anise, brown sugar, cilantro, dill, honey, saffron, and tarragon.*

---

*Kosher salt is about half as salty in taste as table salt and is preferred by some cooks for rubbing into meats because of its coarse-grained texture.*

---

*This rich mushroom sauce enhances any fried or grilled meat — filet mignon, pork chops, even open-faced hamburgers.*

*If you like, double the amount of olive oil and butter and add sliced baby carrots, zucchini, and summer squash during last 20 minutes of baking.*

# WILD RICE MEDLEY WITH TOASTED PINE NUTS, DRIED APRICOTS, AND GOLDEN RAISINS

*The literal translation of Basmati is "Queen of Fragrance" — a befitting name for this aromatic rice.*

*Kashi is a 5-grain mix found in the cereal section of health-food stores. If not readily available, white rice can be substituted.*

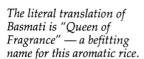

Combine chicken stock, both rices, and Kashi in medium saucepan. Cover and bring to boil over high heat. Reduce heat and simmer until rice is just cooked through, 20-30 minutes. Strain any remaining liquid. Add pine nuts, apricots, raisins, and celery to cooked rice. Mix well and serve.

**SERVES:** 6

## INGREDIENTS

| | |
|---|---|
| 3 | cups chicken stock |
| ½ | cup wild rice |
| ½ | cup Basmati rice |
| ½ | cup Kashi |
| 1 | cup toasted pine nuts |
| 1 | cup dried apricots, chopped |
| ½ | cup golden raisins |
| 1 | cup celery, finely chopped |

*Seasoned Pork Roast, p. 178; Baked Acorn Squash, p. 178.*

*Seasoned Pork Roast with Mushroom Sauce, p. 178; Baked Acorn Squash, p. 178; Wild Rice Medley with Toasted Pine Nuts, Dried Apricots, and Golden Raisins, this page.*

*Seasoned Pork Roast, p. 178; Baked Acorn Squash, p. 178;*
*Bakery-Fresh Cloverleaf Rolls, p. 181.*

# COOL-RISE WHOLE WHEAT BREAD

*Heavenly-smelling from the oven, this bread is wonderful smothered with any of our flavored butters: Cinnamon Honey Butter (p. 257); Herb Butter (p. 203); Orange Honey Butter (p. 13); or Strawberry Honey Butter (p. 13).*

*For Bakery-Fresh Cloverleaf Rolls, start by preparing the dough for Hot Butter Croissants (p. 203).*

*After the dough has rested overnight in the refrigerator, simply pinch off small pieces and shape into smooth 1-inch balls. Dip into melted butter and then place 3 balls in each cup of a greased standard muffin pan.*

*Bake at 400 degrees until golden brown (12-15 minutes).*

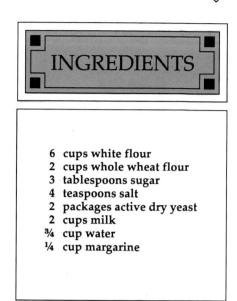

**INGREDIENTS**

| | |
|---|---|
| 6 | cups white flour |
| 2 | cups whole wheat flour |
| 3 | tablespoons sugar |
| 4 | teaspoons salt |
| 2 | packages active dry yeast |
| 2 | cups milk |
| ¾ | cup water |
| ¼ | cup margarine |

Combine both flours in large bowl. Mix 2 ½ cups of flour mixture with sugar, salt, and yeast. Set aside.

Heat milk, water, and margarine in medium saucepan to 120-130 degrees. (Can be done in microwave.) Gradually add liquid to flour/yeast mixture. Beat with electric mixer 2 minutes. Add 1 ½ cups more flour. Beat 2 minutes and gradually stir in remaining flour.

Turn out dough onto floured board and knead 8-10 minutes until smooth and elastic. Cover with plastic wrap and towel. Let rest 20 minutes. Divide dough into 2 loaves and put into greased pans. Brush tops with oil, cover with plastic wrap, and refrigerate up to 24 hours.

Preheat oven to 400 degrees.

Allow loaves to come to room temperature. Bake 40 minutes. Cover with aluminum foil tent for softer crust. Remove tent last 10 minutes to brown.

**YIELD:** 2 loaves

*Apple Cranberry Tart, p. 183.*

# APPLE CRANBERRY TART

### FOR CRUST:

Preheat oven to 400 degrees.

Cream butter, sugar, and salt in large bowl until smooth. Add flour and mix just until combined. Divide dough into 3 equal portions. Wrap 2 portions well and refrigerate or freeze for later use. (*Dough can be refrigerated 2 weeks or frozen 3 months.*)

Pat remaining dough into greased 10 x 2-inch tart pan, keeping crust at even thickness throughout. Bake until crust is golden brown, approximately 15 minutes.

### FOR FILLING:

Preheat oven to 350 degrees.

Fan apple slices on baked crust in tart pan. Add cranberries in between apple slices.

### FOR TOPPING:

Whisk eggs and sugar together lightly. Add cream and milk. Continue to whisk until smooth. Pour over fruit, tapping pan to settle mixture on bottom. Sprinkle with cinnamon sugar and allspice. Bake 1 hour or until custard is set. Garnish with dollop of sweetened whipped cream.

**SERVES:** 6

# RUM-BUTTERED LEMONADE

Combine all ingredients, except cinnamon sticks, in large saucepan. Stir over moderate heat until mixture is hot. Serve with cinnamon stick stirrers, if desired.

**YIELD:** 8 drinks

*The best apples for a pie are Granny Smith, Gravenstein, Peppin, Greening, and Northern Spy.*

*North Carolina is one of the top apple-producing states in the nation.*

*Cherokee Indians used cranberries for dye and war paint as well as food.*

*One average lemon will normally yield about 2 ½ tablespoons of juice.*

## INGREDIENTS

**CRUST**

- 1 pound butter
- 1 ¼ cups sugar
- 1 teaspoon salt
- 5 ½ cups cake flour

**FILLING**

- 4-5 large apples, peeled, cored, and sliced
- 1 cup cranberries

**TOPPING**

- 6 eggs
- 1 cup sugar
- 2 cups heavy cream
- 1 cup milk
  cinnamon sugar to taste
- ½ teaspoon allspice

  sweetened whipped cream for garnish

## INGREDIENTS

- 1 cup sugar
- ½ teaspoon lemon peel, finely grated
- 1 cup lemon juice
- ½ cup light rum
- 6 cups water
- 3 tablespoons butter
  cinnamon sticks (optional)

# The Best Housewarming Gift :

## Dinner In A Basket For Those On The Move

The movers are gone
and they've hung all the pictures
so let's christen their home
with fun, food, and fixtures.
Saturday, May 6
7:00 p.m.

A housewarming dinner for Missy and Fitzhugh
at their new address.
Please bring a whimsical (or practical,
if you must!) gift for their home.

✳ Basket menus can be a wonderful way to welcome new neighbors and babies or to help out with sick friends.

✳ An hour after the moving van arrives, you will be a welcome sight with a thermos of coffee and a few disposable cups (but wait till later to visit)!

✳ A few days afterward, you will earn undying gratitude and lasting friendships when you delight the new neighbors with "dinner in a basket." Remember to pack all the food in disposable containers such as the aluminum ones found in the grocery store. If you desire to go the extra mile, tuck in colorful cloth napkins and placemats or dish cloths. Remember to include a note, "Nothing to Return" and complete recipe cards for the delectables found in the basket. If young children are a part of the household, slip in a bag of jelly beans or gummy bears and a new coloring book with bright new crayons.

✳ Include some treasured lists for out-of-town newcomers. Provide a spiral notebook covered with pretty paper that shares useful secrets: phone numbers for the best take-out/delivery pizza, who to call to sign up for T-ball or the swim club, where to buy homemade bread and pasta, the best laundry in town . . . and so on. If you want to be considered an angel of mercy, include names and phone numbers of your most trusted baby-sitters!

## The Best Housewarming Gift:
(Serves 4-6)

## MENU

**For A Spring / Summer Move:**
Seafood Salad with Honeydew Cantaloupe
in Poppyseed Dressing
or
Chilled Vegetable Rotini Salad
with Sesame Chicken

Tomatoes Stuffed with Artichoke Hearts,
Onions, and Bacon

White Chocolate Brownies
*Wine suggestion:*
*Preston - Cuvee de Fume*
*(This Sonoma County Sauvignon Blanc*
*has been barrel fermented to give a rich*
*tropical fruit yet dry taste.)*

**For An Autumn / Winter Move:**
Monterey Jack Chicken Lentil Chili
or
Lasagne Beef Crowns with Pesto Cream Sauce

Minted Green Bean and Onion Salad

Honey Pecan Squares
*Wine suggestion:*
*Dry Creek Zinfandel*
*(The spicy finish on this red wine blends nicely*
*with chili or lasagne.)*

**INGREDIENTS**

**SALAD**

1   pound fresh lump crabmeat, picked over and cleaned
1   pound medium shrimp, cooked, peeled, and deveined
1   cup celery, diced
6   green onions, chopped
1   red bell pepper, finely diced
2   small cantaloupes, seeded and cubed
1   large honeydew melon, seeded and cubed

1   bunch red leaf, green leaf, or Boston lettuce
2   limes, quartered

**DRESSING**

¼   cup honey
¼   cup cider vinegar
2   tablespoons prepared mustard
3   tablespoons poppyseeds
½   small white onion, finely grated
1   teaspoon salt
¾   cup vegetable oil

# SEAFOOD SALAD WITH HONEYDEW AND CANTALOUPE IN POPPYSEED DRESSING

**FOR SALAD:**

Combine all ingredients, except lettuce and limes, in large bowl. Cover and refrigerate until ready to serve. *(Can be made early in day.)* At time of serving, pour enough dressing over salad mixture to coat thoroughly. Mound salad mixture on lettuce-lined platter. Garnish with lime quarters.

**FOR DRESSING:**

Combine all ingredients, except oil, in glass jar with lid and blend well. Slowly add oil and shake vigorously. Chill. *(Can be made 3 days ahead.)*

**SERVES:** 6

*Cooked chicken breast cubes are just as delicious with this light and sweet salad.*

*When purchasing melons, select those that seem moderately hollow when thumped. If too hollow, the melon may not be fully developed, while a too solid melon may indicate it is full of water.*

*Try this poppyseed dressing with virtually any green or fruit salad — always adored!*

# CHILLED VEGETABLE ROTINI SALAD WITH SESAME CHICKEN

**INGREDIENTS**

Combine sesame seeds and ¼ cup oil in small skillet. Cook over moderate-low heat, stirring until seeds are coated. Combine sesame seed mixture, remaining ¼ cup oil, soy sauce, vinegar, sugar, salt, and pepper in small bowl. Cool. Pour over cooked pasta. Add chicken and toss gently. Cover and chill at least 6 hours. *(Can be made 1 day ahead up to this point.)* At time of serving, add parsley, green onion, and spinach. Toss.

**SERVES:** 6

¼ cup sesame seeds
½ cup vegetable oil
⅓ cup soy sauce
⅓ cup wine vinegar
2 tablespoons sugar
½ teaspoon salt
¼ teaspoon pepper
8 ounces vegetable rotini pasta twists, cooked and drained
3 cups chicken breast, cooked and shredded
½ cup fresh parsley, chopped
¾ cup green onion, thinly sliced
8 cups fresh spinach leaves, torn into bite-sized pieces

*"For centuries when youngsters asked the inevitable, 'Where did I come from, Mommy?' — the answer was likely to be, 'From the parsley bed, my dear.' "*
—*English folk tale*

*For a vegetaria[n] this chili, you n[eed] one can of whit[e] beans and one [can of] beans for the ch[...]*

# TOMATOES STUFFED WITH ARTICHOKE HEARTS, ONIONS, AND BACON

**INGREDIENTS**

Combine artichoke hearts, celery, onions, and mayonnaise in medium bowl. Cover and refrigerate until ready to use. *(May be prepared one day ahead up to this point.)*

Peel and scoop out tomatoes. Allow to drain. Stuff with artichoke mixture. Sprinkle crumbled bacon on top of each. Serve on bed of lettuce leaves.

**SERVES:** 6

2 cups canned artichoke hearts, drained and coarsely chopped
½ cup celery, chopped
½ cup green onions (including tops), chopped
1 cup mayonnaise
6 medium tomatoes
3 slices bacon, cooked and crumbled

lettuce leaves

*When selecting tomatoes ideal for stuffing, be sure they are not overripe. They should be more firm than those you would typically purchase for a tossed salad.*

*Gingerbread People, pp. 268-269; Citrus Cheesecake, p. 270; Brandy Snaps with Cream Filling, p. 268; Creamy Pecan Tartlets, p. 272; Peppermints, p. 273.*

# HOLIDAY AND BUFFET ENTERTAINING

*Hot Butter Croissants, p. 203; Garlicky Accordian Potatoes,
p. 202; Lobster-Stuffed Tenderloin of Beef, p. 199;
Asparagus, Leek, and Tomato Compote, p. 201.*

# ASPARAGUS, LEEK, AND TOMATO COMPOTE

**INGREDIENTS**

| | |
|---|---|
| 4 | ripe tomatoes |
| 40 | asparagus spears, washed and trimmed |
| 3 | medium leeks, white part only |
| 3 | tablespoons butter |
| ½ | pound bacon, cut into ½-inch slices, cooked and drained |
| | salt to taste |
| | pepper to taste |

*If money is no object for your "Movable Menu," and host houses are scattered throughout the city, consider hiring a limo to transport guests from one house to the next.*

Bring large pot of water to boil over high heat. Using a fork, hold each tomato in boiling water 15-20 seconds to help remove peel. Finish peeling with knife. Seed and slice peeled tomatoes and cut into ½-inch thick pieces.

Let water return to boil. Plunge asparagus into water and cook 3 minutes. Remove, place in colander, and rinse under cold water briefly. Drain and cut into ¾-inch pieces.

Clean leeks well and cut into 4 pieces lengthwise and then into ¾-inch pieces diagonally. Plunge leeks into boiling water and cook 2 minutes. Remove, place in colander, and rinse under cold water briefly. Drain well. *(Recipe may be prepared early in day up to this point. Refrigerate vegetables in large covered bowl.)*

Melt butter in large skillet over moderate heat. When butter begins to foam, add asparagus, tomatoes, leeks, and bacon. Cook 3 minutes and place in serving dish. Season with salt and pepper to taste. Serve immediately.

**SERVES:** 10

## INGREDIENTS

10 medium baking potatoes, peeled
1 cup butter, melted
3 tablespoons olive oil
2 cloves garlic, minced
 salt to taste
 pepper to taste
6 ounces Parmesan cheese, freshly grated

# GARLICKY
# ACCORDIAN POTATOES

Preheat oven to 375 degrees.

Thinly slice each potato ¾ of the way through crosswise, carefully leaving bottom of potato whole.

Combine butter, olive oil, and garlic in medium shallow bowl. Roll potatoes in butter mixture. Place potatoes in large shallow roasting pan. Pour remaining butter mixture over potatoes. Season with salt and pepper.

Bake potatoes, basting frequently, until tender and golden, about 1 ½ hours.

Sprinkle with Parmesan cheese just before serving. *(Can be baked earlier in day and reheated just before serving.)*

**SERVES:** 10

*Remember the phrase, "An apple a day keeps the doctor away"? Well, the same holds true for garlic! Recent medical studies show that eating 3-6 cloves of garlic a day will substantially lower cholesterol, prevent hardening of the arteries, and reduce the risk of cancer. Just keep plenty of breath mints on hand!*

## INGREDIENTS

4 sprigs fresh rosemary, at least 4 inches each
4 cups new potatoes, cut into quarters
4 tablespoons butter, melted
4 tablespoons olive oil
 salt to taste
 pepper to taste
½ teaspoon curry powder (optional)

# ROSEMARY
# NEW POTATOES

Preheat oven to 350 degrees.

Remove rosemary leaves from woody stem. Toss rosemary leaves with rest of ingredients in large bowl. Place mixture in large casserole dish and bake 45 minutes, stirring occasionally.

**SERVES:** 10

*"Are you going to Scarborough Fair? Parsley, sage, rosemary, and thyme. Remember me to the one who lives there. She once was a true love of mine."*
 —*Scarborough Fair*
 *Paul Simon, 1965*

# HOT BUTTER CROISSANTS

Dissolve yeast and 1 teaspoon sugar in 1 cup warm water. Set aside.

Combine shortening, ½ cup sugar, and 1 cup boiling water. Mix and cool to lukewarm. Add dissolved yeast and stir in beaten eggs. Sift together flour and salt and add to yeast mixture. Cover and refrigerate overnight.

Using ¼ of dough at a time, roll out a circle ¼ inch - ½ inch thick on lightly-floured surface. Cut circle into 8 pie-shaped wedges. Starting with wide end, roll up each wedge jelly-roll fashion to form a crescent shape. Place on cookie sheet, cover lightly with waxed paper, and let rise in warm place until doubled in size, about two hours.

Preheat oven to 400 degrees.

Brush croissants with melted butter and bake 10 minutes or until golden. *(Can be frozen after baking and reheated before serving.)*

**YIELD:** 24 rolls

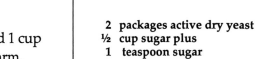

## INGREDIENTS

    2  packages active dry yeast
    ½  cup sugar plus
    1   teaspoon sugar
    2  cups water
    1  cup shortening
    2  eggs, well beaten
    6  cups flour
    2  teaspoons salt
    ½  cup butter, melted

# ENGLISH TOFFEE

Grease large cookie sheet with sides. Heat brown sugar and butter in large saucepan over moderate heat to the hard-to-crack stage (300 degrees on candy thermometer), about 15 minutes. Stir constantly. Pour onto cookie sheet and immediately lay chocolate bars on toffee mixture. As chocolate melts, spread to smooth and sprinkle almonds on top. Cool in refrigerator and break into pieces. *(Can be stored in airtight container in refrigerator 1 week.)*

**YIELD:** 3 pounds

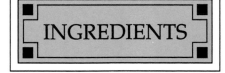

## INGREDIENTS

    1  16-ounce box brown
       sugar
    2  cups butter
   12  ½-ounce milk chocolate
       bars
    1  4-ounce package slivered
       almonds

*For herb-buttered croissants, brush dough with the following herb butter before rolling into crescent shape.*

*Herb Butter*
½  *cup butter, softened*
2  *tablespoons chives, chopped*
1  *tablespoon fresh parsley, chopped*

*Combine all ingredients in small bowl.*

# CHOCOLATE CRESCENTS WITH INDIVIDUAL CHEESECAKES IN STRAWBERRY SAUCE

## CHOCOLATE CRESCENTS

4 ounces sweet baking chocolate
4 ounces semisweet chocolate
⅓ cup cold water
8 eggs, separated
1 cup sugar
¼ cup unsweetened cocoa, sifted

## INDIVIDUAL CHEESECAKES

24 ounces cream cheese, softened
1 cup sugar
3 eggs
1 teaspoon vanilla

## STRAWBERRY SAUCE

20 ounces frozen unsweetened strawberries, thawed
4 tablespoons sugar
2 tablespoons lemon juice
2 tablespoons Grand Marnier

sliced strawberries for garnish

### FOR CHOCOLATE CRESCENTS:

Preheat oven to 350 degrees.

Oil bottom of jelly roll pan (15 ½ x 10 ½ x 1-inch). Cut pastry paper to fit pan plus extend 1 inch over sides. Heat chocolates with water in top of double boiler until melted. Let cool.

Lightly beat egg yolks in large bowl. Gradually add sugar and beat until thick. Stir in melted chocolate.

Beat egg whites in small bowl until stiff peaks form. Carefully fold egg whites into chocolate mixture. Spread batter evenly in lined pan and bake 20 minutes. Remove from oven and let cool 30 minutes. Dust top of cake with sifted cocoa. Cover top with wax paper, then cookie sheet, and invert. Cut crescent shapes from cake using cookie cutter. Store in airtight container until ready to use. *(Can be prepared 2 days ahead.)*

*Sauce Design: To make a string of hearts, place drops of heavy cream in a line around outer edge of sauce. Draw toothpick through the center of the string of drops, shaping each into a heart.*

### FOR CHEESECAKES:

Preheat oven to 350 degrees.

Mix cream cheese and sugar in large bowl. Add eggs one at a time, beating well. Add vanilla. Pour batter into cupcake pans. Place in large pan of warm water. Bake 30 minutes. Immediatley cover and chill until ready to unmold. To unmold, cut around edges of cupcakes with knife. Hold bottom of cupcake pans in warm water 1 minute to loosen cakes from pan. Turn out onto waxed paper.

### FOR STRAWBERRY SAUCE:

Process all ingredients, except Grand Marnier, in blender or food processor until smooth. Strain and discard seeds. Stir in Grand Marnier and refrigerate, covered, until cold. *(Can be prepared 2 days ahead.)*

To serve, nap individual dessert plates with thin layer of strawberry sauce. Top with 1 chocolate crescent and 1 cheesecake on each plate and serve. Garnish with strawberries and serve.

**SERVES:** 10

*English Toffee, p. 203; Chocolate Crescents with Individual
Cheesecakes in Strawberry Sauce, p. 204.*

# What Are Your Roots?

## An Ethnic Dinner For Eight

You must have been a beautiful baby!

Get out your old scrapbooks; call Mom if you need,
Choose a prized baby picture for your friends to see.
We'll dine among chatter of family roots and old times
An evening of laughter, good food, and good wine.

An Ethnic Dinner
Saturday, August 27 7:30 p.m.
Hosted by Brentley and Tommy Harper
101 Pinewood Road
Please bring a baby picture of yourself.

* Host your friends to a "What Are Your Roots" potluck party. Everyone brings a dish which heralds from their "roots." All guests must bring a baby picture to put on display — can the baby be matched with the adult? Decorate the table with flags from different countries, trinkets, dolls, and anything with an international or ethnic flavor.

* The roots of many inhabitants of Waccamaw, James, Johns, Wadmalaw, Edisto, St. Helena, and Hilton Head Islands in South Carolina are of ethnic origin. They can be traced directly to the west coast countries of Africa.

* The dialect, Gullah, spoken on these islands has remained intact almost 300 years. Even as late as 1932, there were inhabitants on some of the islands that had never visited the mainland.

* The communication age in which we live has played a role in making the Earth "a small, small world." Countries seek to communicate and learn about each other. Through this education comes understanding and friendship. For example, Charlotte shares a unique relationship with the city of Voronezh in Russia. Voronezh became Charlotte's "Sister" City in June 1991. Residents of both localities now visit together, and learn about each other's culture, history, and business climate.

206

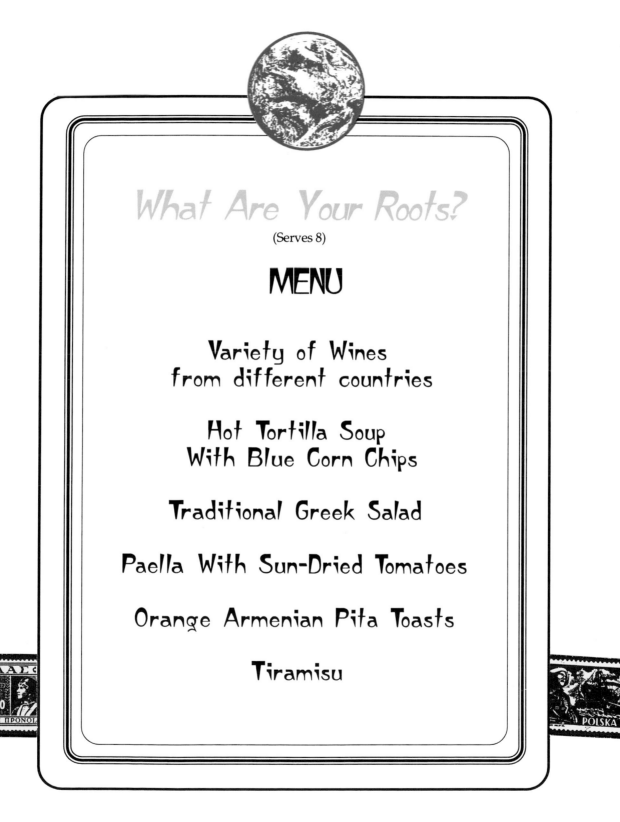

# What Are Your Roots?

(Serves 8)

## MENU

Variety of Wines
from different countries

Hot Tortilla Soup
With Blue Corn Chips

Traditional Greek Salad

Paella With Sun-Dried Tomatoes

Orange Armenian Pita Toasts

Tiramisu

## INGREDIENTS

- ¼ cup vegetable oil
- 12 corn tortillas (6-inch), cut into ¼-inch wide strips
- ¼ cup sherry
- ½ Spanish onion, finely chopped
- 1 teaspoon fresh or canned jalapeño, chopped
- 1 teaspoon garlic, minced
- 2 pints chicken stock
- 5 fresh or canned tomatillos, chopped
- ¼ cup fresh cilantro, chopped
- ¼ teaspoon cumin
- ¼ teaspoon white pepper
- 3 teaspoons chicken-flavored soup base

- 1 thinly sliced avocado for garnish (optional) blue corn tortilla chips for garnish

# HOT TORTILLA SOUP WITH BLUE CORN CHIPS

Heat oil in large skillet over high heat and fry tortilla strips 15-30 seconds until golden. Drain on paper towels. Add sherry to large pot and sauté onion, jalapeño, and garlic. Reduce heat and add chicken stock, tomatillos, cilantro, and spices. Simmer 20 minutes.

Process tortilla strips in blender. Add soup mixture and continue to process until puréed. Reheat if necessary. Pour into bowls and garnish with avocado slices, if desired. Serve with blue corn tortilla chips.

**SERVES:** 8

*Created by an L.A. chef, this soup is a favorite among the stars!*

*Blue corn is one of the oldest strains of corn grown in North America. Held sacred by ancient Native American civilizations, its striking blue color derives from natural plant pigments in the corn.*

*To serve hot tortilla chips (or recrisp stale ones), simply heat in the microwave 15-30 seconds.*

# CREATE A MENU

*Be creative! Make up your own menu for a special occasion using your favorite recipes.*

| Occasion: | | |
|---|---|---|
| Recipe Title | | Page |
| | | |
| | | |
| | | |
| | | |
| | | |
| | | |
| | | |

# TRADITIONAL GREEK SALAD

Combine tomatoes, zucchini, cucumbers, olives, onion, and feta cheese in large 3-quart bowl and toss. Add artichoke hearts, reserving marinade.

Combine reserved marinade, vinegar, pepper, and oregano in small bowl or jar and mix well. Pour over vegetables and toss. Cover and chill at least 8 hours, stirring occasionally. *(Should be prepared 1 day ahead.)*

**SERVES:** 8

*This salad is amazingly light and refreshing!*

*Kalamata (also spelled Calamata) olives are black Greek olives packed in vinegar. Available in the specialty section of most supermarkets, they add a tangy, salty flavor to salads, pasta sauces, and stews.*

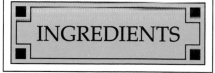

## INGREDIENTS

2 large tomatoes, cut into wedges
1 large zucchini, cut into julienne strips
2 large cucumbers, sliced
1 cup Kalamata olives, pitted
1 medium sweet or purple onion, sliced into rings
¾ cup feta cheese, crumbled
1 6-ounce jar marinated artichoke hearts, undrained
¼ cup balsamic vinegar
¼ teaspoon fresh black pepper
1 ½ teaspoons oregano

# PAELLA WITH SUN-DRIED TOMATOES

Heat oil in large skillet or Dutch oven over moderate heat. Cut chicken into bite-sized pieces and sauté until brown, about 10 minutes. Add onion, bell pepper, and garlic and sauté 3 minutes. Add rice, broth, tomatoes, wine, oregano, and thyme. Bring to boil. Reduce heat and simmer 20 minutes or until liquid is almost absorbed. Stir in shrimp and peas and simmer 4-6 minutes. Season with salt and pepper. Serve immediately.

**SERVES:** 8

*Traditional Spanish Paella also includes saffron threads (½ teaspoon added to the broth) to impart a rich golden color and exceptional flavor to the rice. Sausages, clams, and mussels may be added to the Paella during the last 15 minutes of cooking.*

## INGREDIENTS

1 ½ tablespoons olive oil
8 boneless chicken breast halves
1 ½ cups onion, chopped
1 ¼ cups green bell pepper, chopped
3 cloves garlic, minced
2 cups long grain rice
4 cups chicken broth
1 ¾ cups sun-dried tomatoes, chopped
1 ¼ cups dry white wine
1 ¼ teaspoons oregano
1 ¼ teaspoons thyme
1 ¼ pounds medium shrimp, peeled
1 cup frozen peas, thawed salt to taste pepper to taste

# Buon Appetito !

## A Gourmet Pizza Fest

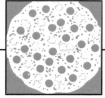

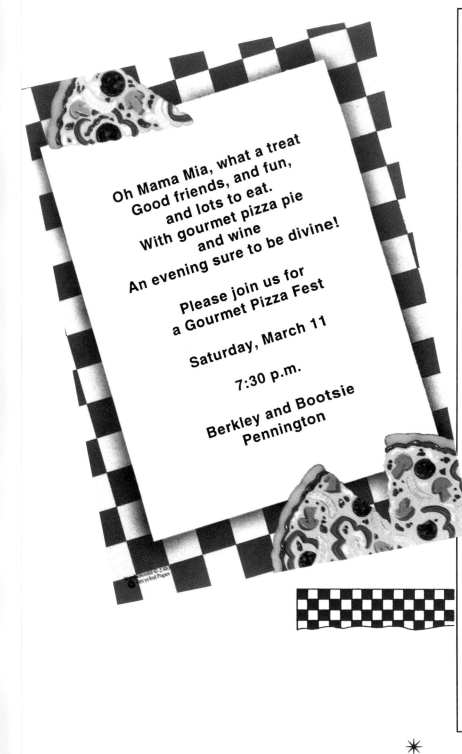

Oh Mama Mia, what a treat
Good friends, and fun,
and lots to eat.
With gourmet pizza pie
and wine
An evening sure to be divine!

Please join us for
a Gourmet Pizza Fest

Saturday, March 11

7:30 p.m.

Berkley and Bootsie
Pennington

✳ Believe it or not, pizza has actually been a part of the Italian diet since the Stone Age. The first pizzas were baked under stones in the fire and then seasoned. Plato even mentions pizza in *The Republic*.

✳ Table decor for your Pizza Fest should capture the colors of Italy — red, white, and green. Place tri-colored pasta in different size glass jars and tie with raffia and ribbon. Arrange in the center of the table, and, at the end of the evening, give each guest a jar with a recipe tied to the ribbon.

✳ Set the mood! Take old wine bottles and place different colored candles (such as red, green, orange, and yellow) in each. Light the candles and lightly blow the wax so that it melts and falls down the sides of the bottles. Repeat until each color has been used on each bottle.

✳ Not all of the pizzas listed in the menu would be used to serve the 10 people here. Probably 3 would do very nicely. But it was too difficult to choose, and variety is, as they say, the spice of life! So enjoy, and, don't forget, pizza (cut into small squares) makes stupendous buffet eating.

# *Buon Appetito !*

(Serves 10)

## MENU

**Red And White Italian Wines**

*Wine Suggestions:*
*White - Pinot Grigio*
*(A dry, crisp Italian white wine with a light taste.)*
*Red - Chianti Classico*
*(A dry, soft red wine with flavors*
*of blackberries and plums.)*

**Fresh Fruit with Prosciutto**

**Honey and Garlic Glazed Chicken Pizza**

**Seafood Scampi Pizza with Two Cheeses**

**Black Bean and Bacon Pizza**

**Kielbasa Pizza with Black Olives, Artichoke Hearts,
and Sun-dried Tomatoes**

**Crumbled Feta, Roma, and Onion Salad Pizza**

**Brown Sugar Brie, Pear, and Pecan Pizza**

**Red and Green Leaf Lettuces
with Garlic Dressing**

**Frozen Peppermint Parfaits**

## INGREDIENTS

1 package skinless Polish
   kielbasa, sliced
8 ounces tomato sauce

1 Homemade Pizza Dough
   Crust (see recipe), or
1 purchased unbaked pizza
   crust

2 cups mozzarella cheese,
   grated
3 ounces sun-dried tomatoes
8 ounces feta cheese
6 ½ ounces black olives,
   chopped
1 red onion, thinly sliced
4 ounces quartered artichoke
   hearts, drained and
   separated

# KIELBASA PIZZA WITH BLACK OLIVES, ARTICHOKE HEARTS, AND SUN-DRIED TOMATOES

Preheat oven to 350 degrees.

Lightly brown kielbasa in large skillet. Pour tomato sauce over prepared pizza crust. Place kielbasa on pizza. Sprinkle with mozzarella cheese. Reconstitute or plump sun-dried tomatoes according to package directions and chop. Top pizza with tomatoes, feta cheese, olives, red onions, and artichoke hearts. Bake 15-20 minutes or until done. Slice and serve immediately.

**SERVES:** 8-10

*Kielbasa is the Polish word for sausage. If you are health conscious, there are many varieties of "lite" sausages now on the market that can be substituted.*

*Crumbled Feta, Roma, and Onion Salad Pizza, p. 220.*

What do Princess Diana, Martha Stewart, and Paul McCartney have in common? It's the Aga Stove, featured in the background of this photograph. Introduced over 60 years ago in England, it is considered one of the most efficient sources of heat for cooking.

# THE PETER PRINCIPLE AT WORK?
## *Pop The Cork For A Job Promotion*

Cornelia has worked quite hard
and now it shows.
A couple rungs up
the ladder she goes.

Please join with me to celebrate.
To her new job we'll make a toast.
Friday, the third, at half past eight.
We will dine and of her boast.

The Corporate Headquarters of
Gigi and Sutton Stockton

✳ Although we are sure it doesn't apply to you, the "Peter Principle" asserts that other people tend to be promoted until they reach a level beyond their competence.

✳ Regardless of your situation, your table might hold a miniature ladder reaching to a chandelier glittering with a string of stars. A briefcase holding champagne may sit on the sideboard amid a pool of confetti. If you're really ambitious, write out the menu on company letterhead.

✳ Rising like huge ladders of confetti in the nighttime sky, the "uptown" Charlotte banks and businesses sparkle and shine. Charlotte is the nation's third largest financial center and serves as the subsidiary headquarters for many major national and over 400 international companies.

✳ Known as the "Banking Capitol of the South," Charlotte is heavily capitalized with six of the nation's top 200 banks operating here and two of the top 25 actually headquartered here.

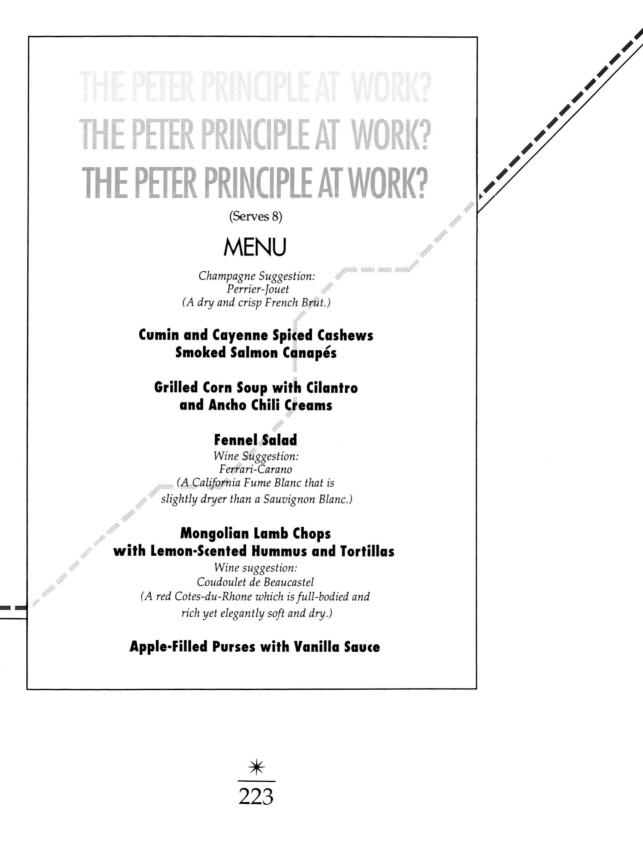

THE PETER PRINCIPLE AT WORK?
THE PETER PRINCIPLE AT WORK?

# THE PETER PRINCIPLE AT WORK?

(Serves 8)

## MENU

*Champagne Suggestion:*
*Perrier-Jouet*
*(A dry and crisp French Brut.)*

**Cumin and Cayenne Spiced Cashews**
**Smoked Salmon Canapés**

**Grilled Corn Soup with Cilantro**
**and Ancho Chili Creams**

**Fennel Salad**
*Wine Suggestion:*
*Ferrari-Carano*
*(A California Fume Blanc that is*
*slightly dryer than a Sauvignon Blanc.)*

**Mongolian Lamb Chops**
**with Lemon-Scented Hummus and Tortillas**
*Wine suggestion:*
*Coudoulet de Beaucastel*
*(A red Cotes-du-Rhone which is full-bodied and*
*rich yet elegantly soft and dry.)*

**Apple-Filled Purses with Vanilla Sauce**

## INGREDIENTS

**GRAPEFRUIT STRIPS**

- 1 grapefruit
- 1 cup water
- 1 cup sugar

**APPLE PURSES**

- 8 large Granny Smith apples, peeled and cored
- 2 tablespoons butter
- 2 tablespoons sugar
- ½ cup heavy hazelnuts, ground
- ½ cup raisins
- ¼ teaspoon ground cinnamon
- 8 8-inch diameter crêpes

**VANILLA SAUCE**

- 6 egg yolks
- ½ cup granulated sugar
- 1 pint half-and-half
- 2 teaspoons vanilla

**GARNISHES**

- 1 mango, peeled and sliced
- 1 kiwi, peeled and sliced
- 8 whole strawberries, washed
- 8 chocolate truffles (optional)

# APPLE-FILLED PURSES WITH VANILLA SAUCE

**FOR GRAPEFRUIT STRIPS:**

Cut 8 long strips from grapefruit peel with citrus stripper. Combine water and sugar in small saucepan and bring to boil. Add grapefruit strips and simmer until tender. Remove from heat and let strips cool in syrup.

**FOR APPLE PURSES:**

Preheat oven to 350 degrees.

Cut apples into thin slices and sauté in large skillet with butter. Add sugar and sauté until golden brown. Add hazelnuts, raisins, and cinnamon. Toss well.

Divide filling among crêpes. Fold crêpes into neat pouches and tie with blanched grapefruit strips into purses. Bake purses in oven 15 minutes until golden.

To serve: pour a pool of vanilla sauce on each plate. Garnish with mango and kiwi slices, whole strawerry, and chocolate truffle, if desired. Place purses on plates and serve while still hot.

## FOR VANILLA SAUCE:

Combine  egg yolks and sugar in medium bowl.  Whip until light and fluffy. Bring half-and-half to scalding point and very gradually add to yolk mixture while stirring rapidly. Place mixture in top of double boiler and heat slowly but constantly until thick enough to coat back of spoon. (Be careful not to get mixture too hot or it will curdle.)  Immediately pour custard into another container and continue stirring for at least 1 minute.  Stir in vanilla.  Set aside to continue cooling, stirring occasionally. Store in refrigerator.  *(Sauce can be refrigerated for 1 week.)*

**SERVES:**  8

## IMPORTANT CAREER CELEBRATIONS

| DATE | PROMOTION | MENU SELECTIONS |
|------|-----------|-----------------|
|  |  |  |
|  |  |  |
|  |  |  |
|  |  |  |
|  |  |  |
|  |  |  |
|  |  |  |
|  |  |  |
|  |  |  |
|  |  |  |
|  |  |  |
|  |  |  |

# Pumpkins *and* Palates
## Carve A Jack-O-Lantern Over Dinner

Ten little pumpkins sitting on the walk.
They look so real, they just might talk.

Ten little pumpkins to welcome our guests,
All dressed up in their Trick-or-Treat best.

Join us for a harvest feast
on the night of Halloween

Ghosts and goblins should appear at 7:00 p.m.
Betsy and Archie Huffstetler
23 Eastover Drive

Pumpkins provided. Be prepared to carve
a take-home Jack-O-Lantern!

✳ Invite your friends for supper to share in the fun of Halloween and the joy of cool fall breezes. If you decide to include children, plan fun activities, and order pizza for your young guests while the adults enjoy fare for more mature palates. (Although little ghosts and goblins will love the Pumpkin Pecan Fudge!)

✳ Your guests will feel a tingle when they arrive to see your walkway lit with pumpkin luminaries. Carve small pumpkins with a simple design and put candles or small flashlights inside.

✳ Celebrate the season by making your own soup bowls! Take small pumpkins, cut ⅓ of the top off and carve out the insides. For a centerpiece purchase a large pumpkin, prepare the same way, and fill it with flowers. For place cards take fall colored leaves and write guests' names with a gold paint pen.

✳ Napkins may be tied with raffia, grape-vine, or other natural material. Gourds or miniature pumpkins can be hollowed out to hold votive candles. Fill a grape-vine basket with an assortment of pumpkins and gourds for an additional fall-fest look.

✳ If children "haunt" your house, send the little ones on a bone hunt! Spray paint large dog bones with white paint and hide them in the back yard. Give a prize for the most found and reward the other players with special treats.

✳ And make sure each guest under six leaves with a copy of Tasha Tudor's book, *Pumpkin Moonshine.*

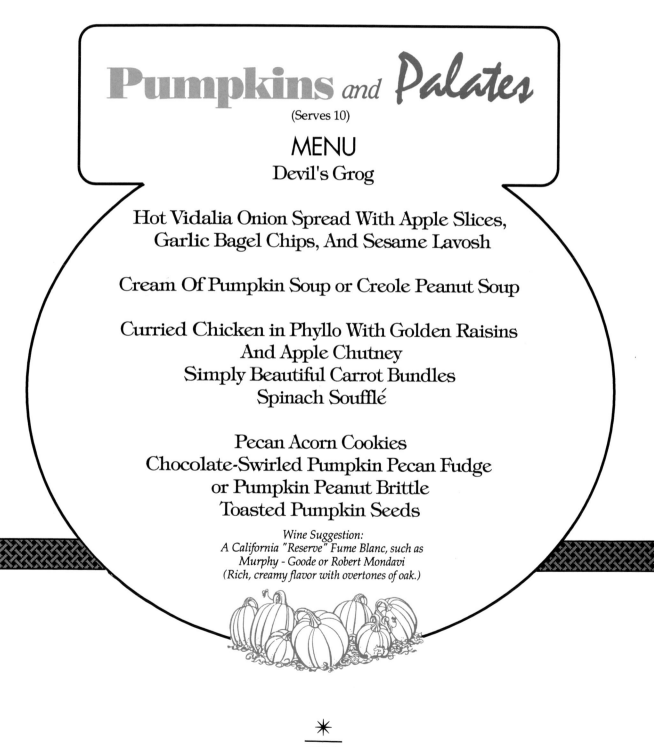

# Pumpkins *and* Palates

(Serves 10)

## MENU

Devil's Grog

Hot Vidalia Onion Spread With Apple Slices,
Garlic Bagel Chips, And Sesame Lavosh

Cream Of Pumpkin Soup or Creole Peanut Soup

Curried Chicken in Phyllo With Golden Raisins
And Apple Chutney
Simply Beautiful Carrot Bundles
Spinach Soufflé

Pecan Acorn Cookies
Chocolate-Swirled Pumpkin Pecan Fudge
or Pumpkin Peanut Brittle
Toasted Pumpkin Seeds

*Wine Suggestion:*
*A California "Reserve" Fume Blanc, such as*
*Murphy - Goode or Robert Mondavi*
*(Rich, creamy flavor with overtones of oak.)*

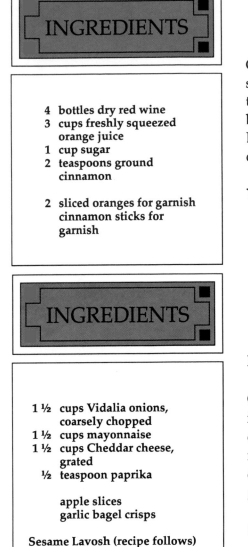

## INGREDIENTS

4 bottles dry red wine
3 cups freshly squeezed
   orange juice
1 cup sugar
2 teaspoons ground
   cinnamon

2 sliced oranges for garnish
   cinnamon sticks for
   garnish

## INGREDIENTS

1 ½ cups Vidalia onions,
      coarsely chopped
1 ½ cups mayonnaise
1 ½ cups Cheddar cheese,
      grated
  ½ teaspoon paprika

   apple slices
   garlic bagel crisps

Sesame Lavosh (recipe follows)

# DEVIL'S GROG

Combine first 4 ingredients in large, heavy saucepan over moderate heat. Bring almost to simmer, stirring occasionally. (Do not boil.) Taste and add more sugar, if desired. Ladle into heat-proof mugs. Garnish with orange slices and cinnamon sticks.

**YIELDS:** 20 drinks

# HOT VIDALIA ONION SPREAD

Preheat oven to 350 degrees.

Combine onions, mayonnaise, and cheese in medium bowl. Pour into 1-quart baking dish. Sprinkle with paprika and bake 25 minutes. Blot with paper towel to absorb excess oil. Serve hot with apple slices, garlic bagel chips, and Sesame Lavosh.

**SERVES:** 10

*Vidalia onions are a hybrid onion grown in Vidalia, Georgia. They are milder than regular onions because of the soil and climate of the region. Georgia's early spring provides a young harvest so the onions never develop a "bite." Vidalia onions are a real treat because they have a short season, from May to July, and do not store well due to their high water content. So enjoy while you can! White onions may be substituted.*

*Devil's Grog, p. 232; Hot Vidalia Onion Spread, p. 232.*

# SESAME LAVOSH

## INGREDIENTS

Preheat oven to 400 degrees.

*These are crispy thin delicious and simply prepared.*

Combine flour, salt, baking soda, sugar, and seasoned salt in large bowl. Cut in butter until mixture resembles course meal. Add marjoram leaves and buttermilk. Blend into stiff dough. Roll tablespoon-sized pieces of dough onto floured board until very thin. Sprinkle with sesame and poppy seeds and roll again. Place on cookie sheet and brush lightly with melted butter. Bake 10 minutes until golden brown. Cool on a wire rack. *(Can be stored in airtight container 1 week.)*

| | |
|---|---|
| 2 ¾ | cups flour |
| 1 ½ | teaspoons salt |
| ½ | teaspoon baking soda |
| 1 | tablespoon sugar |
| ½ | teaspoon seasoned salt |
| ½ | cup butter, softened |
| ½ | teaspoon marjoram leaves |
| 1 | cup buttermilk |
| | dash sesame seeds |
| | dash poppy seeds |
| 4 | tablespoons butter, melted |

## INGREDIENTS

7 tablespoons butter
3 ⅓ cups onions, chopped
8 ⅓ cups vegetable boullion
3 ⅓ cups pumpkin, cooked and
      mashed or canned
⅓ teaspoon thyme
    dash nutmeg
    dash salt
    dash pepper
1 cup light cream

chopped peanuts for
garnish (optional)

# CREAM OF PUMPKIN SOUP

Melt butter in large saucepan and sauté onions until translucent. Add boullion, pumpkin, and seasonings. Mix well. Cover and simmer 40 minutes. Process in food processor until smooth. Return to saucepan and add cream. Reheat to serving temperature. Ladle soup into bowls and garnish with chopped peanuts, if desired. *(May be prepared one day ahead and refrigerated. Gently reheat before serving.)*

**SERVES:** 10

*Everyone thinks that pumpkins are sweet because they are most often eaten in pie. Actually, pumpkins are not as sweet as one might imagine, and this soup closely resembles potato soup because of its lack of sugar.*

## INGREDIENTS

1 cup onion, finely chopped
2 teaspoons oil
1 tablespoon all purpose
    flour
2 cups milk, divided
½ cup crunchy peanut butter
2 cups V-8 Juice
1 teaspoon salt
5-6 dashes hot sauce

curry powder for garnish
sour cream for garnish
chopped parsley for
garnish

# CREOLE PEANUT SOUP

Sauté chopped onion in oil in large saucepan over moderate heat until light brown, 4-5 minutes. Sprinkle flour over onions and stir rapidly to prevent burning. Remove from heat and mix thoroughly into dry paste. Return to moderate-high heat and gradually add 1 cup milk. Mix until smooth. Add peanut butter and stir until melted. Gradually add remaining milk and bring to boil. Cook 1-2 minutes until thick. Add V-8 juice and salt and bring to boil. Add hot sauce and mix well.

Ladle soup into bowls or hollowed out and baked squash halves. Sprinkle with curry powder, top with dollop of sour cream, and garnish with parsley.

**SERVES:** 10

*ream of Pumpkin Soup, p. 234.*

# CURRIED CHICKEN IN PHYLLO WITH GOLDEN RAISINS AND APPLE CHUTNEY

## INGREDIENTS

½ cup butter
1 medium onion, diced
1 large red apple, diced
1 4-ounce can green chiles, diced
2 large cloves garlic, minced
1 tablespoon ground turmeric
1 tablespoon fresh ginger, minced
2-4 tablespoons curry powder
1 teaspoon coriander
1 teaspoon ground cumin
¾ cup chicken stock
2 pounds skinless, boneless chicken breasts, cubed into bite-sized pieces
½ cup whipping cream
½ cup half-and-half
¾ cup golden raisins
1 tablespoon sugar
salt to taste
pepper to taste
1 pound phyllo dough sheets
1 cup butter, melted

Apple Chutney (recipe follows)

Melt butter in medium saucepan over moderate heat. Add onion, apple, chiles, and garlic. Cook until tender, about 5 minutes. Add spices and stir until well blended. Add stock and simmer 20 minutes. Add next 7 ingredients. Simmer until chicken is cooked but tender, about 15 minutes. Cool completely, cover, and chill at least 1 hour or overnight.

Preheat oven to 500 degrees.

Lightly grease 2 baking sheets. Set one phyllo sheet on work surface. Top with second phyllo sheet. Brush with melted butter. Mound ½ cup chicken filling in center of phyllo sheet about 6 inches from one end. Fold both sides over filling cross-wise and roll, starting at filling end, into a package. Generously brush with melted butter while rolling. Set package, seam side down, on prepared baking sheet. Brush top with melted butter. Repeat with remaining phyllo sheets and filling to make 10 packages. *(Can be made one day ahead up to this point by wrapping packages in plastic wrap and refrigerating.)*

Bake until crisp and golden brown, about 15 minutes. Serve immediately with Apple Chutney.

**SERVES:** 10

*Economical and not difficult (but a bit time consuming) to prepare, this do-ahead recipe is heavenly.*

*The phyllo "package" is butter-crisp tender on the outside while the chicken filling on the inside is rich, aromatic, and delicious.*

*If time does not permit to make the Apple Chutney at home there are many marvelous chutneys to choose from at the supermarket. Any would be appropriate.*

*Curried Chicken in Phyllo with Golden Raisins and Apple Chutney, pp. 236, 238; Simply Beautiful Carrot Bundles, p. 238; Spinach Soufflé, p. 239*

*The Carolinas coast is filled with legends of ghosts and apparitions. Cape Fear is named for the treacherous ship-dooming sandbars off its shores. Further south, the coast from Georgetown to Charleston has been called the "most haunted section of the United States." During hurricane season dangerous storms threaten off the coast and reported ghosts-sightings are common. For example, "The Gray Man" warns land dwellers of an impending hurricane from August through October. An unbelievable number of Carolinians have either seen "The Gray Man" or know someone who has.*

## INGREDIENTS

| | |
|---|---|
| 10 | medium Granny Smith apples, peeled and chopped |
| 1 | cup onion, diced |
| 1 | cup red bell pepper, diced |
| 1-2 | hot peppers |
| 1 ½ | pounds dark raisins |
| 4 | cups light brown sugar |
| 3 | tablespoons ground ginger |
| 2 | teaspoons allspice |
| 2 | teaspoons salt |
| 1 | clove garlic, crushed |
| 1 | quart apple cider vinegar |
| 3 | tablespoons mustard seed |

## INGREDIENTS

| | |
|---|---|
| 2 | pounds carrots, peeled and trimmed |
| 10 | green onions |
| ⅔ | cup fresh lemon juice |
| 6 | tablespoons butter |
| 4 | tablespoons sugar |
| ½ | teaspoon salt |

# APPLE CHUTNEY

Combine all ingredients in large stockpot and bring to boil. Reduce heat and simmer 90 minutes. Stir frequently. Spoon hot chutney into hot, sterilized jars. Leave ½ inch head space. Wipe rims and seal lids. Do not process. The heat from the chutney will seal lids.

**YIELD:** 6 pints

*Mention the word chutney and everyone immediately thinks East Indian spicy!*

*Chutney tastes fabulous with barbecued meats of all kinds and makes a very special hostess gift any time of year.*

# SIMPLY BEAUTIFUL CARROT BUNDLES

Cut carrots into 3-inch sticks. Steam until tender but crunchy. Rinse immediately in cold water. Dry on paper towels and separate into 10 bundles.

Remove white bulbs from green onions and save for another use. Dip green stems into boiling water for 30 seconds and tie around each carrot bundle while still limp. Double knot and trim.

Combine lemon juice, butter, sugar, and salt in large saucepan and bring to boil. Simmer until sugar and salt have dissolved. Carefully add carrot bundles and cook until just heated through. Spoon lemon mixture over carrots often. Carefully remove each bundle from pan with spatula and serve hot.

**SERVES:** 10

*Carrots will keep refrigerated in a ziplock bag for several weeks in the vegetable crisper. When selecting carrots, avoid those that are rubbery, split, or darkly colored around the stem — signs which indicate age.*

# SPINACH SOUFFLÉ

Preheat oven to 350 degrees.

Combine butter and flour in large saucepan over low heat. Stir until smooth and bubbly. Add salt, pepper, Cheddar cheese, and milk. Stir constantly over moderate heat until melted. Remove from heat. Add spinach and onion. Gradually add egg yolks, mixing well. Cool. Beat egg whites until stiff. Fold whites into spinach mixture. Pour into lightly-greased, 2-quart soufflé dish or individual soufflé dishes. Bake 35 minutes and serve.

**SERVES:** 10

# PECAN
# ACORN COOKIES

Preheat oven to 350 degrees.

Combine butter, brown sugar, 1 cup pecans, and vanilla in large bowl. Cream well. Add sifted flour and baking powder. Beat well. Make acorn shaped cookies by pressing bits of dough into a teaspoon. Bake on ungreased cookie sheet 13 minutes. Melt chocolate in top of double boiler. Dip top ⅓ of each cookie in melted chocolate and immediately dip into reserved pecans. Cool on wax paper until hardened.

**YIELD:** 6 dozen

*Since spinach is grown in sand, wash leaves thoroughly to remove grit and dry well if using in salads.*

*Children will love the following Halloween dessert treats too:*

*(1) Hollow out large oranges and cut eyes and a mouth like a Jack-O-Lantern. Fill with ice cream and place in the freezer.*

*(2) Cover a pumpkin with gum drops! Using toothpicks, stick one toothpick into each gumdrop, and then stick the toothpicks into the pumpkin.*

*(3) Make caramel popcorn balls and let children decorate them like Jack-O-Lanterns using raisins, candy corn, and marshmallows to make faces.*

## INGREDIENTS

¼ cup butter
¼ cup flour
½ teaspoon salt
  dash pepper
1 cup sharp Cheddar cheese, grated
¾ cup milk
10 ounces chopped spinach, cooked and well drained
2 tablespoons onion, chopped
4 eggs, separated

## INGREDIENTS

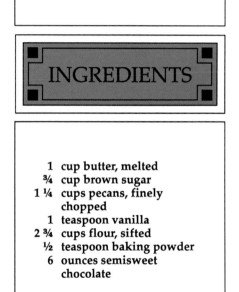

1 cup butter, melted
¾ cup brown sugar
1 ¼ cups pecans, finely chopped
1 teaspoon vanilla
2 ¾ cups flour, sifted
½ teaspoon baking powder
6 ounces semisweet chocolate

*Chocolate-Swirled Pumpkin Pecan Fudge, this page; Pumpkin Peanut Brittle, p. 241.*

## INGREDIENTS

4 cups sugar
1 cup milk
3 tablespoons light corn syrup
1 cup canned pumpkin
pinch salt
3 tablespoons unsalted butter, cut into small pieces
1 teaspoon vanilla
2 cups pecans, chopped
6 ounces semisweet chocolate, melted

# CHOCOLATE-SWIRLED PUMPKIN PECAN FUDGE

Combine sugar, milk, corn syrup, pumpkin, and salt in 4-quart heavy saucepan. Cook over moderate heat, stirring until sugar is dissolved. Continue cooking until candy thermometer registers 238 degrees. Remove from heat, and add butter but do not stir into mixture. Allow mixture to cool until it reaches 140 degrees. Then stir in vanilla and pecans. Beat mixture 30 seconds-1 minute or until it begins to lose its sheen. Pour immediately into a buttered 9-inch square pan. Let fudge cool until it begins to harden. Swirl melted chocolate over top. Cut into squares and let cool completely. *(Fudge can be stored between sheets of wax paper in airtight container for 2 weeks.)*

**YIELD:** 2 pounds

✳

# PUMPKIN PEANUT BRITTLE

Combine sugar, corn syrup, salt, and baking soda in medium saucepan. Stir with wooden spoon until sugar has dissolved. Add peanuts and pumpkin seeds. Cook over moderate heat until candy thermometer reaches 293 degrees. Quickly pour into well-greased 9 x 13-inch pan. Let cool and break into pieces. Store in airtight container.

**YIELD:** about 3 cups

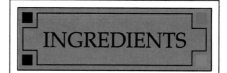

## INGREDIENTS

2 cups sugar
1 cup corn syrup
½ teaspoon salt
1 teaspoon baking soda
½ cup raw peanuts
½ cup toasted pumpkin seeds (recipe follows)

# TOASTED PUMPKIN SEEDS

Preheat oven to 250 degrees.

Toss seeds with oil in small bowl until seeds are well-coated. Spread seeds onto ungreased baking sheet. Bake 1-1 ¼ hours, stirring occasionally until golden and crisp.

**YIELD:** 2 cups

## INGREDIENTS

½ cup fresh pumpkin seeds
1 tablespoon vegetable oil

*For snacking, toss seeds with 2 teaspoons ground dried rosemary and seasoned salt before baking.*

# PUMPKIN CARVING

For carving the perfect pumpkin:

• Cut a hole in the back of the pumpkin to put the candle inside. This keeps the front and top of the pumpkin in tact.

• Draw a face on the pumpkin before carving. Use stencils, cookie cutters, or other Halloween cut-outs to trace designs onto the pumpkin.

• When removing insides from the pumpkin, an ice cream scoop is a good tool to use.

• If you carve a piece out of the pumpkin by mistake, simply secure it back with a toothpick.

# It's All In The FINISH !

## A Pre-Race Affair For 20

Ladies and Gentlemen
BEFORE You Start Your Engines
Make A Pit Stop
At The "Garage" Of
Kit and Pierce Farthing
For A Pre-Race Buffet

Twelve Noon

Race Day

The Checkered Flag
Will Be Waving!

✻ Grab your checkered flags and head out to the Speedway! Charlotte racing fans are particularly proud of the Charlotte Motor Speedway. In use almost every day of the year by either NASCAR races, professional race car driving schools, or auto fairs, the "Speedway" is home to three NASCAR events, including the Coca-Cola 600. Attended by more than 162,000 fans, the Coca-Cola 600 is the second largest single day sporting event in the country.

✻ To decorate for your pre-race affair, use a black and white checked tablecloth. If unavailable, make your own with an inexpensive white cloth and black fabric paint. Use masking tape to mark the squares.

✻ Also, inexpensive toy cars can be placed about the table and even spray painted silver and gold for a glitzy effect. Top off the decor with red, yellow, and green napkins — the racing signal colors, of course!

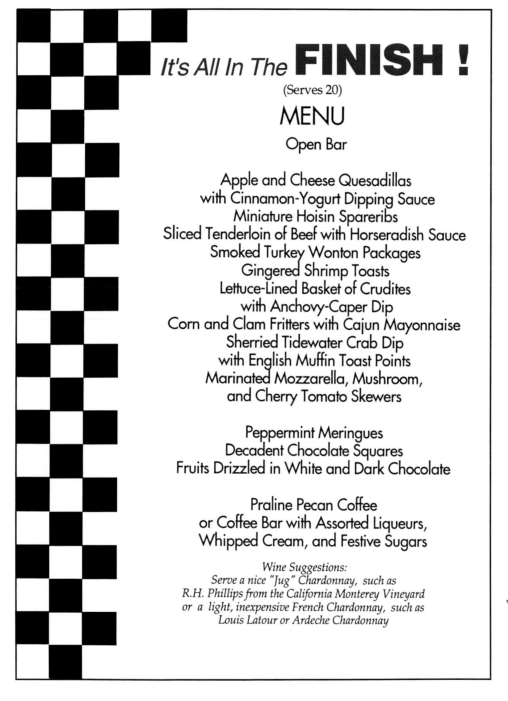

# It's All In The **FINISH !**

(Serves 20)

## MENU

Open Bar

Apple and Cheese Quesadillas
with Cinnamon-Yogurt Dipping Sauce
Miniature Hoisin Spareribs
Sliced Tenderloin of Beef with Horseradish Sauce
Smoked Turkey Wonton Packages
Gingered Shrimp Toasts
Lettuce-Lined Basket of Crudites
with Anchovy-Caper Dip
Corn and Clam Fritters with Cajun Mayonnaise
Sherried Tidewater Crab Dip
with English Muffin Toast Points
Marinated Mozzarella, Mushroom,
and Cherry Tomato Skewers

Peppermint Meringues
Decadent Chocolate Squares
Fruits Drizzled in White and Dark Chocolate

Praline Pecan Coffee
or Coffee Bar with Assorted Liqueurs,
Whipped Cream, and Festive Sugars

*Wine Suggestions:*
*Serve a nice "Jug" Chardonnay, such as*
*R.H. Phillips from the California Monterey Vineyard*
*or a light, inexpensive French Chardonnay, such as*
*Louis Latour or Ardeche Chardonnay*

# APPLE AND CHEESE QUESADILLAS WITH CINNAMON-YOGURT DIPPING SAUCE

**INGREDIENTS**

- 2 tablespoons butter, softened
- 16 7-inch flour tortillas
- ⅓ cup orange marmalade
- 1 cup Monterey jack cheese, shredded
- 1 cup Cheddar cheese, shredded
- 1 large apple, peeled and finely chopped
- ⅓ cup golden raisins

**DIPPING SAUCE**

- 1 cup vanilla or lemon yogurt
- ¼ teaspoon cinnamon

Preheat oven to 350 degrees.

Spread butter on one side of each tortilla. Place tortillas, butter side down, on wax paper. Spread marmalade on non-buttered side of each tortilla.

Combine cheeses in small bowl. Sprinkle evenly over tortillas. Top each with apples and raisins. Fold tortillas in half. Place on ungreased baking sheet and bake 12 minutes or until cheese is melted and tortillas are golden brown. Cut each tortilla in half and serve with Cinnamon-Yogurt Dipping Sauce.

**FOR DIPPING SAUCE:**

Combine yogurt and cinnamon in small bowl. Cover and refrigerate until serving.

**YIELD:** 32 quesadillas

*The cinnamon-yogurt dipping sauce is also a wonderful dressing for fruit salad.*

# MINIATURE HOISIN SPARERIBS

**INGREDIENTS**

- 4 pounds pork spareribs
- 12 ounces beer
- ½ cup hoisin sauce
- 1 cup honey
- 1 cup soy sauce
- 1 cup green onions, minced

Preheat oven to 350 degrees.

Cut spareribs in half horizontally and separate into individual, miniature ribs.

Combine beer, hoisin sauce, honey, and soy sauce in medium saucepan over moderate heat. Add onions and cook until sauce is hot. Place ribs in large baking dish. Pour sauce over ribs and bake 1 hour. Baste with sauce from pan every 30 minutes or so.

**YIELD:** 60 pieces

*Ask your butcher to cut the spareribs for you.*

*Hoisin sauce, packed in cans or jars, adds a combination of sharp, spicy, and sweet flavor to seafood, chicken, pork, and vegetable dishes. Based on fermented soy beans and spices, it keeps indefinitely in the refrigerator.*

# SLICED TENDERLOIN OF BEEF WITH HORSERADISH SAUCE

**FOR TENDERLOIN:**

Combine all ingredients, except tenderloin, in large, shallow pan. Place tenderloin in pan, cover, and marinate in refrigerator at least 2 hours or overnight, turning occasionally. Remove beef from refrigerator 1 hour before cooking.

Preheat oven to 450 degrees.

Place beef on rack in large baking pan and bake 10 minutes. Lower oven temperature to 400 degrees and continue baking to desired doneness (approximately 30 minutes for medium rare). Remove beef from oven and let cool. Wrap with foil and refrigerate until ready to serve.

To serve, slice beef thinly and arrange on platter. *(Can be kept covered and chilled 2 hours.)* Serve with Horseradish Sauce.

**SERVES:** 20

**FOR SAUCE:**

Combine first 3 ingredients in medium bowl and mash with fork to mix well. Whip cream until stiff peaks form in small bowl. Gently fold cream into horseradish mixture. Cover and refrigerate until ready to serve.

**YIELD:** 4 cups

1 ½ cups vegetable oil
¾ cup soy sauce
¼ cup Worcestershire sauce
2 tablespoons dry mustard
2 cloves garlic, minced
½ cup red wine vinegar
2 ½ teaspoons salt
2 tablespoons freshly ground pepper
¼ cup cider vinegar
1 tablespoon fresh parsley, chopped
5 pound beef tenderloin

**HORSERADISH SAUCE**

2 cups sour cream
1 cup prepared horseradish, drained
3 slices fresh white bread, crusts removed, finely diced
1 cup whipping cream, chilled

## INGREDIENTS

    2  cups smoked turkey, finely
       chopped
  2-3  cloves garlic, minced
    4  green onions (with tops),
       finely chopped
  ⅓  cup Parmesan cheese,
       grated
    1  4-ounce can green chiles,
       drained and chopped
    1  teaspoon salt

    1  16-ounce package wonton
       wrappers
       vegetable oil for frying

       Purchased Duck Sauce,
       Honey Mustard, or
       Horseradish Sauce for
       dipping

## INGREDIENTS

   30  strips or triangles thin-
       sliced bread, crusts
       removed and reserved
    1  pound medium shrimp,
       peeled and deveined
    1  small onion or 2 green
       onions, minced
    1  ½-inch slice fresh ginger
       root, minced
    1  tablespoon white wine or
       sherry
  ½  teaspoon salt
  ¼  teaspoon ground pepper
    2  egg whites
       vegetable oil for frying

       fresh parsley sprigs for
       garnish

       Purchased Plum Sauce

# SMOKED TURKEY WONTON PACKAGES

Combine first 6 ingredients in medium bowl. Mix well and let stand 30 minutes. Place a wonton wrapper on counter with one corner towards you. Place 1 teaspoon of filling in lower center of wrapper and fold bottom corner up. Fold in sides with points overlapping. Fold top corner over to assemble one package. Wet edges to seal. Repeat until all packages are assembled. *(Wontons can be refrigerated, covered, 1 day ahead.)*

Deep fry a few packages at a time in vegetable oil in large skillet until golden. Drain on paper towels. Serve hot with Duck Sauce, Honey Mustard, or Horseradish Sauce. *(Packages can be made ahead and reheated in 375 degree oven until hot.)*

**YIELD:** 50 wontons

# GINGERED SHRIMP TOASTS

Process reserved bread crusts in food processor. Set aside ½ cup fine bread crumbs. Process next 6 ingredients in food processor until finely chopped. With motor running, pour in egg whites and process until well combined. Spread mixture ¼-inch thick on bread pieces. Dip mixture-coated sides in bread crumbs. Place on cookie sheet and cover with plastic wrap. Chill until time to fry. *(May be refrigerated 1 day or frozen 2 weeks. Do not thaw before frying.)*

Heat 1 ½ to 2 inches oil in large skillet over moderate heat. Fry toast in batches until golden brown on both sides. Drain on paper towels. Place on large platter, garnish with parsley, and serve with plum sauce.

**YIELD:** 30 appetizers

*For a variation, substitute crabmeat or shrimp for the smoked turkey and add 4 ounces of softened cream cheese to the filling mixture.*

*Enjoy your shopping trip for the wontons! If unavailable in the supermarket (usually located near the fresh bean sprouts and snow peas), visit the local Chinese grocery and you're sure to be amazed at the variety of items sold there.*

*Deep purple in color and sweet-tart in flavor, plum sauce is generally available, bottled or canned, in the Asian section of most supermarkets. It serves as a pungent basting sauce for duck, pork, and spareribs or as a dipping sauce for egg rolls and shrimp toasts. Once opened, it will keep stored in the refrigerator for up to a year if placed in an airtight plastic or glass container.*

*Serve the dip in a hollowed-out cabbage or hollowed-out red, green, and yellow bell peppers nestled amongst the crudités.*

---

*If you are planning to use cucumbers with your Anchovy-Caper Dip, pull a sharp fork down the sides of the cucumber before slicing to create a "flower" look for the crudité.*

---

*Finger foods are perfect for outdoor occasions such as a tailgate party or reception. Crudités are among the most popular finger foods, especially served with dips. When arranging crudités, be sure the vegetables are well chilled. Some vegetables are briefly blanched for better texture, flavor, and more vibrant color.*

# LETTUCE-LINED BASKET OF CRUDITÉS WITH ANCHOVY-CAPER DIP

## FOR CRUDITÉS:

Select several vegetables from suggested list. The variety and quantity should be determined by availability and individual taste. Try to have a mixture of colors and textures.

Line a basket with lettuce leaves and arrange vegetables in the leaf-lined basket. Serve with Anchovy-Caper Dip.

## FOR DIP:

Combine all ingredients, except olive oil, in food processor until smooth. With machine running, add olive oil in continuous trickle until mixture emulsifies.

**SERVES:** 20

**INGREDIENTS**

### CRUDITÉS

green beans, blanched
broccoli florets, blanched
small leeks, blanched
tiny new potatoes, blanched
fresh, thin asparagus spears, blanched
cauliflower florets
red cabbage, cut into small wedges
fennel, cut into strips
red and green bell peppers, sliced into strips
radishes, cleaned, with roots trimmed off
endive spears
lettuce leaves for garnish

### DIP

| | |
|---|---|
| 1 | small can anchovies |
| 3 | cloves garlic, crushed |
| ½ | teaspoon fresh thyme leaves |
| ½ | teaspoon fresh ginger, chopped |
| ½ | teaspoon fresh basil, chopped |
| 1 | tablespoon Dijon mustard |
| 1 | tablespoon lemon juice |
| 1 | egg |
| 2 | teaspoons capers |
| ½ | teaspoon sugar |
| ½ | teaspoon freshly ground pepper |
| 6 | ounces olive oil |

## INGREDIENTS

1 cup bread flour
½ teaspoon salt
2 tablespoons sugar
2 eggs
1 cup beer
1 cup clams, chopped
½ cup corn kernels
¼ cup red bell pepper, minced
3 tablespoons onion, minced
½ teaspoon lemon pepper
1 large clove garlic, minced
¼ cup fresh parsley, chopped
safflower oil, for frying

lemon wedges and fresh parsley for garnish

### CAJUN MAYONNAISE

⅛ cup capers, finely chopped
6 cornichons, or
3 baby dill pickles, finely chopped
½ small onion, finely chopped
1 cup mayonnaise
2 tablespoons fresh lemon juice
2 tablespoons tarragon vinegar
1 tablespoon Dijon mustard
3 tablespoons parsley, chopped
2 teaspoons prepared horseradish
1 teaspoon Worcestershire sauce
½ teaspoon dried tarragon
½ teaspoon dried oregano

# CORN AND CLAM FRITTERS WITH CAJUN MAYONNAISE

**FOR THE FRITTERS:**

Mix flour, salt, and sugar in small bowl. Separate eggs, placing whites in medium bowl and yolks in large bowl. Add beer to yolks. Mix well. Gradually stir flour mixture into yolk mixture and carefully blend until smooth. Refrigerate 30 minutes.

Whip egg whites until stiff. Remove batter from refrigerator and stir in clams, corn, red pepper, onion, lemon pepper, garlic, and parsley. Fold egg whites into mixture.

Heat ½ inch safflower oil in large, deep skillet or electric frying pan to 375 degrees. Scoop about 2 tablespoons of batter and drop into heated oil. Repeat with remaining batter but do not crowd pan. Fry uncovered about 2 minutes on each side. Remove with slotted spoon and drain on paper towels.

Arrange fritters on platter with Cajun Mayonnaise for dipping and garnish with lemon wedges and parsley.

**FOR CAJUN MAYONNAISE:**

Combine capers, cornichons or pickles, and onion in medium bowl. Add mayonnaise, lemon juice, vinegar, and mustard. Stir in remaining ingredients, cover, and chill. Make one day ahead to blend flavors. *(Keeps refrigerated for at least 1 week.)*

**YIELD:** 20 fritters

# SHERRIED TIDEWATER CRAB DIP WITH ENGLISH MUFFIN TOAST POINTS

*Even top quality backfin crabmeat should be picked through for shell prior to using.*

Heat cream cheese in large saucepan over low heat until softened. Stir in garlic, onion, mayonnaise, mustard, and crabmeat. Add wine and sherry. Stir until blended. Pour into chafing dish and serve warm with English muffin toast points or melba toast rounds.

**SERVES:** 20

## INGREDIENTS

24 ounces cream cheese
1 clove garlic, finely minced
1 tablespoon grated onion
½ cup mayonnaise
3 teaspoons dry mustard
1 pound backfin crabmeat, cleaned and picked
¼ cup dry white wine
¼ cup sherry

6 English muffins, split, toasted and quartered, or melba toast rounds

# MARINATED MOZZARELLA, MUSHROOM, AND CHERRY TOMATO SKEWERS

Combine all ingredients, except cherry tomatoes, in medium bowl. Cover and refrigerate overnight.

Thread mozzarella cube, mushroom, and cherry tomato onto each wooden skewer and arrange on large platter. *(Can be made 4 hours ahead, covered, and refrigerated.)*

**YIELD:** 50 appetizers

## INGREDIENTS

¾ pound fresh mozzarella, cut into ½-inch cubes
2 pounds small fresh mushrooms, washed and trimmed
⅔ cup tarragon vinegar
½ cup light olive oil
2 cloves garlic, minced
1 tablespoon sugar
1 ½ teaspoons salt
½ teaspoon freshly ground pepper
2 tablespoons water dash hot pepper sauce
1 teaspoon fresh parsley, chopped
2 pints small cherry tomatoes, washed and stemmed
50 wooden skewers

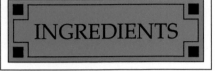

**INGREDIENTS**

4 large egg whites, room temperature
¼ teaspoon cream of tartar
⅛ teaspoon salt
½ teaspoon vanilla
¾ cup superfine sugar
½ teaspoon peppermint extract

**INGREDIENTS**

32 ounces milk chocolate bars
1 cup butter, softened
3 cups sugar
8 ounces cream cheese, softened
6 eggs
3 cups flour
1 tablespoon vanilla
1 tablespoon almond extract
4 teaspoons cocoa powder
¼ teaspoon baking soda

# PEPPERMINT MERINGUES

Preheat oven to 225 degrees.

Beat egg whites, cream of tartar, and salt in large bowl until soft peaks form. Gradually beat in remaining ingredients until mixture is well combined. Cover cookie sheet with parchment paper, foil, or brown paper grocery bag cut in half. Pipe or mound meringues in small dollops onto cookie sheet. Bake 1 ½ hours until very dry. Store in airtight container. *(Best if made on a day with very low humidity.)*

**YIELD:** 36 small meringues

# DECADENT CHOCOLATE SQUARES

Preheat oven to 350 degrees.

Break chocolate bars into pieces and freeze. Blend butter and sugar in large bowl. Add cream cheese and beat well. Add eggs, one at a time, beating well after each addition. Gradually add flour. Blend in remaining ingredients, except chocolate.

Pour half the batter into greased 9 x 13-inch baking pan. Place half the frozen chocolate pieces on top. Pour in remaining batter. Bake 40 minutes and remove from oven. Place remaining chocolate pieces on top, pushing them into the cake. Bake an additional 10 minutes. Cool. Cut into squares.

**YIELD:** 36 squares

*Cream of tartar is an acid used to stabilize egg whites in angel food cake, meringues, and some frostings. Cream of tartar can be mixed with baking soda and cornstarch to create baking powder. (To make one tablespoon of baking powder, substitute ½ teaspoon of cream of tartar, ¼ teaspoon of baking soda, and ¼ teaspoon of cornstarch.)*

# FRUITS DRIZZLED IN WHITE AND DARK CHOCOLATE

*When melting chocolate, never allow water to boil or steam to rise and settle in container of chocolate. If there is even a tiny droplet of water in the melted chocolate, the chocolate will tighten into an unworkable mass. To save tightened chocolate, stir in one teaspoon of vegetable shortening per ounce of chocolate.*

Cover baking sheets with foil or parchment paper and place fruit on prepared sheets.

Melt semisweet chocolate in top of double boiler over hot (not boiling) water. Remove from heat and whisk in 3 tablespoons shortening. Transfer melted chocolate into clean, small plastic bag. Snip a hole in one corner of bag. Drizzle melted chocolate over half of the fruits placed on covered baking sheets. Follow the same procedure with the white chocolate and remaining 3 tablespoons shortening.

After chocolate hardens, arrange fruit on platter to serve.

**SERVES:** 20

## INGREDIENTS

20 large fresh strawberries, with long stems
8 ounces fresh raspberries
4 fresh apricots, cut into wedges
2 fresh oranges, sectioned

Other optional fruits: sweet plums, sectioned; dried or fresh figs; seedless grapes; prunes; candied ginger; candied citrus peel

12 ounces semisweet chocolate, chopped into pieces
6 tablespoons vegetable shortening
12 ounces white chocolate, chopped into pieces

# PRALINE PECAN COFFEE

*If praline-flavored liqueur is unavailable, substitute hazelnut-flavored liqueur.*

Add coffee and chopped pecans to brewing basket. Brew 10 cups of coffee. Pour liqueur into brewed coffee. Serve with cream and sugar.

**YIELD:** 10 cups

## INGREDIENTS

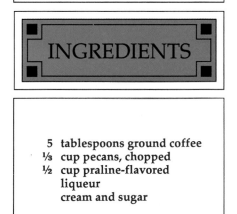

5 tablespoons ground coffee
⅓ cup pecans, chopped
½ cup praline-flavored liqueur
cream and sugar

# COFFEE BAR

Try a coffee bar instead! Have a tray of your favorite after-dinner liqueurs, such as Kahlua, Irish Whiskey, Grand Marnier, or Peppermint Schnapps, next to the coffee urn along with sweetened whipped cream and colored sugar crystals. Then let your guests make their own coffee concoctions. If you want to really spice it up, add chocolate pieces, lemon or orange peel strips, brown sugar, candied ginger, or maple syrup, in separate containers.

# Shoppers Anonymous:

## A Holiday Break For The Ladies

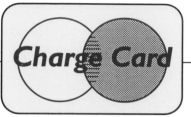

To market to market, off shopping we went,
See all the presents and money we spent!
So join us for lunch, to relax is the reason,
No crowds or long lines,
Share the holiday season.

Drop by for lunch
Thursday, December 10
12:00 til 2:00

Priestley Bossong, 101 Pine Road

* When your guests come for their "holiday break," have each one bring a roll of wrapping paper, a roll of ribbon, a pair of scissors, and any unwrapped gifts. Set up a wrapping station and follow the luncheon with a wrapping party. Or, better yet, hire someone to wrap for each guest during lunch. They will all be eternally grateful.

* Even if you did not select a Christmas china when you were married, it's not too late. Pick out the pattern you have been admiring and let your family and closest friends know. They will leap with joy at knowing what to get you for the next few special occasions, such as birthday or Christmas. You just made their shopping much easier!

* Turn your holiday event into a philanthropic occasion to benefit a favorite community cause. You and your friends can be "Super Santas" for Christmas while sharing your blessings with others.

* Each guest could bring a check made out to his or her college and drop it into Santa's hat. Or, the group could set a goal beforehand and designate their combined gift to a specific project, such as books for a women's shelter, toys for a children's hospital, or the library fund. The "Super Santas" can set the example for other philanthropic friends to follow.

* Also keep in mind that gifts to a favorite charity made in honor of friends or family members make a wonderful Christmas present for the person who has everything.

# *Shoppers Anonymous :*
### (Serves 15 Or More)

## MENU

*Peppermint Nog*
*Burgundy Wassail*
*Cheese and Pimento Biscuits*

*Ham-Green Onion Chedder Cake*
*Shrimp and Green Chile Mini-Quiches*

*Bacon, Date, and Pecan Chicken Sandwiches*
*Olive, Chopped Tomato, and Watercress Sandwiches*
*with Lemon Pepper Mayonnaise*

*Cold Poached Orange Sections*

*Winter Cranberry Bread with Cinnamon Honey Butter*

*Miniature Chocolate Éclairs*
*Brown Sugar Frosted Pecan Sandies*
*Almond Chocolate Joys*
*Old Fashioned Gingerbread with Lemon Fondue*

### *Recipes For Gifts From Your Kitchen For Friends And Neighbors*

*Spiced Pumpkin Granola*
*Homemade Kahlua*
*Cranberry Chutney*
*Chocolate Cherry Chippers*
*Peppermint Hot Chocolate Mix*

*Wine Suggestions:*
*Hess Select California Chardonnay*
*Louis Jadot Macon-Village (French)*
*Seppelt Reserve Bin Chardonnay (Australian)*
*(These are all moderately priced dry white wines.)*

## INGREDIENTS

2 pints vanilla ice cream, softened
6 cups eggnog
5 ¼ cups carbonated water, chilled
1 ½ cups heavy cream, whipped
1 cup broken peppermint sticks

# PEPPERMINT NOG

Spoon ice cream into large punch bowl. Stir in eggnog and carbonated water. Top with puffs of whipped cream and sprinkle with candy. This nog may also be poured into individual cups and then topped with whipped cream and candy.

**YIELD:** 16 drinks

## INGREDIENTS

1 gallon apple cider
1 gallon Burgundy wine
1 cup brown sugar
1 6-ounce can frozen lemonade concentrate
1 6-ounce can frozen orange juice concentrate
1 teaspoon nutmeg
1 tablespoon cinnamon
1 tablespoon whole cloves
1 tablespoon whole allspice
15 or more cinnamon sticks

# BURGUNDY WASSAIL

Combine cider, wine, sugar, lemonade, orange juice, nutmeg, and cinnamon in large stockpot. Tie cloves and allspice in cheesecloth and add to liquid. Simmer, covered, 30 minutes. Remove cheesecloth and discard spices. Serve hot with a cinnamon stick. *(Can be prepared ahead and reheated before serving.)*

**YIELD:** 30 drinks

*Allspice, the dried unripe berry of the West Indian pimento, was first brought to Europe by Christopher Columbus, who found the reddish-brown peppercorn in Jamaica. The berry adds a spicy zest to stews, sauces, relishes, marinades, hot beverages, and baked goods.*

## INGREDIENTS

3 cups flour, sifted
5 teaspoons baking powder
1 ½ teaspoons salt
½ teaspoon cayenne pepper
½ cup shortening
1 cup cheddar cheese, grated
¼ cup pimento, finely chopped
1 to 1½ cups milk

# CHEESE AND PIMENTO BISCUITS

Preheat oven to 450 degrees.

Sift together dry ingredients in large bowl. Cut in shortening. Stir in cheese and pimento. Add milk gradually to make dough. Roll out to ½-inch thickness. Cut with biscuit cutter and place on greased cookie sheet. Bake 15 minutes. *(Can be prepared ahead and frozen after baking. Reheat before serving.)*

**YIELD:** 3 dozen

*For a festive touch, cut biscuits with Christmas shaped cookie or canapé cutters.*

# HAM-GREEN ONION CHEDDAR CAKE

### FOR CRUST:

Butter 9-inch springform pan. Mix breadcrumbs and cheddar cheese in medium bowl. Coat pan with crumb and cheese mixture and refrigerate.

### FOR FILLING:

Preheat oven to 350 degrees.

Dice half of ham and reserve remaining slices. Mix diced ham with remaining ingredients in large bowl until smooth. Pour half of filling into pan. Top with reserved ham slices and cover with remaining filling. Set pan on baking sheet and bake 1 hour 15 minutes. Turn oven off and cool cake 1 hour with oven door ajar. Remove from oven and cool.

To serve, release cake from pan and place on serving platter. Sprinkle top of cake with green onions. Garnish with parsley around bottom edge of cake. Serve with crackers.

**SERVES:** 15

### INGREDIENTS

CRUST

- ¼ cup fine breadcrumbs
- ¼ cup sharp Cheddar cheese, finely grated

FILLING

- 6 ounces ham, thinly sliced (Virginia Baked is best)
- 3 8-ounce packages cream cheese, softened
- ¾ pound sharp Cheddar cheese, grated
- 1 cup cottage cheese
- ¾ cup green onion, chopped
- 4 eggs
- 3 tablespoons jalapeños, finely chopped
- 2 tablespoons milk
- 1 clove garlic, minced

- ¼ cup diced green onion for garnish
  parsley for garnish

# SHRIMP AND GREEN CHILE MINI-QUICHES

Preheat oven to 425 degrees.

Prepare pastry according to directions. Cut pastry into 35 3-inch circles, re-rolling pastry scraps. Use pastry circles to line mini-muffin pans. In each cup, layer cheeses, chiles, green onions, and shrimp.

Beat eggs in medium bowl until foaming. Stir in half-and-half. Spoon filling into cups. Bake 15 minutes. Turn oven down to 325 degrees and bake 20 minutes longer or until golden brown and puffy. May be served hot or at room temperature.

**YIELD:** 35

*To save time, this dish may be baked in a 9-inch pie shell.*

### INGREDIENTS

- 1 pie crust mix for 2 pies
- 1 cup Cheddar cheese, grated
- 1 ½ cups Monterey jack cheese, grated
- 1 4-ounce can green chiles, chopped and drained
- 1 cup tiny shrimp, cooked and peeled
- 3 eggs
- 1 cup half-and-half
- 3 green onions, minced

## INGREDIENTS

1 cup chicken, cooked and diced
½ cup dates, finely chopped
¼ cup pecans, chopped
¼ cup crisp bacon, crumbled
½ cup mayonnaise
¼ teaspoon salt
12 slices thin white bread, buttered and crusts trimmed

## INGREDIENTS

**MAYONNAISE**

1 large egg
½ teaspoon freshly ground black pepper
¼ teaspoon cayenne pepper
¼ teaspoon salt or to taste
2 tablespoons fresh lemon juice
2 green onions, minced
¾ cup vegetable oil

**SANDWICH FILLING**

8 ounces ripe olives, chopped
2 tomatoes, seeded, drained, and finely chopped
1 bunch watercress, hard stems removed and finely chopped
    salt to taste
    pepper to taste
12 slices whole wheat bread, crusts trimmed and buttered

# BACON, DATE, AND PECAN CHICKEN SANDWICHES

Mix all ingredients, except bread, in medium bowl. Spread on buttered bread slices. Cut each slice into two triangles and serve.

**YIELD:** 24

# OLIVE, CHOPPED TOMATO, AND WATERCRESS SANDWICHES WITH LEMON PEPPER MAYONNAISE

**FOR MAYONNAISE:**

Combine egg, peppers, salt, lemon juice, and onions in food processor or blender. With motor running, add oil in a stream and blend until thick. Cover and chill 1 hour. *(Can be refrigerated up to 3 days.)*

**FOR FILLING:**

Mix all ingredients, except bread, in medium bowl. Add enough mayonnaise to hold filling together (about four tablespoons). Spread filling over 6 bread slices. Top each with second slice of bread, buttered side down. Cut each sandwich diagonally into fourths, forming triangles. *(Can be prepared 6 hours ahead if covered with a slightly damp dish towel and refrigerated.)*

**YIELD:** 24 sandwiches

## COLD POACHED ORANGE SECTIONS

Combine 4½ tablespoons reserved orange rind slivers, sugar, and water in large saucepan. Cook over moderate heat, without stirring, 8 minutes or until slightly thickened. Add orange sections to syrup and cook over low heat 5 minutes, basting constantly. Oranges should be warm but firm. Remove from heat and add liqueur. Chill, basting occasionally with syrup. Serve cold. *(Can be prepared up to 2 days ahead.)*

**SERVES:** 20

## WINTER CRANBERRY BREAD WITH CINNAMON HONEY BUTTER

Preheat oven to 350 degrees.

Process first 6 ingredients in food processor until mixture resembles coarse meal. Transfer to large bowl.

Whisk peel, juice, and egg in small bowl. Add to flour mixture and stir until just combined. Stir in cranberries and walnuts. Pour into well-greased 9 x 5-inch loaf pan. Bake 1 hour 15 minutes or until tester comes out clean. Let cool in pan 15 minutes and turn out onto rack. Slice and serve with Cinnamon Honey Butter. *(Can be prepared 3 days ahead, wrapped, and refrigerated or frozen.)*

**FOR CINNAMON HONEY BUTTER:**

Combine all ingredients in small bowl and beat with mixer until creamy. Cover and refrigerate. Let stand to soften before serving. *(Can be prepared 1 week ahead.)*

**YIELD:** 1 loaf

*Valued as a superb orange for eating, the navel orange peels easily, separates easily, and is seedless. It received its name because of the navel-like appearance of the blossom end.*

*Oranges may also be peeled and poached whole.*

*Know your cranberries! The best way to test a cranberry is to check its bounce. If it is ripe, it should bounce like a rubber ball.*

### INGREDIENTS

9 navel oranges, cut into sections (rind removed, slivered and reserved)
2 ¼ cups sugar
1 ⅛ cups water
3 tablespoons orange-flavored liqueur

### INGREDIENTS

2 cups flour
1 cup sugar
1 ½ teaspoons baking powder
1 teaspoon salt
½ teaspoon baking soda
½ cup unsalted butter, cut into pieces

1 teaspoon orange peel, freshly grated
¾ cup orange juice
1 large egg

1 cup cranberries, coarsely chopped
⅓ cup walnuts, coarsely chopped

**CINNAMON HONEY BUTTER**

1 cup butter, softened
3 tablespoons honey
1 teaspoon ground cinnamon

## INGREDIENTS

**ÉCLAIRS**

- 1 cup water
- ½ cup butter
- 1 cup all purpose flour
- 4 large eggs

**CUSTARD FILLING**

- ½ cup sugar
- ⅓ cup flour
-   dash salt
- 4 egg yolks
- 2 cups milk
- 1 teaspoon vanilla

**CHOCOLATE GLAZE**

- ½ cup semisweet chocolate morsels
- 1 tablespoon butter
- 1 ½ teaspoons light corn syrup
- 1 ½ teaspoons milk

# MINIATURE CHOCOLATE ÉCLAIRS

**FOR ÉCLAIRS:**

Preheat oven to 375 degrees.

Combine water and butter in medium saucepan over moderate heat and bring to boil. Remove from heat. Add flour all at once and stir vigorously with wooden spoon until mixture forms a ball. Add eggs, one at a time, beating well after each addition, until batter is smooth.

Spoon batter into pastry bag with large tip. Pipe batter onto greased cookie sheet in 3-inch long éclairs. Bake 20 minutes or until golden.

**FOR CUSTARD FILLING:**

Combine sugar, flour, and salt in top of double boiler. Whisk egg yolks and milk in medium bowl and add to sugar mixture, a little at a time, until blended. Cook, uncovered, until thick, stirring constantly. Reduce heat and cook 5 minutes more. Remove from heat and stir in vanilla. Cover and chill in refrigerator.

When filling is cold, put in pastry bag. Cut slit in one side of each éclair pastry. Pipe filling into éclair. Ice or drizzle top with chocolate glaze.

**FOR CHOCOLATE GLAZE:**

Heat all ingredients in medium saucepan over low heat, stirring frequently, until melted. Pour into ziplock bag and seal. Cut small hole in corner of bag. Squeeze bag to drizzle glaze over pastry.

*If time does not allow for preparation of traditional custard filling, the following may be substituted:*

- *1 cup whipping cream*
- *1 small package vanilla instant pudding mix*
- *1¼ cups milk*

*Whip cream in small bowl until stiff peaks form. Set aside. Prepare pudding mix, as directed, in large bowl, using only 1 ¼ cups milk. Gently fold in whipping cream and quickly fill éclairs before pudding sets.*

258

# BROWN SUGAR FROSTED PECAN SANDIES

**FOR COOKIES:**

Preheat oven to 350 degrees.

Cream butter and sugars in large bowl with mixer until well blended. Beat in egg and vanilla. Combine flour, soda, and salt in small bowl and gradually add to creamed mixture. Mix well after each addition. Stir in chopped pecans and chill dough 30 minutes.

Shape dough into 1-inch balls and place on ungreased cookie sheet. Bake 10-12 minutes. Cool on wire racks. When completely cool, spread cookies with Brown Sugar Frosting and top with a pecan half.

**BROWN SUGAR FROSTING:**

Combine brown sugar and half-and-half in small saucepan. Cook over moderate heat, stirring constantly, until mixture comes to a boil. Continue to boil 4 minutes. Remove from heat and stir in butter. Add 1 ½ cups powdered sugar and beat with mixer until smooth. Add remaining powdered sugar to desired spreading consistency.

**YIELD:** 5 dozen

## COOKIES

- 1 cup butter, softened
- ½ cup brown sugar, firmly packed
- ½ cup sugar
- 1 egg
- 1 teaspoon vanilla
- 2 cups flour
- ½ teaspoon baking soda
- ¼ teaspoon salt
- ½ cup pecans, finely chopped

## FROSTING

- 1 cup brown sugar, firmly packed
- ½ cup half-and-half
- 1 tablespoon butter
- 1 ½-1 ⅔ cups powdered sugar, sifted

pecan halves for garnish

## INGREDIENTS

60  whole almonds
 1  can sweetened condensed
    milk
 1  pound powdered sugar
 2  14-ounce bags flaked
    coconut
½  cup butter
12  ounces semisweet
    chocolate chips
⅓  block paraffin

# ALMOND CHOCOLATE JOYS

Preheat oven to 350 degrees.

Place almonds on cookie sheet and roast 5-10 minutes.  Let cool.

Combine next four ingredients in large bowl. Refrigerate until firm.  Form into slightly oblong balls.  Place balls on wax paper and refrigerate.

Melt chocolate and paraffin in top of double boiler.  Place a ball on fork and barely submerge in chocolate.  Spoon chocolate over ball.  Lift fork out and scrape under fork with toothpick.  Slide ball off fork, using toothpick, onto wax paper.  Top each with a roasted almond.  Freeze on cookie sheets to harden. *(Can be stored in freezer in airtight container.)*  Serve at room temperature.

**YIELD:**  5 dozen

# OLD FASHIONED GINGERBREAD WITH LEMON FONDUE

## INGREDIENTS

*The light and tangy Lemon Fondue may also be served with poundcake or fruitcake cubes or as a sauce over cake slices.*

**FOR GINGERBREAD:**

Preheat oven to 350 degrees.

Cream butter and sugar in large bowl. Add egg and molasses. Combine dry ingredients in medium bowl. Gradually add to butter and sugar mixture. Add water and beat thoroughly. Pour into greased 9 x 13-inch pan. Bake 30-40 minutes. Cool and cut into small cubes. Serve with Lemon Fondue.

**FOR LEMON FONDUE:**

Combine water, sugar, cornstarch, and lemon peel in medium saucepan and stir to dissolve cornstarch. Add butter. Cook on low heat until butter melts and sauce thickens. Stir in lemonade and heat 1-2 minutes. Pour into fondue pot to keep warm.

**SERVES:** 15

**GINGERBREAD**

- ½ cup butter, softened
- ½ cup sugar
- 1 egg
- 1 cup molasses
- 2 ½ cups flour, sifted
- 1 teaspoon ground ginger
- ½ teaspoon cloves
- 1 teaspoon cinnamon
- ½ teaspoon salt
- 1 ½ teaspoons baking soda
- 1 cup water

**LEMON FONDUE**

- 4 ½ cups water
- 3 cups powdered sugar
- ⅔ cup cornstarch
- 4 tablespoons lemon peel, grated
- 1 ½ cups butter
- 2 6-ounce cans frozen lemonade concentrate, thawed

*Recipes For Gifts From Your Kitchen For Friends And Neighbors*

*Pages 262-263*

Spiced Pumpkin Granola
Homemade Kahlua
Cranberry Chutney
Chocolate Cherry Chippers
Peppermint Hot Chocolate Mix

## INGREDIENTS

3 cups old fashioned oats
½ cup almonds, sliced
1 cup pecan pieces
½ cup pumpkin pie mix
¼ cup honey
3 tablespoons vegetable oil
2 tablespoons light brown sugar, firmly packed
2 teaspoons vanilla
2 teaspoons cinnamon
¼ teaspoon ground ginger
¼ teaspoon ground nutmeg
¼ teaspoon ground coriander
¾ cup raisins
½ cup dried cranberries

# SPICED PUMPKIN GRANOLA

Preheat oven to 250 degrees.

Spread oats in 15x10-inch pan. Toast in oven 20 minutes, stirring at 10-minute intervals. Pour toasted oats into large bowl. Add almonds and pecans; set aside.

Blend pumpkin pie mix in medium bowl with remaining ingredients. Mix thoroughly with toasted oats. Divide mixture into 2 pans, spreading to make a thin layer. Bake 30 minutes, stirring at 10-minute intervals. Cool and store in airtight container.

**YIELD:** 4 ½ cups

*For gift-giving, place the Spiced Pumpkin Granola in colorful cellophane and tie with elegant lace ribbon, inexpensively purchased by the yard at your local fabric store (great for gift-wrapping as well). Or give the granola in a festive holiday tin.*

## INGREDIENTS

3 cups sugar
3 cups boiling water
2-3 ounces instant coffee
⅓ 100-proof vodka
1 vanilla bean, or
2 tablespoons vanilla extract

# HOMEMADE KAHLUA

*(Must be made 1 month in advance.)*

Mix sugar, water, and coffee in large bottle or container. Add vodka and vanilla bean. Let stand 1 month. (Does not need to be refrigerated.) Serve as a beverage or over ice cream.

*Buy pretty decorative bottles in which to give your Homemade Kahlua as treasured holiday treats, or recycle used bottles and tie their necks with gorgeous cascades of ribbon and a Kahlua recipe.*

## INGREDIENTS

1 12-ounce bag cranberries
2 cups sugar
1 cup water
1 cup pecans, chopped
1 cup celery, chopped
1 cup dark raisins
1 cup orange juice
1 large apple, peeled and chopped
1 teaspoon fresh ginger, grated
1 teaspoon orange rind, grated

# CRANBERRY CHUTNEY

Combine cranberries, sugar, and water in large saucepan and bring to boil. Reduce heat and simmer 15 minutes. Remove from heat and stir in remaining ingredients. Cool and pour into jars. *(This will keep up to 2 weeks in refrigerator.)*

**YIELD:** 6 jars

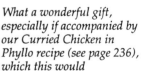

*What a wonderful gift, especially if accompanied by our Curried Chicken in Phyllo recipe (see page 236), which this would complement beautifully!*

*Start a new tradition — try serving the Cranberry Chutney at Thanksgiving.*

# CHOCOLATE CHERRY CHIPPERS

Preheat oven to 350 degrees.

Cream butter and sugar in large bowl. Add eggs and vanilla, mixing well. Add cherries. Combine flour, baking soda, salt, and baking powder in small bowl. Gradually add to batter, mixing well. Fold in pecans and chocolate chips. Drop, by teaspoonful, on greased cookie sheet. Bake 10-15 minutes. Remove cookies at once and cool on rack. Store in airtight container.

**YIELD:** 6 dozen

**INGREDIENTS**

| | |
|---|---|
| 1 | cup butter, softened |
| ½ | cup light brown sugar, firmly packed |
| 2 | eggs |
| 4 | tablespoons vanilla |
| 1 ½ | cups dried cherries, chopped |
| 2 | cups all purpose flour |
| 2 | teaspoons baking soda |
| 2 | teaspoons salt |
| ½ | teaspoon baking powder |
| 1 ½ | cups pecans, chopped |
| 3 ½ | cups semisweet chocolate chips |

*Kids and adults alike adore these! For special friends, wrap the cookies up prettily on a holiday tray which can then be used as a keepsake for years to come.*

# PEPPERMINT HOT CHOCOLATE MIX

Place candy sticks in ziplock bag and crush with mallet. Combine crushed candy with remaining ingredients in large bowl. Store in airtight container. To make hot chocolate, combine 3 heaping spoonfuls of mix with 1 cup boiling water. Garnish with whole peppermint stick, if desired.

**YIELD:** 4 ½ cups

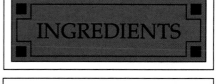
**INGREDIENTS**

| | |
|---|---|
| 6 | 4 ½-inch sticks peppermint candy |
| 2 | cups powdered non-dairy coffee creamer |
| 2 | cups powdered sugar, sifted |
| ½ | cup cocoa |
| | whole peppermint sticks for garnish |

*For a gift, place the hot chocolate mix (sealed in a ziplock bag) in a coffee mug or burlap material purchased from your local fabric store. Tie burlap with twine and attach a small bag of candy canes dipped half way in chocolate for stirring along with the recipe for making hot chocolate.*

# Home Sweet Home
## Build A Gingerbread House And Come For Dessert

Welcome Hansel and Gretel too.
Come in, come in, come in, please do!
So you like my house of gingerbread, eh?
Do come in, you'll have a lovely stay!

If you've lost your way. . .
find your way to our house.
December 12
7:30 p.m.
Join us for dessert and build
your own gingerbread house.

Drury and Randolph Gilchrist
23 Cherokee Road

✳ Depart from the ordinary holiday cocktail party for something intimate and unforgettable. Invite your best friends over to decorate a gingerbread house and serve them an array of delicious desserts in the process.

✳ With a little time and effort you and your guests can make a gingerbread house just as magical as the one first glimpsed by Hansel and Gretel! The hostess should bake the walls and roofs several days in advance. Cut pattern pieces out of lightweight cardboard. Roll out the gingerbread cookie dough on a cookie sheet to ⅛ inch thickness and cut out front, back, 2 sides and 2 roof pieces. Don't forget to cut doors and windows! Bake 10-12 minutes at 350 degrees until deep brown.

✳ For your guests, provide gingerbread pieces, a cardboard base purchased from a cake decorating supply or craft store, and lots of frosting "glue" (see p. 269 for recipe).

✳ For decorating, have on hand bowls of hard candies, red hots, pretzels, gum drops, candy canes, etc.

✳ All guests will leave with a happy holiday memory and a special decoration for their table at home.

# Home Sweet Home
(Serves 8-10)

## MENU

*Cranberry Slushes, Hot Buttered Rum,*
*or Dairy Eggnog*

*Rose And Chocolate Truffle Tree*
*Brandy Snaps with Cream Filling*
*Gingerbread People*
*White Chocolate Cheesecake*
*or Citrus Cheesecake*
*Creamy Pecan Tartlets*
*Peppermints*

*Nutmeg Muffins*

**INGREDIENTS**

1 quart cranberry juice
6 ounces orange juice
   concentrate
1 cup apple juice
1 cup vodka

# CRANBERRY SLUSHES

Mix juices and vodka together in large pitcher and freeze. Remove from freezer about 45 minutes before serving. Allow mixture to soften, stir, and serve.

**YIELD:** 10 drinks

*Rose and Chocolate Truffle Tree, p. 267; Dairy Egnogg.*

# HOT BUTTERED RUM

Put cloves, allspice, cinnamon stick, and sugar in mug and add 1 ounce boiling water. Let mixture stand 5 minutes. Add both rums, 2 ounces boiling water, and butter. Stir until butter dissolves. Add more sugar if desired. Repeat in individual mugs for additional servings.

**YIELD:** 1 drink

INGREDIENTS

2 whole cloves
2 whole allspice
1 cinnamon stick
1 teaspoon sugar
3 ounces boiling water
1 ½ ounces light rum, hot
½ ounce dark Jamaican rum, hot
1 teaspoon sweet butter

# ROSE AND CHOCOLATE TRUFFLE TREE

INGREDIENTS

### FOR TRUFFLES:

Melt chocolate squares over low heat in heavy saucepan. Remove from heat and add butter, stirring until smooth. Stir in whipping cream. Cover and chill two hours or until firm.

Dust hands with cocoa and shape chocolate mixture into one-inch balls. Freeze 30 minutes or until firm. Roll balls in cocoa and place in airtight container in refrigerator.

Melt chocolate chips in top of double boiler. Using toothpick, dip truffles, one at a time, into melted chocolate. Remove and place on wax paper to cool. Store truffles in refrigerator until ready to assemble tree. (White candy coating may be melted, tinted with food coloring, and piped through a pastry bag to decorate truffles, if desired.)

**YIELD:** 24

**TRUFFLES**

16 ounces semisweet chocolate squares
½ cup butter, softened
½ cup whipping cream
1 cup cocoa, sifted
1 12-ounce package semisweet chocolate chips

white candy coating (optional)
red and green food coloring (optional)

*For tree assembly, you will need:*

*styrofoam cone*
*package u-shaped florist pins*
*curly leaf lettuce*
*toothpicks*
*red rosebuds*
*ribbon bow (optional)*

*Cover styrofoam cone with curly leaf lettuce securing with florist pins. Stick toothpicks in truffles and arrange on tree. Place red rose buds in various places between truffles all around tree. Top with ribbon bow, if desired.*

## BRANDY SNAPS WITH CREAM FILLING

**FOR BRANDY SNAPS:**

Preheat oven to 350 degrees.

Combine brown sugar, melted butter, molasses, and brandy in large bowl and stir. Add flour, ginger, and nutmeg until thoroughly combined.

Drop batter, by teaspoonful, 3 inches apart onto greased cookie sheet, baking only 5 cookies at a time. Bake 5-6 minutes or until cookies are bubbly and deep golden brown.

Cool cookies on cookie sheet until they have set. Quickly remove cookies, one at a time. Place each cookie upside down on a heatproof surface then roll each cookie around metal cone or greased handle of wooden spoon. When cookie is firm, slide off cone or handle and cool completely on wire rack. (If cookies harden before you shape them, reheat in oven 1 minute.)

**FOR CREAM FILLING:**

Combine whipping cream, powdered sugar, and brandy in chilled mixing bowl. Beat with chilled beaters until stiff peaks form. Spoon brandy cream filling into a pastry bag fitted with a large star tip. Pipe filling into each cookie.

**YIELD:** 54 cookies

### BRANDY SNAPS

- ½  cup brown sugar, packed
- ⅓  cup butter, melted
- ¼  cup light molasses
- 1  tablespoon brandy
- ¾  cup all-purpose flour
- ½  teaspoon ground ginger
- ½  teaspoon ground nutmeg

### FILLING

- 2  cups whipping cream
- ¼  cup powdered sugar, sifted
- 2  tablespoons brandy

*For an extra touch of elegance, tie a gold ribbon around each cookie.*

## GINGERBREAD PEOPLE

Mix first 6 ingredients in large bowl. Mix remaining ingredients in medium bowl. Combine both mixtures. Form dough into ball, wrap in plastic wrap, and refrigerate 1 hour or longer.

Preheat oven to 350 degrees.

- 2 ¼  cups all purpose flour
- 2  teaspoons ground ginger
- 1  teaspoon baking soda
- ¾  teaspoon ground cinnamon
- ½  teaspoon ground cloves
- ¼  teaspoon salt
- ¾  cup butter
- 1  cup sugar
- ¼  cup molasses
- 1  egg

*If time is of the essence, make gingerbread cookies instead of "people." Roll dough into small balls (about 2 dozen) and then roll in sugar. Place balls on greased cookie sheet and bake 8-10 minutes.*

*Decorator Icing*
16  ounces powdered sugar
⅓  cup warm water
3  tablespoons meringue
    powder

*Beat all ingredients together until very stiff. Can be tinted with food coloring if desired. Spread on cookies or pipe through pastry bag fitted with desired decorating tip.*

*White chocolate actually is not chocolate at all. It is made of cocoa butter, sugar, milk, and flavorings. It should never be substituted for chocolate in recipes.*

Roll out gingerbread to ¼-inch thickness on lightly-floured surface. Cut out cookies with a floured, 4 ½ inch gingerbread cookie cutter. Place on greased cookie sheet and bake until cookies are lightly browned around edges, about 8-10 minutes. When cool, decorate with icing, if desired. (Cookies may be stored in airtight container several weeks.)

**YIELD:**  1 dozen

# WHITE CHOCOLATE CHEESECAKE

## FOR CRUST:

Combine all crust ingredients in small bowl and press evenly into 10-inch springform pan.

## FOR FILLLNG:

Preheat oven to 350 degrees.

Combine cream cheese and sugar, beating with mixer until fluffy. Add salt and mix well. Add eggs, one at a time, beating with mixer on slowest speed. Add white chocolate and pour into crust. Bake 40-45 minutes. Remove from oven and let cool 10 minutes.

## FOR TOPPING:

Combine sour cream, sugar, and vanilla in small bowl. Spread on cake. Place cake back in oven 10 minutes and then refrigerate immediately. Top with white chocolate shavings before serving.

**SERVES:**  10

*Gingerbread House "Glue"*
2  egg whites
⅛  teaspoon cream of tartar
2  teaspoons water
3  cups powdered sugar, sifted

*Beat first 3 ingredients with mixer at high speed until frothy. Gradually add powdered sugar and beat until mixture reaches spreading consistency. Add more sugar if necessary so icing will hold stiff peaks. (May be made early in day and stored in refrigerator in airtight container.)*

INGREDIENTS

**CRUST**

½  cup butter, melted
2  cups Lorna Doone Shortbread Cookies, finely ground
1  ounce white chocolate, grated
¼  cup sugar

**FILLING**

2  pounds cream cheese, softened
1 ¼  cups sugar
    pinch salt
4  eggs
3  ounces white chocolate, grated

**TOPPING**

2  cups sour cream
¼  cup sugar
1  teaspoon vanilla
1  ounce white chocolate, shaved

**CRUST**

| | |
|---|---|
| 1 ½ | cups graham cracker crumbs |
| ⅓ | cup brown sugar |
| ½ | teaspoon cinnamon |
| 1 | teaspoon orange peel, minced |
| 1 | teaspoon lemon peel, minced |
| ½ | cup unsalted butter, melted |

**FILLING**

| | |
|---|---|
| 2 ½ | pounds cream cheese, room temperature |
| 1 ½ | cups sugar |
| 3 | tablespoons flour |
| 5 | eggs, room temperature |
| 2 | egg yolks, room temperature |
| ¼ | cup whipping cream |
| 2 | teaspoons fresh lemon juice |
| 1 | teaspoon orange peel, minced |
| 1 | teaspoon lemon peel, minced |
| ½ | teaspoon vanilla |

**TOPPING**

| | |
|---|---|
| ½ | cup apricot jam, warmed |
| 10 | strawberries, sliced thinly |
| 3 | kiwi, peeled and sliced thinly |
| 1 | can mandarin oranges, drained |
| | finely chopped nuts (optional) |

# CITRUS CHEESECAKE

**FOR CRUST:**

Combine crust ingredients in medium bowl and press into 10-inch spring form pan. Chill 30 minutes.

**FOR FILLING:**

Preheat oven to 425 degrees.

Combine cream cheese, sugar, and flour in large bowl. Beat until smooth. Blend in eggs and egg yolks, one at a time. Stir in remaining ingredients and pour into chilled crust. Bake 15 minutes and lower oven temperature to 225 degrees. Bake until firm around edges, approximately 1 hour. Refrigerate immediately.

**FOR TOPPING:**

Just before serving, remove cheesecake from pan and place on platter. Brush top of cake with jam. Arrange strawberries, kiwi, and oranges on top, from outer edge to center. Brush jam over fruit. Lightly pat finely chopped nuts around sides of cheesecake, if desired.

**SERVES:** 10

*How do you prevent your cheesecake from developing cracks and fissures? Always refrigerate it directly from the oven. Chill, uncovered, to prevent the top from becoming wet with condensation. And try using dental floss pulled taut to cut your slices.*

*If fresh strawberries and kiwi are not in season, mandarin oranges alone make a beautiful cheesecake topping.*

*ingerbread People, p. 268; Citrus Cheesecake, p. 270;*
*nnamon-Orange Pomanders, p. 272; Brandy Snaps with*
*ream Filling, p. 268; Creamy Pecan Tartlets, p. 272;*
*ppermints, p. 273.*

## INGREDIENTS

**TARTLET SHELLS**

- 3 ounces cream cheese, softened
- ½ cup butter, softened
- 1 cup sifted flour

**FILLING**

- 4 tablespoons butter
- ½ cup sugar
- 4 ounces cream cheese
- 1 cup light corn syrup
- 3 eggs, beaten
- 1 teaspoon vanilla
- ⅛ teaspoon salt
- 1½ cups pecans, whole or coarsly chopped

# CREAMY PECAN TARTLETS

**FOR TARTLET SHELLS:**

Combine cream cheese and butter in small bowl. Stir in flour. Chill dough 1 hour. Shape into round balls and press into miniature muffin or tartlet pans.

**FOR FILLING:**

Preheat oven to 350 degrees.

Melt butter in medium saucepan over low heat. Add sugar, cream cheese, and syrup. Stir until sugar dissolves. Remove from heat. Lightly beat mixture until smooth. Let cool.

Combine eggs, vanilla, and salt in large bowl. Beat well. Stir in syrup mixture and pecans. Spoon into tartlet shells and bake 20-30 minutes until set and golden.

**YIELD:** 2 dozen

*Fill your house with the smell of Christmas by making cinnamon-orange pomanders. Push whole cloves into the oranges in circular or random patterns. Tie with a Christmas plaid ribbon. Group together in a pretty bowl for a holiday decoration or centerpiece.*

# PEPPERMINTS

Combine milk, sugar, and shortening in medium saucepan and bring to boil. Pour mixture into large bowl and stir in powdered sugar. Add peppermint flavoring, food coloring, and salt. Beat with mixer until mixture holds its shape or ribbons. While still warm, put into pastry tube and form into desired shapes, or press into molds. Spread on wax paper and let air dry overnight. Store in airtight container.

**SERVES:** 10

### INGREDIENTS

½ cup milk
1 cup sugar
½ cup vegetable shortening
1 16-ounce box powdered sugar, sifted
18 drops peppermint flavoring
2 drops green or red food coloring
½ teaspoon salt

# NUTMEG MUFFINS

Preheat oven to 350 degrees.

Combine 2 cups flour and brown sugar in medium bowl. Cut in butter until mixture resembles cornmeal. Set aside ¾ cup for topping.

Add 1 cup flour, baking powder, nutmeg, baking soda, and salt to remaining mixture. Add buttermilk and eggs, stirring just until moistened.

Spoon batter into well-greased muffin cups, filling each about half full. Sprinkle each muffin with 1 ½ teaspoons of reserved topping mixture. Bake until toothpick inserted in center comes out clean, about 20 minutes.

**YIELD:** 24

*These are perfect muffins to take as a gift to your holiday hostess — a yummy breakfast treat the "day after."*

### INGREDIENTS

3 cups flour
1 ½ cups brown sugar, firmly packed
¾ cup butter
2 teaspoons baking powder
2 teaspoons ground nutmeg
½ teaspoon baking soda
½ teaspoon salt
1 cup buttermilk
2 eggs, slightly beaten

273

# SPECIAL THANK YOUS

We of the *Dining By Fireflies* Cookbook Committee wish to extend our warmest thanks to the following League members, community individuals, and businesses for their invaluable advice, tireless support, invitation reprint permission, special recipe or sidebar text contributions, or most generous loan of their lovely homes or exceptional props for our photography shoots:

The Aga Works, Inc.
Mr. and Mrs. Richard Alexander
Barnes & Noble Bookstore
Belk Southpark
Mr. and Mrs. John M. Belk
The Biltmore Estate
Ed Bohannon
The Buttercup
Calico Corners
Campbell's Greenhouses
Charlotte Sister Cities Committee
Christie and Company
Circa Interiors & Antiques
Colors By Design
Rachel Rivers-Coffey
Mr. and Mrs. David W. Cunningham
De La Maison
Dr. and Mrs. Philip Dubois
Elizabeth Bruns Jewelers
Elizabeth House Flowers
Englehardt & Co.
Faux Designs
Favorite Things
Mr. and Mrs. Carlton Fleming
Dr. and Mrs. J.H. Smith Foushee, Jr.
Mr. and Mrs. J.H. Smith Foushee, III
Fresh Innovations Designs by Pat McCall
Greeting Graphics
Grodzicki & Co.

Mr. and Mrs. Raymond J. Grodzicki
Gutmann Galleries
Mr. and Mrs. Cameron Harris
Executive Chef Mark
    Harrold, NationsBank
John Dabbs, Ltd.
Jones Paper
The 1993-94 Junior League
    Executive Committee
Debra R. Karney
Barbara Karro
Leagueprint, Inc.
Fran Lemmons
Wardie Martin
Mr. and Mrs. Alex McMillan
Executive Chef Luis Morales, Stanley's
Odd Balls
Pier 1 Imports
The Pottery Barn
Page Renger
Mr. and Mrs. Steve B. Smith
Mr. and Mrs. D. Harding Stowe
Raymond Tom
Debby Wallace
Mary Elfreth Watkins
Williams-Sonoma
Beth Wylie
Sally Ydel
Jennifer Young

## and
### most especially, our wonderful families

# RECIPE CONTRIBUTORS AND TESTERS

We also wish to offer our deepest appreciation to the following recipe contributors and testers who spent countless hours and/or dollars to provide us with the quality recipes featured in *Dining By Fireflies:*

Joseph Aiken
Martha Aiken
Sunny Allen
Kimberly Allen
Tina Allison
Margaraet Almeida
Suzan Anderson
Margueritte Andresen
Terry Andrews
Brenda Appleby
Adria Appleby
Kelley Archer
Lynn Armstrong
Jennie Arnold
Mary Jo Ashcraft
Joanna Ashworth
Kerry Baldwin
Nancy Ballenger
Sarah Barnett
Bailey Barnett
Patty Barnhardt
Elsie Barnhardt
Mabel Barnhardt
Laura Beall
Suzan Becker
Anne Belk
Claudia Belk
Gene Berry
Pam Berry
Leigh Bogucki
Mary Clifford Boyd
Margaret Bradley
Pamela Brady
Karen Breach
Jane Brietz
Gayle Brinly
Kathleen Bromstead
Mary-Stuart Brooks
Nina Browder
Frances Browne
Leigh Bugucki
Joan Burke
Carolyn Butler
Nona Butterworth
Shawn Butterworth
Dianne Byers
Priscilla Bynum
Barbara Carpenter
Cissy Carr
Jean Carrington
Jill Carter
Boots Carter
Anne Carter
Barbara Cash
Bennett Cave
Ellen Chason
Marlene Ciatti
Dorothy Ciatti
Betsy Clardy
Gina Clegg
Rush Coe
Lee Collins
Carla Cornelius
Kimberlye Cornelson
Betty Cowden
Suzanne Crawford
Elizabeth Crenshaw
Priestley Cummings
Elizabeth Cunningham
Sara Daniel
Patricia Daniel
Rebecca Davis
Pamela Dedor
Susan Dell
Lynn DeLoache
Melissa Denney
Emily Dermatas
Frances deWitt
Catherine Diehl
Lory Dillner
Anne Dooley

Betsy Downs
Sharli Drew
Lisa Dubois
Steve Duff
Janet Dulin
Joyee Dunaway
Christe Eades
Ann Edgerton
Janice Elder
Ellie Elmore
Beth Erwin
Bruce Evans
Cam Ewing
Joy Favrot
Tiz Faison
Cydne Farris
Frances Fennebresque
Anna Ferguson
Leigh Finley
Kaye Finnell
Susie Finnell
Myra Finnell
Ann Fleming
Linda Ford-Banner
Katherine Forney
Meredith Forshaw
Julie Francisco
Cantey Gannaway
Cynthia Gass
Katherine Gaston
Susie Gee
Roberto Gianfalla
Marilyn Gideon
Trudy Gilbert
Betty Gilbert
Anne Glenn
Peggy Glover
Kathryn Goode
Gourmet-to-Go
Sharon Graper
Linda Graybill
Linda Grayfield
Laura Greer
Marion Griffin
Anita Griffin
Avis Griffith
Julie Griggs
June Gunter
Spencer Guthery
Elizabeth Haas
Andrea Hall
Carol Hamrick
Meg Hancock
Donna Handford
Ellen Hardison
Amy Harris
Nancy Harris
DeeDee Harris
Patricia Hasty
Kim Hattaway
Dana Hearn
Lori Heinz
Penny Henry
Cecilia Hipp
Amy Hitchens
Jere Hollmeyer
Anne Honeycutt
Mrs. Albert Honsch
Peggy Horsley
Kathy Howe
Teresa Hubbell
Julie Hudson
Diana Huffstutler
Genie Hufham
Leslie Huntley
Doris Hurr
Jean Ives
Lachlan Ivy
Margaret Jackson
Pauline Jackson
Sara Jackson

Cheryl Jensen
SaraBee Johnson
Susan Johnson
Linda Johnson
Nancy Johnston
Anne Jones
Carole Joyner
Debra Karney
Barbara Karro
Charlotte Keenan
Irene Kehoe
Lisa Kehoe
Gloria Keith
Theresa Keller
Wyndall Kenney
Patti Kenney
Wendy Kenney
Dot Kilpatrick
Diane Kiradjieff
Gail Landers
Susan Laney
Ginna LaPorte
Darie Lapp
Pat Lassiter
Elizabeth Laudun
Lee Leggett
Mary Alice Lewis
Elizabeth Lewis
Grant Lewis
Cathy Liang
Anne Linde
Nola Linker
Link Litaker
Nancy Little
Ellen Long
Sallie Lowrance
Lucinda Lucas
Sally Lucas
Natalie Lucas
Nan Luckey
Beverly MacBain
Tamera Majors
Wardie Martin
Frannie Martin
Renna Massey
Fran Mathay
Sheryl Mayberry
Lynne McAdams
Margaret McAlister
Betty McCann
Mary McDonald
Melissa McDonald
Elizabeth McDowell
Mary McElveen
Anne McGrath
Lynn McGugan
Bonnie McKibbon
Beth McKnight
Dottie McLeod
Barbara McManeus
Delia McMullen
Sue Meacham
Elizabeth Meadows
Jenny Merlo
Kim Metts
Katherine Miller
Dawnel Miller
Stuart Milton
Virginia Milton
Pam Misle
Cynthia Mitchener
Mary Charles Montgomery
Cathy Morgan
Trudy Morgan
Mary Alice Morton
Wendy Munce
Becky Mustian
Anne Neal
Laine Neese
Ashley Nelson
Paula Nichol

Susan Nolton
Jane Nye
Mary Beth O'Briant
Roger Overcash
Judy Painter
Karrie Payne
Ruth Pellisario
Martha Player
Allison Poehlein
Irene Politis
Judy Postal
Claudia Putnam
Kathy Ragsdale
Susan Rankin
Carol Ransone
Lila Rash
Darlene Ray
Beth Reigel
Dot Renfro
Page Renger
Lynn Reynolds
Marsha Rich
Wendy Richardson
Liz Ritchie
Meg Roach
Barry Roach
Constance Roads
Donna Robertson
Debbie Robertson
Karen Rockecharlie
Page Rogers
Sharon Rountree
Iris Rountree
Jane Rudisill
Celeste Rudolph
Toni Sanders
Joanne Schlecht
Dana Scott
Ann Seagle
Lisa Seaton
Katy Shannon
Margaret Sherentz
Leslie Shinn
Susie Shoff
Laura Shwedo
Shirley Snead
Molly Snyder
Jack Sommers
Helen Sowell
Colleen Spencer

Musette Steck
Sally Stout
Pam Stowe
Linda Strong
Stacy Sumner
Linda Love Talmadge
Lynn Thompson
Kathy Thompson
Lee Thorpe
Melissa Tolmie
Jenny Tolson
Lisa Tomlinson
Karen Troutman
Mary Tucker
Mickie Turner
Peggy Tuttle
Guyla Vardell
Janet Vazquez
Nita Voskian
Pamela Waller
Marla Walsh
Nancy Walsh
Sarah Wannamaker
Judy Warren
Bennett Waters
Claudia Watkins
Susan Watkins
Mary Elfreth Watkins
Kim Weir
Agnes Weisiger
Jackie Wells
Linda Welton
Warwick Werthmuller
Virginia Whedon
Lydia Whiteside
Laurel Whitmore
Nancy Williams
Jane Williamson
Hannah Wilson
Susanne Wise
Donna Wise
Jayne Withers
Frances Witt
Melissa Woolf
Ann Wrenn
Deborah Wright
Beth Wylie
Frances Young
Terry Young
Martha Zweier

We sincerely hope that none of the many individuals who have made this book possible has been inadvertently overlooked.

**Literary Sources for Sidebar Text:**

Belk, Sarah, *Around the Southern Table.* New York: Simon & Schuster, 1991.

*The Charlotte Observer*

Claiborne, Craig, ed., *The New York Times Cookbook.* New York: Harper & Row, 1961.

Friedman, Rodney M., ed., *The Wellness Engagement Calendar 1994.* New York: Rebus, Inc., 1993.

Horn, Jane, ed., *Cooking A to Z.* California: Chevron Chemical Company, 1988.

Tartan, Beth, and Parker, Fran, *Instant Gourmet and How To Form a Gourmet Society.* Kernersville, NC: TarPar Ltd.

*The Watauga County Library*

*The Watauga Democrat*

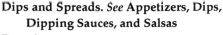

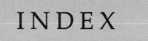